HENSLOWE AND ALLEYN.

VOL. II.

HENSLOWE AND ALLEYN:

BEING

THE DIARY OF PHILIP HENSLOWE,

FROM 1591 TO 1609

Edited by J. PAYNE COLLIER.

AND THE

LIFE OF EDWARD ALLEYN.

By J. PAYNE COLLIER.

TO WHICH IS ADDED

THE ALLEYN PAPERS.

IN TWO VOLUMES.

VOL. II.

PRINTED FOR THE SHAKESPEARE SOCIETY,
AND TO BE HAD OF
W. SKEFFINGTON, AGENT TO THE SOCIETY, 192, PICCADILLY.
1853.

LONDON:
BRADBURY AND EVANS, PRINTERS, WHITEFRIARS.

MEMOIRS

OF

EDWARD ALLEYN,

FOUNDER OF DULWICH COLLEGE:

INCLUDING

SOME NEW PARTICULARS

RESPECTING

SHAKESPEARE, BEN JONSON, MASSINGER,
MARSTON, DEKKER, &c.

BY

J. PAYNE COLLIER, ESQ., F.S.A.

LONDON:
PRINTED FOR THE SHAKESPEARE SOCIETY
1841.

LONDON:
F. SHOBERL, JUN. 51, RUPERT STREET, HAYMARKET,
PRINTER TO H.R.H. PRINCE ALBERT.

PREFACE.

MORE than ten years ago, when the writer of the following Memoir was collecting materials for his "History of English Dramatic Poetry and the Stage," he had an opportunity of inspecting Henslowe's Diary, and some few other original documents preserved in Dulwich College. He was not then, however, aware of the curious sources of information possessed by that institution, in relation to some of our early theatres, and to the life of an individual, who for nearly half a century was more or less prominently concerned in dramatic representations.

His attention was not long since directed to these additional stores; and on examining them, he found that they afforded ample and novel matter for an extended biography of the Founder of Dulwich College, including important and interesting particulars respecting Shakespeare, Ben Jonson, Massinger, Marston, Dekker, and other Dramatists of the reigns of Elizabeth and James I.

It is necessary to mention, in order to account for some of the imperfections in the succeeding pages, that a knowledge of the existence of certain deeds and family papers, left behind him by Alleyn and preserved in the original "Treasury Chest of God's Gift College," did not reach the writer until he had not only drawn up the whole, but actually printed some part, of the present volume. Had he enjoyed the advantage of having all the information before him at once, he might have rendered the narrative in some places more consecutive and satisfactory.

He cannot too emphatically express his obligations to the Master and Fellows of Dulwich College for the facilities they have at all times afforded him in the inspection of their muniments; but his personal thanks are especially due to the Rev. John Image for ready assistance during the search for materials, and for the most patient kindness while the writer was necessarily occupied in going through them.

COUNCIL

OF THE

SHAKESPEARE SOCIETY.

PRESIDENT,

THE MOST NOBLE THE MARQUESS OF NORMANBY.

VICE-PRESIDENTS,

RT. HON. HON. LORD BRAYBROOKE, F.S.A.
RT. HON. LORD F. EGERTON, M.P.
RT. HON. THE EARL OF GLENGALL.
RT. HON. LORD LEIGH.

AMYOT, THOMAS, ESQ., F.R.S. TREAS. S.A.
AYRTON, WILLIAM, ESQ.. F.R.S., F.S.A.
BRUCE, JOHN, ESQ., F.S.A.
CAMPBELL, THOMAS, ESQ.
COLLIER, J. PAYNE, ESQ. F.S.A.
COURTENAY, RT. HON. THOMAS P.
CRAIK, GEORGE L., ESQ.
DILKE, C. W. ESQ TREASURER.
DYCE, REV. ALEXANDER.
HALLIWELL, J. O. ESQ., F.R.S. F.S.A., &c.
HARNESS, REV. WILLIAM.
JERROLD, DOUGLAS, ESQ.
KENNEY, JAMES, ESQ.
KNIGHT, CHARLES, ESQ.
MACREADY, WILLIAM C., ESQ.
MADDEN, SIR F., F.R.S., F.S.A., KEEPER OF THE
   MSS. IN THE BRITISH MUSEUM.
MILMAN, REV. HENRY HART.
TALFOURD, MR. SERGEANT, M.P.
TOMLINS, F. GUEST, ESQ., SECRETARY.
WRIGHT, THOMAS, ESQ., F.S.A.
YOUNG, CHARLES M., ESQ.

MEMOIRS

OF

EDWARD ALLEYN.

CHAPTER I.

Manuscripts in Dulwich College Library—Alleyn's Birth and Pedigree—Fuller's "Worthies"—Alleyn's Education—Number of London Theatres in his Youth—Nash's "Pierce Pennyless," and other proofs of Alleyn's celebrity and excellence as an Actor—Original MS. of his part in R. Greene's "Orlando Furioso"—Other Characters in which he was famous.

WE know little or nothing of Edward Alleyn before his connection with the stage; but, as regards posterity, the later portion of his career seems to be the only important part of his life. Respecting that part, we are now in possession of fuller details than, as far as we are yet aware, exist respecting any of his dramatic contemporaries—even Shakespeare himself.

Nearly all our materials are derived from Alleyn's family papers preserved in Dulwich College, often mentioned, but never hitherto thoroughly examined. Malone had many of them in his possession for some years; but it is impossible to suppose that he saw them all, or he could not have passed them over so carelessly as not to observe how much they contain that is interesting and curious in relation, not only to the history of the stage, but to the biography of many of

his father, an innholder. The old practice of employing inn-yards as theatres had not then been entirely abandoned; and it is not at all impossible that, in the time of their father, the yard of his inn had been converted to that purpose, and was so continued by his son John, who succeeded him. What was the value of the property Alleyn, the father, left to his widow and children is no where stated; but the founder of Dulwich College owned houses in the parish of St. Botolph, Bishopgate; and his father, as we find by extant leases and other writings, had bought one or more of them from a person named William Parker: on the 5th of March, 1565, he purchased of this person a house, for which he gave £90; and the original deed was many years afterwards indorsed by his son, Edward, "An indenture of sale from Parker to my father." Mr. and Mrs. Browne probably endeavoured to make the most of the histrionic talents of Edward Alleyn, and the cultivation of his mind was, therefore, neglected.

The earliest date at which we hear of him, in connection with the stage, is the 3d of January, 1588-9, when he bought, for £37 10s. 0d., the share of " playing apparels, play-books, instruments and other commodities," which Richard Jones owned jointly with the brothers, John and Edward Alleyn, and their step-father. On the 8th of July of the following year, John Alleyn and Edward Alleyn, " sons of Edward Alleyn, citizen and innholder, deceased," mortgaged a house in the parish of St. Botolph to William Horne for £80. This was, perhaps, the same house their father had bought of Parker twenty-five years before. Other papers at Dulwich shew that John Alleyn became a distiller about the year 1594, and resided in the parish of St. Andrew, Holborn. William Alleyn seems to have been dead in 1590.

With reference to the early career of Edward Alleyn, we are to recollect that, not many years after his birth, acting in stage-plays, as they were called, though not a very respectable, became a very common employment. Few of the nobility

were without companies of comedians, performing under the protection of their names, and as their theatrical servants. Even knights had their dependant players, and as early as 1553 we hear of those of Sir Francis Leek, and in 1571 of those of Sir Robert Lane (Hist. Engl. Dram. Poetry and the Stage, i. 160, 196). The first public Theatre upon record was opened about this latter date; and the Curtain (another place purposely constructed for the exhibition of dramatic entertainments) was in use before 1576. Both these playhouses may be said to have been in the immediate vicinity of the place where Alleyn was born, for they were situated near each other in the parish of St. Leonard, Shoreditch. The Blackfriars theatre was also constructed in 1576; and the Whitefriars theatre was in the possession of a theatrical company soon afterwards. The Rose, Hope, and Swan theatres, on the Bankside, were opened either shortly before or after 1580;* so that by the time Alleyn was sixteen years old dramatic representations were extremely frequent and popular in all quarters of the metropolis. When he was in his nineteenth year they received additional encouragement from the direct patronage of Queen Elizabeth, who took into her service twelve players selected from the most distinguished associations of the day.

It no where appears that Alleyn was one of the performers so chosen, and in 1583 he might not have attained sufficient eminence to entitle him to such a situation. Perhaps he began like many others, as the representative of female characters; and all the companies of players of that date, and earlier and later, had boys or very young men attached to them for this purpose. It is quite certain, however, that before 1592 Alleyn had established a very high reputation as

* A document is in the possession of the writer which shews that there was a house called the Rose on the Bankside in 1571; but it may be doubted whether it was then a theatre, or an inn which was converted into a theatre afterwards.

an actor. In that year came out Thomas Nash's "Pierce Pennyless, his Supplication to the Devil;" and as there were three editions of the same date, we may conclude, perhaps, that the first, from which we quote, made its appearance early in 1592. Alleyn is there twice mentioned as a performer of the utmost and most deserved distinction. The marginal note in the tract is "The due commendation of Ned Allen," and the text opposite to it runs thus:—"Not Roscius nor Æsope, those tragedians admyred before Christ was borne, could ever performe more in action than famous Ned Allen* (Sign. H 3). This sentence contains Nash's testimony to Alleyn's merits, and to the fame which attended those merits; and he adds on the next page, "If I ever write any thing in Latine (as I hope one day I shall), not a man of any desert here amongst us but I will have up— Tarlton, Ned Allen, Knell, Bentley, shall be made knowen

* Ben Jonson, in his "Epigram," addressed "to Edward Allen," also couples him with Roscius and Æsop. It was first printed in 1616, but it had been written, no doubt, fifteen or twenty years earlier.

> "If Rome so great, and in her wisest age,
> Fear'd not to boast the glories of her stage,
> As skilfull Roscius and grave Æsope, men,
> Yet crown'd with honors as with riches then;
> Who had no lesse a trumpet of their name
> Then Cicero, whose every breath was fame;
> How can so great example dye in mee,
> That, Allen, I should pause to publish thee?
> Who both their graces in thy selfe hast more
> Outstript, then they did all that went before;
> And present worth in all dost so contract,
> As others speake, but onely thou dost act.
> Weare this renowne: 'tis just, that who did give
> So many Poets life, by one should live."

Ben Jonson was no flatterer, and of course a most competent judge. The Duchess of Newcastle, in one of her Letters, 1664, fol., p. 362, says, "I never heard any man read well but my husband, and I have heard him say he never heard any man read well but Ben Jonson."

to Fraunce, Spayne, and Italie; and not a part that they surmounted in, more than other, but I will there note and set downe, with the manner of their habites and attyre." Thus we see Alleyn put upon a level with Tarlton (who had been one of the leaders of the Queen's Company of Players in 1583, and who died in 1588), the most celebrated comic performer this country had ever produced, as well as with Knell and Bentley, who had also enjoyed an extraordinary reputation. Nash never lived to complete his design of noting the parts "they surmounted in," and we are left to collect them, as well as we can, from other authorities and accidental notices.

One of the parts which Alleyn "surmounted in" we may now assert for the first time, was Orlando, in Robert Greene's play of "Orlando Furioso." It is alluded to, or at all events a play on the same subject seems spoken of, by G. Peele in his "Farewell" to Sir John Norris and Sir Francis Drake, printed in 1589; and when Henslowe in his Diary notices it, under the date of 21st February, 1591-2, he does not treat it as if it were a new production.* Greene was an author in 1584, and if he wrote "Orlando Furioso" in 1588, Peele might well mention it on account of its popularity in 1589.

The evidence to establish that the character of the hero of the piece was performed by Alleyn, may be looked upon as decisive. Among the MSS. at Dulwich College is a large portion of the original part of Orlando, as transcribed by the copyist of the theatre for the actor. It is in three pieces, one much longer than the others, all imperfect, being more or less

---

* The entry by the manager (who, as will be seen by and by, was stepfather to Alleyn's wife) runs exactly thus:—

                                                        s.   d.
"Rd at orlando the 21 of febreary [1591] . : xvj vj."

It is the oldest entry, excepting two, in the Diary; and the mark which Henslowe placed before plays represented on particular days, for the first time, is not found attached to it. Therefore "Orlando Furioso" was not a new play in Feb. 1591-2.

injured by worms and time. Here and there certain blanks have been supplied in a different hand-writing, and that hand-writing is Alleyn's. We may conclude, therefore, that this is the very copy from which he learnt his part; and that the scribe, not being able in some places to read the author's manuscript, had left small spaces, which Alleyn filled up, either by his own suggestion, from the MS., or after inquiry of Greene. It contains no more than was to be delivered by the actor of the character of Orlando, with the *cues* (as they were then, and are still, technically called) regularly marked, exactly in the same manner as is done at the present day by transcribers in our theatres. We need have no hesitation in pronouncing this one of the most singular theatrical relics in existence, and it is therefore printed entire (as entire, we mean, as it has come down to us) in the Appendix. It is not worth while here to point out in what respects, and to what degree, it differs from the copy of the play as published in 1594 and again in 1599, although the variations are numerous and considerable. The Rev. Mr. Dyce has inserted "Orlando Furioso" with great accuracy, from the printed copy of 1594, in his edition of Greene's Poetical Works (2 vols. 8vo. 1834); so that a comparison may be easily made by those who are curious on such points, and who wish to form an opinion from thence of the very imperfect and slovenly manner in which our old plays usually came from the press.*

Another of Alleyn's famous characters was Barabas, in Christopher Marlowe's tragedy, "The Rich Jew of Malta;" and to this fact we have the evidence of his contemporary, Thomas Heywood, the dramatist, who had been an actor in Alleyn's company in 1596, and doubtless recollected the effect

* As this fragment by some extraordinary chance has been preserved, we may not unreasonably conclude that Alleyn's papers at Dulwich College originally contained many such portions of old plays, in the performance of which he was principally engaged.

produced by him in the part. Possibly, Heywood did not recollect the first production of the tragedy, about 1589 or 1590; but it continued a favourite with the town for many years, most likely until Alleyn finally quitted the stage. It was not printed until 1633, when it was revived at the Cockpit Theatre in Drury Lane, and its success there recommended it for representation at Court. Heywood ushered it into the world in 1633 by a Dedication to that impression, and by Prologues and Epilogues at Whitehall and at the Cockpit Theatre. In the Dedication he states that " the part of the Jew was presented by so unimitable an actor as Mr. Allen;" and in the Prologue at the Cockpit he inserted the following remarkable lines:—

> " We know not how our play may pass this stage,
> But by the best of poets in that age
> The Malta Jew had being and was made;
> And he then by the best of actors play'd.
> In Hero and Leander one did gain
> A lasting memory: in Tamberlaine,
> This Jew, with others many, the other wan
> The attribute of peerless; being a man
> Whom we may rank with (doing no one wrong)
> Proteus for shapes, and Roscius for a tongue,
> So could he speak, so vary."——

The sense has hitherto been somewhat obscured by ill pointing,* but the meaning seems to be, that Marlowe gained a lasting memory by his paraphrase of Musæus under the title of " Hero and Leander," (licensed for the press in 1593, but not published till 1598); while Alleyn (whose name is

---

* In the Hist. of Engl. Dram. Poetry and the Stage, iii. 114, an opinion is given by the author that the passage
——— " in Tamberlaine
This Jew, with others many,"

applies to Marlowe, and not to Alleyn, and that the punctuation ought to be regulated accordingly; but this is at least doubtful.

inserted in the margin) " wan the attribute of peerless" by his personation of Tamberlaine, the Jew of Malta, and many other characters; he being a man who could so speak and vary his appearance, that he might be likened to " Proteus for shapes, and Roscius for a tongue."

On the same authority, therefore, we find that Alleyn was also the original representative of Marlowe's " Tamberlaine the Great," which there is every reason to suppose had been acted in or before 1587, (Hist. of Engl. Dram. Poetry and the Stage, iii. 112); and Alleyn's performance of that part ought (if it could have been done conveniently) to have been mentioned before we spoke of his Orlando, or of his Barabas. It is hardly too much to suppose that Alleyn was the actor who sustained many, if not most, of the chief tragic characters in the plays entered in Henslowe's Diary; for, as we have already seen, Fuller informs us that he was especially great in parts requiring a majestic deportment. His countenance and person, as far as we can judge from his full-length portrait in Dulwich College, were admirably adapted to give effect to such impersonations.

It merits observation, that in the preceding quotation from the Prologue to " The Rich Jew of Malta," Heywood calls Marlowe " the best of poets *in that age:*" he is to be understood as meaning " the best of poets" in the age in which Marlowe flourished; for it is not likely that he intended to exclude Shakespeare, and to place him in a rank inferior to Marlowe. Heywood does not seem to have considered Marlowe as in the same age with Shakespeare, and hence an inference might possibly be drawn that Shakespeare did not obtain any great eminence as a dramatic author until after the death of Marlowe. Marlowe was buried on June 1, 1593, (Hist. Engl. Dram. Poetry and the Stage, iii. 144); and there is reason to suppose that previous to that year Shakespeare had done little more than improve the three parts of Henry VI. (if, indeed, he touched the first part of Henry VI.

at all), and had written "The Two Gentlemen of Verona," and "The Comedy of Errors." His "Richard II." has generally been assigned to the year 1593. Marlowe's career was a comparatively short one, but it is very possible that he began to write for the stage six or eight years before that date.

CHAPTER II.

Theatrical Wagers, and Alleyn's concern in them—Shakespeare mentioned under the name of "Will"—Alleyn's Marriage with Joan Woodward—His Wife's Property—Philip Henslowe's connection with Theatres—His Partnership with Alleyn—Original Inventory of Alleyn's Theatrical Wardrobe—Union of Shakespeare's and Alleyn's Companies of Players, and the Dramas represented by them.

OTHER strong proofs of Alleyn's high character as an actor are furnished by documents still preserved at Dulwich College, and one of them has been quoted by Malone, but with some inaccuracies (Shakesp. by Boswell, iii. 335). It relates to a wager which had been laid by some friend of Alleyn, that in the performance of a particular part, which either Bentley or Knell had formerly sustained, he should excel Peele, who, we may perhaps conclude, had plumed himself on his histrionic abilities. Contests of this kind were not uncommon in those days: Meres, in his "Palladis Tamia," 1598, fol. 286, speaks of Wilson's "challenge at the Swan on the Bankside;" and Malone has adduced two passages, one from Dekker's "Gull's Hornbook," and the other from "the Knight of the Burning Pestle," to the same effect. How these wagers and challenges were conducted and decided, we have no precise information: this, in which Alleyn was to be pitted against Peele, must have been given when the latter was in his zenith, and considerably prior to the epistle which

in his distress, and after long sickness, he addressed to Lord Burghley in 1595. (Dyce's Peele's Works, i. xvi. second edition). It is likely that Peele did not recover from this illness, and we know, on the evidence of Meres,* that he was dead in 1598. The following paper has no date, but we may place it in 1590 or 1591 at the latest.

"Your answer the other nighte so well pleased the Gentlemen, as I was satisfied therewith, though to the hazarde of the wager: and yet my meaninge was not to prejudice Peele's credit, neither wolde it, though it pleased you so to excuse it; but beinge now growen in question, the partie affected to Bentley scornynge to wynne the wager by your deniall, hath now given yow libertie to make choice of any one playe that either Bentley or Knell plaide; and least this advantage agree not with your minde, he is contented both the plaie and the tyme shalbe referred to the gentlemen here present. I see not how yow canne any waie hurte your credit by this action, for if yow excell them yow will then be famous; if equall them, yow wynne both the wager and credit; yf short of them, we must and will saie Ned Allen still.

"Your frend to his power,
"W. P."

To this letter the following verses were appended:—

"Deny me not, sweete Nedd, the wager's downe,
  And twice as muche commaunde of me or myne;
  And if you wynne, I sweare the half is thyne,
And for an overplus an English Crowne:
  Appoint the tyme and stint it as you pleas,
  Your labors gaine, and that will prove it ease."

All this is written in a beautiful hand, and "Ned Allen" in the letter, and "sweete Nedd" and "English Crowne" in the verses, are in characters of gold. It is clear that Alleyn at this time had not attained the loftiest point of his celebrity, inasmuch as he is told, that if he excels Bentley and Knell he "will *then* be famous." We have before seen Thomas Nash,

* In his "Palladis Tamia, or Wit's Treasury," fol. 286 b. Peele's death was occasioned by the irregularity of his life.

in a passage already quoted, mention Alleyn in conjunction with Bentley, Knell, and Tarlton, in 1592.

But there is another paper of a very similar kind, apparently referring to the preceding, or to some other like contest, but containing several remarkable allusions, which Malone did not notice. Perhaps it never met his eye, or perhaps he reserved it for his Life of Shakespeare, and was unwilling to forestal that production by inserting it elsewhere. It seems to be of a later date, and it mentions not only Tarlton, Knell, and Bentley, but Kempe, Phillips, and Pope, while Alleyn's rival Burbage is sneered at as "Roscius Richard," and Shakespeare introduced under the name of Will, by which we have Thomas Heywood's authority (in his "Hierarchie of the blessed Angels," 1635, p. 206) for saying he was known among his companions. The paper is in verse, and runs precisely as follows:

> "Sweete Nedde, nowe wynne an other wager
> For thine old frende and Fellow stager.
> Tarlton himselfe thou doest excell,
> And Bentley beate, and conquer Knell,
> And nowe shall Kempe orecome aswell.
> The moneyes downe, the place the Hope,
> Phillippes shall hide his head and Pope.
> Feare not, the victorie is thyne;
> Thou still as macheles Ned shall shyne.
> If Roscius Richard foames and fumes,
> The globe shall have but emptie roomes,
> If thou doest act; and Willes newe playe
> Shall be rehearst some other daye.
> Consent then, Nedde; doe us this grace:
> Thou cannot faile in anie case;
> For in the triall, come what maye,
> All sides shall brave Ned Allin saye."

No explanatory prose accompanies the above slip, which seems to have been an inclosure. The wager was laid by some brother actor, that Alleyn would be adjudged superior

to Kempe, (whom Nash, about 1589, in the dedication to his "Almond for a Parrot," called "Vice-gerent General to the Ghost of Dick Tarlton,") in some part not mentioned; and hence we may gather that Alleyn was "famous" in comedy, as well as in tragedy: all the actors named, excepting Burbage and Shakespeare, (who is only spoken of here as an author,) were comedians. The Hope was a theatre in the occupation of Alleyn, and in the immediate vicinity of the Globe, where "Roscius Richard" was in the habit of performing, and where (and at the Blackfriars Theatre) Shakespeare's plays, as far as we can now learn with certainty, were represented. We need feel little hesitation in believing that the couplet

——— " and Willes newe playe
Shall be rehearst some other daye,"

refers to Shakespeare; but it may be doubtful whether we should take the word "rehearst" in the sense of a private repetition before public performance, which then, as now, it signified, or in the more general sense of *acted*. A mere rehearsal would not attract an audience, nor would be intended to do so; and it would, therefore, have been no disappointment if the "rooms" at the Globe were " empty;" while the words "new play" seem appropriate to the term "rehearst." However, the point of the passage would be lost, were we not to understand "rehearst" as *acted*, and the reference to be to the first night of a new play by "Will" Shakespeare.

We have thus completely established Alleyn's great eminence in his profession, which, doubtless, independently of any patrimony, yielded him such an income as would enable him to marry with every prospect of comfort and competence. This event occurred in the autumn of 1592. On the 1st September, he completed his twenty-sixth year; and on the 22nd of October following he was united to Joan

Woodward, the daughter of the wife of Philip Henslowe, who had married Agnes Woodward, a widow. The entry of the marriage of Edward Alleyn with Joan Woodward stands thus in a Diary or Account Book kept by Henslowe.

"Edward Alen wasse maryed unto Jone woodward the 22 day of octobr 1592   In the iiij and thirtie yeare of the Quenes Matie Rayne, elizabeth by the grace of god of Ingland, france, and Iarland, defender of the fayth."

After his marriage, the house Alleyn was to live in was either extensively repaired or built. At the other end of the book which contains the preceding entry is a statement of figures thus entitled, "The Acount of such Carges [charges] as hathe bene layd owt a bowt edward alenes howsse, as foloweth—1592." It commences on Nov. 4, and a little farther on we meet with "Novmbr. 11:" before it is closed, items, dated February, 1593, and even February, 1594, are inserted, so that the work was going on for more than two years. At the end are some particulars that appear to relate directly to the marriage: thus we have,

> "Itm pd for makinge the writtinges . . . . v s.
> Itm sowld my soune a fetherbead for . . . . xxx s.
> Itm pd for makinge of writinges
>   for my sones parte . . . . xx s."

There is ground for believing that Alleyn's wife, Joan Woodward, possessed property in her own right, which she had derived under her father's will: a portion of this property was, probably, the lease of the parsonage of Firle, in Sussex, before-mentioned, which, four years after his marriage, Alleyn sold to Arthur Langworth for £3000. To this property the writings, above-noticed by Henslowe, may have referred. Henslowe's wife, Agnes, had been a widow, and before her marriage with Henslowe, they stood (as Alleyn himself alleges, in a piece of evidence hereafter to be produced) in the relation of mistress and servant: Philip Henslowe had been the servant of Agnes Woodward, and

we may presume that her first husband had left her and her daughter Joan sufficiently provided for. The very book in which Henslowe, at a subsequent date, made his theatrical memoranda had most likely belonged to her husband, Woodward, who appears from it to have been extensively engaged in the iron mines and founderies in Ashdowne Forest, the dates commencing in 1576. Hence, perhaps, the property in Sussex, which Alleyn seems to have obtained on his marriage with Joan Woodward on the 22nd October, 1592. "The writings," it is true, may not have had any connection with this union, but may have related to other transactions; and the name of "Mr. Langworth" is introduced into the same account, as having received from Henslowe £27 10 0 and £30; but the date of these payments is given as 9th September, 1594. In fact, Henslowe was so illiterate, and kept his accounts (sometimes in his own hand-writing, but oftener in that of some person he employed) so irregularly, that it is frequently impossible to make out at all exactly what they do, or do not establish. The dates upon the page, to which we are now referring, extend from 1592 to 1597.

In what manner, and at what period, Henslowe became connected with theatres nowhere appears; but the earliest entry in his Diary or Account-book, relating to any company of players, is dated 19th February 1591 (or 1592, according to our present mode of calculating the year), about eight months prior to the marriage of Alleyn with Henslowe's wife's daughter. By rough drafts of two bills in Chancery, among the miscellaneous papers at Dulwich College, (without dates, but addressed in the usual form to "Lord Ellesmere," therefore subsequent to July, 1603, when Sir Thomas Egerton was raised to the peerage,) we learn that Henslowe was "free inheritor" of some houses in Southwark, and that he had besides purchased what is called "the Pike Garden, near the Bankside, in Southwark." "A note (in

his Diary) of such charges as I have lay'd out about my play-howsse," dated 1592, shews that he was at that period the proprietor of the Rose Theatre. He had, in fact, been so since 1586, when he entered into partnership with a person of the name of Cholmley, with whose money the Rose, as it stood in 1592, was constructed. It had, however, as has been already stated, been used as a playhouse at a considerably earlier date. Some new and curious particulars regarding it will be found in the Appendix: they are derived from Alleyn's papers. It is quite certain, from a portion of the contents of Henslowe's Diary, that he also acted as a sort of pawnbroker, and advanced money to any parties who were in want of it, upon plate, rings, jewels, and wearing apparel.

From the date of the marriage of Alleyn with Joan Woodward, he and Henslowe entered into partnership in their theatrical concerns; and as far as we can learn from extant letters (most of which appear to have remained till now totally unexamined) the two families, until Alleyn's house was ready, lived together, occupying the same dwelling in Southwark. Upon what terms, and to what extent Alleyn and Henslowe engaged in partnership, it is impossible to ascertain from any of the accounts or documents that have come down to us; but it seems more than probable that Alleyn was sole owner of the wardrobe used by himself in the personation of various characters.

There exists in his own hand-writing at Dulwich College an inventory of his theatrical apparel, which is much more important and interesting than a mere list of dresses would be supposed to be. It has no heading and no date, but it is unquestionably early, and it renders it quite clear that Alleyn acted parts, if not in Shakespeare's Plays (though that has been asserted by Oldys in his account of Alleyn, in the *Biographia Britannica*, and after him by several others,) in plays upon the same stories as those employed by our greatest dramatist. Malone (Shakesp. by Bosw. iii.

331 and 335,) has shewn that in 1599, Dekker and Chettle were employed in writing a play for Alleyn and Henslowe, of which Troilus and Cressida were the hero and heroine; and that, as late as 1602, Ben Jonson had undertaken to write a play upon the events of the reign of Richard III. It will be seen, by what we shall presently subjoin, that Alleyn had probably played Lear, (or Leir, as he spells the name,) Henry VIII. Romeo and Pericles, as if the subjects of those plays had been the common property of the dramatists of the day, the only question being who could make the best use of it. The "Leir" was perhaps that which was licensed to Edward White, May 14th, 1594, under the title of "the moste famous Chronicle Hystorie of Leire, King of England, and his three Daughters." The "Romeo" may have been a play written either before or in rivalry of Shakespeare's Tragedy, which is supposed to have been first acted in 1596: the "Pericles" possibly was the old play of which Shakespeare made use in 1608, especially in the earlier portion of his drama. "The Moore in Venis" may have been another version of "Othello." "The Guises" mentioned in the succeeding document, was no doubt Marlowe's "Massacre at Paris," printed without date; and the "Dido," Marlowe's and Nash's celebrated tragedy, published in 1594.* Regarding other items, such

---

* A good edition of Marlowe's productions is much wanted: a very imperfect attempt of the kind was made in 1826, 3 vols. 8vo. which is full of blunders, some of them of the grossest kind. We will add an instance from the tragedy above-mentioned, "Dido, Queen of Carthage," by Marlowe and Nash. In the scene between Juno and Venus (Act III.) after the speech of Juno, which, in the edition of 1826, ends with the line

"Then in one cave, the Queen and he shall meet,"

leaving the sense imperfect, the following three lines should have been added; but they are wholly omitted.

"And interchangeably discourse their thoughts,
Whose short conclusion will seale up their hearts
Unto the purpose which we now propound."

Other errors are numerous and important, but not quite so glaring as the preceding.

as "a cloth of silver for Har," "Daniel's gowne," "Will Somer's cote," &c. we might indulge conjectures, but there is every chance that they would be fruitless.

CLOKES.

1 A scarlett cloke with ij brode gould laces with gould buttons of the same downe the sids, for Leir.
2 A black velvett cloke.
3 A scarlett cloke layd downe with silver lace and silver buttons.
4 A short velvett cape cloke embroydered with gould and gould spangles.
5 A watched sattin cloke with v gould laces.
6 A purpell sattin welted with velvett and silver twist Romeos.
7 A black tufted cloke cloke [*sic*—q^{re} cloth cloke].
8 A damask cloke garded [def. in MS.]
9 A long blak tafata cloke.
10 A colored bugett for a boye.
11 A scarlett with buttons of gould fact with blew velvett.
12 A scarlett fact with black velvett.
13 A stamell cloke with gould lace.
14 Blak bugett cloke.

GOWNES.

1 Hary the VIII gowne.
2 The blak velvett gowne with wight fure.
3 A crimosin bestrypt with gould fact with ermin.
4 On of wrought cloth of gould.
5 On of red silk with gould buttons.
6 A Cardinalls gowne.
7 Wemens gowns.
8 Blak velvett embroydered with gould.
9 Cloth of gould Candish his stuf.
10 A blak velvett lact and drawne out with wight sarsnett.
11 A blak silk with red slash.
12 A cloth of silver for Har.
13 A yelow silk gowne.
14 A red silk gowne.
15 Angells sute.
16 Blew calico gownes.

Antik Sutes.

1. A cote of crimosen velvett cut in paynes and embroydered with gould.
2. Cloth of gould cote with gould laces.
3. Cloth of gould with oraing tawny lace.
4. Cloth of silver with blew silk and tinsell bases.
5. Blew damask cote for the Moore in Venis.
6. A red velvett horsmans cote.
7. Yelow tafata.
8. Cloth of gould horsmans cote.
9. Cloth of bodkin horsmans cote.
10. Orayng tany horsmans cote of cloth lact.
11. Daniells gowne.
12. Blew embroydered bases.
13. Will Somers cote.
14. Wight embroyd bases.
15. Gilt bases wt.
16. Hedins set with stones.

Jerkings and Dublets.

1. A crimosin velvett with gould buttons and lace.
2. A crymosin sattin case lact with gould lace all over.
3. A velvett dublett with dimond fact with gould lace and spangles.
4. A dublett of blak velvett cut on silver tinsell.
5. A ginger colored dublett.
6. A wight sattin cut on wight.
7. Black velvett with gould lace.
8. Green velvett.
9. Blak tafata cut on blak velvett lact with bugells.
10. Blak velvett playne.
11. Ould wight sattin.
12. Red velvett for a boy.
13. Carnation velvett lacte with silver.
14. A yelow spangled case.
15. Red velvett with blew sattin flower and case.
16. Cloth of silver Jerkin.
17. Faustus Jerkin, his cloke.

French Hose.

1 Blew velvett enlayd with gould paynet, blew sattin stokin.
2 Silver payns lact with carnation, satins lact over with silver.
3 For the Guises.
4 Rich payns with long stokins.
5 Gould payns with blak stript scalings of cary.
6 Gould payns with velvett scalings.
7 Gould payns with red stript scaling.
8 Black angell.
9 Red payns for a boy with yelow scalins.
10 Pryams Hoes in Dido.
11 Spangled hoes in Pericles.

Venetians.

A purpell velvett cut in dimonds lace and spangels.
Red velved lact with gould Spanish.
Purpell vellore emproydered with silver cut on tinsell.
Greene velvett lact with gould Spanish.
Blake velvett.
Cloth of silver.
Green strypt sattin.
Cloth of gould for a boye.

Inventories, not very dissimilar, were printed by Malone; but they were taken from Henslowe's Diary (though not now remaining in it) and consisted of properties and dresses belonging either to the company at large, to himself alone, or to himself and Alleyn in partnership. Neither do they present any such curious points for speculation, as the preceding list, which, as has been stated, is entirely in the hand-writing of the subject of the present memoir.

The probability certainly is, that Alleyn never performed in any of Shakespeare's plays; but, in our present state of information, it is impossible to speak at all decisively upon the point. The "Leir," the "Romeo," the "Henry VIII." "the "Moore in Venis," and the "Pericles," of the preceding inventory, may have been the Lear, Romeo, Henry VIII., Othello, and Pericles of Shakespeare; and there is

one circumstance, in connection with this question, that has never been sufficiently attended to. The agreement between Burbage and Street, the carpenter, for the original construction of the Globe Theatre, is dated 22d Dec. 1593, (Hist. of Engl. Dram. Poetry and the Stage, iii., 296;) so that the building could not have been commenced until 1594. How long it took to finish it, is not known; but, in Henslowe's Diary, there is an account, beginning 3d of June, 1594, and ending 15th Nov., 1596, by which it appears that the Lord Admiral's players and the Lord Chamberlain's players (to which last company Shakespeare belonged) during that interval played together at the theatre in Newington Butts. Whether they acted jointly on the same days, or severally on different days, we cannot determine; but Henslowe's entries are of daily receipts on his part, as if he were entitled to a share of "the takings," whatever company performed. It is remarkable, also, that while the two associations of actors were thus occupying the Newington Theatre, we read the following, among the names of the plays which Henslowe informs us were represented:

"9 June 1594 Rd at Hamlet . . . . viij s.
11 June 1594 Rd at the Tamynge of a Shrowe . ix s.
12 June 1594 Rd at Andronicus . . . . vij s.
25 Augt 1594 Rd at the Venesyon Comodey . ls. vj d.
17 Sepr 1594 Rd at Palamon and Arsett . . lj s.
8 Nov. 1594 Rd at Seser and Pompie . . iij li ij s.
20 June 1595 Rd at Antony and Vallea . . xx s.
26 June 1595 Rd at the 2 pte of Seaser . . xx s.
28 Nov. 1595 Rd at Harry the V. . . . iij li vj s.
22 June 1596 Rd at Troye . . . . iij li ix s.

Thus we see that between 9th June, 1594, and 22nd June, 1596, during which period, it is very likely, the Globe theatre was in a course of construction, no fewer than ten plays were performed, upon the same, or similar, subjects as those which Shakespeare adopted: this remark supposes that "the Vene-

syon Comodey" meant (as has indeed been conjectured) " the Merchant of Venice;" and that Shakespeare was concerned in "the Two Noble Kinsmen." It seems not impossible that some of these may not have been different or older productions, but the very same that proceeded from his pen; and it is capable of distinct proof, from Henslowe's Diary, that five out of the ten plays were new. These are "the Veneçyon Comodey," "Palamon and Arsett," "Seser and Pompie," "Harry the V.," and "Troye." It will be observed that the receipts to Henslowe, as entered by him, were much larger upon these five occasions (in consequence, no doubt, of the greater fulness of the theatre) than when old plays were represented; and he inserts opposite to each of them the usual mark, to denote that it was the first time the piece was produced before an audience. If none of these plays were by Shakespeare, but dramas of which he availed himself in the composition of his own plays, the above list shews that he had perhaps been in some way concerned in the representation of them, and his attention might thus have been especially directed to them.

CHAPTER III.

Alleyn driven into the country by the Plague in 1593—His Letter to his Wife—Carting of Mrs. Alleyn—Another Letter from Alleyn to his Wife—His fondness for Home—Letter from Henslowe and Mrs. Alleyn to Alleyn—Lord Strange's Players—Letter to Alleyn from Henslowe—Mrs. Henslowe and Mrs. Alleyn—Bartholomew Fair—Letter from Henslowe and Mrs. Alleyn to Alleyn.

WE have brought Alleyn's personal history down to October, 1592, when he was married to Joan Woodward, daughter to Henslowe's wife by her first husband. Very

soon afterwards a malignant fever, called the plague, broke out in London, and put a stop to all dramatic performances, which, from the congregation of persons in theatres, were thought to promote and spread the infection. Accordingly, Alleyn and his companions, "Lord Strange's Players," were obliged, as usual in such cases, to quit the metropolis, and to take to a strolling life through the country, where they were frequently little welcome to the inhabitants, under the fear that the players would convey to them the pestilence which was devastating the metropolis. He left his wife residing with his "father," (as he was accustomed to call Henslowe) and with her mother and sister on the Bankside in Southwark. Among the papers at Dulwich College are preserved several letters of about this period, some of them written to Alleyn while he was travelling in the provinces, and two from him to his wife. Only the last have ever been noticed; but they are all highly interesting in reference to Alleyn, his connections, occupation, and prospects. The earliest in the series is from Alleyn to his wife (but addressed as to himself) which adverts to a singular report which had reached him at Chelmsford, that Mrs. Alleyn, "and all her fellowes," (meaning, perhaps, such players as had not accompanied Alleyn into the country) had been *carted* by the Lord Mayor's officers. It is difficult, from the wording of the letter, to decide whether Alleyn was in jest or in earnest; but it is not impossible that his wife, and the remnant of the company in town, had got into disgrace in consequence of the infringement of the order against dramatic performances. The letter is literatim as follows:—

"To E. Alline, on the bank side.

"My good sweet harte and loving mouse, I send the a thousand comendations, wishing thee as well as well may be, and hoping thou art in good helth, with my father, mother, and sister. I have no newes to send thee, but I thank god we ar all well, and in helth, which I pray god to continew with us in the contry, and with you in london. But, mouse, I littell thought to hear that which I now hear by you, for it is well knowne,

they say, that you wear by my lorde maiors officer mad to rid in a cart, you and all your felowes, which I ame sory to hear; but you may thank your ij suporters, your stronge leges I mene, that would nott cary you away, but lett you fall in to the hands of such Tarmagants. But, mouse, when I com hom, Il be revengd on them: tell when, mouse, I bid thee fayerwell. I prethee send me word how thou doste, and do my harty comendations to my father, mother, and sister, and to thy own self; and so, swett hart, the lord bless thee. From Chelmsford, the 2 of Maye, 1593.

"thyn ever, and no bodies els, by god of heaven,
"EDWARDE ALLEYN.

"Farewell mecho mousin, and mouse,
and farwell bess dodipoll." *

"Bess Dodipoll," in the postscript, was doubtless his wife's "syster bease," of whom we shall see that Henslowe speaks in a subsequent letter: Dr. Dodipoll was a character in a play of the time, and hence perhaps the nickname. When Alleyn states above, that it was his wife's (or "mouse's") own fault, if she had fallen into the hands of "such Termagants" as the officers of the lord mayor, because she would not let her "two supporters, her strong legs," carry her away, he may mean to reproach her gently for not having accompanied him into the country. On the 2d May, 1593, Alleyn was at Chelmsford, but he was at Bristol when he dispatched the next letter to his wife, on the 1st August, 1593, which Malone published (Shakesp. by Bosw. xxi. 389), with many minute variations from the original, and with some important errors. It is thus superscribed, with a peculiar sparingness of capital letters:—

"This be delyvered to m^r. hinslo, on of the gromes of hir maist. chamber, dwelling on the bank sid, right over against the clink.

"My good sweete mouse, I comend me hartely to you And to my father, my mother, and my sister bess, hopinge in god, though the sicknes be round about you, yett by his mercy itt may escape your house,

* This letter is very incorrectly printed in "Lysons' Environs," i. 88. The Rev. Author states, that at its date Alleyn had been married "about a year;" but, in fact, he had been married only six months and a few days.

which by the grace of god it shall. therefor use this corse:—kepe your house fayr and clean, which I knowe you will, and every evening throwe water before your dore and in your bake sid, and have in your windowes good store of reue and herbe of grace, and with all the grace of god, which must be obtaynd by prayers; and so doinge, no dout but the Lord will mercyfully defend you. now, good mouse, I have no newse to send you but this, thatt we have all our helth, for which the Lord be praysed. I reseved your Letter at Bristo by richard couley, for the wich I thank you. I have sent you by this berer, Thomas popes kinsman, my whit wascote, because it is a trobell to me to cary it. reseave it with this letter, And lay it up for me till I com. if you send any mor Letters, send to me by the cariers of Shrowsbury, or to Westchester, or to York, to be kept till my Lord Stranges players com. and thus, sweett hart, with my harty comenda. to all our frends, I sett from Bristo this Wensday after Saynt James his day, being redy to begin the playe of hary of cornwall. mouse, do my harty commend. to M^r grigs, his wife, and all his houshould, and to my sister phillyps.

"Your Loving housband,
"E. ALLEYN.

"Mouse, you send me no newes of any things: you should send of your domestycall matters, such things as hapens att home; as how your distilled watter proves, or this or that, or any thing, what you will.

"And, Jug, I pray you, lett my orayng tawny stokins of wolen be dyed a very good blak against I com hom, to wear in the winter. you sente me nott word of my garden, but next tym you will; but remember this in any case, that all that bed which was parsley in the month of september you sowe itt with spinage, for then is the tym. I would do it my selfe, but we shall nott com hom till allholland tyd. and so, swett mouse, farwell, and broke our Long Jorney with patienc."

It is an excellent trait in the character of Alleyn, that he was of so domestic a turn, and, though absent, took such a strong interest in all that was going forward at home. He appears to have preserved the same disposition through life, always thinking that the happiest place in the world was his own fireside. The strange terms of endearment of "mouse," and "mousin," &c., he applies to his wife, and the nickname he gives to his sister proceed from the same amiable and affectionate habit of mind. His anxiety lest they should take the infection, and his earnest and sensible instructions to prevent

it, are very kindly and natural. Richard Cowley, mentioned in the preceding as the bearer of a letter from Mrs. Alleyn to her husband at Bristol, became one of the king's players on the accession of James I., being the last name inserted in the patent of 17th May, 1603. The words "Thomas Popes kinsman," Malone misprinted "Thomas Chockes kinsman." Now we know no such person as Thomas Chocke, but Thomas Pope was a very eminent comedian, who, in 1596, belonged to the same company as that to which Shakespeare was attached, and whose will bears date in July, 1603 (Hist. of Engl. Dram. Poetry and the Stage, iii. 433). Griggs, as we learn from Henslowe's Diary, was a carpenter, and a man of some property, living on the Bankside. There was a very distinguished actor of clown's parts of the name of Phillips, and perhaps he married another of Henslowe's wife's daughters, who was therefore called "sister" by Alleyn.

The contents of a letter without date, written by some scribe jointly for Philip Henslowe and Joane Alleyn* (misspelling both their names), shew that it was an answer to the preceding, and it seems to have been sent by a carrier to Shrewsbury, Chester (then often called West-chester), or York, as Alleyn had given directions. It is merely addressed to him as "one of my Lord Stranges players," without the addition of any place where they were to be found. It runs thus:—

"To my wealle loved Sonne Edward Allen, one of my Lord Stranges Players, this be delyvered with spead.

"Welbeloved Sonne Edward Allen. After owr hartie comendations, bothe I and your mother, and syster bease, all in generall doth hartiely

* The same hand-writing is to be found in many parts of "Henslowe's Diary," and all the principal entries respecting the performance of plays, and Henslowe's proportion of the profits, are made in it. This is a circumstance not hitherto observed, and Malone attributes all the specimens of ignorance contained in the Diary to the old manager. This scribe, whoever he might be, seems to have acted as Henslowe's clerk.

comend us unto you; and for your mowse, her comendationes comes by yt sealfe, which, as she sayes, comes from her harte and her sowle, prainge to god day and nyght for your good heallth, which trewley, to be playne, we doe saie all, hoopinge in the lorde Jesus that we shall have agayne a mery meting; for I thanke god we have be flytted with feare of the sycknes, but thankes be unto god, we are all at this time in good healthe in owr howsse; but rownd a bowte us yt hath bene all moste in every howsse abowt us, and wholle howsholdes deyed, and y[e]t my friend the Baylle doth scape, but he smealles monstrusly for feare, and dares staye no wheare, for ther hath deyed this laste weake, in generall, 1603, of the which nomber ther hathe deyed of them of the plage 113, which hause bene the greatest that came yet; and as for other newes of this and that, I cane tealle youe none, but that Robert Brownes wife in Shordech and all her children and howshowld be dead, and heare dores shut upe; and as for your joyner he hath browght you a corte coberd and hath seat up your portowle in the chamber, and sayes you shall have a good bead stead; and as for your garden yt is weall, and your spenege bead not forgoten. Your orenge colerd stockens died, but no market in Smythfylld, nether to bye your cloth, nor yet to sealle your horsse, for no man wold ofer me a bove fower pownd for hime; therfor I wold not sealle hime, but have seante hime into the contrey, tylle youe retorne backe agayene. This, licke poore peapell rejoysinge that the lorde hath in compased us rownd, and kepeth us all in health we end, prayinge to god to send you all good health, that yet maye pleasse god to send, that we maye all merelye meat; and I praye you do ower comendations unto them all, and I wold gladley heare the licke frome them; and thankes be to god your poore mowsse hath not ben seack seance you weant.

"Your poore and assured frend tell death,
"PHILLIPPE HENSLEY.

"Your lovinge wife tylle deathe,
"JONE ALLEN."

Philip Henslowe (as he usually signed his own name, though his practice was not quite uniform) wrote badly and illiterately, and therefore employed a scribe, who did not write much better; but Mrs. Alleyn could not write at all, for in witnessing a document in 1596, hereafter to be introduced, she affixed her mark to it. At the earliest date at which we have any information regarding Lord Strange's servants, they exhibited feats of activity; but, at this period, and for some

time before, (Henslowe gives a list of plays represented by them in 1592), they had become regular actors of the drama, like the servants of the Lord Chamberlain, the Earl of Leicester, the Earl of Warwick, &c. In the letter, which we shall next subjoin, Henslowe, after referring to Alleyn's illness, and complaining that he did not oftener write (apparently not making due allowance for indisposition) adverts to the difficulty of sending letters to him, because in London it could not be known where Lord Strange's company was performing. He also alludes to points touched by Alleyn in his communication of the 1st of August, especially to the necessity of taking measures against the infection, attending to his garden, &c. Henslowe talks of the poverty of Alleyn's tenants, without mentioning where the property for which rent should have been paid was situated, and regrets that the absence of the players in the country, and the closing of the theatres, kept him poor. The subsequent letter was also the penmanship of the same person who wrote the former communication, and it purports to be the composition of Philip Henslowe, Agnes his wife (their initials being appended), and Joane Alleyn. It is addressed

"For my wealbeloved husbande Mr. Edwarde Allen, on of my Lorde Strange's players, this be delyvered with speade.

"Jesus.

"Welbeloved Sonne Edwarde Allen, I and your mother and your sister Beasse have all in generall our hartie commendations unto you, and very glad to heare of your good healthe, which we praye god to contenew longe to his will and pleasur; for we hard that you weare very sycke at Bathe, and that one of your felowes weare fayne to playe your part for you, which wasse no lytell greafe unto us to heare, but thanckes be to god for amendmente, for we feared yt much, because we had no leatter from you when the other wifes had leatters sente; which made your mouse not to weape a lytell, but tooke yt very greavesly, thinckinge that you hade conseved some unkindnes of her, because you weare ever wont to write with the firste: and I praye ye do so stylle, for we wold all be sorey but to heare as often frome you as others do frome ther frendes; for we wold write oftener

to you then we doe, but we knowe not whether to sende to you, therfore I praye you forgeat not your mouse and us: for you seant in one leatter that we retorned not answeare wheather we receved your or no, for we receved one which you made at seant James tide, wherin mackes mensyon of your whitte wascote, and your lute bockes, and other thinges which we have receved, and now lastly a leater, which Peter browght with your horsse, which I wilbe as carfull as I cane in yt. Now, sonne, althouge longeyt [is] at the laste I remember a hundered comendations from your mowsse, which is very glade to heare of your healthe and prayeth daye and nyght to the lord to contenew the same; and lickewisse prayeth unto the lord to seace his hand frome punyshinge us with his crosse, that she mowght have you at home with her, hopinge then that you shold be eased of this heavey laboure and toylle: and you sayd in your leater that she seant you not worde howe your garden and all your things dothe prosper; very well, thanckes be to god, for your beanes are growen to hey headge and well coded, and all other thinges doth very well; but your tenantes weax very power, for they cane paye no reant, nor will paye no rent while mychellmas next, and then we shall have yt yf we cane geat yt; and lyckwisse your Joyner comendes hime unto you and sayes he will mack you suche good stufe and suche good peneworthes as he hoopeth shall weall licke you and contente you; which I hope he will do, because he sayes he will prove himseallfe ane onest man: and for your good cownsell which you gave us in your leater we all thanck you, which wasse for keping of our howsse cleane and watringe of our dores, and strainge our windowes with wormwode and rewe, which I hope all this we do and more; for we strowe yt with hartie prayers unto the lorde, which unto us is more avaylable then all thinges eallse in the world; for I praysse the lord god for yt, we are all in very good healthe, and I praye ye, sonne, comend me harteley to all the reast of your fealowes in generall, for I growe poore for lacke of them, therfor have no geaftes to sende, but as good and faythfull a hart as they shall desyer to have comen amongste them. Now, sonne, we thanck you all for your tokenes you seant us; and as for newes of the sycknes, I cane not seande you no juste note of yt, because ther is comandement to the contrary; but as I thincke doth die within the sitteye and without of all syckneses to the number of seventen or eyghten hundredth in one weacke: and this, prayinge to god for your health, I ende from London the 14 of Auguste 1593.

" Your lovinge Father and Mother to our powers,

" P. H.   A.

" Your lovinge wiffe to comande till death,

" JOHNE ALLEN."

Every letter serves to prove more and more how attached Alleyn was to his family, with what affection they regarded him, and what a deprivation it must have been to all, for him to be so long absent. Nevertheless, in the following letter Henslowe again blames him for not writing more frequently. This seems to have been only a repetition of the topic before urged, and it will be observed that the old manager (if so he may be called), as to several particulars, goes over the same ground as that he had touched in preceding communications, adding, however, a good deal that is new and curious. Among other things he reiterates what he had said about the disappointment in the sale of Alleyn's horse, and the purchase of cloth in Smithfield, observing that "the fair lasted but three days." Stowe informs us that in 1593 "no Bartholomew fair was kept at London," but we see from Henslowe that this statement is to be received with some qualification: there was a fair, but it continued only for three days. The letter is imperfect near the middle of it, the paper having been quite rotted away by damp.

"This be delyvered unto my welbeloved husband Mr. Edward Allen, one of my lord Stranges players, geve with spede.

"Righte welbe loved Sonne Edward Allen. I and your mother and your sisster beasse have all in generall our hartie commendations unto you, and as for your wiffe and mowse she desieres to send heare commendationes alone, which she sayes comes frome heare very harte; but as for your wellfare and health we do all joyne to geather in joye and rejjoysse ther att, and do all to geather with one consent pray to god long to continew the same. Nowe, Sonne, leate us growe to a lyttell unkindnes with you, be causse we cane not heare frome you as we wold do, that is when others do; and if we cold as serteuly send to you as you maye to us, we wold not leat to vesete you often, for we beinge with in the crosse of the lorde, you lettell knowe howe we do but by sendinge; for yt hath pleassed the lorde to vesette me rownd a bowt, and almoste all my nebores dead of the plage, and not my howsse free, for my two weauches have hade the plage, and yet thankes to god ar very well and ar well, and I my wiffe and my two daughters, I thanke god, ar very well and in good heallth. Nowe to caste a waye

unkindnes and to come to our newes, that is that we hade a very bade market at Smyth fylld, for no monn wold ofer me a bove fower pownd for your horsse, and therfor have not sowld hime, but to save carges I have sent hime downe into the contrey, that be keapte tell you retorne; and as for your clocke, cloth ther wasse none sowld by retaylle, for all wasse bowght up by the wholle saylle in to dayes, so the fayre lasted but iij dayes: and as for your stockings they are deyed, and your joyner hath seate up your portotle in the chamber, and hath brothe you a corte cobert, and sayes he will bring the reaste very shortly, and we beare with hime becausse his howsse is visited: and as for your garden that is very weall, your spenege bead and all sowed: and as for my lorde a Pembrocke's [men] which you desier to knowe wheare they be, they ar all at home, and hauffe ben thes v or sixe weakes, for they cane not save ther carges to travell, as I heare, and weare fayne to pane the parell, for the * * when I wasse in Smythfell a selling of your horsse, I meate with owld * * *

* * * * * * * *

To aske for yt, for yf we dead, we wold have sowght yt owt, but we never had yt: and this I eand, praysinge god that it doth pleasse hime of his mersey to slacke his hand frome veseting us and the sittie of London, for ther hath abated this last two weacke of the syknes iiij hundreth thurtie and five, and hath died in all betwext a leven and twealle hundred this last weacke, which I hoop in the lord yt will contenew in seasynge every weacke that we maye rejoysse agayne at our meating; and this with my hartie comendations to thy own seall, and lickewisse to all the reaste of my felowes in generall I praye yon hartily comende me. From London the 28 of Septembr 1593.

"Your lovinge father and frend to my power tell death,
"PHILLIPE HENSLOW.

" Your asured owne seallife tell deathe,
JOANE ALLEN
comendinge to her munshen.

"Your wiffe prayeth you to send her word in your next leater what goodman Hudson payes you yerley for his reante for the house, the sealer and all, stille in his hand; and as for your tenenantes we cane geat no rent; and as for Greges and his wife hath ther comendations unto you, and your sister Phillipes and her husband hath leced two or thre owt of ther howsse, yt [yet] there in good health, and doth hartily comend them unto you."

What success attended Alleyn and his fellows in the provinces it is not possible to state, but it is evident that the Earl of Pembroke's players thought there was so little chance of " saving their charges" by travelling, that they were willing rather to run the risk of catching the plague by remaining in London.

CHAPTER IV.

Abating of the Plague in London, and renewal of Theatrical Performances — Petition to the Privy Council — The Thames Watermen's Petition to the Lord Admiral — Permission to Lord Strange's Players to return to the Rose Theatre — Alleyn's Property; the Parsonage of Firle sold by him to Arthur Langworth — Commission to Henslowe and Alleyn.

By the end of September 1593, the virulence of the infectious disorder which had visited the metropolis had been considerably subdued; but we do not find that the companies were allowed to act again until the 27th of December, when Henslowe in his Diary records that the Earl of Sussex's men, in whose receipts he appears to have had a large interest, began performing; and, though he does not state in his entry at what theatre on the Bankside, there can be little doubt that it was at the Rose.

But the actors were not permitted to renew their performances in the metropolis without special license, and a paper, still extant in Dulwich College, shows that the " Servants and Players" of Lord Strange petitioned the privy council, on this occasion, for that license. The document (a copy of the original petition) has no date, but it speaks for itself, as well as some others by which it is accompanied.

" To the right honorable our verie good Lords, the Lords of her Ma^{ts} moste honorable Privie Councell.

" Our dueties in all humblenes remembred to your Honors. Forasmuche (righte Honorable) oure Companie is greate, and thearbie our chardge

intollerable in travellinge the Countrie, and the contynuaunce thereof wilbe a meane to bringe us to division and seperation, whearebie wee shall not onelie be undone, but alsoe unreadie to serve her Matie when it shall please her Highnes to commaund us. And for that the use of our plaiehowse on the Banckside, by reason of the passage to and frome the same by water, is a greate releif to the poore Watermen theare, and our dismission thence, nowe in this longe vacation, is to those poore men a greate hindraunce and in manner an undoeinge, as they generallie complaine, both our and theire humble petition and suite thearefore to your good Honnors is that you wilbe pleased, of your speciall favour, to recall this our restrainte, and permitt us the use of the saide Plaiehowse againe And not onelie our selves, but alsoe a greate nomber of poore men shalbe especiallie bownden to praie for your Honnors.

"Your Honors humble Suppliants
"The righte Honorable the Lord Straunge
"His servantes and Plaiers."

The prayer contained in the preceding petition was seconded by the subsequent address from the watermen plying on the Thames to Lord Howard, the Lord Admiral. What follows is from the original, but why it was returned into Henslowe's hands does not appear. Possibly the object was accomplished without the intervention of the watermen.

"To the right honnorable my Lorde Haywarde, Lorde highe Admirall of Englande, and one of her Maties moste honnorable previe Counsayle

"In moste humble manner complayneth and sheweth unto your good Lordeshipp your poore suppliantes and dayly orators Phillipp Henslo and others, the poore watermen on the bancke side: whereas your good L. hathe derected your warrant unto hir Maties Justices for the restraynte of a playe howse belonginge unto the saide Phillipp Henslo, one of the groomes of her Maties Chamber. So it is, if it please your good Lordshipp, that wee your saide poore watermen have had muche helpe and reliefe, for us oure poore wives and children, by meanes of the resorte of suche people as come unto the said playe howse. It maye therefore please your good L., for godes sake and in the waye of charetie, to respecte us your poore watermen, and to give leave unto the said Phillipp Henslo to have playinge in his saide howse duringe suche tyme as others have, according as it hathe byne

accustomed. And in your Honnors so doinge, you shall not onely doe a good and a charitable dede, but also bynde us all, according to oure dewties, with oure poore wives and children, dayly to praye for your honuor in muche happynes longe to lyve.

"William Dowet, M^r of her Majesties barge.
"Isack Towell
"William Tuchenner, M. of her M^{ties} mean.
"James Russell
"Ferdinando Black
"Parker Playne
"Xpfer Topen
"Thomas Iarmonger, on of her M^{ties} wattermen.
"Edward Adysson, on of her M^{ties} wattermen."

Five other signatures (or more properly marks, for the parties could not write) are attached; but, although Henslowe is introduced into the body of the instrument as one of the petitioners, his name is not subscribed, which renders it still more probable that the petition, being unnecessary, was never presented to the Lord Admiral.

We have already referred to the account in Henslowe's Diary thus headed, "In the name of God, beginning at Newington, my lord admirell men, and my lord chamberlen men, as followeth, 1594." As soon as the Globe Theatre on the Bankside was constructed, the Lord Chamberlain's men (including Shakespeare) removed there—probably in the summer of 1596. But, besides the Earl of Nottingham's and Lord Hunsdon's companies, Lord Strange's players had also occupied the theatre at Newington Butts; and we find, by another curious document, that dramatic exhibitions there, at least by the Lord Strange's servants, (who are not mentioned in connection with that theatre by Henslowe) had been in a manner compulsory. They had been forbidden to perform at the Rose, and "enjoined" to exhibit three days at Newington Butts. Perhaps this medium course was adopted when the plague began to abate its ravages, and before theatres, like the Rose, in populous vicinities were allowed to be reopened. The date of the revo-

cation of the order that Lord Strange's servants should perform at Newington is not given, but the following is a contemporaneous copy of the instrument by which they were permitted to return to their old quarters:—

"Wheareas, not longe since, upon some considerations, we did restraine the Lorde Straunge his servauntes from playinge at the Rose on the Banckside, and enjoyned them to plaie three daies at Newington Butts. Now, forasmuch as wee are satisfied that by reason of the tediousnes of the waie, and that of longe tyme plaies have not there bene used on working daies, and for that a nomber of poore watermen are therby releeved, yow shall permitt and suffer them, or any other there, to exercise them selves in suche sorte as they have don heretofore, and that the Rose maie be at libertie, without any restrainte, so longe as yt shalbe free from infection of sicknes. Any commaundement from us heretofore to the contrye notwithstandinge From —

"To the Justices, Bayliffes, Constables and others to whome yt shall apperteyne."

Reverting to the private affairs of Alleyn, we now come to a very important piece of evidence, establishing that, independent of his interest in theatres, he was, at all events in 1596, and, perhaps, owing in a considerable degree to his marriage, a man of property. Money was at that time worth about five times as much as at the present moment, and yet we find him at this period disposing of a single estate in Sussex for £3000, to be paid for in twenty years at the rate of £150 per annum. None of his biographers appear to have been acquainted with this remarkable fact, and all have speculated in what way he could have become possessed of sufficient money and land to enable him to build and endow Dulwich College, besides his other charitable foundations. They have supposed that he had little or no paternal property, and that nearly his whole estate had been derived from his profession; but by what follows, to which previous reference has been made, it will be seen that he held the lease of the parsonage of Firle, near Beddingham, in Sussex; and that he sold it in 1596 to a gentleman of that county, of the name of Langworth, for an amount equal to perhaps

£15,000 of our present money. The subsequent memorandum, written and witnessed by Allen's "father," Henslowe, is inserted in the Diary of which we have before so often spoken, and which was made the receptacle of various agreements, memoranda, and matters of account.

"This agremente and bargen betwene Edward Alleyn and Mr. Arthur Langworth, as foloweth, was made the 5 daye of July 1596. Yt was agreed upon that Mr. Langworth shold geve unto Edward Alleyn for the lease of the parsonege of Furlle iij thowssen powndes of laffull mony of England, to be payd in xx^{ti} yeares in maner folowinge: by a hundred and fiftie powndes a yeare, and to be gine payment at our Ladey daye next folowinge, and so to paye every halfe yeare the hallfe of the hundreth and fiftie powndes, or within one moneth after, beinge xxviij dayes: and for the performence of this xx yeares payment hath promesed to potte hime in suche asuerence, as by his learned cownsell he shall devise at his next cominge to towne after the daye above written. In wittnes whereof to this I have seate to my hand

"Phillippe Henslow."*

This agreement is wholly in the hand-writing of Henslowe's scribe, who made such strange confusion in the wording of it, near the end, that we might suppose Alleyn was out of town

---

* In the preceding year Mr. Arthur Langworth had bought a house, land, and good-will, of Henslowe, for which he agreed to give him £100. The subsequent memorandum on this subject, witnessed by Alleyn's wife who could not write, is found in Henslowe's Diary:—

"Mdm. that Mr. Arture Langworth hath promysed, the 16 daye of Maye 1595, to paye unto me Phillipe Henslow the some of j hundreth powndes for a howsse, and land, and goodwyll he bargened with me, with owt any condicion, but absolutely to paye me so muche mony, and to take such a surence as I have at this time. Wittneses to this promes of payment

"E. Alleyn
"Edward + Allenes wiffes marke."

Where the house and land so bargained for were situated no where appears, but probably in Sussex, where Langworth resided. Henslowe had, perhaps, come into possession of it through his wife, the widow Agnes Woodward.

when it was signed; but Langworth (as we shall see hereafter) lived at a place called "the Brill," in Sussex, and the words, "at his next coming to town," apply to him; while, "as by his learned counsel he shall devise," refers to Alleyn, who was to take counsel's opinion on the subject of securities. At a subsequent date, viz., 2d July, 1601 (as appears by the legal instrument preserved at Dulwich), Langworth reconveyed the same estate to Alleyn; and hence we may be led to infer, that Alleyn required the money for some special purpose in 1596, and was able to repay it in 1601.

In Henslowe's Diary, under date of 1597, is an account of various journeys he made to court, and fees he paid there, headed, "Layd owt at sundry tymes of my owne readey money, abowt the changinge of ower comyssion." This clearly refers to the partnership between himself and Alleyn; but there is some confusion respecting the appointment of "Master &c. of the Queen's Games," which had been given to John Dorington, Esq., in 1573, but of which we find Ralph Bowes, Esq., in possession in 1596.* Soon after this date, as will be seen by a document in the Appendix, Henslowe seems to have been in treaty with Bowes for the surrender of the office, which, however, he did not obtain. One of the items in Henslowe's account is for waiting upon Mr. Cæsar at St. Katherine's. Dr. (afterwards Sir Julius) Cæsar seems to have befriended Henslowe on more occasions than one.

* In Henslowe's Diary occurs the following entry, subscribed by Bowes:—

"Sir,—I praye you cause suche mony as is dew unto me for my quarter's fee, dew to be payd at our ladye daye laste past, to be delyvered unto this bearer, and this shalbe your suficyante discharge. From Grenwiche, the xvij of aprell 1596.

"RAFFE BOWES.

"To our lovinge frende Mr William
　　Kelegraye esquyer."

CHAPTER V.

Alleyn's pecuniary claims upon Thomas Lodge—Some account of Lodge as an Author and Actor—His contest with Stephen Gosson respecting the Stage—His "Fig for Momus," 1595—Topping's Demand against Lodge, and Henslowe's Security for him—Petitions by Topping and Henslowe to the Lord Chamberlain—Extract from the Privy Council Registers regarding Lodge—His Death.

In the papers which next fall under our observation, Alleyn does not appear to have been personally concerned, at least until after the death of Henslowe, when we find, from memoranda in Alleyn's Diary, that the celebrated Thomas Lodge, who had been an actor and dramatic poet, but was then practising as a physician, was indebted to him.* The debt had, most likely, descended to Alleyn from Henslowe, and had arisen out of the transaction to which the singular documents, we are presently about to insert, relate.

Lodge was one of the most distinguished predecessors and contemporaries of Shakespeare. He wrote "The Wounds of Civil War, lively set forth in the true Tragedies of Marius and Scilla" (printed in 1594) alone, and "A Looking Glass for London and England" (also printed in 1594), a play of considerable popularity, in conjunction with Robert Greene. He is, however, chiefly to be admired as a graceful lyrical poet, a writer of severe satires and agreeable pastorals, and of several romantic novels, formerly in great request, and of one of which, as is well known, Shakespeare availed himself in "As you like it." Malone has shewn that Spenser applauded him under the name of Alcon, in his "Tears of the Muses,"

---

* Two entries by Alleyn relating to Lodge run thus:—

                                                                                     li. s. d.

"Mar. 25, 1619. Mathias arested Lodge

    June 4, 1619. For sueing Doc. Lodge's bond . 0 6 10"

It has been doubted whether Lodge, the dramatist, and Lodge, the physician, were the same person; but the information now obtained leaves no room for dispute.

1591, and, in 1593, Lodge thus endeavoured, in his "Phillis," to repay the tribute:—

> "Goe, weeping Truce-men, in your sighing weedes,
>   Under a great Mecænas I have p[l]ast you;
> If so you come where learned Colin feedes
>   His lovely flocke, packe thence and quickly haste you:
> You are but mistes before so bright a sunne,
> Who hath the palme for deepe invention wunne."

We first hear of Lodge some thirteen years earlier, viz. about 1580, as the antagonist of Stephen Gosson, who published his attack upon the stage, under the title of "The School of Abuse," in 1579. Lodge immediately wrote and printed a Defence of Plays and Play-makers; but he was not allowed to publish it, because, as he stated in one of his subsequent productions ("Alarum against Usurers," 1584), "the godly and reverend, that had to deal in the cause, misliking it, forbad the publishing." Gosson, however, obtained an imperfect copy of Lodge's tract, and answered it in his "Plays confuted in five Actions." He there accuses Lodge of being "a vagrant person, visited by the heavy hand of God;" an expression hitherto not clearly understood, inasmuch as it was not known that Lodge had ever been a player, and by statute "a vagrant." We have now, for the first time, evidence to prove that, like many of the dramatists of that day, he had been an actor as well as an author: therefore it was that Gosson called him "a vagrant person, visited by the heavy hand of God;" but how long he continued on the stage, or what class of parts he filled, we know not. As early as 1590, in the dedication to his "Rosalynde," he informs us, that he had, "with Captain Clarke, made a voyage to the islands of Terceras and the Canaries," and that he had been educated under Sir Edward Hobby. In 1591 he was a student "of Lincoln's Inn," and so he continued for some years; but we have no reason to believe that he was ever called to the bar. He was still "of Lincoln's Inn,

gent." when he published his "Fig for Momus," in 1595, and when, under the name of Golde (the letters of his name misplaced), in one of his Pastorals, he vowed to forsake poetry, in consequence of the little encouragement it received. It is a dialogue between Golde (Lodge) and a shepherd called Wagrin, a name, no doubt, intended to denote some person of the time. Golde says—

> "Which sound rewards, since this neglected time
>   Repines to yeeld to men of high desart,
> Ile cease to revel out my wits in rime,
>   For such who make such base account of art:
> And since by wit there is no meanes to clime,
>   Ile hould the plough a while, and plie the cart;
> And if my muse to wonted course returne,
>   Ile write and judge, peruse, commend and burne."

To which Wagrin answers—

> "A better mind God send thee, or more meanes.
>   Oh, wouldst thou but converse with Charles the kind,
> Or follow harvest when thy Donroy gleanes,
>   These thoughts would cease; with them they muse should find
> A sweete converse: then this conceit, which weanes
>   Thy pen from writing, should be soone resignd." *

Golde thus closes the conference:—

> "I rest resolvd: if bountie will, I wright;
> If not, why then my muse shall flie the light."

Who was meant by "Charles the kind" is very doubtful, but Donroy was Roydon, a poet of considerable eminence, and in 1595 apparently prosperous (Chapman had inscribed

---

* I have had the less scruple in making this curious auto-biographical quotation from the original edition of Lodge's "Fig for Momus," because in the only reprint of it (from the Auchinleck press, in 1817), the line,

> "A sweete converse: then this conceit, which weanes,"

is entirely omitted, making the whole passage unintelligible. Other misprints are numerous in the same volume.

to him his "Shadow of Night," in 1594); but we shall see by and by that the ordinary fate of poets and poetry followed him, and that, some twenty years after the date to which we are now adverting, he was glad to receive sixpence as a charitable contribution from Alleyn.

The best account of Lodge, and of his numerous works in prose and verse, is to be found in vol. viii. of the last edition of "Dodsley's Old Plays;" but the compiler of that piece of biography knew nothing of the transaction to which the papers about to be inserted relate. It appears that Lodge was indebted to a tailor of the name of Richard Topping, carrying on business in the Strand, and that Henslowe (in order not to lose Lodge's services by his imprisonment in the Clink), had become security for the money. Lodge, however, as is asserted, went beyond seas (not on the voyage to Terceras and the Canaries, already mentioned), leaving Henslowe liable for the debt and costs, which Topping could not obtain, Henslowe pleading his privilege from arrest, as one of the grooms of the queen's chamber. Such seems to have been the state of things some time prior to the death of Henry Lord Hunsdon (which happened in 1596), and the following petition was presented to him by Topping:—

> "To the right honorable the Lord Hunsdon Lord Chamberlaine to her Matie.

"Most humblie showeth to your honorable Lo. That wheare your poore Suppl. Richard Topping of the Strand, taylor, hath hadd a debte of seaven poundes odd monney for this viij yeares dew unto him by one Thoms Lodge, who hath from tyme to tyme waged lawe and put your Suppl. to extreame charges by meanes of one Phillip Inclow (as he saith) one of the gromes of her Maties Chamber; yet in thend was forced to put your poore Suppl. in securitie, and procured the sayd Phillipp Inclowe to become bound by bond with him, either to bring in the boddye of the sayd Thomas Lodge into the Clynke in Southwarke, or to answere his condemnation, which he hath not accordingly performed; by meanes whereof a judgement hath passed for twelve poundes odd money and execution thereupon graunted forth against them. And the sayd Phillipp Inclowe,

having bene frindly intreated for payment thereof, or to acquaint your Suppl. whear the sayd Lodge is, that some frindly end might be takin therein, utterly refuseth the same, affirming that he will kepe your Suppl. from it this seaven yeares. May it therefore please your Lo, in that the sayd Inclow (as he saith) is her Ma^{tes} servant, to graunt, with your honors favor, leave to your Suppl. either to arrest him or to sett downe such order therein, whereby your Suppl. may have his owne, being most willing to referr the same to your honorable consideration and order. And he, as most bound, shall pray for the preservation of your honorable estate."

This complaint and request having been made, the old Lord Hunsdon required Henslowe to give his answer to Topping's accusation, and the next document contains his defence; which amounted in substance to this, that Lodge having removed the cause into the Court of King's Bench, other bail had been put in and accepted, and Henslowe consequently discharged from liability. Henslowe, in the subsequent representation to the Lord Chamberlain, asserts that Topping knew where to find Lodge, but wished, nevertheless, to compel him (Henslowe) to pay the debt.

"Righte honorable, my duetie in all humblenes remembred. Maie it please your good Lpp. that this complainte and the contentes thereof is in all pointes most untrue, and devised and suggested by the saied Toppinge, of mallice to provoke (if he might) your honnors displeasure against me; for in verie truth, (right honorable) as I will avouch, I never knewe of anie debte or matter twixt Lodge and him, and thearefore could be noe hinderer to him frome the attayneinge to his debte supposed, as he hath first suggested. But aboute half a yeare nowe past, Toppinge haveing arrested Lodge to the Clincke, in Southwarke, uppon an action of debte, att Lodge his earnest request, and for meere goodwill, beeinge somewhat acquainted with him, I became his bayle, and before any issue theare tried, Lodge removed the action by Habeas Corpus to the Kinges Benche, and theare (by the acceptaunce of the Judges) putt in newe baile. Toppinge, mislikinge that baile, procured a procedendo to trie thaction in the Clinck, wheare it first began; and theare (as it seemeth) hath proceeded, onelie of purpose to laie thexecution on me for the money he hath recovered, albeit he knoweth wheare Lodge, the principall, ys, and howe he maie easelie come by him. In other sorte, then thus as baile, I never became bounde to him. Nowe, my good Lord, I am advised by my learned

Counsell that by reason of thacceptaunce of the last baile uppon the Habeas Corpus, I am discharged and cleere of the first baile, and in that respect (I doe confes) I have been unwillinge to paie another mans debte, wherein I trust your Honnor will holde me excused. And thus, beeinge readie to make further aunsweare face to face with Toppinge, yf it shalbe your Lpps pleasure, I rest

"Your Honnors in all humblenes att comaundment,

"PHILLIPP HENSLEY."

So the matter appears to have stood up to the time of the death of Henry, Lord Hunsdon, in 1596; but as soon as his successor came to the title, Topping renewed his complaint and suit against Henslowe, and what succeeds is his petition to George, Lord Hunsdon, who wrote his order, dated 29 Jan. 1597, at the top of it.

"The humble petition of Richarde Toppin.

"Hensley, you are to satisfie this Petitioner in what shalbe due unto him; or otherwise he is to take his remedie by course of lawe against you. Courte, this 29th Januarie, 1597.

"G. HUNSDON."

"To the right Ho. the Lo. Hunsdon, Lord Chamberlayne of his Maties Howshold.

"In all humilitie besecheth your good Lo, your dailie Sup. Richarde Toppin. That whereas your Sup., about iij yeres past, was constrayned to prosecute sute against one Thomas Lodge for a debt of vij^{li} and upwardes, principall debt, which with charges of lawe surmounteth xij^{li}, the debt the first vij yeres forborne before your Sup. attempted any sute. Nowe, so it is, Right Ho., that one Phillip Hinchlow, one of the groomes of her Maties chamber, of his owne willingnes, and with intent to delaie your Supp., became bayle for the saide Lodge, and bothe unconscianablie and very arrogantly protesteth to spende 1C^{li} to kepe your Supp. from his saide debt; althoughe the saide Lodge affirmeth that he hathe made Henchley full satisfaction to thende your Sup. might be paide. Uppon those injuries your Sup. complayned to your late father (of Right H. memorie) by petition, and then Henchley entreated your Sup. staie, vowinge your Sup. should be paide; neverthelesse, contrarie to all honestie and equitie, ymediatly after procured a Writt of Error for further delaye, and inforced your Sup. to make his further sute to the L. Cobham, late L. Chamberlaine, who tooke the cause into his hearinge, and ordered the saide Henchley

should other paie your Sup. his debt, or bringe in Lodge, uppon warrant which his Lo. graunted, and Henchley thereof possessed; but nothinge performed, so greatly Henchley beareth him selfe of his place. He therefore most humblie beseecheth your Honnour to extende your Lordship's releefe herein to your Sup., as to your Ho. wisdome shall seeme good, and most agreeinge with equitie. And he shall ever praie that your Ho. maie most honorablie [and] happelie long live."

It is evident that Lord Hunsdon did not come to the determination, expressed at the commencement of the foregoing document, without calling upon Henslowe to show cause against it; and the paper next to be inserted (which is slightly defective in some places) was Henslowe's statement of the case, in which he admits that Lodge had escaped beyond seas to avoid arrest and imprisonment. Here it is that we find that Lodge had been "a player." Lord Hunsdon thought that the merits were with Topping, or, at all events, that Henslowe ought not to be allowed to prevent the course of law by pleading his privilege as one of the Queen's household.

"To the righte honorable my verie good Lord the Lord of Hunsdon, Lord Chamberlen.

"Wheareas, righte honourable, one Richard Toppin did of late prefer unto your honor a petition against me suggestinge therein divers untruthes, to thintent to bringe your Lpp. into some hard conceipt of me. The truth is, right honorable, that one Thos. Lodge beinge aboute a yeare nowe paste arrested within the Libertie of the Clinck (wheare I am a dweller) att the suite of the said Toppin, upon an action of debte, and haveinge some knowledge and acquaintaunce of him as a player, requested me to be his baile. Before anie yssue theare tried, Lodge removed the action by Habeas Corpus to the Kinges benche, and theare (by thacceptaunce of the Judges) put in newe baile. Toppin mislikinge that baile, procured a procedendo to trie thaction in the Clinck, wheare it first begon, and theare hath proceded onelie of purpose to laie the execution on me. Nowe, forsomuche as I am advised by my Councell that by reason of thacceptaunce of the newe baile upon the Habeas Corpus I am cleere in lawe and that the debte (if theare be anie) noe waie concerneth me, I have been unwilling frome tyme to tyme (I must needs confes) to yeeld satisfaction without lawfull compulsion, as anie man ells would in like case: by means whearof Toppin hath made sondrie severall complaintes to your late honorable father, the late Lo.

Cobham, before whome, in this * * * reasonable manner, I made my excuse. But wheare Toppin affirmeth that Lodge hath lefte sufficient in my handes to paie the debt, and that I have wilfully refused to satisfie the same with pretence to put him to chardge and trouble; and that therefore the Lord Cobham did enjoyne me either to paie the debt or bring forth Lodge, my good Lo the * * * are in all points most untrue; onelie this was doen. For that Toppin suggested that I was privie to the place of Lodge his hiding (which was alsoe untrue) the Lord Cobham enjoyned me to doe my endevor to attache him, and to that end gave me his proper warrant, which accordingly I putt in execution, but by no meanes could attaine to him; for that he is (as I heare) passed byond the seas; and more then this his Lpp. did not enjoyne me unto. Nevertheles, if it please your Lpp. to order the cause, albeit I never had nor am like to have any manner of restitution, I shalbe content to submitt my self to your Honor's judgement, with hope of your Honor's favorable consideration for the mittigation of the execution, which being pryvily recorded is brought to xij^{li} and all [odd ?] money, the debte beeing meerly vij^{li} and noe more; soe that theare is above v^{li} awarded besides the debt. And thus I rest, in all dutie,

"Your Honors most humble
"Phillipp Henslowe."

The preceding appears to have been Henslowe's rough draft of his answer, which he preserved after he had sent the fair copy to the Lord Chamberlain. What was the issue of the affair, is not shown by any of the papers preserved at Dulwich; but it is most likely that there had been a running account between Lodge, as dramatist and actor, and Henslowe. That Henslowe was still Lodge's creditor, when the former died in January, 1616, there can be little doubt; and the bond which Alleyn put in force in 1619 had very possibly been one of the securities he had inherited from his wife's step-father. In the Privy Council Registers, under date of January 10, 1616, is the following memorandum.

"A passe for Tho. Lodge, Doctor of Physic, and Henry Sewell, gent, to travell into the Arch Dukes Country to recover such debts as are due unto them there, taking with them two servants and to returne agayne within five moneths."

This was immediately after Henslowe's decease; and it is much more likely that Lodge quitted England to avoid process

on the part of Alleyn, than that he went to receive debts due to himself abroad. After his return, in March, 1619, Alleyn, as we find by his Diary, arrested Lodge; but nothing remains to show that he ever obtained any money from Lodge, who is supposed to have died during the great plague of 1625.

CHAPTER VI.

Alleyn's temporary retirement from the Stage, and return to it—His visit with his Wife to the Langworths at the Brill, Sussex—Letter to him there—Illness of Mr. Bowes, and Henslowe's hopes of obtaining the place of Master of the Queen's Games—Another Letter to Alleyn at the Brill—Ben Jonson's Duel with Gabriel Spenser, and death of the latter—Ben Jonson's copy of Sir Henry Watton's Verses—Epigram in Ben Johnson's hand-writing.

THERE is reason for supposing that in the autumn of 1597, or winter of 1597-8, Alleyn, if he did not for a short time secede entirely from the stage, quitted the company of the Earl of Nottingham's players. Henslowe thus entitles a short account in his Diary:—" A not [note] of all such goods as I have browght for playinge, *sence my sonne Edward Allen leafte playinge*, 1597;" and on the next page Henslowe thus inserts the names of all the members of the dramatic association, omitting Alleyn:—" A juste a cownt of all suche money as I have layd owt for my lord Admeralles players, begynyng the xi of october, whose names ar as foloweth—Borne, Gabrell [Spenser] Shaw, Jonnes, Dowten, Jube, Towne, Synger, and the ij Geffes, 1597." The precise date when Alleyn returned to the stage it is very difficult to ascertain; but we find him again a member of the same company in 1601; and he had probably rejoined it, when they began to act at the new theatre, the Fortune, of which we shall speak hereafter.

He certainly spent the summer of 1598 in Sussex, where

he owned property, as may be supposed, in right of his wife. Two letters to him while in that part of the country have fortunately been preserved among his papers at Dulwich. They are addressed to him at the Brill, in the parish of Ringmer, near Lewes, where Mr. Arthur Langworth resided, who, two years before, as already mentioned, had purchased from Alleyn the parsonage of Firle.

The Brill was a house (part of which is still standing) built during the reign of the Tudors, formerly surrounded by a park of 1100 acres, and occupied by the Archbishops of Canterbury. Soon after Elizabeth came to the throne they exchanged it for lands at Croydon. Alleyn's wife accompanied him on the occasion, and, as far as we can now judge, it was an expedition of pleasure. His sojourn was of several months' duration, and while he was absent, an important event for Henslowe and Alleyn occurred—Mr. Bowes, the "Master, &c. of the Queen's Games of Bulls and Bears, died; and Mr. (afterwards Sir John) Dorington, succeeded him. Henslowe had hopes of obtaining the office through the Lord Admiral, and made considerable interest for it, but unsuccessfully. The subsequent letter from him to Alleyn, then at the Brill, is principally upon this subject, and upon the disappointments Henslowe had experienced in his suit. It also adverts to "our other matter," which is confusedly mixed up with the question as to the succession to the Mastership of the Games, but which, no doubt, related to a plan they contemplated of building the Fortune theatre in the parish of St. Giles, Cripplegate, a scheme which they carried into effect not very long afterwards. Mr. Langworth, who had been in London, assisting Henslowe in his suit, seems to have been the bearer of the letter to Alleyn.

> "This be dd. unto Mr. Edwarde Alleyn, at Mr. Arthur Langworthes at the Brille in Sussex, d. this.
>
> "Sonne Edward Alleyn, I commend me unto you and to my daughter, and very glade to heare of your healthes, which god conteuewe. The

causse whie I writte unto you is this: Mr. Bowes liesse very sycke, and every bodey thinckes he will not escape; in so muche that I feare I shall losse all, for Doctor Seassar hath done nothinge for me; and as for ower other matter betwext us, I have bene with my lord Admeralle a bowte yt, and he promyssed me that he wold move the quene a bowte yt; and the next daye he rides from the corte to Winser, so that ther is nothinge ther to be hade but good wordes, which trobelles my mynd very muche, for any losse you knowe is very muche to me. I did move my laday Edmones in yt, and she very onerably ussed me, for she weant presentley and moved the quene for me; and Mr. Darsey of the previ chamber crossed her and made yt knowne to her that the quene had geven yt all readey in reversyon to one Mr. Dorington a pensener; and I have talked with hime and he confesseth yt to be trew, but as yet Mr. Bowes lyveth, and what paynes and trobell I have tacken in yt Mr. Langworth shall macke yt knowne unto you, for I have had his heallpe in yt for so muche as in hime lyesse, for we have moved other great parsonages for yt, but as yeat I knowe not howe yt shall pleasse god we shall spead, for I ame sure my lord Admerell will do nothinge. And thus I comitte you bothe to god, leavinge the wholle descord to be unfolded to you by Mr. Langworth. From London, this 4 of June, 1598.

"Yours to my power
"PHILLIPPE HENSLOW.

"I pray you commend me unto
 Mrs. Langworth, and to all
 the reast of our frendes ther."

From the expression used by Henslowe in the above letter, " for any loss, you know, is very much to me," we might be led to conclude that his circumstances at this date were not flourishing. His Diary shows that, in the spring of the year 1599, he had made various inventories of his theatrical properties, apparel, &c.; but this step might have been adopted either to ascertain their value, and thus " to take stock," or (which is more probable) with a view to the projected removal of the company and their appurtenances to the Fortune Theatre in Goulding Lane, Cripplegate, as soon as it should be ready to receive them.

The next letter from Henslowe to his " son" is dated more than three months after the last, at which time Alleyn and his wife were still with Mr. Langworth at the Brill. It is a very

remarkable communication, which Malone could not even have glanced at, or he must have seen in an instant what new light it throws upon a dark transaction in which one of the greatest names in our dramatic poetry was concerned.

In Ben Jonson's conversation with Drummond of Hawthornden (as published by Mr. D. Laing in the *Archæologia Scotica*, vol. iv.) occurs the following passage: " In his service in the Low Countries he had, in the face of both the campes, killed ane enemie, and taken *opima spolia* from him; and, since his coming to England, being appealed to the fields, he had killed his adversarie, which hurt him in the arme, and whose sword was ten inches longer than his; for the which he was emprisoned and almost at the gallowes." This story has been related in all the biographical accounts of Ben Jonson, and Gifford observes (Ben Jonson's Works, i. xix.) that " the rank or condition in life of his antagonist was not known, but that he was commonly supposed to be a player:" the witness upon this point is Dekker in his " Satiromastix," printed in 1602, where Tucca asks Horace (who was meant for Ben Jonson) " Art not famous enough yet, my mad Horastratus, for killing a player, but thou must eat men alive?" On the authority of Aubrey, some have thought that this player was Marlowe. The following letter (after urging Alleyn to return to London, that he and Henslowe might combine their endeavours respecting the office mentioned in the previous communication) makes the matter regarding Ben Jonson's duel quite clear: he had killed Gabriel, a member of Henslowe's company of players, in Hoxton Fields. The date, be it remarked, is 1598, whereas Gifford places the recontre in 1595.

" To my welbelovde sonne Mr. Edward Alleyne, at Mr. Arthure Langworthes at the Brille, in Susex, give this.

" Sonne Edward Alleyne. I have Rec. your leatter, the which yow sente unto me by the Caryer, wher in I understand of both your good healthes, which I praye to god to contenew; and forthir I understand yow have considered of the wordes which yow and I had betwene us conservnynge the bear-

garden, and accordinge to your wordes yow and I and all other frendes shall have as much as wee can do to bring yt unto a good eand: therfore I wold willingley that yow weare at the bancate, for then with our losse I shold be the meryer. Therfore, yf yow thincke as I thincke, yt weare fytte that we weare both here to do what we mowght, and not as two frendes, but as two joyned in one. Therfor, Ned, I love not to macke many great glosses and protestacions to yow, as others do, but as a poore frend yow shall comaunde me, as I hoope I shall do yow. Therfore I desyre rather to have your company and good wisses then your leatters. For ower laste talke which we had abowte Mr. Pascalle, assure yow I do not forgeatte now to leat yow understand newes, that I will teall yow some, but yt is for me harde and heavey. Sence yow weare with me I have lost one of my company which hurteth me greatley, that is Gabrell, for he is slayen in hogesden fylldes by the hands of bergemen Jonson, bricklayer; therfore I wold fayne have a littell of your cownsell, yf I cowld. Thus with hartie comendations to you and my dawghter, and lyckwise to all the reast of our frends, I eande. From london the 26 of September 1598

" Your assured frend to my power,
" PHILLIPPE HEGLOWE."

Gifford, in his anxiety to uphold the character of Ben Jonson, endeavours to throw discredit on all that Dekker imputes to him in his "Satiromastix;" but those who look at the matter impartially can have little doubt that there was some foundation for most of the charges and insinuations in that personal drama, even to the borrowing of a gown of Roscius (probably Alleyn) and other trifles of the same kind; for unless there had been a portion of truth in the stories, there would have been no joke in their repetition, and no point in the satire. In the preceding letter we see a confirmation of this opinion, for Ben Jonson had killed a player, and that player was named Gabriel (or *Gabrell*, as Henslowe spells it), and a member of the association with which Henslowe was connected. "I have lost," he says, "one of my company, which hurteth me greatly, that is Gabrell, for he is slain in Hoxton Fields by the hands of Benjamin Jonson, bricklayer."

The first point that strikes us as remarkable in the paragraph is, that Henslowe calls Ben Jonson "bricklayer" merely,

as if that were his trade, and apparently without meaning it as any reproach. When Dekker so frequently throws bricks and mortar in Jonson's teeth in " Satiromastix," we know that he wishes thereby to bring him into ridicule; but Henslowe only seems to speak of it as a matter of course. This is very singular, because Ben Jonson, two years before the date of the letter just quoted, had written his " Every Man in his Humour" for Henslowe's theatre (Malone's Shakesp. by Boswell, iii. 307: the play is called " the Comedy of Humours," under date of 11th May, 1596, in Henslowe's Diary); and, in 1597 and 1598, he had received several sums of money on account of dramatic productions in progress. It would almost appear as if Henslowe, when he wrote to Alleyn, did not know that it was the same Benjamin Jonson, who was and had been an author in his own pay. Besides, at this date Ben Jonson was in his twenty-fourth year; and it has always been supposed that it was only for a short time after he returned from Cambridge to his step-father, and before he embarked for Flanders, that he followed the trade of bricklaying. According to the mode in which Henslowe speaks of him, it would be thought that Ben Jonson was a bricklayer at the period when he killed Gabriel.

A question then arises, who was Gabriel? It was in all probability a christian name, and we find that there were, about this date, two Gabriels in Henslowe's company—Gabriel Spenser and Gabriel Synger (Hist. Engl. Dram. Poetry and the Stage, i. 350). They are both frequently mentioned in Henslowe's Diary in and prior to 1598, but after that year we only hear of one of them *—Gabriel Synger; and in the same book occurs an entry regarding him in 1602, when he produced what was known by the name of " Synger's Voluntary." Therefore the actor whom Ben Jonson killed must, in all probability, have been Gabriel Spenser.

* The latest entry in Henslowe's Diary respecting Gabriel Spenser bears date on 24th June, 1598, up to which date the old manager received Spenser's share of the galleries. The account begins on the 6th April, 1598.

Among other points in Drummond's account of his conversation with Ben Jonson, it is said, "Sir Edward (Henry) Wotton's verses of a happie lyfe, he [Jonson] hath by heart." It so happens that among the MSS. at Dulwich College is a copy of these very verses in Ben Jonson's beautiful hand-writing; and as his authority must be considered good, and as the lines differ materially from the copies as printed in the various editions of "Wotton's Remains," it will be well to quote them exactly in the form in which they stand in the manuscript Ben Jonson left behind him, and which was very likely given by him to Alleyn.

" How happy is he borne and taught,
    That serveth not another's will!
    Whose armor is his honest thought,
    And silly truth his highest skill.

" Whose passions not his Masters are,
    Whose soule is still prepar'd for death,
    Untied to the world with care
    Of princes grace or vulgar breath.

" Who hath his life from humors freed,
    Whose conscience is his strong retreate;
    Whose state can neyther flatterers feed,
    Nor ruine make accusers great.

" Who envieth none whome chance doth rayse,
    Or vice; who never understood
    How swordes give sleighter wounds than prayse,
    Nor rules of state, but rules of good.

" Who God doth late and early pray
    More of his grace, then guifts to lend;
    And entertaynes the harmlesse day
    With a well-chosen booke or freind.

" This man is free from servile bandes
    Of hope to rise or feare to fall;
    Lord of himselfe, though not of landes,
    And having nothing, yet hath all."

It is impossible to assign the precise date to these verses, but they seem to have fallen in with Alleyn's taste and notions, and hence perhaps the fact that a copy of them, so well authenticated, is found among his papers. There is evidence that he himself had written them out, possibly before Ben Jonson gave him the perfect transcript, for a fragment remains of the first stanza, or rather of part of it, in Alleyn's hand-writing, upon a scrap of paper on the back of which is a memorandum respecting some agricultural implements bought by him, bearing date in 1616. The oldest known production by Sir Henry Wotton is inserted in Davison's "Poetical Rhapsodie," edit. 1602. Drummond's conversation with Ben Jonson, during which he probably recited the verses, took place, as is well known, in January, 1619.

On the same paper as that which contains Sir H. Wotton's verses, and also in Ben Jonson's hand-writing, is the following:—

" Martial.

" The things that make the happier life are these,
  Most pleasant Martial; Substance got with ease,
  Not labour'd for, but left thee by thy Sire;
  A soyle not barren; a continuall fire;
  Never at Law; seldome in office gownd;
  A quiet mind, free powers, and body sound;
  A wise simplicity; freindes alike stated;
  Thy table without art, and easy rated:
  Thy night not dronken, but from cares layd wast;
  No soure or sollen bed-mate, yet a chast;
  Sleepe that will make the darkest howres swift-pac't;
  Will to be what thou art, and nothing more;
  Nor feare thy latest day, nor wish therefore."

It is very possible that these lines are also by Sir Henry Wotton, though they read more in the terse and forcible style of Ben Jonson. They are not contained in any edition of "Wotton's Remains."

CHAPTER VII.

The Fortune Theatre built — New Documents relating to its origin and construction — Alleyn's interest in it — His return to the Stage — His Plot of Tamar Cam — Bowes and Dorington, Masters of the Games — Accession of James I., and the three Companies of Players — The Plague, and cessation of playing in London — Letter of Mrs. Alleyn to her husband in the country, in which Shakespeare is mentioned.

WE now come to an important event in Alleyn's life—the building of the Fortune Theatre in Cripplegate — from which, until the day of his death, he seems to have received a considerable income, and which ultimately formed part of the endowment of Dulwich College. The ground had been purchased not long before from a person of the name of Gill, who resided in the Isle of Man; and some of the documents at Dulwich College, which it is not necessary to quote, contain various particulars of the bargain.

Such details as were previously known, are inserted in the "History of English Dramatic Poetry and the Stage," i. 311; but the papers preserved at Dulwich present several new particulars. The earliest of these is dated 12 January, 1599—1600, and is addressed by the Earl of Nottingham, on behalf of his players, to the Justices of Middlesex, requiring them to permit his servant, Edward Alleyn, (for Henslowe at this date is not mentioned,) to build a new theatre near Redcross Street; assigning as reasons, that the situation was very convenient, and that the house they had hitherto occupied (the Rose) was in a dangerous state of decay. It runs as follows:—

"Whereas my servant, Edward Allen, in respect of the dangerous decaye of that howse which he and his Companye have nowe on the Banck, and for that the same standeth verie noysome for resorte of people in the wynter tyme, hath thearfore nowe of late taken a plott of grounde neere Redcrosse streete London (verie fitt and convenient) for the buildinge of a

new howse theare, and hath provided tymber and other necessaries for theffectinge theareof, to his greate chardge. Forasmuche as the place standeth verie convenient for the ease of people, and that her Matie (in respect of the acceptable service, which my saide servant and his Companie have doen and presented before her Highenes to her greate lykeinge and contentment, as well this last Christmas as att sondrie other tymes) ys gratiouslie moved towardes them, with a speciall regarde of favor in their proceedinges. Theis shalbe thearefore to praie and requier you, and everie of you, to permitt and suffer my saide servant to proceede in theffectinge and finishinge of the saide newhowse, without anie your lett or molestation towardes him or any of his workmen. And soe, not doubtinge of your observation in this behalf, I bidd you right hartelie farewell. Att the Courte at Richmond, the xij^th of Januarye 1599.

"NOTINGHAM.

" To all and every her Maties Justices, and other Ministers and officers within the Countye of Middx, and to every of them. And to all others whome it shall concerne."

It is very evident that some of the Justices of Middlesex and others did what they could to impede the execution of this project; and three months afterwards, we find the authority of the Lord Admirall again employed in aid of his servants. At this time it appears that Alleyn and his associates had ceased to perform at the Rose, possibly owing to the decayed state of the house, but more probably in order to strengthen their claim to be allowed to erect a new building for the same purpose.

Much complaint had been made against the number of playhouses in and near London; and the Earl of Nottingham, in his second letter to the Justices of Middlesex, is anxious to impress upon them that the Fortune was only to supply the place of a theatre which had been pulled down. How far such was the fact, we cannot now determine; but it is certain that the Rose was standing some time afterwards, that Lord Pembroke's players acted in it, and that in 1603, Henslowe renewed his lease of the ground on which it stood.

(Hist. Engl. Dram. Poetry and the Stage, iii. 318). In April, 1600, when the subsequent document was prepared (to give which more effect, the names of Lord Hunsdon and Sir Robert Cecill were subscribed with that of Lord Nottingham,) we gather that some progress had been made with "the frame and workmanship of the Fortune." In January, 1599—1600, "timber and other necessaries" had been provided; but by the following April, considerable progress had been made in the undertaking.

"After our hartie comendations. Whereas her Matie (haveinge been well pleased heeretofere at tymes of recreation with the services of Edward Allen and his Companie, servantes to me the Earle of Nottingham, wheareof of late he hath made discontynuance) hath sondrye tymes signified her pleasuer, that he should revive the same agayne. Forasmuche as he hath bestowed a greate some of money, not onelie for the title of a plott of grounde scituat in a verie remote and exempt place neere Goulding Lane, theare to erect a newe house, but alsoe is in good forwardnes aboute the frame and warkmanshipp theareof, the conveniencie of which place for that purpose ys testified unto us under the handes of manie of the Inhabitantes of the Libertie of Finsbury, wheare it is, and recomended by some of the Justices them selves, Wee thearfore, haviuge informed her Matie lykewise of the decaye of the howse wherein this Companye latelie plaied, scituate uppon the Bancke, verie noysome for the resorte of people in the Wynter tyme, have receaved order to requier yow to tollerate the proceedinge of the saide newhowse neere Goulding Lane, and doe heerbye requier you, and everie of yow, to permitte and suffer the said Edward Allen to proceede in theffectinge and finishinge of the same newehowse, without anie your lett or interruption towardes him or anie of his woorkmen; the rather because an other howse is pulled downe instead of yt. And soe, not doubtinge of your conformitye heerin, wee comitt you to God: frome the Courte at Richmond, the viij^th of Aprill 1600.

"Your loveinge freindes
"NOTINGHAM.
"G. HUNSDON
"RO. CECYLL.
"To the Justices of Peace of the Countye of Middx, especially of St. Gyles without Creplegate, and to all others whome it shall concerne."

The foregoing document refers to a certain testification "under the hands of many of the inhabitants of the Liberty of Finsbury" in favour of the completion of the Fortune: that instrument is also found at Dulwich, and it is indorsed "The Certificate of the Inhabitants of the Lp. of Fynsburie of theire consent to the Tolleration of the Erection of the newe Plaihouse theare;" the principal ground of "consent to the toleration" being, that the undertakers had agreed to contribute liberally to the maintenance of the poor of the parish. It is in the following form.

"To the righte honorable the Lordes and others of her Ma^{ts} most honorable privie Councell.

"In all humblenes, wee the Inhabitants of the Lordshipp of Fynisburye, within the parishe of St Gyles without Creplegate, London, doe certifie unto your honnours, that wheare the Servantes of the right honorable the Earle of Nottingham have latelie gone aboute to erect and sett upp a newe Playhouse within the said Lp, wee could be contented that the same might proceede and be tollerated (soe it stande with your honnours pleasuers) for the reasons and causes followeinge.

"First, because the place appoynted oute for that purpose standeth very tollerrable, neere unto the Feildes, and soe farr distant and remote frome any person or place of accompt, as that none cann be annoyed thearbie.

"Secondlie, because the erectours of the saied howse are contented to give a very liberall portion of money weekelie towards the relief of our poore, the nomber and necessity whereof is soe greate, that the same will redounde to the contynuall comfort of the said poore.

"Thirdlie and lastlie, wee are the rather contented to accept this meanes of relief of our poore because our Parrishe is not able to releeve them. Neither hath the Justices of the Sheire taken any order for any supplie out of the Countye, as is enjoyned by the late Acte of Parliamente.

"Hary Stapelforde
"Anthonie Marlowe
"Willm Browne Constable
"George Garlande, Overseer for our Poore
"John Hitchens, Overseer for our Poore
"Nicholas Warden" &c. &c.

The Lord Admirall seems to have known nothing of Henslowe in the transaction; but it is quite certain, from the agreement between Alleyn and Henslowe on the one part, and Peter Streete, the carpenter, on the other part, for building the Fortune, that Henslowe was from first to last concerned in it as Alleyn's partner. According to this document, Streete's work was to cost £440; but it appears by an existing memorandum in Alleyn's hand-writing, that his sole share of the expense was £520; but that perhaps included all the fittings-up and ornaments. Contrary to what is said in the History of Dramatic Poetry and the Stage, iii. 308, it seems likely that, in making the memorandum there quoted, Alleyn was only recording his half of the charge for rendering the Fortune fit for theatrical performances.

We are without any means of knowing the precise date when the new theatre, the Fortune, was opened. It was unquestionably anterior to October, 1602; for, at that date, Henslowe records that he paid 40s. to Alleyn for his book of Tamar Cam, which was played there, and of which "the plott," as it is termed, is extant, and is printed in Malone's Shakespeare by Boswell, iii. 356. The entry in Henslowe's Diary is this:—

"Pd unto my sonne Alleyn, at the apoyntment of the company, for his boocke of Tambercam, the 20 of Octobeer 1602, the some of xxxx s." *

Hence we see, that Alleyn was separately paid for whatever he did for the company in the way of authorship, if it

---

* It was probably only the revival in 1602 of a popular piece, with additions and changes. In Henslowe's Diary we read as follows:—

s.
"6 of Maye 1596   ne   Rd at Tambercamme xxxxvij"

The letters ne indicate that it was then a new piece, and was acted for the first time. From another item in the same MS. we learn that the success of it very soon led to the production of "a second part of Tambercam," which was brought out on the 11 June 1596. It is the "plott of the first parte of Tamar Cam," which was printed by Malone.

may be so called. It is supposed that Tamar Cam (like Tarlton's "plott" of "the Seven Deadly Sins," &c.) was an entertainment made up of dumb shew, action, and extempore performance. Alleyn was the principal actor in Tamar Cam, as well as the contriver of the whole representation, and he was supported in it by W. Cartwright, Towne, Jubie, Parsons, Singer, Marbeck, Parr, and several inferior actors. The names of the different members of the company, Alleyn's immediate associates, were these, as we find them enumerated in Harl. MS. No. 252:— Thomas Towne, Thomas Downton (or Dowton), William Byrde (or Borne), Samuel Rowley, Edward Jubye, Charles Massy, Humphrey Jeffes, Edward Colbrand, William Parr, Richard Pryor, William Stratford, Francis Grace, and John Shanke.

Henslowe, in his letter to Alleyn, at the Brill, on the 4th June, 1598, mentions, as will be recollected, the extreme illness of Mr. Bowes, the then "master of the game of bulls and bears;" adding, with some disappointment, that the place had already been granted in reversion to Mr. Dorington. Dorington came into the office soon afterwards, but he seems to have acted upon a grant made to him in reversion in 1573; and on the accession of James I. a new patent was made out to him. The date of the patent to Bowes (a copy of which is found at Dulwich) bears date on the 8th November, 1586. In March 1600 we find Dorington writing in a very urgent manner to Henslowe for his assistance, the queen having suddenly required "her majesty's games" to be exhibited at court. Henslowe was therefore to assist Dorington in his emergency with his dogs and bears from Paris Garden. The letter of the Master of the Game is addressed,

"To my very good frend Mr. Henslow geve thees.

"Mr. Henslow. I have recevid a letter to have hir Ma^{tes} games to be at the court of monday next, so short a warning as I never knew the lyke, and my self not well, having had a fytt of agew on Frydaye at night; but yf ther be no remedye, then good Mr Henslow pull up your

speryttes and Jackcobe to furnyshe yt as well as yow canne, and I have wrytten to my sister Hide to lett hir Ma^ty understand of the losse we had in this wynter of our best beers, and to sygnyfy so much to them that executes my Lord Chamberlins place; and so I will leve you for this time, hoping you will dow all your best indevors to so satisfy hir Ma^ty in this servisse. From Wigall, this [torn] of marche 1600.

"Your very frend,
"JOHN DORINGTON."

We are unable to state what precise interest Alleyn, at this date, had in Paris Garden; he was unquestionably a partner in the concern, and after the death of Henslowe it seems to have devolved entirely into his hands.

On his accession, James I. took into his pay the Lord Chamberlain's servants, and they were afterwards called the King's Players: this was the company to which Shakespeare was attached. Queen Anne adopted Lord Worcester's players (of whom Thomas Heywood was one) as her theatrical servants; and Prince Henry allowed Alleyn and thirteen of his associates, who had previously belonged to the Earl of Nottingham, to act under his name.† Very soon after this

* In Henslowe's Diary we meet with the following memorandum, which seems to shew that Henslowe, in 1602, paid Dorington rent; which may mean a consideration for being allowed by the Master of the Queen's Games to bait bears, bulls, &c. at Paris Garden.

"Received of Mr. Henslow, the xj^th daye of aprill 1602, the some of ten pounds, dew to me at our lady abouff wrytten, for that quarter then dewe to me for Rent. "JOHN DORINGTON."

† "Nay, see the beauty of our kinde Soveraigne: not only to the indifferent of worth and the worthy of honour did he freely deale about these causes, but to the meane gave grace; as taking to him the late Lord Chamberlains servants, now the King's Actors; the Queene taking to her the Earl of Worster's servants, that are now her actors; and the Prince, their son, Henry Prince of Wales, full of hope, tooke to him the Earl of Nottingham his servants, who are now his actors: so that of Lords' servants, they are now the servants of the King, Queene and Prince."—Gilbert Dugdale's *Time Triumphant*, 1604, *Sign.* B.

arrangement had been made, the plague broke out in London with so much virulence that the theatres were closed, and the actors driven to procure subsistence as they could. Alleyn, as usual, went with a selection from his company into the provinces upon a strolling expedition. Of this date we have a very interesting letter from Mrs. Alleyn to her husband, written and subscribed by the person ordinarily employed: it is remarkable, because it contains a mention of Shakespeare, who is spoken of as " of the Globe;" and though it throws no new light upon our great dramatist's character, excepting as it shews that he was on good terms with Alleyn's family, any document containing merely his name must be considered valuable. The paper on which the letter was written is in a most decayed state, especially at the bottom, where it breaks and drops away in dust and fragments at the slightest touch. The notice of Shakespeare is near the commencement of a postscript on the lower part of the page, where the paper is most rotten, and several deficiencies occur, which it is impossible to supply: all that remains is extremely difficult to be deciphered. We will insert it, and defer further remarks until afterwards, only premising that the address has completely disappeared, so that we cannot tell where Alleyn was at the time; nor indeed, excepting from internal evidence, can we decide that it was sent to him. Upon this point, however, there can be no doubt.

" Jhesus

" My intyre and welbeloved sweete harte, still it joyes me and longe, I pray god, may I joye to heare of your healthe and welfare, as of ours. Allmighty god be thanked, my own selfe, your selfe and my mother, and whole house are in good h ..lhe, and about us the sycknes dothe cease and likely more and more by gods healpe to cease. All the companyes be come home and well for ought we knowe, but that Browne of the Boares head is dead, and dyed very pore. He went not into the countrye at all, and all of your owne company ar well at there owne houses. My father is at the corte, but wheare the corte ys I know not. I am of your owne

mynde, that it is needles to meete my father at Basynge: the entertaynment beinge as it is, I comend your discreation. It weare a sore journey to loase your labour, besyde expenses, and change of ayre mighte hurte you; therfore you are resolved upon the best course. For your cominge hoame I am not to advyse you, neither will I: use your owne discreation, yet I longe and am very desyrous to see you; and my poore and simple opinion is, yf it shall please you, you maye safely come hoame. Heare is none now sycke neare us; yet let it not be as I wyll, but at your owne best lykynge. I am glad to heare you take delight in hauckinge, and thoughe you have worne your appayrell to rags, the best ys you knowe where to have better, and as wellcome to me shall you be with your rags, as yf you were in cloathe of gold or velvet. Trye and see.

"I have payd fyfty shillings for your rent for the warfe, the Lordes rent. Mr Woodward, my Lordes bayly, was not in towne but poynted his deputy who receaved all the rentes. I had witnesses with me at the payment of the money, and have his quittance, but the quyttance cost me a groat: they sayd it was the baylives fee. You knowe best whether you were wont to paye it; yf not, they made a symple woman of me. You shall receave a letter from the Joyner hym selfe, and a pryuted bill; and so with my humble and harty comendations to your owne selfe, Mr Chaloners and his wyfe, with thankes for your kynde usage, with my good mothers kyndest comendations with the rest of your househould * * he is well but can not speake, I ende prayinge allmighty god to blesse you for his mercyes sake, and so sweete harte * * noe more. Farwell till we meete, which I hope shall not be longe. This xxth of October 1603.

"Aboute a weeke a goe there came a youthe who said he was Mr Fbrauncis Chaloner who would have borrowed x^{li} to have bought things for * * * and said he was known unto you, and Mr Shakespeare of the globe, who came * * * said he knewe hym not, ouely he herde of hym that he was a roge * * * so he was glade we did not lend him the monney * * * Richard Johnes [went] to seeke and inquire after the fellow, and said he had lent hym a horse. I feare me he gulled hym, thoughe he gulled not us. The youthe was a prety youthe, and hansom in appayrell: we knowe not what became of hym. Mr Benfield commendes hym; he was heare yesterdaye. Nicke and Jeames be well, and comend them: so doth Mr Cooke and his wiefe in the kyndest sorte, and so once more in the hartiest manner farwell.

"Your faithfull and lovinge wiefe,

"JOANE ALLEYNE."

We learn from this letter that Henslowe, at its date, was absent from London, following the king and court. The plague had somewhat abated, and most of the companies of actors had returned to London, including Alleyn's associates, though he himself lingered in the country (after having worn out his clothes), to enjoy the sport of hawking. Meanwhile, his careful and loving wife had been attentive to her duties; the wharf, for which she had paid the rent, Alleyn held under Lord Montague. The young rogue, who vainly attempted to borrow £10 of her, and regarding whom Shakespeare coming in just afterwards spoke to her, probably pretended to be some relation to the "Mr. Chaloners and his wife," mentioned near the close of the body of the letter. Benfield, who sent his commendations in the postscript, might be the father of the actor of that name: he died in 1619. Cooke was, perhaps, the author of the celebrated play which is known by the name of "Greene's Tu Quoque."

CHAPTER VIII.

Lion-baiting by Alleyn before James I. in the Tower — Permission to the Kings, Queens, and Prince's Players to act again — Blackfriars Theatre — Shakespeare an Actor up to the 9th of April, 1604 — Players of the Duke of Lennox, and Henslowe's connection with them — Purchase by Alleyn and Henslowe of the office of Master of the King's Games — Their Patent and Petition to the King.

IN Stowe's Chronicle, under date of March, 1603-4, is inserted a very minute and picturesque account of a barbarous and revolting exhibition before King James in the Tower, when Alleyn was sent for, that he might bring his dogs from the Bear Garden to bait a lion in his den. As this description has never been quoted by any biographer of Alleyn, and as he personally

superintended the singular exhibition, it will not be out of place to insert it here.

"Whereupon the King caused Edward Allen, late servant to the Lord Admirall, now sworne the Princes man and Maister of the Beare Garden, to fetch secretly three of the fellest dogs in the Garden, which being done, the King, Queene, and Prince with 4 or 5 Lords, went to the Lions Towre, and caused the lustiest Lion to be seperated from his mate, and put into the Lions den one dog alone, who presently flew to the face of the Lion, but the Lion suddenly shooke him off, and graspt him fast by the necke, drawing the dog vp staires and downe staires. The King now perceiving the Lion greatly to exceede the dog in strength, but nothing in noble heart and courage, caused another dog to be put into the den, who prooved as hotte and lusty as his fellow, and tooke the Lion by the face, but the Lion began to deale with him as with the former; whereupon the King commanded the third dog to be put in before the second dog was spoiled, which third dog more fierce and fell then either of the former, and in despight either of clawes or strength, tooke the Lyon by the lip, but the Lion so tore the dog by the eyes, head, and face, that he lost his hold, and then the Lion tooke the dogs neck in his mouth, drawing him up and downe as he did the former, but being wearied, could not bite so deadly as at the first, now whilest the last dog was thus hand to hand with the Lion in the upper roome, the other two dogs were fighting together in the lower roome, whereupon the King caused the Lion to be driven downe, thinking the lion would have parted them, but when he saw he must needs come by them, he leapt cleane over them both, and contrary to the King's expectation, the lion fled into an inward den, and would not by any means endure the presence of the dogs, albeit the last dogge pursued egerly, but could not finde the way to the Lion. You shall vnderstand the two last dogs whilst the Lion held them both under his pawes, did bite the Lion by the belly, whereat the Lion roared so extreamly that the earth shooke withall, and the next Lion rampt and roared as if she would have made rescue. The Lion hath not any peculiar or proper kind of fight, as hath the dog, beare, or bull, but onely a ravenous kinde of surprising for prey. The 2 first dogs dyed within few dayes, but the last dog was well recovered of all his hurts, and the young Prince commanded his seruant E. Allen to bring the dog to him to S. James, where the Prince charged the said Allen to keepe him, and make much of him, saying, he that had fought with the King of Beasts, should never after fight with any inferior creature."

The plague having been checked by the winter of 1603-4,

began so far to disappear in the spring, that permission was again given for the opening of the theatres in and near London. We now come to a paper which Malone saw, and to the general import of which he adverts in his "Inquiry," p. 215, but which, as he tells us, he reserved for publication at large in his projected life of Shakespeare, which he never completed. He does not state where he had found it, but it was in fact among the MSS. which he procured from Dulwich College. It is the copy of a letter from the Council, consisting of Lords Nottingham, Suffolk, Shrewsbury, Worcester, &c. to the Lord Mayor of London and the magistrates of Middlesex and Surrey, directing them not to interfere with three companies of players, but to permit those of the King, the Queen, and the Prince, to act at the Globe on the Bankside, at the Fortune in Golding Lane, and at the Curtain in Shoreditch, notwithstanding any previous prohibition. Malone does not seem to have been aware on what particular occasion this order had appeared, but it was issued after the plague had in a considerable degree abated its violence. The document is so much damaged as to be illegible in two places at the beginning, but the rest of it runs as follows :—

"After our hartie * * * Wheras the Kings ma^{ties} Plaiers have given * * * highnes good service in ther Quallitie of Playinge, and for as much likewise as they are at all times to be emploied in that service, whensoever they shalbe commaunded, We thinke it therfore fitt, the time of Lent being now past, that your L doe permitt and suffer the three Companies of Plaiers to the King, Queene and Prince, publicklie to exercise ther plaies in ther severall usuall howses for that purpose and noe other; viz the Globe, scituate in Maiden Lane on the Banckside in the Countie of Surrey, the Fortune, in Golding Lane, and the Curtaine, in Hollywell in the Cowntie of Middlesex, without any lett or interruption in respect of any former Letters of Prohibition heertofore written by us to your Lop., except there happen weeklie to die of the Plague above the number of thirtie, within the Cittie of London and the Liberties therof. Att which time we thinke itt fitt they shall cease and forbeare any further publicklie to playe, untill the sicknes be again decreaced to the saide number.

And so we bid your Lo. hartilie farewell. From the Court at Whitehalle, the ixth of Aprill 1604.

" Your very loving Frends,
" NOTTINGHAM
" SUFFOLK
" GILL SHROWSBERIE
" E. WORSTER
" W. KNOWLES
" J. STANHOPP.

" To our verie good L the Lord Maior of the Cittie of London, and to the Justices of the Peace of the Counties of Middlesex and Surrey."

Here we see that the Globe, the Fortune, and the Curtain, are designated as the " several usual houses" of the three companies; and Malone would infer, from these only being mentioned, that the King's players, of whom Shakespeare was one, had not, in April 1604, possession of the Blackfriars Theatre. He did not advert to the important point that the Blackfriars, like the Whitefriars, was what was called " a private theatre," and, therefore, did not fall within the same regulations as a public theatre. It is much more likely that the Blackfriars Theatre should have been in the hands of the King's players (formerly the Lord Chamberlain's servants) from the time it was built by James Burbage, the father of Richard Burbage, in 1576, until the period of which we are now speaking, than that the company should have purchased it, as Malone supposes, in the winter of 1604-5. He, however, was not acquainted with the fact, since discovered, that the Blackfriars Theatre, having been originally constructed by James Burbage, was actually in possession of Shakespeare and his fellows in 1596. (Hist. of Engl. Dram. Poetry and the Stage, iii. 298.)

Malone also appears to have reserved another circumstance, of very considerable importance in relation to Shakespeare, for his life of the poet. To the last quoted document, but in a different hand and in different ink, is appended a list of the King's players. The name of Shakespeare there occurs

second; and as it could not be written at the bottom of the letter of the Council to the Lord Mayor, &c. prior to the date of that letter, it proves that up to 9th April, 1604, our great dramatist continued to be numbered among the *actors* of the company. Hitherto the last trace we have had of Shakespeare as actually on the stage, has been as one of the performers in Ben Jonson's "Sejanus," which was produced in 1603. We will insert the list as it stands at the foot of the Council's letter to the Lord Mayor, &c.—

"Ks Comp.
"BURBIDGE
"SHAKSPEARE
"FLETCHER
"PHILLIPS
"CONDLE
"HEMMINGES
"ARMYN
"SLYE
"COWLEY
"HOSTLER
"DAY."

It seems doubtful whether this enumeration was made out according to the comparative prominence and importance of the individuals in the company. In the patent of King James of 17th May, 1603, the order of the three first of the above names is exactly reversed—viz., Lawrence Fletcher, William Shakespeare, and Richard Burbage; and there are other variations of minor consequence. Of Hostler (or Ostler) and Day, in connection with the King's Players, we now hear for the first time. William Ostler was one of the children of the Chapel in 1601, and either joined the King's company after 17th May, 1603, or was included in the general words of the Patent, "and the rest of their associates." Precisely the same may be said of Thomas Day, who never seems to have attained eminence: he was possibly some relation to John Day, the prolific dramatist. The reason why we are not furnished with corresponding lists of the Queen's and Prince's Players may be, that Alleyn and Henslowe were certainly connected with the one body, and possibly with the other.

On the 15th March, 1603, Alleyn, attired as Genius, delivered a speech to King James, as he passed through London; and Dekker, giving an account of the ceremony, printed in 1604, says, " Genius by M. Allin (servant to the young Prince) his gratulatory speech, which was delivered with excellent action, and a well tunde audible voice." We do not recollect that the quality of Alleyn's voice is elsewhere noticed.

In the autumn of 1604, we hear of another company of actors, mentioned in no earlier authority than that we are about to notice—the players of the Duke of Lennox. Whether Alleyn had any interest in their performances is not stated; but it is quite clear from the papers at Dulwich, that Henslowe had, and that his brother Francis Henslowe (several times mentioned by Philip Henslowe in his Diary,) was at the head of them, though probably not as a performer. Prior to the 13th Oct. 1604, this company had been forbidden to perform (whether in London or elsewhere cannot now be determined,) in consequence of which the ensuing official letter was obtained from the Duke of Lennox to all Mayors, Justices of the Peace, &c. desiring that no obstruction might be offered to his players.

" To all maiors, Justeces of peas, Shreefes, Balifes, Constabells, and all other his highnes officers and lofing subjects, to whome it shall, or may in any wise appertaine.

" Sir. I am given to understand that you have forbidden the Companye of Players (that call themselves myne) the exercise of their Playes. I praie you to forbeare any such course against them, and seeing they have my License to suffer them to continue the use of their Playes; and untill you receave other signification from me of them, to afforde them your favour and assistance. And so I bidd you hartely farewell. From Hampton Courte, the xiij of October 1604.

" Your loving freende,
" LENOX."

The above seems to have come into Henslowe's possession in consequence of the pecuniary interest he had in the company, which possibly performed for a short time at one of his

theatres. They continued in existence in March following the date of the foregoing letter; for on the 17th of that month Francis Henslowe entered into a bond to his brother, with the penalty of £60, "well and trulie to holde, performe, fulfill and keepe all such agreementes matters and things, as are conteyned and specified in certen Articles of Agreemente, bearing date with theis presentes, made and agreed uppon by and betweene the said Francis Henslowe and John Garland and Abraham Saverie, his fellowes, servantes to the most noble Prince, the Duke of Linnox, and subscribed with all theire handes."

Garland and Saverie are both names new in our dramatic history;[*] and after this date, we hear no more of the Players of the Duke of Lennox, or of the connection of either of the Henslowes with them. Whether they were put down by authority of the Council (which not long before had restricted theatrical performances in public theatres to the three companies of the King, Queen, and Prince) nowhere appears: possibly the speculation did not answer, and they therefore relinquished their performances.

Sir John Dorington, as we have seen, was ill of an ague in March, 1600:[†] he died soon after James I. came to the throne, and Sir William Stuart was appointed to the vacant office of "Master, &c. of the King's Games of Bears, Bulls, and Dogs," and Henslowe and Alleyn, not having a license for

[*] To this period is probably to be assigned the following undated entry in Henslowe's Diary or Account-book:—

"Lent unto Frances Henslow to goyne with owld Garland and Symcockes and Savery, when they played in the Dukes name at the laste goinge owt, the some of vij^{li} : I saye lent. vij^{li}"

[†] The writer has in his possession the original appointment of John Dorington, Esq., to "the room or office of Cheif Master, Overseer and Ruler of all and singular our game, pastimes and sports, that is to say of all and every our bears, bulls and mastiff dogs, meet for the purpose." It bears date at Westminster, 2d June, A° 15. Eliz. 1573. Dorington, as appears by the same instrument, succeeded Cuthbert Vaughan, Esq.

the purpose, were, as they afterwards alleged, unable to employ Paris Garden for the chief purpose to which it had for many years been applied. They then offered to sell their house, bears, and dogs to Sir William Stuart, but he refused to buy them, and thus compelled Henslowe and Alleyn* to purchase the office he held for £450, which they insisted was a very bad bargain on their part. The following is a copy of the "acquittance" Sir William Stuart gave for the £450. It will be observed that one of the witnesses subscribes his name John Alleyn; and Edward had an elder brother John, who was entered in the pedigree furnished at the visitation of Surrey in 1624: John Allen had died, and this was perhaps his son.

"Be it knowne unto all men by theis presents, that I, Sir William Steward, Knight, have receaved and had the day of the date hereof, of Phillip Henslowe and Edward Allen of the parishe of S$^{t.}$ Saviours in Southwarke in the County of Surrey, Esquiers, the somme of four hundreth and fiftye poundes of lawfull money of England, in full satisfaction payment and discharge for the absolute bargayne, sale and assignement of a certen Patent to me made and graunted by our soveraigne Lord the Kinges Matie that now is, of the Mastership of his Ma^{ts} games of Beeres Bulls and dogges, and the fees proffitts and appurtenances whatsoever to the same place or office belonginge or appertayninge, the receipte of which foure hundreth and fiftye poundes, in forme aforesaid receaved, I doe acknowledge by theis presents, and thereof and of every parcell thereof I clerelye acquite and discharge the said Phillip Henslowe and Edward Allen and either of them, their executors and administrators for by theis presents. And further I the said Sir William Steward, Knight, have remised, released and altogeather for me my executors and administrators for ever quite claymed, unto the said Phillip Henslowe and Edward Allen and either of them, their executors and administrators, all and all manner of actions sutes, debts accompts reccon-

* After 1617, but at what precise date does not appear, Alleyn presented a petition to James I. in "the Court of Requests," alleging his partnership with Henslowe, and claiming, as such partner, a sum of £13. 5. 0 (the balance of an account) from a person of the name of Hobday, upon whose credit bears and dogs had been furnished to one Starkey, who conveyed them to France, in order to amuse the King in Paris with the sport of bear-baiting. Alleyn in his own hand indorsed the petition, "satisfied and payd."

ings somme and sommes of money claymes dutyes and demaunds whatsoever, which againste the said Phillip Henslowe and Edward Allen or either of them ever I have had, now have, or hereafter shall or may move or have, by reason or force of anye matter, cause, bargaine, contract or thing whatsoever, from the beginninge of the worlde untill the day of the date hereof. In witnes whereof I have hereunto sett my hand and seale, dated the eight and twentieth daye of November 1604, and in the second yere of the Raigne of our soveraigne Lorde Kinge James &c.

         " WILLIAM STEUART (L. S.)
" Sealed and delivered in the
 presence of us
  " EDW. TAYLOR servant to
" Tyarman Davies Notar. Public.
  " JOHN ALLEN
   " JACINTHE BRADSHAWGHE."

It is somewhat remarkable, that the Patent to Henslowe and Alleyn, constituting them jointly and severally Masters of the King's Games, should be dated four days anterior to the instrument we have just quoted; so that they were, in fact, appointed before they paid the £450 to Sir William Stuart. It is very possible that the sum stipulated had previously been deposited in the hands of some third party; and Henslowe had seen too much of the world to be likely to part with his money beyond controul, until he was sure of the office. Originally there must have been a complete and perfect copy of the patent to Henslowe and Alleyn at Dulwich College on four sheets, but only the three last of these now remain. They are indorsed in a strange hand, " Mr. Henslowe bergarden," and by Alleyn " a draft of the patent:" in fact, they contain all that is material, and are as follow, the absent introduction being of course mere matter of form.

  ———— " and advantages whatsoever to the said office of Cheefe Mr. Overseer and Ruler of our Beares, Bulls and Mastiffe Dogges in any wise belonginge, in as large and ample manner as Sir William Steward, Knight, or before him Sir John Darrington, Knight, deceased, or as Raphe Bowes, or any other at any tyme ever had, used, perceaved or enjoyed, in for or by reason of the same office. Givinge by these presentes, for us our heires and

successors, unto the said Phillip Henslow and Edward Allen, and to either of them, joyntly and severallye, and to the deputie or deputies of them or either of them, during the naturalle lives of the said Phillipe Henslowe and Edward Allen, and the life of the longer liver of them, full power comission and authoritie, not onlie to take up and kepe for our service pastyme and sporte any mastife dogge or dogges and mastife bitches, beares, bulls and other meete and convenient for our said service and pastymes, or any of them, beinge within this our realme or other our dominions, at and for such reasonable prices as our said servauntes or either of them, there deputie or deputies, or the deputie or deputies of either of them, can agree with the owner or owners of the beares and bulls; but also to staye, or cause to be stayed at theire or either of theire discretions all and every such mastiffe dogges and bitches as the said Phillip Henslow and Edward Allen, or either of them, or there assignes or the assignes of either of them, shall fortune at any tyme hereafter to take or fynde goinge, passinge or conveyinge, or to be conveyed in any wise into any partes of beyond the seas without our special warrant and commission for conveyinge of the same. Willinge and straightly charging and commaundinge, that as well all our officers, ministers and subjects and every of them, from henceforth doe ayde from tyme to tyme, assiste strengthen and helpe the said Phillip Henslowe and Edward Allen, or either of them, in exercisinge of the same office and other the premisses, as also other our officers and ministers in any wise appertayninge to our said games shall diligently obey, be attendinge and do any thing and thinges reasonable that the said Phillip Henslow and Edward Allen, joyntly and either of them severally, as masters and cheefe rulers of our said games shall comaunde for our better service therein. And further, we doe give and graunt full power and authoritie by these presentes to the said Phillip Henslow and Edward Allen, and to either of them, to bayte or cause to be bayted our said beares and others beinge of our saide games, in all and every convenient place and places at altymes meete, at there and either of there discretions, and that no other officer or under officer belonginge, or any manner of waies appertayninge to our said beares and games for the tyme being, nor any of them, shall from henceforth baite or cause to be baited any of our said beares, or others of our games aforesaid, in any yarde or place or places without the speciall lycence and appoyntment of the said Phillip Henslow and Edward Allen, or one of them; nor that any of them shall from henceforth take up any beare or beares, or any other appertayninge to our said games, or for any service and commoditie, without the like appointment of the said Phillipe Henslowe and Edward Allen or of one of them as is aforesaide, any manner of graunt or lycense heretofore made, or hereafter to be made to any of them for the same to the

contrarie hereof in any wise notwithstanding. And of our further grace certaine knowledge and meere motion, we doe by these presentes, for us our heires and successors, give and graunt to the said Phillip Henslow and Edward Allen, joyntly and severally, the office and roome of Keeper of our Bandoggs, Mastiffes and Mastiffe Bitches, and the said Phillipe Henslow and Edward Allen and either of them Kepper and Ruler of our Mastiffes and Bandoggs and of the Mastiffes and Bandoggs of us our heirs and successors, we do ordaine and make by these presentes. To have and to holde, occupie and injoye the saide roome to the saide Phillip Henslow and Edwarde Allen joyntly and severallie, aswell by them selves as by there sufficient deputie or deputies, or by the sufficient deputie or deputies of either of them, duringe theire lives and the longer longer lives of them. Moreover, we do by these presentes for us our heires and successors give and graunt to the saide Phillipe Henslowe and Edwarde Allen, for occupyinge and exercisinge of the saide office and keppinge of twentie mastiffe bitches, the fee and wages of tenn pence sterlinge by the daie, and for there deputie for exercisinge of the saide roome under them the fee and wages of fower pence by the daie. To have and enjoye the saide severall fees and either of them by the saide Phillip Henslow and Edward Allen and theire assignes, duringe theire lives and the liffe of the longer liver of them; and the saide fee to be had and yerelie receaved out of the treasure of our Chamber, and of our heires and successors, by the hands of our Treasurer of the saide Chamber for the tyme beinge, quarterly by even portions, together with all fees advantages profitts and comodities thereunto belonginge, in as large and ample manner as the said Sir William Steward, or as before him the saide Sir John Dorrington, Knight, deceased, or as the saide Ralphe Bowes, or any other person or persons heretofore have had and enjoyed, in and for thexercisinge of the same; althoughe expresse mention of the true yerely valew, or of any other valew or certentie of the premisses, or any of them, or of any other guiftes or graunts by us or any of our progenitors made before this tyme to the aforesaid Phillip Henslow and Edwarde Allen in these presentes is not made, or any other statute acte, ordinance provision, proclamation or restrainte to the contrarie hereof, before this tyme had made sett forth, ordayned or provided, or any other thinge matter or cause whatsoever in any wise notwithstandinge. In witnes whereof we have caused theise our letters to be made pattents. Witnes our selfe at Westminster, the fower and twentith daie of November, in the yere of our raigne of England Fraunce and Ireland the seconde, and of Scotlande the eight and thirteeth."

The date of the document we shall next quote is not given, and perhaps cannot now be ascertained with precision,

but it must have been subsequent to the preceding patent. It is a petition from Henslowe and Alleyn to the King, in their joint capacity of Masters of his Majesty's Games, by purchase from Sir William Stuart; and we may conjecture that it was presented not very long after they became so in 1604, and when they found that their fees and emoluments were insufficient. They complain of the "high rate" at which they had been obliged to buy the office, of not being permitted to bait bears on Sunday, and of the injury done to them by vagrants going about the country with bears and dogs without their licence. They also ask, that the old daily fee of 1s. 4d. should be increased by the addition of 2s. 8d. The original is in Henslowe's illiterate writing.

"To the Kinges moste exsellent magestie.

"The humble pettition of Phillipe Henslow and Edward Alleyn, your Maties servantes.

"Wheras it pleased your moste exselent Matie, after the death of Sir John Dorington, to grant the offes of M^r of your game of beares, bulles and doges, with the fee of xvj^d per dium, unto Sir W^m. Steward, knight, at which tyme the howse and beares being your Maties pettitioners, but we not licensed to bayte them, and Sir Wm Steward refusynge to tacke them at our handes upon any resonable termes, weare therfore inforsed to bye of hime the said office pastime and fee at a very highe ratte.

"And wheras in respecte of the great charge that the kepinge of the saide game contenewally requirethe, and also the smalnes of the fee, in the late quenes tyme fre libertie was permited with owt restrainte to bayght them, which now is tacken away frome us, especiallye one the sondayes in the after none after devine service, which was the cheffest meanes and benyfite to the place; and in the tyme of the sicknes we have bene retrayned many tymes one the workey dayes. Thes hinderances in generalle, with the losse of divers of thes beastes, as before the Kinge of Denmarke, which loste a goodlye beare called Gorge Stone; and at our laste beinge before your Matie weare kylled iiij of our beaste beares, which in your kingdom are not the licke to be hade, all which weare in valley worth 30^{li}; and also our ordenary charges amounteth yearly unto ijC^{li} and beatter: thes losses and charges are so heavey upon your pettitioners, that wheras formerly we cowld have leatten it forth for 100^{li} a yeare, now none will

tacke it gratis to beare the charges, which is your pore servantes undoinge, unles your M^tie of your gratious clemensey have consideration of us.

"Thes cawsses do in forse us moste humblie to be come sewters to your Matie in respecte of the premisies, and for that we have, ever sence your gratious enterance into this kingdom, done your Matie service with all dewtie and observance, it wold pleasse your Matie in your moste rialle bowntie now so to releve us, as we maye be able to contenew our service unto your Matie as hereto fore we have done, and to that eand to grant unto us free libertie, as hath byun geaven us in the late quenes tyme, and also in respecte of our great and dayle charge, to ade unto our sayd fee ij^s viij^d, beinge never as yet incresed sence the firste fowndation of the office.

"And wheras ther ar divers vagrantes, and persones of losse and idell liffe, that usalley wandreth throwgh the contreyes with beares and bulles with owt any lycence, and for owght we know servinge no man, spoyllinge and kyllinge doges for that game, so that your Matie cane not be served but by great charges to us, fetchinge them very fare, which is directly contrary to a statute made in that behallfe: for the restrayninge of suche your Matie wold be pleassed, in your moste gratious favor, to renew unto your pettitioners our pattyne, and to grant us and our deputies power and atoritie to apprehend suche vagrantes, and to convent them before the next Justice of pece, therto be bownd with suerties to forfet his said beares and bulles to your Maties usse, yf he shalbe tacken to go a bowt with any suche game, contrary to the lawes of this your Maties Realme, and your pore servantes will dayle praye for your Maties longe and hapey Rayne.

Another less authentic copy, in the hand-writing of some scrivener, is also preserved at Dulwich, and it is printed in "Lysons' Environs," vol. i. p. 92. How far the petition was successful on other points, we are without the means of knowing; but from Alleyn's Diary we find, that he never received more than £24 2s. 6d. per annum as his fee, after the death of Henslowe, and when the office devolved into his sole hands. While Henslowe was living, if they paid the £450 to Sir W. Stuart in equal proportions, only half of this yearly fee would belong to Alleyn.

CHAPTER IX.

Alleyn's Skill on the Lute—His Residence—Rebuilding of Paris Garden in 1606 — Agreement with Peter Streete — Alleyn's first Acquisition of Property at Dulwich—Bear-baiting in the Country—Annuity to Thomas Towne, the Actor— Indenture between Henslowe and Alleyn, and Thomas Downton, as a Sharer at the Fortune.

PROFICIENCY in music, both vocal and instrumental, was much more usual in the time of Elizabeth and James I., than at present. The lute was commonly played upon, and one proof, among many, is, that at that period and earlier, a lute, a gittern, or a cittern, were ordinarily part of the furniture of every barber's shop, in order that the customers, who were waiting for their turn, might amuse themselves with it. Alleyn was a performer upon the lute, (his " lute-books " are mentioned in Henslowe's Letter, the 14th of August, 1593, p. 30) and while in Sussex he, perhaps, became acquainted with some members of the Pointz family, one of whom, from the subsequent note, seems to have employed him when in London, either to repair a lute, or to get it repaired. At the conclusion it gives Alleyn's then address very particularly:—

" Good Mr Allen, delevir my lute unto this bearer, whoe will convaye it unto me, and looke what it comes two the mendinge, I shall not be longe from London and then, god willinge, I will defraye it, with manie thanks, and soe in hast doe rest.

" Your verie loveinge freinde,
"Jo. POYNTZ.

" Woodbatche this
vjth. of marche 1605.

"Mr. Allen dwells harde by the Clynke by the bank syde, neere Wynchesterhowse, where you must deliver this note." *

* In Alleyn's Diary, from 1617 to 1622, are several entries of money paid for lute-strings: when he died he left behind him " a lute, a pandora, a cythern, and six vyols." He was fond of music, entertained singers at his table, bought an organ for his chapel, and went to a considerable expense for a " music room."

The house in which Alleyn at this time resided was, probably, the same, for the extensive repair or construction of which there is an account in Philip Henslowe's Diary. He seems to have occupied it without intermission until he finally removed to Dulwich, though there is some trace of his having for a short time resided at Kensington.

How long prior to 1606 the building at Paris Garden had been standing it is impossible now to decide; but it is not unlikely that it was in great part reconstructed after the accident on January 13th, 1583, when five men and two women were killed by the falling of the "old and underpropped" scaffolds. (Hist. of Engl. Dram. Poetry and the Stage, iii., 382). In the three-and-twenty years between that catastrophe and 1606, as the structure was principally of wood, no doubt it would have become much decayed, and in 1606 (according to the original instrument still existing at Dulwich College) Henslowe and Alleyn entered into an agreement with Peter Streete, the carpenter (who had built the Globe in 1593, and the Fortune in 1599) for the rebuilding of Paris Garden. It gives so minute and so particular an account of all that Streete was to perform, that a most accurate notion may easily be formed of the size, convenience, and even general appearance of the fabric. Any artist of moderate skill could with facility make drawings from it of the whole frontage towards the Thames, as well as of most parts of the interior. The carpenter's work was to cost only £65, or about £300 of our present money, so that it could hardly be of the most finished kind, nor in such a place and for such a purpose would it be required. Though somewhat long, we cannot refrain from quoting the whole of this curious document:—

"Indorsed 'Peter Streetes covenantes and bond for the building of the bearegarden.'

"This Indenture made the second day of June 1606, and in the yeres of the raigne of our Soveraigne Lord, James by the grace of god Kinge of

England Fraunce and Ireland, defender of the faithe &c the fowerth, and of Scotland the nyne and thirteth. Betwene Peter Streete, cittizen and carpenter of London on thone party, and Phillipp Henslowe and Edward Alleyn, of the parishe of St. Saviors in Southwark in the County of Surrey, Esquiers, on thother party. Witnessethe that it is covenanted, graunted concluded and agreed by and betweene the said parties to theis presentes, and the said Peter Streete (for the consideration hereunder specified) for him and his executors and administrators covenauteth and graunteth to and with the said Phillipp Henslowe and Edward Alleyn and either of them, their executors and assignes, by their presentes in manner and forme following, as hereunder from article to article is specified and declared; that is to say:—That he the said Peter Streete, his executors administrators or assignes, before the thirde day of September next comynge after the date hereof, shall at his owne or their owne proper costes and charges, not only take and pull downe for and to the use of the said Phillipp Henslowe and Edward Alleyn their executors or assignes, so much of the tymber or carpenters worke of the foreside of the messuage or tenemente called the Beare garden, next the river of Thames in the parishe of St. Saviors aforesaide, as conteyneth in lengthe from outside to outside fiftye and sixe feete of assize, and in bridth from outside to outside sixeteene feete of assize; but also in steade and place thereof, before the saide thirde day of September, att his or their like costes and charges, shall well sufficiently, and workemanlike, make or erect sett up and fully finishe one new frame for a howse, to conteyne in length from outside to outside fyftie and sixe feete of assize, and in bridth from outside to outside sixteene foote of assize, which frame shalbe made of good, new sufficient and sounde Tymber of oke, to be fynished in all thinges as hereunder is mentioned; that is to say: that the saide frame shall conteyne in height two storyes and a halfe, the two whole storyes of the same frame to be in height from flower to flower ten foote of assize a peece, and the halfe story to be in height fower foote of assize, and all the principall rafters of the same frame to be framed with crooked postes and bolted with iron boltes thorough the rafters, which iron boltes are to be provided at the costes and charges of the saide Peter Streete his executors or assignes. And also shall make in the same frame throughout two flowers with good and sufficient joystes, the same flowers to be boarded throughout with good and sounde deale boardes to be plained and closely laid and shott. All the principall longe upright postes of the saide frame to be nyne ynches broade and seaven ynches thicke: and shall make in the same frame three maine summers, that is to say in the uppermost story twoe summers, and in the lower story one summer, every summer to be one foote square; all the brest summers to be eight ynches broade and seaven ynches thick.

The same frame to jetty over towardes the Thames one foote of assize. And also shall make on the south side of the saide frame a sufficient staire case, with staires convenient to leade up into the uppermost romes of the saide frame, with convenient dores out of the same staire case into every of the romes adjoyninge thereunto, and in every rome of the same frame one sufficient dore; and also by the same staire case shall make and frame one studdy, with a little rome over the same, which studdy is to jetty out from the same frame fower foote of assize, and to extend in lengthe from the saide staire case unto the place where the chimneyes are appoynted to be sett, with a sufficient dore into either of the romes of the same studdy. And the nether story of the same frame shall seperate and devide into fower romes: that is to say, the first towardes the east to be for a tenemente, and to conteyne in length from wall to wall thirteene foote of assize; the next rome to be for a gate rome, and to conteyne in length ten foote of assize; the third rome twenty foote of assize, and the fowerth westward thirteene foote of assize. And the second story shall seperate into three romes, the first, over the rome appoynted for a tenemente on the east end of the said frame, to conteyne in length thirteene foote of assize, the midle rome thirty foote of assize, and the third rome westward thirteene foote likewise of assize. And the halfe story above to be divided into two romes, namely over the said tenement thirteene foote, to be seperated from the rest of the said frame, and the residue to be open in one rome only. And out of the said frame towardes the Thames shall make twoe dores, and one faire paire of gates with twoe wickettes proportionable. And also att either end of the lower story of the same frame shall make one clere story windowe [to] either of the same clere storyes, to be in height three foote of assize, and sixe foote in length, and the middle rome of the same frame, conteyninge twenty foote, to have a clere story windowe throughout of the height of the saide former clere storyes: and in the second story of the same frame shall make three splay windowes, every windowe to be sixe foote betweene the postes; and in the same second story shall make seaven clere story windowes, every clere story to be three foote wide a peece, with one mullion in the midest of every clere story; and every of the same clere storyes to be three foote and a halfe in depth. And over the foresaid gate shall make one greete square windowe, to be in length ten foote of assize and to jetty over from the said frame three foote of assize, standinge upon twoe carved Satyres, the same windowe to be in wheight according to the depth of the story, and the same windowe to be framed with twoe endes with mullions convenient; and over the same windowe one piramen with three piramides, the same frame to have fower gable endes towards the Thames, and upon the top of every gable end one piramide, and betweene every gable end to

be left three foote for the fallinge of the water, and in every gable end one clere story, and backward over the gate of the same frame towardes the south one gable end with a clere story therein, and under the same gable end backward in the second story one clere story windowe. And also in that parcell of the saide frame as is appoynted for a tenement shall make twoe paires of staires, one over an other by the place where the chimneyes are appoynted to be sett. And that he the saide Peter Streete, his executors administrators or assignes, shall before the saide thirde day of September next comynge after the date hereof fully fynishe the saide frame in and by all thinges as aforesaid, and all other carpenters worke specified in a plott made of the said frame, subscribed by the saide Peter and by him delivered to the said Phillipp Henslowe and Edward Alleyn, in such comely and convenient manner and sorte as by the same plott is figured, without fraude or covyn, and at his or their owne charges shall fynd all nayles to be used in and aboute the carpenters worke of the same frame. For and in consideration of which frame and worke to be made performed and fynished in forme aforesaide, the saide Phillipp Henslowe and Edward Alleyn for them and either of them, their executors and administrators, doe covenaunte and graunte to and with the saide Peter Streete, his executors and assignes, by theis presentes, that they the saide Phillipp Henslowe and Edward Alleyn or either of them, their executors or assignes, shall and will well and truly paie or cause to be paide to the saide Peter Streete, his executors or assignes, at the now dwellinge howse of the said Phillipp Henslowe in the parishe of St Saviors aforesaide, the some of threeskore and five powndes of lawfull mony of England in manner and forme followinge, that is to say; in hand at thensealinge hereof the some of ten powndes of lawfull mony of England, the receipte whereof the saide Peter Streete doth acknowledge by theis presentes; upon the delivery of the   saide frame at the Beare garden aforesaid other ten powndes thereof, and when the same frame shalbe fully and wholly raised twenty powndes thereof, and upon the full fynishinge of the same frame in forme aforesaid twenty and five powndes residue, and in full paymente of the saide some of threeskore and five powndes. In witness whereof the saide parteis to theis present Indentures interchaungeably have sett their handes and seales. Yeoven the day and yeres first abo e written.

"Signum P. S.
"Petri Streete.

"Sealed and delivered in the presence of me Thomas Bolton Scr.
"John Allyn."

By indorsements upon this agreement, we find that the first payment of £10 was made on the day after its date; and

various other sums are subsequently entered, in Henslowe's handwriting, amounting, in the whole, to £50 10s .8d. For the remainder, we may conclude that a separate receipt was given by Streete. The work was not completed until 9th January, 1606—7; but it included finishing the stables, sheds, a dormer, and a kitchen. If it be true that, before 1602, when Dekker in his "Satiromastix" asserts that Ben Jonson had played Zulziman at Paris Garden, dramatic performances had been given there, it is singular that in the preceding document nothing is said about adapting the building in some way to such exhibitions. At a not long subsequent date Paris Garden was re-modelled for the purpose.

Nobody has yet been able to fix the time when Alleyn first began to acquire property in Dulwich, which property he afterwards kept constantly increasing. It is, however, a fact established by a bond, given jointly by himself and Henslowe, dated as early as the 18th October, 1606, that he was then "Lord of the Manor of Dulwich;" and he is therein so styled. An unexecuted deed of sale of the manor, from Sir Francis Calton to Alleyn, is preserved in the College, bearing date 2d June, 1606; and doubtless the purchase was completed by Alleyn in the autumn of that year. On the 4th August, 1607, we find him adding to his property there, by buying, for £410 10s., three tenements and twenty-two acres of land, copyhold of the manor of Dulwich, and four acres and one rood of freehold ground, from Ellis Parry, "citizen and weaver." Parry had become possessed of them, by purchase, from Sir Francis Calton, who was also Lord of the Manor of Lewisham, which Alleyn subsequently acquired. The subjoined memorandum of agreement contains all the circumstances of the bargain with Parry.

"Vicesimo quarto die Augusti, 1607, Annoque R. Regis Jacobi Anglie, &c quinto, et Scotie quadragisimo primo.

"Memorandum the day and yere above written Ellis Parrey, citizen and weaver of London, (for the consideration hereunder written) hath bargained

and solde unto Edward Alleyn Esquier three tenementes, scituate and beinge in Dulwich in the parishe of Camerwell in the County of Surrey, now in the severall tenures or occupations of John Lewes —— Kitchen and widdow Ambler with all barnes stables orchards, gardens backsides and twoe and twenty acres of land and pasture, to the same three tenementes belonginge or apperteyninge, beinge coppy hold land holden of the mannor of Dulwich aforesaide; and also fower acres and one rood of land and pasture, beinge freehould, which the saide Ellis Parrey late purchased to him and his heires of Sir Frauncis Calton now in the tenure of the saide —— Kitchen. Which tenementes landes and premisses the saide Ellis Parrey and his heires are to surrender, convey and assure unto the said Edward Alleyn his heires and assignes when and in such sorte and manner as he the saide Edward or his heires shall devise and require, either at the nexte Courte to be holden for the mannor of Dulwich, or sooner if it shall seeme good to the saide Edward Alleyn his heires or assignes: for and in consideration of which bargaine and sale, and assurance to be made thereof as aforesaid, the said Edward Alleyn is to pay to the said Ellis Parrey the somme of fower hundreth and ten powndes and ten shillinges in forme followinge, that is to say; two hundreth powndes on the nyne and twentith day of September next, ten powndes and ten shillinges thereof one moneth after, which ten powndes and ten shillinges the said Edward is to receave of the tennantes, viz of widdowe Ambler one whole yere att michaelmas next, and of Lewes and Kitchen one halfe yeres rent: then, on the five and twentith day of March next one hundredth powndes more, and on the xxiiijth day of June next one other hundreth powndes, residue and in full payment of the said somme of CCCCX^{li} x$^{s.}$ In witnes whereof the saide parties have hereunto subscribed their names the day and yere above written.

"Signum   E P Ellicij   E. ALLEYN
                Parrey

"Subscribed in the presence of us
    "THOMAS BOLTON Scr.
    "ISAAC THORP
    "PETER REYNOLDS
    "MATHIAS ALLEN."

The last witness to the preceding agreement, Mathias Alleyn, was nephew to Edward Alleyn, and succeeded him as Master of God's Gift or Dulwich College.

On a previous page it has been shewn, that Henslowe and Alleyn, in their petition to the King, remonstrated against

the invasion of their exclusive privileges, as Masters of the Royal Games, by unlicensed vagrants, who went about the country with bears and dogs. The Masters claimed the right of sending bearwards into the provinces, who accounted to them for their receipts and expenditure; and among the MSS. at Dulwich is a small memorandum book, kept by one of these itinerant exhibitors in the summer of 1608, the blank leaves at the end of which Alleyn subsequently applied to a different purpose. At the commencement is written "Auguste 1608. The be giminge of the book;" and it is kept most irregularly, and obviously by a very ignorant accountant. The earliest entry is this:—

"Satterday the 27 of Auguste

	s.	d.
R. at Keinsintonn as wee went . . .	x	x"

By which we are to understand, that at starting they were paid 10s. 10d., probably by Alleyn himself; for there is reason to suppose that at this date he had a temporary residence at Kensington. The bearwards, Borne and Bryant, (for more than one man was employed to take charge of the bears and dogs) from thence proceeded westward, and it appears that on Sunday, at Colnbrook, they received 23s., and on Monday, at Maidenhead, 10s. Their expenses were only "for breade for the beares 1s. 6d.," and 2s. which they were charged for lodging and for "the yard," where doubtless the animals were exhibited. They "lay still" at Reading, and at Salisbury spent 1s. 2d. for "oil for the blynd bare." They sometimes stopped at the houses of the nobility and gentry, and one item runs as follows:—

"Tuesday at Sir John Traces.

	s.	d.
Some, gave us for bating before him . .	7	4"

from which was to be deducted 7d., which the bearwards paid " to the drummer for his drum." It is very difficult,

from the confused and illiterate manner in which the account is kept, to make out the balance upon these journeys; but in one instance it is clearly stated as follows:—

	l.	*s.*	*d.*
"R. in the wholle	16	9	9
And dd. him to goe	0	5	0
	16	14	9
Layd owt	13	14	9
	3	0	0."

the difference being the balance of profit to Henslowe and Alleyn on the expedition.

At the end of these accounts we come to a part of the book where entries of a different kind are made. They relate to an annuity of £12 per annum to a person of the name of Thomas Towne (who had been a player with Alleyn in 1597), the quarterly payments of which began on the 28th October, 1608, and were regularly continued until his death, which must have happened before November 5th, 1612, when "the widow Towne" received 20s. This annuity had been purchased by Towne from Alleyn, as we find by the extant deed, on the 20th October, 1608, for £90 in money, and the surrender of some copyhold lands belonging to Towne. The earliest receipt is this:—

"xxviij° die Octobris, 1608.

"Rd by me Thomas Towne, the day and yere abovewritten, of Edward Alleyn Esquer, the somme of Three powndes of lawfull money of England for one quarters payment of the yerely Annuity of Twelve powndes, to me to be due att the feast of the birth of our Lord God now next ensuinge, according to a deed by him, the said Edward, made to me. I say receved } iij^{li}

"THOMAS TOWNE."

This entry appears to have been drawn up by some scrivener, but later in the book, the receipts are written by Alleyn, and subscribed by Towne.

The name of Downton (or Dowton, as it is sometimes written) first occurs as a player at the time when Henry Prince of Wales adopted the theatrical servants of the Earl of Nottingham, in 1603.* Alleyn was undoubtedly looked upon as the leader and master of the company, and, as has been observed, he is not in the list of the members contained in Prince Henry's Household Book (MS. Harl. 252); but Downton's name there immediately follows that of Towne, so that we may infer that they were both distinguished performers. In 1608 Henslowe and Alleyn appear to have been anxious to secure Downton's services permanently at the Fortune, and for that purpose an "indenture" was drawn up, which is the oldest precedent of the kind on record. A copy of it, ready for execution, is among Alleyn's papers; but excepting the year it has no date, and is without signatures. We may suppose, therefore, that for some reason, not explained, the design of the parties was never accomplished. It stipulates that Downton was to receive a thirty-second share of the profits of all dramatic representations at the Fortune for thirteen years, on condition that he paid £27 10s. down, and 10s. annually; and he, on his part, agreed to perform constantly at the Fortune, and in no other "common playhouse," erected or to be erected in London, or within two miles of it. In fact, he thus became a considerable sharer in the theatre, and we insert the document at length, on account of the light it throws upon the relations of manager and actor at the time.

"This Indenture made the   day of   1608, and in the yere of the raigne of our soveraigne Lord, James, by the grace of God

* Although Downton's name does not occur in any list of players anterior to 1603, there is every probability that he had been an actor under Henslowe and Alleyn in 1599, if not earlier. In that year also we find him joining with William Bird and William Juby, two other actors, to write a play, called "The lamentable Tragedy of Page of Plymouth," or "Peg of Plymouth," as Malone misprints it. (Shakesp. by Bosw. iii. 323.)

king of England, Fraunce and Ireland, defender of the faith &c. the sixt and of Scotland the two and fortith. Betweene Phillipp Henslowe and Edward Alleyn of the parishe of S^t. Saviors in Southwark in the County of Surrey, Esquiors, on thone partye, and Thomas Downton of the parishe of S^t. Gyles without Criplegate London, gentleman, on th'other partye. Witnesseth that the said Phillipp Henslowe and Edward Alleyn (for and inconsideration of the somme of twenty and seaven pownds and ten shillinges of lawfull mony of England to them in hand, att or before thensealinge hereof, by the saide Thomas Downton paid, whereof and wherewith they the saide Phillipp Henslowe and Edward Alleyn doe acknowledge themselves well and truly contented satisfied and paide) by theis presentes have demised, leased and to farme letten, and by these presentes doe demise lease and to farme lett unto the saide Thomas Downton, one eight parte of a fowerth parte of all such clere gaynes in mony as shall hereafter, duringe the terme hereunder demised, arrise growe accrew or become due or properly belong unto the saide Phillipp Henslowe and Edward Alleyn or either of them, their or either of their executors or assignes, for or by reason of any stage playinge or other exercise comoditie or use whatsoever, used or to be used or exercised within the play howse of the saide Phillipp Henslow and Edward Alleyn commonly called the Fortune, scituate and beinge betweene Whitcrosse streete and Golding lane in the parishe of St Gyles without Criplegate, London, in the county of Midd. And the saide eighte parte of a fowerth parte of all the saide cleregaynes properly belonginge to the saide Phillipp Henslowe and Edward Alleyn, to be paid by the saide Phillipp Henslowe and Edward Alleyn or one of them, their or one of their executors or assignes, unto the said Thomas Downton or his assignes every day that any play or other exercise shall be acted or exercised in the play howse aforesaide, upon the sharinge of the monyes gathered and gotten att every of the same playes and exercises, as heretofore hath byn used and accustomed. To have and to houlde and receave the saide eight parte of a fowerth parte of the saide clere gaynes to be gotten by playinge or by any other exercise whatsoever, and to be paide in manner and forme aforesaid unto the saide Thomas Downton, his executors and assignes, from the feast of S^t. Michaell Tharchangell last past before the date hereof, unto thend and terme of thirteene yeres from thence next ensuinge and fully to be compleate and ended, in as full large ample and beneficiall manner and forme to all intentes, constructions and purposes as they the saide Phillipp Henslowe and Edward Alleyn, or either of them or the executors or assignes of them or either of them, might should or ought to have had held and enjoyed received and taken the same as aforesaide, if this present Indenture had never beene had nor made. Yeald-

inge and prayinge therefore yerely duringe the said terme unto the saide Phillipp Henslow and Edward Alleyn, their heires executors or assignes, att the saide playe howse called the Fortune, ten shillinges of lawfull mony of England att fower feastes or termes of the yere (that is to say) att the feastes of the birth of our lord god, thannunciation of our lady, the nativity of St. John Baptist and St. Michaell Tharchangell, or within fowerteene dayes next ensuinge every of the same feast dayes, by even portions. And the saide Thomas Downton for him his executors and administrators doth covenante and graunte to and with the saide Phillipp Henslowe and Edward Alleyn and either of them, their and either of their heires executors and assignes, by theis presentes in manner and forme followinge (that is to say) That the saide Thomas Downton, his executors administrators or assignes, shall att his or their owne proper costes and charges beare and discharge one equall eighte parte of a fowerth parte of all such necessary and needfull charges as shalbe bestowed or layed forth in the new buildinge or repairinge of the saide play howse duringe the saide terme of thirteene yeres without any fraud or covyn. And that he the saide Thomas Downton shall not att any tyme hereafter duringe the saide terme give over the faculty or quality of playinge, but shall in his owne person exercise the same to the best and most benefitt he can within the play howse aforesaide, duringe the tyme aforesaide, unles he shalbe come unliable, by reason of sicknes or any other infirmity, or unles it be with the consent of the saide Phillipp Henslowe and Edward Alleyn or either of them, their executors or assignes. And that he the saide Thomas Downton shall not att any tyme hereafter, duringe the saide terme of thirteene yeres, play or exercise the facultye of stage playinge in any common play howse now erected or hereafter to be erected within the saide cittye of London or twoe myles compasse thereof, other then in the saide play howse called the Fortune, without the speciall licence will consent and agreement of the saide Phillipp Henslowe and Edward Alleyn or one of them, their or one of their heires executors or assignes, first therefore had and obteyned in wrytinge under their handes and seales. And that the saide Thomas Downton shall not att any tyme hereafter duringe the saide terme give graunte bargaine sell or otherwise doe away or departe with the saide eight parte of a fowerth parte of the saide clere gaynes before demised, nor any parcell thereof, to any person or persons whatsoever without the consent licence will and agreement of them the said Phillipp Henslowe and Edward Alleyn or either of them, their or either of their heires executors administrators or assignes, first therefore had and obteyned in wrytinge under their handes and seales for the same as aforesaide • • • • Phillipp Henslowe and Edward Alleyn for them and either of them, their and either of their heires executors and

administrators, doe covenante and graunte to and with the saide Thomas Downton, his executors and assignes, by theis presentes that he the saide Thomas Downton, his executors and assignes (payinge the saide yerely rent of ten shillinges in forme aforesaide, and performinge all other the covenantes, grauntes articles and agreementes abovesaide on his and their partes performed) shall or may, duringe the saide terme of thirteene yeres have hold receave and injoye the saide eight parte of a fowerth parte of all the saide clere gaynes to be gotten by playinge or any other exercise as aforesaide, in manner and forme aforesaide, accordinge to the true intent and meaninge of theis presentes without the lette, trouble, molestation, deniall, or interruption of the saide Phillipp Henslowe and Edward Alleyn or either of them, their or either of their heires or assignes, or of any other person or persons by their either or any of their meanes righte tytle interest or procuremente. Provided alwaies that if it shall happen the saide yerely rent of ten shillinges or any parcell thereof to be behinde and unpaide, in parte or in all, by the saide space of fowerteene dayes next over or after any feast day of paymente thereof above saide, in which the same ought to be paide (beinge lawfully demaunded at the place aforesaide) or if the saide Thomas Downton, his executors administrators or assignes or any of them, doe infrindge or breake any of the covenantes, grauntes articles or agreementes abovesaide on his or their partes to be performed, contrary to the tennore and true meaninge of theis presentes, that then and from thenceforth this present lease demise and graunt, and every covenante graunt and article herein conteyned on the parte and behalfe of the said Phillipp and Edward or either of them, their or either of their heires executors or assignes, from henceforth to be performed, shalbe utterly void frustrate and of none effect to all intentes constructions and purposes, any thinge herein conteyned to the contrary thereof in any wise notwithstandinge. In witnes whereof the said partyes to theis present Indentures sunderly have sett their handes and seales. Yeoven the day and yere first above written."

Downton's value might be increased by the fact, that he could upon occasion put pen to paper for the production of a play. He continued on the stage, at all events, until 1615, when he was summoned before the privy council (Hist. of Engl. Dram. Poetry and the Stage, i. 395), so that his premature death did not prevent the execution of the agreement above inserted.

CHAPTER X.

Shakespeare an Inhabitant of Southwark in 1609, and rated to the Poor — Alleyn Churchwarden for the Liberty of the Clink in 1610 — Immorality of the Liberty — Alleyne's Loans to Sir Francis Calton — Letter to him from Sir Francis Calton — Alleyn's final Retirement from the Stage — Disputes with Country Magistrates respecting Bear-wards — Letters from the Earl of Suffolk, Thomas Dutton, Thomas Brooke, and Sir Anthony Cooke, on the same subject.

In his "Inquiry," (p. 215), Malone observes: "From a paper now before me, which formerly belonged to Edward Alleyn, the player, our poet (Shakespeare) appears to have lived in Southwark, near the Bear Garden, in 1596. Another curious document in my possession, which will be produced in the History of his Life, affords the strongest presumptive evidence that he continued to reside in Southwark to the year 1608." The papers at Dulwich go farther than this: they may be said to establish that Shakespeare was living in Southwark in 1609,* for in a document indorsed, "1609. The Estate of the poores booke, the 8 of Aprill, for the Clinke," it is stated that he was rated as an "inhabitant" at 6*d.* per week. Thus we also see that he then resided within what was called the Liberty of the Clink, Henslowe being in that year churchwarden, and receiving the "brief note" of assessments from Francis Carter, one of the late overseers. The account is divided into three compartments, the names in each compartment, most likely, being those of the inhabitants of a particular district of the Liberty. "Mr. Shakespeare" stands at the head of the list to which he belongs, and as he is rated at the

---

* It is not unlikely that Malone may have erred in the date he has given, 1608, and that he in fact alluded to the document now under consideration, which belongs to the year 1609. It was one of the miscellaneous documents restored to Dulwich College by Mr. Boswell after the sale of Malone's books.

highest sum paid by any body, we are warranted in concluding that he lived at that time in as good a house as any of his neighbours: Henslowe, Alleyn, Shakespeare, Collins, and Burrett, are the only persons rated as high as 6*d*. The paper is in this form:—

" A breif noat taken out of the poores booke, contayning the names of all thenhabitantes of this Liberty wch arre rated and assesed to a weekely paim^t towardes the relief of the poore. As it standes now encreased, this 6th day of Aprill 1609. Delivered up to Phillip Henslowe Esquior, churchwarden, by Francis Carter, one of the late Ovreseers of the same Liberty.

" Phillip Henslowe esquior assesed at weekely	vj *d*
Ed Alleyn assesed at weekely	vj *d*
The Ladye Buckley, weekly	iiij *d*
Mr Cole	iiij *d*
Mr Lee	iiij *d*
Mrs Cannon	iij *d*
Mrs White	iij *d*
Mr Langworthe	iij *d*
Mr Benfield	iij *d*
Mr Corden	iij *d*
Mr Chauncye	iij *d*
Mrs Sparrowhauke	ij *d*
Mr Mason	ij *d*
Mr Watfoord	ij *d*
Mr Badger	ij *d*
Mr Heynes	ij *d*
Mr Dauson	ij *d*
Mr Hovell	ij *d*
Mr Griffin	ij *d*
Mr Toppin	ij *d*
Mr Cevis	ij *d*
Mr Lyman	ij *d*
Mr Louens	ij *d*
Mr Simpson	ij *d*
Mr Maynard	ij *d*
Mr Burkett	ij *d*
Francis Carter	ij *d*
Mr Stock for halfe the parke	ij *d*

Huighe Robbinson for halfe the parke	ij d
Mr Carre	ij d
Gilbert Catherens	ij d
Mr Shakespeare	vj d
Mr Edw. Collins	vj d
John Burrett	vj d
Roger Johnes	ij d ob
Mychaell Elsmoore	ij d ob
Mr Towne	ij d ob
Mr Jubye	j d ob
Mr Mansfeild	j d ob
John Dodson	j d ob
Richard Smith	j d ob
Richard Hunt	j d ob
Simon Bird	j d ob
Peter Nasam	j d ob
Jeames Kiddon	j d ob
Tho Stoakes	j d ob
John Faeye	j d ob
Phillip Philcoks	j d ob
Wm Stevens	j d ob
Mr Godfrey Richards for the long slip of ground	j d ob
Mr Coggen weekly	j d
Ferdynando Moses	j d
Edw. Nevell	j d
John Bacon	j d
Mrs Davison	j d
Rafe Trott	j d
John Judkin	j d."

Of the preceding names Alleyn, Lee, Benfield, Louens (or Lowins), Towne, Jubye, Hunt, and Bird, were players, not including Shakespeare, who had then quitted the stage, nor Henslowe, who, as far as we know, had never trodden it. Considering that so many inhabitants are enumerated, and that the Globe, Rose, Hope, and Swan Theatres, and Paris Garden were so near, it is perhaps strange that so few actors are contained in this list; but several of those mentioned

were rated at only a penny per week, and others of a still lower grade in the profession were, no doubt, not rated at all. Besides, many might live in parts of Southwark beyond the limits of the Liberty of the Clink, or indeed in other parts of the metropolis; R. Burbage, for instance, lived in Shoreditch.

In the next year, 1610, Alleyn was churchwarden; and John Lee, the sideman, seems to have been very sedulous in bringing under his notice the disorderly persons and houses within the district. These steps may have been taken at Alleyn's instigation; for, player as he was, or had been, he always seems to have borne the best private character, and to have given no encouragement to the immorality which prevailed in the vicinity of theatres, and for which the Bankside had been long notorious.* Among his papers is found the subsequent presentment to him, with a view that in his official capacity of churchwarden he should institute ulterior proceedings to punish the delinquents, and to correct the evil.

"The 29th of May 1610

"I John Lee, being Sidman of the Liberty of the Clinke, present theise persons unto the Church warden, Mr Allenn Esquire.

"Imprimis. In Robert Tukes house was found one Elizabeth Ayliefe, supposed to be with child, and is reported to live there at her own handes.

One Henery Jones and his wife was dwelling in father Powell's house, whoe weare thought to live losely together before mariage. And alsoe for receving one Elizabeth Williams into his house, whoe was there brought a bed.

——— kepinge a common house of dicing and bouling, and for suffering of the same in time of devine service, and is forwarned of the same

John Noble, for disorder in his bouling Ally, is in like sort forwarned of the same.

* See note to p. 12 of William Rowley's "Search for Money," reprinted by the Percy Society, where a curious passage is quoted from "Cock Lorells Bote," printed by Wynkyn de Worde about 1506.

William King and Sisly his wife are thought fitt to be presented for kepinge of a house suspected for bauderies, and allsoe for keping Margrett Tomkins and Elizabeth Gaunt, the first a suspitious person.

John Roades and Agnes his wife suspected for baudery.

Hall Watty and his wife for harboring of Isabell Lawes, a woeman big with [def. in MS.] and for keping Alise Blackden and Susan Darking • • maides at theire owne handes."

Upon the back of this paper Alleyn made various memoranda, not at all relating to the subject, but to the purchase or sale of hay, straw, wheat, barley, &c.; for we are to recollect that he had been for some time lord of the manor of Dulwich, and a considerable landed proprietor there. The extant letters and notes from Sir Francis Calton to Alleyn requesting loans of money are numerous, and year after year the knight seems to have grown poorer and more importunate, until at last he was obliged to sell his estate, and the lordships of both his manors of Dulwich and Lewisham. What follows is one of the communications of Sir Francis Calton; but it is evident, from the tenor of it, that it was by no means the first of its kind. In the present instance he had a design of advantageously marrying his daughter, if Alleyn would consent to advance him £250, required by his intended son-in-law, who had hopes of being appointed one of the Physicians to the Queen.

" To my very good frend Edward Allen Esqr. these be dd.

" Mr Allen, there is one Doctor Mollyers, a phisition with whom for good reasons I have a purpose to match my seconde daughter, and the reason why it hath not yet taken effecte is bycause his demaundes did still exceede my habilitie, howebeit hes is now contente to accepte of my offer, so as he maye be assured to have 250 li against the 24 of this presente monethe, meanes to doe which yow knowe I have none yet, but by your selfe, whom I very hartelye requeste to stedde me herein. The cause both of this my shorte warninge to yow and his sodaine agreemente with mee is for that he hathe a very good confidence to have [def. in MS.] Doctor Martins place, who died sodainlye the laste Sondaye nighte: hee was Phisition to the Queene. Wherefore nowe presentlye to furnishe him

convenientlye as wilbe fittinge, and happelye to bestowe som gratuities, for both yow and I knowe that places in Courte fall not into mens mouthes for gapinge, he is contente to abate 100 li of what he hathe hitherto insisted upon. Nowe, for somuch as the matter fallethe oute bothe to my ease of charge and the hopefull preferment of my childe, I make no doubte but that yow will advaunce your best meanes to fulfill my desyre; and the rather for that before that daye, the fyve yeares wilbe fullye accomplished for your securitie, which wilbe even as good as fifteene. Thus hopinge yow will have a due consideration hereof, with a disposition awnswerable to themportance of the busines, I hartelye commende me to yow and your good wyfe, expectinge your resolution in wrytinge either by this bearer or som other, for the which I comitte yow to God. In haste this 9 of Maye 1611.

"Your verye frend,
"Fran. Calton."

What is here said about Alleyn's "security," and the "five years" which were to expire, is not very intelligible, but it cannot be doubted that in May 1611 he was considerably in advance to Sir Francis Calton beyond the price Alleyn paid for the manor of Dulwich, which we find from other documents had been in possession of Calton's family since the reign of Henry VIII. and the dissolution of the monasteries.

There is one point upon which we are without distinct evidence derived from any quarter: the MSS. at Dulwich, including Henslowe's Diary, are all silent regarding it—we mean the date when Alleyn finally quitted the stage. He had become lord of the manor of Dulwich in 1606, and we might be led to conjecture that he had retired from the profession, as an actor, even at that comparatively early date. Supposing him to have commenced in 1580, when he would be in his fourteenth year (and Fuller says that he was bred to the stage) he would have been more than a quarter of a century on the boards in 1606. Shakespeare had seceded entirely as a performer for about two years, and Alleyn might wish to follow his example, as soon as he could do so with a due regard to his interests. He had always been an applauded and popular actor; and independently of his own

disposition, Henslowe had constantly been a pattern to him of worldly prudence, so that Alleyn had no doubt made considerable savings even before James I. ascended the throne. Though generous and charitable,* he was careful and frugal, and seems to have indulged in no luxuries for mere selfish gratification. In these views he was seconded by his excellent wife, who, as far as we have the means of judging, was watchful and economical, and was always regarded by her husband with respect and affection.

From the year 1592, to the date to which we are now adverting, Alleyn had been joint owner with Henslowe at least in two theatres, the Rose and the Fortune; and the exhibitions at Paris Garden, notwithstanding what may occasionally appear

---

* His fellow-actors constantly made appeals to him, and not in vain. Malone found and printed, though, as usual, far from accurately, the subsequent letter from an actor of the name of Richard Jones to Alleyn: it is without date, but it was no doubt prior to 1600. There was another actor of the name of Richard Jones in 1633, and possibly he was the son of the writer of the following.

"Mr Allen I commend my love and humble duty to you, geving you thankes for your great bounty bestoed upon me in my sicknes, when I was in great want: god blese you for it. Sir, this it is: I am to go over beyond the seas with Mr browne and the company, but not by his meanes, for he is put to half a shaer, and to stay hear, for they ar all against his going: now, good Sir, as you have ever byne my worthie frend, so helpe me nowe. I have a sut of clothes and a cloke at pane for three pound, and if it shall pleas you to lend me so much to release them, I shall be bound to pray for you so longe as I leve; for if I go over and have no clothes, I shall not be esteemed of, and by gods help the first mony that I get I will send it over unto you, for hear I get nothinge: some tymes I have a shillinge a day, and some tymes nothinge, so that I leve in great poverty hear, and so humbly take my leave praeinge to god, I and my wiffe, for your health and mistris allenes, which god continew.

"Your poor frend to command

"RICHARD JONES."

It would be easy to multiply proofs of the same kind, and some of them will necessarily be noticed hereafter.

to the contrary, must have been to both a productive source of emolument.

It may be doubted whether Alleyn ever really liked his profession, and, as has already been remarked, Henslowe's Letters, as well as his Diary, show that in 1598 he withdrew, for a time, at least, from its more ostensible and public duties. The question is, how long he continued them after he had been prevailed upon to resume them, and it is a question which we have no means of determining satisfactorily. The later portion of his life presents a singular contrast to the earlier portion of it, and there is every ground for believing that after he withdrew from public life, he gave way to the natural bent of his disposition. On the death of Henslowe (which, we shall find, occurred in the beginning of 1616) and of Agnes Henslowe, his widow, in the year following, Alleyn succeeded, if not to the whole, to the greater part of the property in the Rose, the Fortune, and Paris Garden.* Besides the houses, &c. he had derived from his own father, he had also acquired other valuable theatrical property, (of which we shall speak in its place) and, although this acquisition did not occur until 1612, there is good ground for concluding that for some years before that date he was in such easy circumstances as to require no addition to his income from his own personal appearance and exertions on the stage.

Whatever date we may be disposed to assign to Alleyn's retirement, there is proof that in 1611 he ceased in a con-

* The following receipt, dated about the period of which we are now speaking, relates to his leasehold property on the Bankside, which he held under Lord Montague.

"R. the xxvth. day of October 1611 of Mr. Edwarde Allen Esquier, for one halfe yeares rent of his howse and wharfe within the Cloose of S^t. Maryoveries, dewe to the Ryghte Honnorable Antony Lorde Viscounte Monntague, att the feast of S^t. Mychaell Tharchaungell last past, the some of fiftye shillings of lawfull Englishe money: I say R. l. s.

"Per me MATHEWE WOODWARDE."

siderable degree to interfere with the management of the theatres, in which he had with Henslowe a pecuniary interest. Henceforward we shall see that he left the control of the company or companies very much to Henslowe, and the earliest piece of evidence on the point is the following bond entered into between Henslowe and the players of Prince Henry, for the fulfilment of certain articles which have not survived. Nothing is said in it of Alleyn, although, at a posterior date and in one instance, he was called upon by the association to interpose in their favour against a person of whose proceedings they had reason to complain. The date of the subjoined instrument is ascertained from the Latin form by which it is preceded to be the 29th of August, 1611:—

"The condition of this obligation is suche that if the within bound John Townsend, William Barksted, Joseph Taylor, Giles Cary, Robert Hamlytt, Thomas Hunte, Joseph Moore, John Rice, William Carpenter, Thomas Basse, and Alexander Foster, their executors administrators and assignes, and each and every of them, doe for their and every of their partes well and trulie hould observe, paie, performe, fulfill and keepe all and every the covenantes, grauntes, articles, paymentes and agreementes which on their and each and every of their partes are or ought to be houlden, observed, perfourmed, paid, fulfilled and kepte, mentioned and contayned in certen Articles indented bearinge the date within written, made betweene the within named Phillipp Henslowe on thone parte, and the parties abovementioned on thother partes, and that in and by all thinges according to the tenor effect purport and true meaning of the same Articles in every respect, that then this present obligation to be void and of none effect, or elles to remayne in full force and vertue.

"JOHN TOWNSEND
"WILL. BARKSTED
"JOSEPH TAYLOR
"WILLIAM ECCLESTON
"GILLES CARY
"THOMAS HUNT
"JOHN RICE
"ROBT. HAMLETT
"WILL. CARPENTER
"THOMAS BASSE
"JOSEPH MOORE
"ALEXANDER FOSTER."

But although Alleyn might cease to take a prominent part in the management of the companies of players in whose receipts he still had an interest, he was compelled by virtue of the office of Master of the Games, which he filled jointly with Henslowe, to superintend the affairs of the Bear Garden. We have seen that under the patent to Henslowe and Alleyn, after they had bought the office of Sir W. Stuart, they were authorized "to take up" any bears, bulls, or dogs, in any part of the kingdom for the service of his majesty, on payment of what might be considered a reasonable price. For this purpose they had granted a license to a person of the name of Bryan Bradley, but, as he was unable to discharge the duty alone, Henslowe and Alleyn, by the following instrument dated the 18th of April, 1612, under their hands and seals, sent two others named Morgan and Tyler to his assistance. Why assistance in this particular instance became necessary we shall see presently :—

"Whereas wee Phillipp Henslowe Esquier, one of the Sewers of his highnes Chamber, and Edward Alleyn Esquier, servant to the highe and mightie Prince of Wales, Cheif M^{rs}. Rulers and Overseers of his Maties game of Beares Bulls and dogges, have deputed lycensed and authorised our servant Bryan Bradley to take upp and provide for his highnes Beares, Bulls and Dogges, whersoever the same shall or may be found, as by our deputation to that effect made at larg appeareth. And forasmuch as our saide servant is not of him self able and sufficient to take upp keepe and provide suche dogges as shalbe taken and thought fitt for his Maties saide game, wee have therefore sent our servantes John Morgan and Richard Tyler, the Bearers hereof, to be aiding and asisting unto him in the execution of the premisses, that by their asistance his highnes said service may be the better effected. Wherefore wee, the said Phillipp Henslowe and Edward Alleyn, according to the tenor of his highnes Letters Pattents to us graunted, and by force and vertue of the power and authority therby to us given, doe will and requier all his Maties officers and loving subjectes to be aiding and asisting unto our saide servantes in the execution of the premisses, and to permitt and suffer them quietly to passe and repasse to and from any place or places whatsoever about his Maties saide service without any your lett or interruption, behaving them selves well and honestly as wee trust they will. In witnes whereof wee the said Phillipp

Henslowe and Edward Alleyn have hereunto sett our handes and seales. Yeoven the Eighteenth daie of Aprill 1612, and in the tenth yeare of the Raigne of our soveraigne Lord King James &c.

"PHILLIPPE HENSLOWE "ED. ALLEYN
(L. S.) (L. S.)

" Sealed and subscribed by the above
named Phillipp Henslowe and
Edward Alleyn in the presence of
"THOMAS MASON Scrivener."

We can have no hesitation in believing that persons like Bradley, Morgan, and Tyler, sent down from the Bear Garden into distant parts of the country, to seize upon any dogs they pleased, under pretext that they were required for the king's service, often exercised the power entrusted to them in a most arbitrary and unwarrantable manner. We cannot wonder, therefore, that they sometimes met with strong resistance, and it was owing to some opposition of the kind, particularly in appropriating to themselves a dog belonging to a Mr. Venables, a gentleman of Cheshire, that the assistance of Morgan and Tyler was considered necessary by Henslowe and Alleyn. Even then the dog-deputies from Paris Garden were unable to accomplish their object, and it appears from the subsequent communication, that Henslowe solicited the interposition of the Lord Chamberlain, the Earl of Suffolk, in his behalf:—

"To my lovinge freindes Thomas Dutton, John Ireland, Thomas Brooke, Edward Stanley, Thomas Marbery, and John Ashton esquiers, Justices of the peace in the Counties of Chester and Lancaster, or to any fower or two of them, these.

" After my hartie comendations. I have bene informed by Mr. Phillipp Henslowe, one of the Maisters of the game of Beares Bulls and Mastiffe dogges by pattent from his Matie, that his deputies and servants have bene very much abused in the execution of his Comission for taking up of dogges in Lancashire and Cheshire. Forasmuch as he is an officer under my chardge, and his place under my direction for his Ma^{ts} sport, so long as his servants do not misbehave themselves I most and will see their wronges redressed; and at this tyme did purpose, though the waye be farr, to send for the offendors by pursevant and to punishe them here above; but under-

standing that you are gent. judicious and discreete in the admynistration of Justice in those places you hold, I have thought good to recomend the examination, punishement of the offendors, and redresse of the wronges comitted unto yow, as in your discretions yow shall thinke fitt and finde cause. The names of the principalls that have repugned the comission, and abused and beaten the servants, as I understand, were theis:—One Lathome, Richard Penketh of Penketh, Richard Massy his servant, and Raph Barnes of Warrington. By thexamination of these yow shall finde the rest, and I pray you take such a corse as to equitie and justice shall apperteyne, that there may be no further cause of complaint in that behalf. And so I rest

"Your loving freind,

"T. SUFFOLKE.

"Whitehall xiijth. of July 1613."

The delivery of the above was entrusted to Bryan Bradley and Thomas Bradford (whose name now appears for the first time in the transaction), as deputies to Henslowe and Alleyn: they placed it in the hands of the magistrates to whom it was addressed, and the reply of the magistrates, which is subjoined from the original, evinces no great willingness on their part to support the authority of the agents of the Masters of the King's Games; particularly as Mr. Venables, in spite of the Great Seal which was appended to the deputation of Bradley and Bradford, had charged them with felony in stealing his dog, and had threatened to prosecute them at the assizes for the theft.

"To the Right Ho. our verie good Lord, the Earle of Suffolke, Lord Chamberlayn to his Matie.

"Right Ho: having seen your Lpp lettre by the delyverie of Bryan Bradley and Thoms Bradford, deputies, as appeires unto us, under Mr Henslow and Mr Allen, Maisters of the game for Beares, Bulls and Dogges, wee shall endeavour our selves to accomplish your Honors request, although hitherto wee have not much delt therin, for that all the parties offendors named in your Lps lettre dwell in Lankashire, and must be proceaded withall before we can well deale with anie other. And withall we have been hindered by accydent of taking a dog from Mr John Venables of Agdon in this county, who hath brought the takers (the said deputies) before us and will, as he affirmeth, prosecute them for felonie for taking

his dog, and did importune us to have bound them over to aunswere at our next assizes for Chester, which doth comence the xxth of September next. But wee, seeing the greate Seale of England and their deputations, neither of which wee are willing to questyon or withstand, have only taken thexamination of some witnesses produced uppon Mr Venables behalfe, whereof wee have sent your Ho. true copies, and (to our understandings conceiving noe such misdemeanour) have gyven our promis that the parties shalbe readie at thassizes to aunswere what Mr Venables shall then object against them: wherein wee humbly pray your Honors consideration, and that they may be presente with their deputation and lettres patentes already shewed unto us (with your Lps further directions if so it seeme good to yow) to justifie before the Judges of thassizes what they have donne. And soe wee shalbe excused for our proceedings herin. Thus craving pardon for our boldnes, we take leave and rest

"Your Honors ever ready,

"Tho. Dutton

"Dutton 17° Auguste 1613."   "Thos Brooke.

The following letter from Sir Anthony Cooke appears to refer to a somewhat similar transaction in a different part of the kingdom. It is, like the others, preserved at Dulwich College, and, doubtless, came into Alleyn's hands from the Lord Chamberlain:—

"To the right hon. the Earle of Suffolke, Lorde Chamberlayne to his Matie, and one of his Highnesse moste honorable pryvey Counsayle att Courte, give these.

"Righte Honorable and my verye good Lorde &c.

"Your Honors letter, sente me this presente morninge by one John Skales, keeper of the beere garden, I have receyved, whereby I perceyve your Honor hath receyved a verye synister and unjust information agaynst me, conserninge the staye of certeyne persones, who have sundrye wayes mysbehaved them selves within this place, both in the manner and in the matter, as also in particular abuse to my selfe (which I doe least respecte); but when your honorable Lordshipp shalbe trewelye informed that what I have done is onelie juste, and what in this place I houlde here I am bounde in dewetye unto, I nothinge dowght but that your Honor will in your nexte lett me here from you in a more myelde manner, then theise your former lyenes nowe receyved. For first, my honorable Lord, I have not made staye of the dogges in generall taken by them elles where, but onelye of one dogge taken by them in this place of pryvyledge, wherein

no dogge can be taken, as more at lardge I shall make knowen unto your Honor, when it shall please your Honor to commaunde mee. Next, that they have taken anye dogges at all by your Honors authoretye hath not yett appeared to me in auie thinge that they ever shewed me, but that I understande soe muche now by your Honors letter. But I doe nothinge dowghte, but that they whoe have so badelye behaved them selves heere, will alsoe as unhonestlye proceede in abusing your honorable Lordship with untrewe informations. For conclusion, pleaseth yt your honorable Lordshipp to understande, the dogges I have all sente awaye by this messenger that came with your Honors letter, which for anye staye I made of them might have beeue theire sooner yf theye woulde them selves, onely I doo make staye of that dogge taken by them heere, which I maye not parte withall, without breache of our Lybertyes and pryvyledges, graunted by the Kinges Matie under his greate seale. Thus nothinge dowghtinge but that your Honor will conceyve of me, both in this and in all thinges els, as of a man that hath beene bredd to knowe better manners then to give the least suspecte of forgettinge the dewetye I owe to a persone of your dignytie and place, my humbleste dewetye remembred, I cease your Honors farther trouble, restinge now and alwayes,

"Your Honors poore kynseman
"and servaunte to commaunde,
"Antho: Cooke."

What was the result in either case we have now no means of knowing. We have inserted these documents, not merely because Alleyn was immediately concerned in the transactions to which they relate, but because we are not aware of the existence of any others of a similar description.

CHAPTER XI.

Shakespeare's Retirement from London to Stratford-upon-Avon—His Purchase and Mortgage of the Tenement in the Blackfriars—Facts tending to prove that Alleyn became the Purchaser of Shakespeare's Property in the Blackfriars Theatre—Alleyn interested in the Receipts at the Red Bull Theatre—Charles Massy's (the Actor) Letter to Alleyn for a Loan of £50—Massy's intimacy with Alleyn.

It may almost be taken for granted, that about the time Shakespeare finally quitted London for his native town,

Stratford-upon-Avon, he was possessed of a large interest in the two houses at which his plays had been usually performed—the public theatre, called the Globe, on the Bankside, and the private theatre, called, after the name of the precinct in which it stood, the Blackfriars. In settling the question at what date Shakespeare permanently left the metropolis, nobody seems to have adverted sufficiently to the fact, that in both the latest documents (excepting his will) yet discovered, in which his name occurs, he is called " William Shakespeare of Stratford upon Avon, in the Countie of Warwick, Gentleman." This was in March 1612-13, and, taken by itself, it really seems to decide the question; for if he had been living in Southwark at the time he executed the conveyance and the mortgage (Malone's Shakesp. by Bosw. ii. 585 and 592) in London, why should he have been described as "of Stratford-upon-Avon?" No answer can be made to this inquiry, and the truth, no doubt, is, that in March 1613 he had for some time retired to the place of his birth. He probably went there not very long after the production of his last play, which may have come out in 1611, and was perhaps a Roman or a Greek drama, Coriolanus or Timon. The Tempest and the Winter's Tale would both seem (for reasons not necessary to be detailed here) to have been earlier, although hitherto placed last by the best authorities; therefore we should be disposed to fix the date of his departure perhaps a year prior to March 1613—the spring of 1612—when the country was beginning to present its natural invitation to its admirers.

Why Shakespeare returned to the metropolis for the purpose of purchasing, and on the next day mortgaging the tenement in the Blackfriars, is a question that does not appear to have occurred to his biographers. One of the parties named in both the deeds was John Hemming (or Hemyng, as it is there spelt), who was a principal manager of the King's Company occupying the Globe and the Blackfriars

theatres; and it is very possible that both the purchase and the mortgage were in some way, not now easily explained, connected with the sale of Shakespeare's theatrical property, of which, of course, he was desirous to dispose, with a view to his undisturbed residence at Stratford. What then became of that property, and into whose hands did it devolve?

Shakespeare's property in the Globe might be sold to some principal members of the company, before that theatre was burned down on the 29th June, 1613 (Hist. of Engl. Dram. Poetry and the Stage, iii. 298); but it seems very likely, from evidence now for the first time to be adduced, that Alleyn became the purchaser of our great dramatist's interest in the theatre, properties, wardrobe, and stock of the Blackfriars. Among the miscellaneous scraps of paper at Dulwich College is one which appears to be a rough memorandum, in Alleyn's hand-writing, of various sums paid by him in April, 1612, for the Blackfriars; and though the theatre is not there expressly named, it will be rendered evident hereafter that it was the "play-house." The paper is precisely in this form:—

" April 1612
Money paid by me E. A. for the Blackfryers . 160*li*
More for the Blackfryers . . . 126*li*
More againe for the Leasse . . . 310*li*
The writinges for the same and other small charges 3*li*. 6*s*. 8*d*."

The whole sum is £599 6*s*. 8*d*., which would be equal to nearly £3,000 of our present money; and would, no doubt, entitle him to a very considerable share of the property. To whom the money was paid, is nowhere stated; but, for aught we know, it was to Shakespeare himself, and just anterior to his departure from London.

The preceding memorandum is not unlike several others existing at Dulwich; and it was, perhaps, made with a view to an entry of the total amount in a book, which Alleyn may have kept for the purpose. One of these is still preserved, with religious care, at the College; but it applies (and we

shall have occasion to advert to it frequently hereafter) to a date considerably posterior to this transaction, beginning in 1617, and ending in 1622. However, during those years it is kept so regularly and systematically, that any person inspecting its contents can feel no hesitation in believing that Alleyn had long previously been in the habit of minutely recording his daily payments and expenses. It is to be presumed that the other books of the same kind have unfortunately been lost or destroyed; but this, which is still extant, affords strong confirmation, indeed, indisputable proof, that Alleyn was a considerable owner of leasehold property in the Blackfryers: the only question here is whether it included the theatre. The following are some of the entries, which are here given, out of their place, in point of date, but not of subject: the first item occurs regularly, though not precisely in the same words, every quarter.

		li	s.	d.
"Oct. 22. [1617.]	Pd Mr. Travise rent for the Blackfryars	40	0	0
Aug. 27. [1618.]	Pole brought me word that the building would be puld downe, so I went to London—first water to the Strond to Coronell Cussell	0	0	6
	He being gone I followed to Chelsey	0	3	0
	From the Fryers to La. Clarks att Supper	0	0	2
Sep. 28. [1618.]	More disbursed for the building of the Blackfryars for this yeare, and in anno 1617 when itt first begane with the 200*li* first disbursed by my father buyeng in off leases: charges in lawe: and the building itt selfe, with making meanes to kepe them from being puld downe is	1105	0	2
Oct. 9. [1620.]	Bere at the Fryers	0	0	6
Sep. 24. [1621.]	Disbursed 2 years att the Fryars, last ending at Mic.	23	6	6
July 23. [1622.]	Jones and I mett at the Fryers on our scytation by Mr. Hicks, Mr. Place, and Mr. Traviss: the dinner coast 8*s.* 6*d.* I spent 6*s.* 6*d.* and was paid, so	0	7	2"

Hence we learn that the rent paid by Alleyn to a Mr. Travise, was £160 per annum, a large sum in those times; that some building, or the repair of some building, was commenced in 1617; that in the next year Alleyn received information that it would be pulled down, perhaps because it had been left in a dangerous condition; that a very large amount was expended upon it in 1618; that in this sum Alleyn included £200 which his "father"—(meaning, in all probability, Henslowe)—had spent in buying in of leases; and that Alleyn and a person of the name of Jones (perhaps Inigo Jones, employed by Alleyn as his architect,) in July, 1622, received what Alleyn calls "a citation" from three persons, one of them, Mr. Travise, (to whom he regularly paid rent), most likely in reference to the same property. It seems evident, therefore, that Alleyn's "father," Henslowe, had become possessed of some portion of the Blackfriars property, and that, in April, 1612, Alleyn increased it, by expending nearly £600 in the purchase of additions; which additions may have been the share Shakespeare owned in the Blackfriars Theatre and its appurtenances, which he disposed of before he withdrew from London to Stratford. The coincidences of time and place are, at all events, remarkable.

In fact, Alleyn seems to have been a general owner of theatrical property in different parts of the town; and, in his Account-book of disbursements, quoted above, two of the earliest entries establish that he had some interest in the receipts at the Red Bull Theatre, which was situated at the upper end of St. John Street, Smithfield. Under the dates of October, 1st and 3rd, 1617 (the book begins on the 29th September in that year,) we read as follows:—

"Oct. 1. 1617. I came to London in the Coach and went to the red Bull 0. 0. 2
Oct. 3. I went to the red bull and R [i e received] for the younger brother but 3*li*. 6*s*. 4*d*. water . . . . . 0. 0. 4"

What expense was covered by two-pence in the first entry, it is difficult to say:—the price of admission to some parts of the house was that sum; but we must suppose that Alleyn was free, considering the share of the receipts to which the second entry shews he was entitled. "Water," in the second entry, refers to the cost of conveying him, probably, from Southwark to the landing-place nearest to the Red Bull Theatre. The play performed was "The Younger Brother;" and such a drama was entered at Stationers' Hall for publication in 1653, about which date several plays were printed that had long remained in manuscript. The theatres at that time were closed by authority; and the poor actors and booksellers thus sought to raise a little money, as well as to gratify the public curiosity. Alleyn records that he received but £3 6s. 4d., as if he were greatly disappointed in the amount he expected to obtain. It is to be remarked that, subsequent to this date, we find no entries in Alleyn's Account-book regarding the Red Bull; and we may be tempted from this circumstance to conjecture that, as the concern proved unprofitable, he soon afterwards sold such shares as he held in it.

We have already had evidence that when any member of the profession was in pecuniary difficulty, resort was sometimes had to Alleyn and to his known liberality. Among the members of the theatrical association which Prince Henry took into his service in 1603, was Charles Massye (Hist. Engl. Dram. Poetry and the Stage i. 351,) who continued long afterwards a performer; and finally, as we shall see, became one of Alleyn's tenants at the Fortune in 1617, and on its re-construction after the fire of 1621. About 1612 he was embarrassed in his affairs, and applied to Alleyn for an advance of £50. The letter containing his urgent request is extant at Dulwich, but in a most mutilated state from damp: it is without date, but we can ascertain the time when it was written pretty exactly, because Alleyn made some memoranda on the back

MEMOIRS OF EDWARD ALLEYN.   109

of it in July, 1613; and the letter itself speaks of Mrs. Towne as a widow, and her husband died before November, 1612. It was written, therefore, in the following supplicatory form (as far as that form can be made out, in consequence of the decay of the paper) to Alleyn, between November, 1612, and July, 1613.

"To his worshipfull good frende Mr. Edwarde Allen, at his house at Dulledg, give these.

"Ser. I beseche your pardon in that I make boulde to wryte to yow wordes consernynge my selfe, and it may be distastfull to yow, but necesete hath no lawe, and therfore I hope the contrarye. Ser, diverse ocasions before the Prynces * * man * crosses sense hath brought me in tow debt * * * and danger * * * if yow woulde please to helpe me * * * not withstandinge I ever shall rest ever to be com * * * with the world I desire yow should hasard the * * * * by me * * * by such for, ser, I know you understand * * * * compositions betwene oure compenie that if * * * * * ever with consent of his fellowes he is to paye the * * score and ten pounds antony Jeffes hath paid so much * * if any one dye his wife or frends whome he appoyntes it tow reseve fyfte pounds. M^{res}. Pavye and M^{res}. Toune hath had the lyke, be sides that lyke moste I have in the play housses, which I would willingly pas over unto you by dede of gifte, or any course you would set doune for your securete, and that you should be shure I do it not withoute my wiffes consent, she wilbe willinge to set her hand to any thinge that might secure it to you. Ser, fifte poundes would pay my detes, which for one hole twelvemonth I would take up and pay the intreste, and that I might the better pay it in at the yeares ende, I would get Mr. Jube to reserve my gallery mony, and my quarter of the housse mony for a yeare to pay it in with all, and if in * * monthes, I say, the gallery mony would not dowble * * * the other six monthes he should reserve * * * share, only reservinge a marke a weke * * * my house with all the eyghtenth of this * * * pay to Mr. Bankes thurte pounds and other * * * other dettes I owe, if ether you serve * * * the monye or any other whome yow shall appoynt, for I know wher you will you may. I shall ever reste your poore servant to perform any offyse you shall comand me. Ther is one Mr. Mathers, at the bell in newgate market, that six wekes agoe did offer me fifte poundes for a twelf-

month grates, but be desird good securete. Ser, I beseche howsoever pardon me in that bouldly I have presumd to wryte unto you. Thus not darynge to troble you any longer, I comyt you to god, to home I will ever pray to blese you.

"Ever to be comded by you,
"CHARLES MASSYE."

Alleyn most likely complied with this urgent request, and Massye fulfilled his engagement with respect to repayment, for they continued friends ever afterwards; and from Alleyn's Diary we learn that Massye was not unfrequently a guest at his table, from 1617 to 1622. As before stated, he became one of Alleyn's tenants for the Fortune.

We may take it for granted, although Paris Garden was not originally built for the purpose of theatrical representations, that plays had been occasionally acted there from an early date. The Globe Theatre in its vicinity was burnt down on the 29th June, 1613; and, in less than a month afterwards, Henslowe and a person of the name of Jacob Meade, taking advantage of the opportunity, entered into an agreement with Gilbert Katherens, a carpenter, to convert Paris Garden into "a play-house," as well as "a game place." All the particulars are inserted in the Hist. of Engl. Dram. Poetry and the Stage, iii. 284; and it is not necessary here to state more than the fact. How Meade came into the concern, we know not; but, perhaps, as Alleyn (though still called the Prince's servant in 1612) had at this date withdrawn from all that related to theatrical management, and Henslowe had grown old and infirm, he took Meade into partnership to assist him, and Meade's name will henceforwards frequently occur. Paris Garden thus became a theatre, as well as a place for the baiting of animals.

CHAPTER XII.

The Building of Dulwich College—Sutton's Hospital — Original Contract for Building Dulwich College — College of St. Saviour's — Letter to Alleyn from Samuel Jeynans, on behalf of Chelsea College—Agreement between Henslowe, Meade, and Nathaniel Field, the Actor, for Paris Garden—Bond given in 1615 by Daiborne and Massinger to Henslowe, for a Loan of £3.

THE building of God's Gift College at Dulwich, and the endowment of it with the greater part of his property, was unquestionably the most important event of Alleyn's life.

We now arrive at the period when he seems to have taken the first step to carry this great and benevolent project into execution. How long anterior to this date he had contemplated the possibility of such an undertaking, we cannot determine; but, having considerable estates and no family, it was natural that in his 47th year, which he had now attained, he should take into consideration the best and most beneficial mode of disposing of his possessions. The story told by credulous Aubrey, that Alleyn was worked upon by having seen the apparition of the Devil, while playing a dæmon in one of Shakespeare's plays, is merely ridiculous: first of all, Alleyn had left off playing before he appears to have entertained the intention of devoting his affluence to purposes of charity: next, he would not have condescended to play such a part as that of a dæmon; and, thirdly, we have no direct evidence to establish that he ever played in any of Shakespeare's plays, though there is little doubt he represented the hero in dramas founded upon some of the same stories or events. It is possible that the absurd report originated in an event recorded in "The Blacke Booke," by Middleton, printed in 1604, where it is said (Sign. B. 4,) that on one occasion "the old theatre" (the Rose) "cracked and frighted the audience," while a devil was upon the stage in

Marlowe's "Faustus," the hero of which, there is no doubt, Alleyn sustained. *

This incident may have been exaggerated and distorted into Aubrey's tradition; and we may be quite sure that when Alleyn avowed his purpose of establishing his College, the Puritans, and the other enemies of theatrical performances, did not fail to impute it to remorse for his long career of wickedness and profanity.

It has been said that he took his first notion of Dulwich College from Sutton's Hospital, the Charterhouse; but the only hint to that effect was furnished by himself, when he had nearly completed his design. It is to be found in his own Diary, which begins at Michaelmas, 1617: at the very opening, he makes the following note.

"29th Sep. My wife, Mr. Austin, Mr. Young and my self
    went to see Sutton Hospitall—water . . . 0. 1 0."

From the terms used in this entry, we might be led to conclude that Sutton's Hospital was then a novelty to Alleyn, and that he had never seen it before. But there is no need to suppose that he was governed or influenced by any particular precedent in his undertaking, or that he would not have expended his money upon the College, if he had not previously witnessed what others had done elsewhere in a similar benevolent spirit.

We are told in the "General Biographical Dictionary," (ii. 13) that Alleyn "began the foundation of the College under the direction of Inigo Jones in 1614." The fact is, that he began the foundation of the College in the summer of 1613, as appears upon the unquestionable evidence of the original indenture for the brick-work between Alleyn and

* This passage from "The Blacke Booke" has been cited and commented upon by Oldys, in his Life of Alleyn, in the Biographia Britannica: "The Blacke Booke" has been reprinted by Mr. Dyce, in his edition of Middleton, from the only known copy in the possession of the writer of the present memoir.

John Benson, a bricklayer of Westminster, which bears date on the 17th of May, 1613. This document still exists at Dulwich College, and it is stipulated in it that Benson was to commence his work on or before the last day of May: that he did so we need not doubt, as Alleyn paid Benson £20 on the 19th of June, on account of work already done, Alleyn having agreed to pay £10 for every five rods as the undertaking proceeded. Therefore, we may conclude that ten rods of work had been finished by the 19th of June, 1613. Alleyn was to dig the foundation, to find materials and scaffolding, and to allow Benson forty shillings for every rod of brickwork. The indenture is extremely minute in its specifications, so as to give an exact notion of the whole edifice as originally constructed, consisting of a chapel, a school-house, a kitchen, offices, and twelve alms-houses. It will be found in the Appendix, being somewhat too long for insertion here, and it includes a number of curious details. At the back are eleven endorsements in Alleyn's hand-writing (subscribed by Benson) of sums paid as the work went on; and, as they show exactly the progress towards the completion of the College between the 19th of June, 1613, and the 22nd of April, 1614, we shall not hesitate to quote them :—

"Received this 19th of June 1613 of Ed. Alleyn in part of payment   20l
            "John Benson"

"Receved more this 14 of August 1613   .   .   .   .   10l
            "John Benson"

"Receved more this 28th of August 1613   .   .   .   .   10l
            "John Benson"

"Receaved more this 11th of September 1713   .   .   .   10
            "John Benson"

"Receaved more this 18th of September 1613   .   .   .   10l
            "John Benson"

"Receaved more this 9th of October 1613, the sum of   .   .   20l
            "John Benson"

"Receaved more this 30th of November 1613, the sum of   .   .   20l
            "John Benson"

I

"Receaved more this 15th of December 1613, the sum of . . .05¹
"John Benson"

"Receaved more this 24 of December 1613, the sum of . . 05¹
"John Benson"

"Receaved more this 10th of Jannuarie 1613, the sum off . . 10¹
"John Benson"

"Receaved more this 22 of aprill 1614, the some of . . . 7¹
"Receaved from the Kostermonger."

The last item is not receipted by Benson, but the money appears to have been sent to him; and perhaps it was the balance of the account between the founder of God's Gift College and the bricklayer he employed. The whole sum paid by Alleyn was £127; and it is to be recollected that this was for workmanship only, and it does not include the account of the plasterer, the carpenter, the plumber, or the glazier. With regard to the statement that the building was erected under the direction of Inigo Jones, we are without any documentary evidence of the fact: on the contrary, it appears by the contract between Alleyn and Benson, that "the plott" of the building had been "made and drawn" by the latter.

In March 1613-14, shortly before the completion of the brickwork of the College, Alleyn, perhaps with a view to his own Patent, procured that of the Hospital of the Poor of St. Saviour's parish to be delivered into his hands.

"ix° Marcij 1613

"Memorand: there was delivered, the daye and yeare aforesaid, to Mr Edward Allin in the vestrye the letters Patentes of the Corporation of the Colledge or Hospitall of the pore of St. Savioures in Southwark, and also the copie of the booke of order for the Colledge.

"Edward Alleyn."

This was ten months after the signature of the contract with Benson, and if Alleyn were incited to this splendid act of charity by any thing but the naturally benevolent and generous impulses of his own mind, it was, probably, by observing what had been done for the assistance of those who required it in the very parish, for a liberty of which he had been churchwarden only three years before.

It is pretty clear, from the contents of the following undated letter, preserved at Dulwich, that when it was written Alleyn had not distinctly promulgated his intention as to the appropriation of his known fortune. That he entertained some charitable purpose seems to have been understood, and he was therefore earnestly applied to by the writer, Samuel Jeynens, who was probably a zealous divine, to contribute a sum toward the completion of Chelsea College, which had been founded in 1610 for the maintenance of polemical clergymen, bound to advocate the doctrines of the church against the Roman Catholics. About the date of which we are now speaking the design languished for want of funds, Dr. Sutcliffe, the originator of the scheme, having expended upon it a very large sum out of his own private purse. It will be seen that Jeynens also makes other suggestions to Alleyn, respecting the application of his money to religious purposes.

"To the worshipfull and well affected to all good purposes, Mr Allen, all health and happines in this life and in another.

"Blessed be god who hath stirred up your hart to do so many gracious and good deedes to gods glory, the relief of many which ar bound to pray for you, and the good example of many which may do good and do not; and to your owne comfort at the latter day, when it shalbe said, Come ye blessed of my father, inherit ye the kingdome prepared for you; for when I was hungry ye fed me, naked ye clothed me, sick and in prison and ye visited me, and so forth. Beside, this is a thing more acceptable to god and more comfortable to you, that in your life tyme you se this worke perfourmed, which many deferre till after deth, which some devines do hold to be no deedes of theres, being left to others, nor so acceptable to god, rathar regarding the good deedes of the living, then of the dead. Againe, ether there executours do very slowly perfourme that which they would have done, or do it not at all.

"Among all which deedes of almes, though all be good, yet in my conceit those are most to be thought on as ar most necessary, that is, which ar most for god's glory, the good of the church, and common weale. Wherein, yf it might stand with your good liking and it might please you so to accept it and thinke of it, I would gladly move you to a worke of charity toward Chelsey Colledge, neere London, which was founded, though not yet finished, to this intent, that learned men might there have main-

tenance to aunswere all the adversaries of religion. Mʳ Doctor Sutcliffe, that spent all his meanes about it, coming short of the full perfourmance, got the Kings letter to the Maior of London that then was: he told me he could not obtaine so much as on deuier. I framed petitions of my oune accord and privat motion (the worke being so proffitable and commendable) to the Lord Maior, Recorder and others, yet fearing that little or no good would come to passe, I did forbeare to exhibit them. What may fall out hereafter I kno not.

"Since Mʳ Doctor hath got leave to make a collection in the countries and shires for the effecting of this busines, and the contribution being brought into the Bishops hands is yet kept back, that he cannot go forward with the worke, as he himself told me, although the bishops themselves were the meanes to set him on to build. So, because it goes not forward as it begun, the Papists in derision gave it the name of an Alehouse. But yet he saith, yf I could be a meanes to helpe him to a hundred pounds, a hundred pounds he hath of his owne, he saith he would establish maintenauce for 4 learned men. In which worke I would humbly beseech you to helpe him.

"Or yf I might move another project to your self, that it would please you to build some half a score lodging roomes, more or lesse neere unto you, yf it be no more but to give lodging to divers schollers that come from the University. Some would be ministers and some schoolemasters, and for want of meanes to staye heere about London till they could be provided, they are forced to go away againe and to looce all opportunities that might fall out. Yf they had chamber roome, which heere in London is hard and costly, diet would be more easy, and so ether by preaching they might put forth themselves, or by harkening how they might place themselves to tech schollers, they might have helpe till some preferment might be obtained.

"Amongst those lodgings, yf it pleased you, you might build a library and furnish it with some bookes, now some, then some, as you saw cause, as might be very beneficiall, not only for strangers, but for those that ar maintained by you.

"To all theis good workes I pray god incline your hart, and I pray you give me leave to be a petitioner for them and a remembrancer to you, as King Phillip had every morning on to call at his chamber doore and to tell him he was but a mortall man. Which is a good memorandum to put all of us in minde to do all the good we can in our life, for as our Saviour Christ saith, The night cometh wherein no man can worke.

"Yours in his devotion, and to be
"comaunded at your pleasure,
"SAMUEL JEYNENS."

There is no reason to believe that Alleyn lent a favourable ear to this request: it is much more likely that having already matured his plan, he resolved to complete his undertaking at Dulwich.

At about the date of which we are now speaking, we meet with the following memorandum, the whole of which, excepting the signatures, is in Alleyn's hand-writing: it seems to be the final settlement of all accounts between him and the Calton family, in respect of the property he had purchased of them in the vicinity of the spot he had selected for the site of his college of God's Gift :—

"Md. that this 9th. of november, 1614, all reckinings, debts and demaundes what so ever, from the begining of the world to this present daye, due unto me, Thomas Calton, from Edw. Alleyn, is in all threeskore powndes, wheroff receved this 9th afore sayd xxx^{li}: rest dew to me more in all 30^{li}.

"By me THO. CALTON."

"Receved more this 18th. of november, 1614, the sum of twentye powndes, I say R xx^{li}.

"By me THO. CALTON."

"Receved this 26th of november, 1614, in full payment and satisfaction, the sum of tenn powndes of lawfull money off England, I say R. x^{li}.

"By me THOMAS CALTON."

Before we proceed farther upon this subject, it is necessary to revert to theatrical affairs, the long prosperity of which had enabled Alleyn to indulge his favourite design in the village of which at this time he was, no doubt, the chief proprietor. We have noticed the conversion of Paris Garden into a regular theatre under Henslowe and Meade in the summer of 1613. At this date the actors who had been the players of Prince Henry (who died on the 6th of November 1612) had become the theatrical servants of the Palatine of the Rhine, who had married the daughter of James I. The company continued to perform at the Fortune; and Henslowe and Meade, wanting a company for Paris Garden, after it was altered so as to answer the double purpose, seem to have entered into an

engagement with Nathaniel Field, a very celebrated actor, (whose portrait still hangs in Dulwich College) who, as the leader of the association, came to terms with Henslowe and Meade on behalf of himself and his fellows. Field is first heard of in 1600, when he played in Ben Jonson's "Cynthia's Revels," but in 1609 he had become one of the children of the Queen's Revels, occupying the Whitefriars theatre, where he continued, perhaps, until Henslowe and Meade proposed to him to perform with others at Paris Garden. The following is a copy of the instrument, in the title of which it is stated that Henslowe and Meade had lately raised a company of players: in fact they were only raising a company.

> "Articles of Agreement made concluded and agreed uppon, and which are on the part and behalfe of Phillip Henslowe Esqre. and Jacob Meade, Waterman, to be performed touching and concerning the Company of Players which they have latelie raised viz;

"Imprimis the said Phillip Henslowe and Jacob Meade doe for them their executors, and administrators covenante promise and graunt by these presentes, to and with Nathan Feilde Gent, that they the saide Phillip Henslowe and Jacob Meade, or one of them, shall and will during the space of three yeares at all times (when noe restraynte of playinge shall be) at there or some of there owne proper costes and charges fynde and provide a sufficient house or houses for the saide company to play in: and also shall and will at all tymes duringe the said tearme disburse and lay out all suche some and somes of money as fower or five sharers of the same company, chosen by the said Phillip and Jacob, shall thynk fittinge for the furnishinge of the said company with playinge apparell towardes the setting out of their newe playes. And further, that the saide Phillipe Henslowe and Jacob Meade shall and will at all tymes during the saide terme, when the said company shall play in or near the cittie of London, furnish the saide company of players, as well with such stock of apparell and other properties as the said Phillip Henslowe hath already bought; as also with such other stock of apparell as the saide Phillip Henslowe and Jacob Meade shall hereafter provide and buy for the same company during the saide tearme. And further, shall and will, at such tyme and tymes during the saide tearme as the saide company of players shall by meanes of any restraynte or sicknes go into the country, deliver and furnishe the saide

company with fitting apparell out of both the sajde stockes of apparell. And further, the saide Phillip Henslow and Jacob Meade doe, for them their executors and administrators, covenant and graunt to and with the saide Nathan Feilde by theis presentes in manner and forme followinge, that is to saye: that they the saide Phillip Henslowe and Jacob Meade or one of them shall and will, from tyme to tyme during the said tearme, disburse and lay out such somme or sommes of money as shalbe thought fittinge by fower or five of the sharers of the saide company, to be paide for any play which they shall buy or condition or agree for, so alwaies as the said company doe and shall truly repay unto the said Phillip and Jacob, their executors or assignes, all such somme or sommes of money as they shall disburse for any play, uppon the second or third daie whereon the same plaie shalbe plaide by the saide company, without fraud or longer delay. And further, they the said Phillip Henslowe and Jacob Meade shall and will at all tymes, uppon request made by the major parte of the sharers of the saide company, * * * remove and putt out of the said company any of the saide company of players of the said Phillip Henslowe and Jacob Meade shall fynde saide requests to be just, and there be no hope of conformity in the partie complayned of. And further, that they the saide Phillip Henslowe and Jacob Meade shall and will at all tymes, uppon request made by the saide company or major parte thereof, pay unto them all such sommes of money as shall come unto their hands * * * of any forfeitures for rehearsals or such like paymentes. And also shall and will, uppon the request of the said company or the major parte of them, * * * the persons by whom such forfeiture shalbe made as aforesaid, and after or uppon the recovery and receipt thereof (their charges disbursed about the recovery of the same being first deducted and allowed) shall and will make satisfaction of the remaynder thereof unto the said company without fraud or guile. And further, that they the saide Phillip Henslowe and Jacob Meade doe covenant and agree that there shalbe a due accompt given every night to any one that shall by the said company be appointed thereunto * * * * * halfe of the galleries allowed toward the payment of the said sum of one hundred twenty and four pounds," &c.*

This document, as the asterisks imply, is in a very imperfect state, and the conclusion of it has entirely disappeared.

* To this date, or somewhat earlier, may be assigned the interesting letter tripartite, which Malone found at Dulwich College, addressed by Field, Daborne, and Massinger to Henslowe for a loan of money. It has been printed in vol. iii. p. 337, of Boswell's edition of Malone's Shakespeare, and in Gifford's Introduction to Massinger's Works, copied from Malone, but in both instances with so many variations (though some of them minute)

It establishes that Henslowe was ostensibly proceeding without the interference of Alleyn. Whether he had any share in the new theatrical speculation by Henslowe and Meade at Paris Garden may, therefore, be doubted, but he certainly retained his interest in the exhibitions of baiting bears, bulls, &c. at that place.

What was the age of Henslowe we have no means of ascertaining, but we shall see presently that he died in the very commencement of 1616, according to our present mode

that it may be worth while here to insert it accurately from the original. It is addressed by Field:—

"To our most loving frend Mr Phillipp Hinchlow Esquire these."

And at the back, below the direction, is written the subsequent receipt:—

"Rec. by mee Robert Dauison of Mr Hinshloe for ye use of Mr Dauboern Mr Feeld Mr Messenger the some of v^l

"ROBERT DAUISON."

The body of the letter runs literatim as follows:—

"Mr Hinchlow.

"You vnderstand o^r vnfortunate extremitie, and I doe not thincke you so void of christianitie, but that you would throw so much money into the Thames as wee request now of you; rather then endanger so many innocent liues; you know there is x^l more at least to be receaued of you for the play, wee desire you to lend vs v^l of that, wch shall be allowed to you w^howt wch wee cannot be bayled, nor I play any more till this be dispatch'd, it will loose you xx^l ere the end of the next weeke, beside the hinderance of the next new play, pray Sr Consider our Cases wth humanitie, and now giue vs cause to acknowledge you our true freind in time of neede; wee haue entreated Mr Dauison to deliver this note, as well to wittnesse yor loue, as o^r promises, and allwayes acknowledgment to be ever

"Yo^r most thanckfull; and louing freinds

"NAT: FIELD

"The mony shall be abated out of the mony remayns for the play of Mr Fletcher & ours

"ROB. DABORNE

"I have ever founde you a true lovinge freinde to mee & in soe small a suite it beeing honest I hope yow will not faile vs

"PHILIP MASSINGER."

of computing the year; and one of his latest known acts was to take a bond from Robert Daborne and Philip Massinger, for the advance of only £3. It was lent to them, we may conclude, on the day the bond bears date, 4th July, 1615, and they stipulated to repay it on or before the 1st August, at Henslowe's house on the Bankside. If Malone saw this document, he passed it over without notice, and Gifford knew nothing of the Dulwich papers but from Malone. Malone, indeed, discovered and transcribed many notes from Daborne, Rowley, Shaw, Day, and other dramatists; but they were printed with marvellous inaccuracy in vol. xxi. of Boswell's edition of Malone's Shakespeare. The copies vary from the originals, still extant, in hundreds of instances, and sometimes the errors are important.* None of them are posterior to 31st December, 1613; whereas the following shews that Massinger was in pecuniary distress two years and a half subsequent to that date:—

Noverint Universi, &c. 4° die Julij 1615.

"The condition of this obligation is such, that if the above bownden Robert Daborn and Phillip Massinger, or eather of them, shuld pay or cause to be payd unto the above named Phillip Henehlow, his exors administrators or assignes, the full and intier somm of three powndes of lawfull mony of England, at or upon the first day of August next insuing the date of these presents, at the now dwellinge howse of the said Phillip Henchlow, scituate one the Banksyde, without fraude or farther delay, then and from thencforth this present obligation to be voyd and of noe effect, or ells to remayn and abide in full power strength and virtue

"Rob: Daborne   (L. S.)
"Philip Massinger   (L. S.)

"Sealed and delivered in the
  presence of us
    "Walter Hopkins"

* The following may be taken as a specimen. On p. 393, of vol. xxi., is a note, without date, though marked by Malone as of November, 1599, from Robert Shaw (or Shaa, as he spells his own name) to Henslowe, respecting the price of a play; and at the back is a singular memorandum, clearly referring to some projected drama on the reign of Richard III. Faithfully

CHAPTER XIII.

Death of Philip Henslowe—Bill filed by John Henslowe against Agnes Henslowe, Alleyn, and Roger Cole—The Answer, with Particulars of Henslowe's Death and Property—Depositions of Witnesses—Alleyn's Liberality to the Prince Palatine's Players—Agreement of Alleyn with them, signed by the whole Company.

The bond with which the preceding chapter concludes was the last act of the life of Henslowe, in relation to theatres, of which we have any information. He was afflicted with the palsy before his death,[*] and perhaps it rendered him for some months incapable of attending to business. He must have died about the 9th January, 1615-16, for a bill was filed in Chancery on the 23d January of that year, in which it is stated that he had then been dead " about fourteen days." This bill was filed by John Henslowe against Agnes Henslowe, Alleyn, and a person of the name of Roger Cole, executrix and overseers of the last will and testament of Philip Henslowe, and it is asserted in it that he died worth about £10,000 or £12,000; but, according to the answer of Agnes Henslowe, Alleyn, and Cole, the precise value of Henslowe's property at the time of his death was

---

copied it runs thus, and the remarkable differences may be seen on comparison.

" 1 Sce. W^m. Wor. and Ansill, and to them the plowghmen.

" 2 Sce. Richard and Q. Eliza. Catesbie, Lovell, Rice ap Tho., Blunt, Banester.

" 3 Sce. Ansell, Daug^r. Denys, Hen. Oxf. Courtney, Bouchier and Grace. To them Rice ap Tho. and his Souldiers.

" 4 Sce. Milton, Ban. his wyfe and children.

" 5 Sce. K. Rich. Catesb, Lovell, Norf. Northumb. Percye."

Besides other mistakes, Malone omitted the whole of the characters who were to be engaged in the fourth scene. The above was probably the scheme of an entire act, drawn up by concert, and as a guide, between two or more dramatists engaged on the same play.

[*] It appears from Henslowe's Diary that he had a sister who died of the same disorder.

£1700 12s. 8d. Two brief sheets of paper (the last unluckily imperfect), entitled,

"The Breviat of the Cause depending in Chancery between

"John Henchlow Pl. { Edward Allin, Agnes Henchlow, Roger Cole } Deff."

are preserved at Dulwich. They contain the whole of the Bill, and apparently all that was very material of the Answer; and as they throw much light upon the relations of the parties, and shew precisely how and under what circumstances Henslowe disposed of his property, they are here inserted.

"The Bill exhibited 23 Januari 1615.

"Bill.

"That Phillip Henchlow, one of the Sewers to the Kinge, having taken to wif the deff. Agnes, widdow to one Woodward, by whome she had one onely daughter named Joan married to the Deff. Edward Allin, being seized in fee of divers lands and tenements and possessed of divers leases goods and chattells to the valew of ten or twelv thowsand pownds about 14 days last past deceased without issue; after whose death the sayd estate ought to descend to the Pl. as his heyr at the common law, to which purpose the sayd Phillip Henchlow had made a former will in the tyme of his health and perfect memory.

"That the Deff Edward Allin did confederate and practise with the defendants Agnes and Roger Cole to draw the sayd Phillip Henchlow to alter the sayd former will, and to setle his estate by a new will upon the sayd Agnes, an old decrepit woman, unable to governe such an estate, whearby all the estate of the sayd Phillip Henchlow might by this means come to the defend^t Allen, as the man that having married hir daughter should have the governing of the sayd Agnes during hir lif, and after hir decease the possession of all in right of his wif.

"That to this purpose the sayd Allin and Cole cawsed a draught of a will to be made, whearin they made the sayd Agnes his sole executrix and them selves his overseers, conveing thearby the estate of his freehold lands to the sayd Agnes for term of her lif, as all the rest of his estate whatsoever, and brought the sayd will, so made betwixt them, to the sayd Phillip Hinchlow 2 or 3 howrs before his death, being past all sence and understanding; in soe much that the deff Allin put a pen into his hand, and would

hav guided the same to the subscribing of his name, but that he was otherways advised, in so much that the sayd Phillip Hinchlow made onely some mark, like a dash with the penn, whoe in his perfect health was well able to write his name.

"That the sayd Phillip Hinchlow, being demaunded, wheather it wear his will or noe, made a pawse, not being able to speak, and at last cried, noe will, noe will.

"That to prov the confederacy, the deff Allin of his own devise cawsed the deff Cole to insert a clawse to his own advantage, of the legacy of such a one as should refuse to be orderd by the overseers, in case thear rose any question amongst any of them.

"That the deff Allin cawsed the will to be proved the next morning after the decease of the sayd Phillip Hinchlow, although it wear sabaoth day.

"AWNSWER.

"The effect of the Awnswere.

"That the Pl being a man of an ill carriadge towards Phillip Hinchlow, his unkle deceased, the sayd Phillip had in his lif tyme often sayd he, the sayd Pl, should never have penny of his goods.*

"That Phillip Henchlow maried Agnes at such tyme as she was his M^{rs} and he hir servant, being wholy advanced by hir, whoe ever acknowledged the same and promised, if he died before hir, to make hir amends.

"That the goods and leases of the sayd Phillip wear, by sworn praysers and the neighbors, prised and valewd only at 1700^l xij$s$ 8d whearof 400^l was desperat debts; and as for the fee simple, the Pl sonn is to hav the greatest part thearof, after the decease of the sayd Agnes.

"That there never was any confederacy betwixt them, neither did any of them ever perswade the sayd Phillip Hinchlow to alter any former will; only the deff Cole sayth, that being sent for to the sayd Phillip Hinchlow in the tyme of sicknes, as a frynd and neighbor he advised him to settle his estate and make his will, upon whose motion the sayd Phillip Henchlow did willingly prepare himself, and named what legacies he would giv, which the deff Cole set down in wrightinge; as also nominated the deff Agnes for his sole exor, and the deff Allin and Cole for twoe of his overseers, without any provocation or ordging of the deff, the sayd Phillip being of perfect memory.

"That the deff Cole, reading the will after it was drawn up according to the former dyrections of the sayd Phillip, excepted at twoo things: one was

* In Henslowe's Diary at different dates are entries for money paid for John Henslowe's clothes, &c. One account is for law expenses, when John Henslowe disputed his father's will.

at the setting down only of 20 gownes for 20 poor men, saying he would be buried like the kings servant, and cawsed 40 to be sett downe. The 2 exception was, that wheareas the overseers and others advised to put in a clawse into the will, that in case any question should arise about legaces, such a one as should refuse to be orderd by the overseers should forfeyt his or hir legacy, and the deff Agnes should hav the same. Now, the sayd Phillip altered the same and would have such legacy so forfeyted come to the deff Alleyn, alleadging this reason, that Agnes was old and unable to curbe them that should be turbulent in this case.

"That the deff Allin cawsed the will to be proved the next morning, though it wear Sunday, bycawse the deff Agnes was so sick and weak, that he dispayred of hir lif till the next day.

"That the sayd Phillip Hinchlow was stroken sick with the palsy, and could not write his name by reason of the violent shaking of his hand, which maide the deff. Allin offer to guide him, after the sayd Phillip had of him self called for pen and ink to subscribe his sayd last will * * *."

What we have inserted above obviously formed a portion of the brief given to Alleyn's counsel, who made some notes on a blank space, from which we gather that proceedings had been directed by the Lord Chancellor to try the validity of Henslowe's will. Among other notes are what appear to be memoranda of the depositions of witnesses on both sides, and, though they are incomplete, it may be well to quote them just as they stand in the hand-writing of the counsel, whoever he might be:—

"1 Pl not prejudiced by the obtaining of the will, for there is no devise to him.

"2 The guifte of the land not *ad bonum* of Allen.

"3 landes and leases during her life: the residue to the wife.

"4 Not of memorie in the forenoone.

"5 A will precedent suppressed.

"Robert Moore (a kinsman) had no legacie. He hath heard that the Pl is heere.

"6 The Thursday before he died he said he had made a will, written with his owne hand, but not finished, but he would doe it.

"7 Uppon the Saterday Allen tolde him that he and Mr Cole had gotten him to make his will. The will being brought he made a scratch. P. H. beinge asked if it were his will, sayd yea: if he lived it was noe will: he setto his name, not as a witnesse, but to knowe it agayne.

" 9 To the 9th. interr: he was not of perfitt memorie to his understandinge.

" Mich Shepd. 6. he knoweth not, but hath heard of a former will: he hath heard that Allen and Cole perswaded P. H. to make a will.

" He sealed and subscribed the will in his presence: he ingrossed the will, but had not his instructions from the testator.

" The will read by Mr. Cole the afternoone next before his death.

" Ph. Hen. pulled of the seale, his understandinge reasonable good.

" 40 gownes, the question how many gownes.

" Noe thinge leafte out nor added, except the devise of his sowle. and the power to the overseers.

" W^m. Gooden 6. he was with him the morninge before his death.

" 22. Uppon Saterday morninge, at 8 of the clocke, Mr Allen sayd he was sicke and not fitt to receive money: he is perswaded he was not fitt at that tyme to have disposed of his estate.

" Edw. Griffin. 22. he was but once with him, one the Saterday at 3 of the clocke: he questioned with him to trye his memorie. He knewe him, and called him by his name.

" He beinge asked if he heard them pray for him, he answered noe."

The result probably was to establish the will, but upon this question we have little better than conjecture for our guide: no other documents regarding the suit are extant; but Alleyn, after the death of his wife's mother in 1617, (as established by other papers at Dulwich), seems to have come into most of Henslowe's property, which was added to his own [*] while the College was in a course of construction.

The death of Henslowe necessarily re-involved Alleyn in theatrical affairs, and led to some painful and expensive disputes. His first act was one of liberality and generosity. The company of the Prince Palatine's players had become indebted to Henslowe to the extent of £400; and, on the 20th of March, 1615-16, about three months after the

---

[*] It appears by the original lease preserved at Dulwich College, that on the 19th of June, 1615, Alleyn let to Henry Harris two dwelling-houses, together with " Pye Alley" and garden, " standing next the mansion, place, or house, called Fisher's Folly," in the parish of St. Botolph, for £30 per annum. These he had derived from his father.

death of Henslowe, we find Alleyn forgiving them at once £200 of what they owed, and accepting from the company an undertaking to pay the reduced sum by degrees, by allowing him one-fourth of the receipts of the galleries until the debt was liquidated. Jacob Meade was also a party to the deed, as far as related to the observance of certain articles previously entered into by the company with him and Henslowe; for at the time of Henslowe's demise he appears to have been in partnership with Meade, not only in Paris Garden, but in the Hope Theatre on the Bankside. The instrument itself, with all the original signatures of the players, is preserved at Dulwich, and the subsequent is a copy of it.

> "Articles of Agreement indented, had, made, concluded and agreed uppon the twentith daye of Marche, Anno Dom 1615, betwene Edward Allen Esqr. and Jacob Meade of the one partie, and William Rowley, Robt. Pallant, Joseph Taylor, Robt. Hamlett, John Newton, Hugh Attewell, William Barksted, Thomas Hobbs, Antony Smyth and William Penn, gents, of thother partie, as followeth viz.

> "Wheare the said William Rowley Robt. Pallant, Joseph Taylor, Robert Hamlett, John Newton, Hugh Attewell, William Barksted, Thomas Hobbs, Antony Smyth and William Penn, together with others, as well for divers sommes of monnye lent them by Phillip Henchlowe Esqr deceassed, as for a stock of apparell used for playinge apparell to the valewe of 400 li pounds, heretofore delivered unto them by the said Phillip, are and doe stand joyntlye and severally bound unto the said Phillip and to the said Jacob Meade or one of them, in and by divers and sundry obligations of great sommes of monnye, to the somme of 400 li and upwards, as also for performance of certen Articles of Agreement on their the said William Rowley, Robert Pallant, Joseph Taylor, Robert Hamlett, John Newton, Hugh Attewell, William Barksted, Thomas Hobbs, Antony Smyth and William Penn and others their parts and behalfe to be observed performed and kept, as in and by the same obligations and Articles of Agreement more at large it doth and may appeare: Item wheare there is at the speciall intreaty of them the said William Rowley, Robt Pallant, Joseph Taylor, Robert Hamlett, John Newton, Hugh Attewell, William Barksted, Thomas Hobbs, Antony Smyth and William Penn, the daie of the date hereof, a quiet and peaceable agreement had and made by and betwene all the said parties to

these presents, and that he the said Edward Allen is contented and pleased to take of them the said William Rowley, Robert Pallant, Joseph Taylor, Robert Hamlett, John Newton and other the parties to these presents the somme of twoe hundred pound only, to be paid in manner and forme herein after mentioned. First the said William Rowley, Robert Pallant, Joseph Taylor, Robt Hamlett, John Newton, Hugh Attewell, William Barksted, Thomas Hobbs, Antony Smyth, and William Penn for themselves joyntlye, and everye of them severallye their severall executors, and administrators, doe covenant promis and agree to and with the said Edward Allen and Jacob Meade, their executors and administrators, by these presentes that they the said William Rowley, Robert Pallant, Joseph Taylor, Robert Hamlett, John Newton, Hugh Attewell, William Barksted, Thomas Hobbs, Antony Smyth and William Penn, their executors and administrators, shall and will dayly and everye daye well and truly satisfye content and paye unto the said Edward Allen his executors, administrators and assignes, the fowerth parte of all suche somme and sommes of monnye, proffit and gayne shalbe gathered or taken, by playinge or otherwise, out and for the whole galleryes of the Playe House comonly called the Hope, scituate in the parishe of St. Savior in the countye of Surrey, or in anye other house, private or publique, wherein they shall playe, as the same shalbe dayly gathered or taken, accordinge to the full rate and proportion of the gayne and proffitt of the fowerth parte of the said galleryes, untill the said somme of 200^{li} shalbe there with fully satisfyed and paid. And that they shall and will at all tymes from and after the sealinge hereof, well and truly observe performe, fullfill and kepe all and every the said Articles of Agreement heretofore made with the said Phillipp and Jacob or eyther of them, on their or any of their partes hereafter to be observed performed or kept. And that they the said William Rowley, Robert Pallant, Joseph Taylor, Robt. Hamlett, John Newton, Hugh Attewell, William Barksted, Thomas Hobbs, Antony Smyth and William Penn shall and will playe at the said House called the Hope, or elswheare with the likinge of the said Edward and Jacob, accordinge to the former Articles of Agreement had and made with the said Phillipp and Jacob or eyther of them, and their late promis synce in that behalfe made with the said Edward and Jacob. Item the said Edward and Jacob, for them their executors and administrators, doe promis and agree to and with them the said William Rowley, Robt. Pallant, Joseph Taylor, Robt. Hamlett, John Newton, Hugh Attewell, William Barksted, Thomas Hobbs, Antony Smyth and William Penn, their executors and administrators, by these presentes that all and everye the bonds writings obligations and articles of agreement wherein and whereby they or anye of them stand

bound, or by which they doe owe to them, the said Phillipp or Jacob or eyther of them, anye somme of monney (except suche bonds bills and writings by which they or anye of them stand bound to the said Phillipp and Jacob or eyther of them for anye private dett borrowed of the said Phillipp, to or for his or their owne particuler use) shall from and after the full payment of the said somme of 200^{li} in forme aforesaid, and performance of the said articles of agreement, aswell heretofore made as herein and hereby promised to be kept hereafter on their parts to be observed performed and kept, be utterly voide frustrate and of none effect, only against them the said William Rowley, Robt Pallant, Joseph Taylor, Robert Hamlett, John Newton, Hugh Attewell, William Barksted, Thos Hobbs, Antony Smyth and William Penn, their executors and administrators. And that then they shall or may have to their own use all such stock of apparell as they or anye of them had or receaved of or from the said Phillip, Edward and Jacob or anye of them. Provided that yf the said William Rowley, Robt. Pallant, Joseph Taylor, Robert Hamlett, John Newton, Hugh Attewell, William Barksted, Thomas Hobbs, Antony Smyth and William Penn, their executors and administrators and everye of them, shall not well and trulye paie the said somme of 200^{li}, as before the same is herein lymitted tobe paid, and performe the said articles of agreement, as well heretofore as by these presents promised tobe performed as aforesaid, that then the said Edward and Jacob their executors and administrators shalbe at free libertye to have and take all advantage in lawe against them the said William Rowley, Robt Pallant, Joseph Taylor, Robt Hamlett, John Newton and all other the said parties, their executors and administrators, and everye or anye of them, uppon all and every such bonds writings obligations and articles of agreement, and everye or anye of them, by which they or anye of them, by themselves or with others, are and doe stand bound or doe owe unto the said Phillip and Jacob, or either of them, anye somme of monnye. And also have full power and lawfull authoritye to take and seize into their, or some or one of their hands and possession all such stocke of playinge apparrell as they or anye of them now have or shall have, and the same detayne and keepe for and towards the payment of the sommes of monnye in the said bonds and obligations and every or anye of them mentioned, untill they shalbe thereof fully satisfied and paid, as if this present agreement had never byn had nor made.

"Lastlye, it is agreed betweene all the said parties to these presents that they the said Edward and Jacob, their executors and administrators, shall and maye at all tymes hereafter have and take to their owne use all advantage and benefitt uppon the said bonds, obligations and articles of agreement, and every or anye of them, against anye person or persons, their

executors and administrators, named in the said bonds obligations and writings of agreement or anye of them, not beinge parties to these presents In witnes whereof the said parties aforesaid to these presents enterchangeablye have sett their hands and seales, the daye and yeare first above written.

"WILLIAM ROWLEY	ROBᵗ PALLANT
"JOSEPH TAYLOR	
"ROBᵗ HAMLETT	JOHN NEWTON
"WILL BARKSTED	
"ANTHONY	T. HOBBS
"SMITH	
"WILLIAM PENN	HUGH ATWELL

"Sealed and delivered in the
  presence of
  "ROBERT DABORNE
  "THO. FOSTER   EDW. KNIGHT."

Thus we see, in this instance as in many others, a strong desire on the part of Alleyn to remain on the best terms with the parties with whom he was connected, and to make considerable pecuniary sacrifices for the sake of promoting peace and good-will. By this agreement he at once relinquished a sum equal to about £1000 of our present money.

CHAPTER XIV.

Progress and near completion of Dulwich College—Letter from Thomas Dekker to Alleyn—The Earl of Arundel's Letter to Alleyn on behalf of an Orphan—Stephen Gosson's (Rector of St. Botolph) early Attacks upon Theatrical Performances—His Letter to Alleyn respecting proper objects of his Charity—Second Letter from Gosson and certain Inhabitants of St. Botolph—Alleyn's Letter to Serjeant Greene respecting the Claim of a Person of the name of Burnett.

By the autumn of 1616, the construction of Dulwich College, which Alleyn named "The College of God's Gift," must have been considerably advanced, and it must have been then ready for the reception of some of the objects of the founder's

bounty. At this date Alleyn received a letter from one of Shakespeare's most popular and distinguished contemporaries, whose name will be very familiar to the ears of all who are only slightly acquainted with our ancient drama and its poets—Thomas Dekker. He was a playwright of great celebrity some years before the death of Queen Elizabeth, and had written most of his pieces for companies with which Alleyn and Henslowe were connected. Like many of his class, he seems to have been a man of careless habits, as regarded his pecuniary affairs, living from hand to mouth, by turns affluent and needy, and supplying his pressing wants by the produce of his prolific pen. At the date of the following communication he was a prisoner in the King's Bench; and it was, no doubt, intended to induce Alleyn to make Dekker a present in return for some inclosed verses " in praise of charity," and in celebration of the benevolent work which was now approaching completion. The verses themselves have not survived, but the letter containing them was this:—

"To my worthy and wor^ll freind Edw. Allin Esquier, at his house at Dullidge."

"S^r

"Out of that respect wch I ever caryed to yor Worth (now heightned by a Pillar of yor owne erecting) doe I send theis poore testimonies of a more rich Affection. I am glad (yf I bee the First) that I am the first to Consecrate to Memory (yf at least you so embrace it) So noble and pious a Work, as This, yor last and worthiest is. A passionate desire of expressing gladnes to See Goodnes so well delivered having bin long in labour in the world made mee thus far to venture. And it best becomes mee to Sing any thing in praise of Charity, because, albeit I have felt few handes warme thorough that complexion, yett imprisonment may make me long for them. Yf any thing in my Eûlogium (or Praise) of yo^u and yor noble Act bee offensive, lett it bee excused because I live amongst the Gothes and Vandalls, where Barbarousnes is predominant. Accept my will howsoever And mee

"Ready to doe yo^u any service
"Tho. Dekker

"King's Bench Sept 12. 1616."

Dekker was a poet of ability, and a prose writer of great variety: he always " scribbled for bread," and has left behind him much that is utterly worthless in point of literary merit, but much also that well deserves preservation. It is to be regretted that his tribute to Alleyn has shared the fate of many things he and his contemporaries composed. We need entertain little doubt that Alleyn took steps to relieve his old friend's necessities, and, as it is stated that Dekker was released from prison in the very year his letter bears date,* it may not be too much to suppose that Alleyn had a hand in his liberation.

Another proof that the establishment of Dulwich College was so far completed as to be in a state for the reception of those for whom it was erected, is to be found in the subsequent note from the Earl of Arundell to Alleyn. This worthy nobleman had, doubtless, a great respect for Alleyn's sterling character, and subscribes himself " your loving friend," a style not very usual at that time for a peer to adopt towards a person who had been an actor, and in point of station so much his inferior. The intimacy was long kept up between them, and Alleyn mentions in his Diary, that he was at Arundell House in 1621, and that he had taken his lordship's opinion on the plan for rebuilding the Fortune theatre.

" To my loving frend, Mr. Allayne Esquire, these.

" Mr Allayne; wheras I am given to understand that you are in hand with an hospitall for the succouring of poore old people and the mainteynance and education of yong, and have now almost perfected your charitable worke: I am, at the instant request of this bearer, to desire you to accept of a poore fatherles boy to be one of your number, of whose case and necessitie this saed bearer will better informe you, which if yow shall doe at my request I shall take it kindely at your hands, and uppon occasion requite it, and rest

" Your loving frend

" T: ARUNDELL.

" Arundell house, the xvij[th] of
September 1616."

* By Oldys in his MS. notes to Langbaine.

The poor of the parish in which Alleyn was born, St. Botolph, Bishopsgate, were objects of his earliest attention and regard, and in deciding upon fit persons to receive the benefit of his charity, he called to his aid the rector, whose advice would of course be valuable. Singularly enough the incumbent of the living in 1616, and for some years afterwards, was Stephen Gosson, who, having written plays himself, which were publicly acted, became as early as 1579 the bitter enemy of theatrical representations. He then printed his " School of Abuse, containing a pleasant Invective against Poets, Pipers, Players, Jesters," &c. which he followed up at a later date by other attacks. He subsequently entered the Church; and, in 1598, when he printed a sermon called " The Trumpet of War," he called himself " Parson of Great Wigborow in Essex."

By what means, or in what year, he obtained the living of St. Botolph, is not known; but, as far as we can learn, he was conscientious and zealous in the discharge of his sacred duties. It is a strange coincidence, that this violent and vigorous adversary of the stage should, in the end, become a willing witness of the christian piety and humanity of one of its greatest ornaments, who derived much of his wealth from theatres, and who was anxious to apply it to such an admirable purpose. Gosson must have rejoiced in being an instrument towards its accomplishment, and in bearing testimony to the private virtues of a man who had belonged to a class which he had formerly so vehemently maligned. The earliest letter from him to Alleyn is in these terms:—

"To the worshipfull Edward Allen Esquire, at his howse at Dulwich, give theis with speed."

"Salutem in Christo.

"Sir, I have now sente you a personale view of those three poore persons whose names were presented unto yow from the Churche uppon Sunday laste. Mawde Lee, a very poore widow and a pensior of our parish, aged threescore yeares, and upward: Henrie Philippes, an almes man also of owers, uppon the point of three score yeares; and John Muggleton of the

lyke age, trusting that uppon this enterview yow will give them their direction when they shall be admitted unto your hospitale of poore folkes, which are the pledges Christ hath lefte with yow in his absence, whoe hath told us longe agoe that the poore you shall alwayes haue amonge yow corporally present, untill he come agayne in body to judge the world and give recompence to those that have for his sake shewed any mercy heere to his images, and needy members heere. Thus recommendinge to the grace of ower good god, I rest,

"Your verie lovinge and ancient freend,
"Steph : Gosson Rect.

" At my howse in St.
Botolphes withowte
Bishopsgate, 2 Octb.
1616."

Hence we find that on the Sunday preceding the date of the above letter Alleyn had visited St. Botolph's Church, when the names of the poor candidates for his bounty, whom he afterwards saw personally at Dulwich, were given to him. We may conclude that they were admitted to the benefit of the charity; but another letter from the rector, the churchwardens, and five of the parishioners, dated nearly a year afterwards, shews that John Muggleton, one of the persons previously recommended, had been, for some unexplained cause, removed.* A successor was, therefore, recommended in the person of Edward Cullen, who was a single man; for, at this date, (1st September, 1617,) Alleyn had come to the determination that no poor man who was encumbered with a wife should be entitled to the advantages afforded by the College. The testimonials of the churchwardens and inhabitants were added to the recommendation of the rector, possibly because, in the case of Muggleton, the latter only had not been found sufficient.

* On the 21st July, 1620, the subsequent entry was made by Alleyn, shewing that the "removal" of Muggleton was not a solitary case:—
" Pd the pore ther pension, all but one man who was expulsed, and Boane that was drounk—7^h. 0^s. 0^d." When paid without any deduction the monthly pension of the poor brothers and sisters was £8 8s. Boane was again fined 12d. for drunkenness on the 14th October, 1621.

" To the worshipfull Edward Allin Esquire.

" Our very harty Commendations beinge Rendered. Whereas the Last weeke (upon the Removall of Mugleston) wee did commend unto yow one John Woodhouse, who, for that hee hath a wife, could not obtayne your acceptance to bee one of your Beadsmen. Wee have therfore made Choyce of one Edward Cullen, the bearer heerof, who is a Single man and hath longe time bin one of our pentioners: and for hee is aged and therfore past his labour, and withall knowne to us to bee of good Conversation, wee are the more Imbouldened to Commend him to yow, desireinge that yow would be pleased to admit of him to bee a participator of your deedes of Charitye, not doubtinge but hee will bee a very thankfull man both to god and yow, and so with our best wishes for your wellfare, we take our Leave, this first of September 1617.

" Your worships very Loveinge frendes,
" Steph: Gosson Rect.
(and seven others.)

Alleyn seems to have had a readier and abler use of his pen than might have been expected from his want of education, and from the active nature of his early life. He sometimes kept copies of his letters, or rather he made rough drafts of them, when they were upon any matter of importance, and did not destroy the drafts after he had sent away the fair copies. Several of these rough drafts are still in being, but until now they appear to have escaped all observation, and it certainly was no easy task to decipher them. Not long after the death of Henslowe, Alleyn was pestered for money by a person of the name of Burnett, who formerly was a man of property, and had expectations of getting into parliament. Elizabeth had been dead about five years, when a negociation was entered into between Burnett and Henslowe for the purchase of the Sewers' Office, which the latter had long held;*

* At Dulwich College is preserved a bond given by Henslowe (witnessed by Alleyn and others), stipulating that he would relinquish his office of Sewer of the King's Chamber to Thomas Burnett, in consideration of the sum of £220. Alleyn is therein said to be " of the parish of St Saviour's Southwark;" but the money was to be paid to him at the house of Henslowe, as if he had himself no residence there in 1607.

but as the bargain was not completed, a sum of money, which Burnett had paid in anticipation, was returned. Subsequently, Burnet having consumed his estate applied to Henslowe twice for pecuniary assistance, and twice obtained it, not as a matter of right, but of compassion. When Burnett could procure no further supplies by entreaty, he appealed to a nobleman (most probably the Duke of Lennox), who heard the claim and Henslowe's answer to it, and decided against Burnett. Nevertheless, at the instance of Alleyn, Henslowe afterwards consented to make Burnett a present of an additional sum, taking, as he had done before, an acquittance against all future demands. After the death of Henslowe, in January 1615-16, Burnett resorted to Alleyn, and failing by solicitation had recourse to threats; upon which occasion Alleyn wrote the following letter (transcribed from his own rough draft) to Mr. Serjeant Greene (who is named in it) and another individual, not named (for no address is given), explaining exactly and clearly how the case stood: it will be found a very manly and straightforward statement, consistent with the plain dealing, plain sense, and plain language of the writer. It has no date, but it evidently belongs to the period at which we have now arrived.

"Sir, att the first sight of the Letter you sent me, I was driven into an admiration to consider the bouldness of that audacius persone, whome nether tyme nor trouble can stop the swift current of his false and undeserved clamour; and although I have manye tymes sufficiently satisfied both hym and his frends concerning this matter, yett one more I ame contented to deliver you the naked trueth of this busines.

"About the first coming in of the King ther wase som contrackt between my father Hensloe and Tho. Burnett for his place of a Sewer, my selfe being but only a stander by and a wittnes to the bargayne; and for his money I never had itt one nigh in my custody, for itt aperteyned nott unto me, but only to my father Hensloe, as will apere by a great mans letter whoe writt to my father about the staying off the same money, for nott doing the which he purchast no small hate of the said party.

"Afterwards I wase a wittnes that my father dd. and payd to the said Tho. Burnett, and to his use, all the said moneys back againe as the said

Tho. Burnett in theys wordes or the like dd. to me; I asking hym whether they 2 wear agreed, and he answered me yea, and that all matters wase fully satisfied and ended between them; and so itt aperd, for they continewed lovers and frendes a great while after that. But when the said Tho. Burnett had consumed his estat and living in great want, his witts began to wrest his honesty, and looking back to the former agreement would needes pick a quarrell with the trewth, yett never so bowldly as in this fashion he now doth, for he entreated me to move my father to consyder of his estat, in regard off the acquaintance was had with hym, which I faythfully did and procured a some of money tobe then given hym; but my father, verie wisely understanding by his letters in this busines his clamors nature, att the delyverie off the said some recevd off hym a generall release and acquitance, which I have to show. Some 3 or 4 yeere after that, having nothing to work on but his witts, [he] begon againe to harpe on the owld string, complaynd to my Lord Duke off supposed wrong don to hym by my father Hensloe, wher they often mett and wher, to the great disgrace of the said Burnett, my father verie sufficiently clerd hym selfe.

"Yett after this, in a verie mean fashion I was againe sowght by hym selfe and some frends off his, one Mr. Hindson Josin of S*t*. Ellings and others, to move my father, that allthough ther did acrew to hym nothin off right, or dwty, yett in regard off his poverty he would doe some thing for gods [sake], which I did so effectually, that allthough I found hym extreamly unwilling, by the reson he had charged hym so unjustly before my Lord Duke, I procured him once more to give hym an other som of money, he pretending itt wase for his so great good as possible could be, or to furnish hym into the Parlmt, and that he would, if god ever made hym able, requitt with all thankfullnes. And uppon the rec. of the moneys the said Tho. Burnett made hym another aquittance and release. Nowe in all this progress he never demaunded any off me, but still made me the meane to move my father; but now my father Hensloe is gone, belike he thinkes to work on me for soome spending money: if he do, he wilbe much deceaved. For the terrors of complaynt, which he would make me stand in fear off, he knowes is to no purpose, for the last tyme he spoke to me in the Strond, about a yeare and a half sinc, I then bid hym doe his worst, and so I do and will, for I fear no complaynt wher I haue made no offenc. And for a full conclusion to all his demaunds in breef thus:—I never delt with hym for on farthing, and therefore owe hym nott a farthing, but if I or my father had, I haue 2 sufficient releases that will aquitt all his demaunds. And so much for the law: for conscienc, which is the Chancellor in every mans brest, iff that could tell me I ever ought hym on mitte, I would give hym 2 for itt, for, I thank god off his bounty, I am both able and willing to paye every man his owne. Thus

much have I thoght good to wright unto your self and Mr Sergiant Greene, that you might not be carried away with the stream of slander, and with all to give you some information of the matter of his demaund, resting my self contented that they and such like false aclamations, being the theames of envie, hapen to me and others, ar rewards for hum[ility] and to cut of our love to earthly ambition, springing our desiers forward to the harbor of peac. And so, with my love and kind remembranc to you both, I comitt you to God, and shall alwayes continue your trewe frend

"E. A."

Alleyn seems to have been governed by a praiseworthy economy in all his domestic arrangements, and he made the rough copies of his letters upon paper which had previously been applied to some other purpose, and was then of no apparent value. Thus the preceding letter was scribbled upon the back of an old bond given by Francis Henslowe to his relative Philip, dated the 16th of March, 1604.

CHAPTER XV.

Alleyn's Diary in his own Hand-writing — Cost of the Patent for Dulwich College, and Difficulties in obtaining it — Lord Bacon's Opposition — Completion of the College celebrated by a Banquet — Alleyn's Letter to Sir Francis Calton, respecting the Purchase of the Manor of Dulwich — Letter from the Rev. John Harrison, Alleyn's Chaplain, proposing to marry his Niece.

It will have been observed that the last document we have inserted, with a date, is Stephen Gosson's letter to Alleyn, of the 1st of September, 1617. Alleyn's Diary commences on the 29th of that month, and from it we shall now glean some particulars not yet touched upon. To a few points established by this very curious and authentic record,* we have already adverted in the course of our narrative.

* It is a long, narrow folio, bound in parchment, the cover being made of an old lease which had been cancelled.

On the 30th of September, when Alleyn went to Croydon to dine with "the borough men," as he calls them, he paid Gilpin, the mace-bearer to the Archbishop of Canterbury, "his fee of the consecration," that is, of the consecration of the chapel of the college, which was then, of course, finished. We may infer that this ceremony was performed by the archbishop himself, Dr. Abbott, with whom Alleyn was upon intimate terms, for he not unfrequently registers that he went to dine with his grace. On the 6th of August, 1619, Alleyn says, "I dind with my Lo. of Canterbury, and red to hym the Corporation and the foundation," meaning the Patent under the Great Seal, which he had obtained on the 16th of July preceding, and for which under that date he enters the following charges :—

"July 16. Mathias [Alleyn] fetcht the Great Sealle—
water 0. 0. 6

"The charge for the Great Seale.

The Seale	8. 13. 0	
The Dockett and rec. . .	0. 3. 0	
The inrowlment . . .	2. 0. 0	
The divident . . .	2. 0. 0	
The officers fee . .	2. 13. 4	
For drawing, ingrossing and entering the dockett	0. 3. 4	18ˡⁱ. 16ˢ. 10ᵈ"
Vellome and Strings . .	0. 17. 6	
The clarck . . .	1. 0. 0	
	17. 10. 2	
For vellome and ingrossing of the first patent . . .	1. 6. 8	

Alleyn did not accomplish this great object of his life without much difficulty, for he had to encounter and overcome the opposition of Lord Chancellor Bacon, to which we shall advert more particularly presently. On the 8th of July, 1617, Alleyn informs us that he had gone to the Attorney General

"about my foundation," and on the 11th he received it from him, who liberally refused to accept any fee; but to Mr. Beale and other officers Alleyn paid £6 17s. 6d. for it. At this time the royal signature was wanting, and on the 14th of July Alleyn "rode to Wanstead, where the Marquis of Buckingham undertook the king's hand" to it. He left it with the Marquis, and sent Mathias Alleyn for it two days afterwards, but he came back without it, and Alleyn went to London several times, being still unable to procure it. On the 16th of August he paid Mr. Anthony £8 "for the Patent, and for putting the signet and privy seal," and on the next day he "went to London to the Lord Chancellor's about staying the Patent."

Lord Bacon's letter to the Marquis of Buckingham, explaining why he had "stayed the Patent at the Great Seal," bears date on the 18th of August, the very day after he had seen Alleyn. He tells the Marquis, "I now write to give the King an account of a Patent I have stayed at the Seal: it is of license to give in mortmain £800 land, though it be of tenure in chief, to Allen that was the player, for an hospital. I like well that Alleyn playeth the last act of his life so well; but if his Majesty give way thus to amortize his tenures, the Court of Wards will decay, which I had well hoped should improve. But that which moved me chiefly is, that his Majesty now lately did absolutely deny Sir Henry Saville for £200, and Sir Edward Sandys for £100 to the perpetuating of two lectures, the one in Oxford, the other in Cambridge, foundations of singular honour to his Majesty, and of which there is great want; whereas hospitals abound, and beggars abound never a whit less. If his Majesty do like to pass the book at all, yet if he would be pleased to abridge the £800 to £500, and then give way to the other two books for the universities, it were a princely work, and I would make an humble suit to the King, and desire your Lordship to join in it, that it might be so."

On the 18th of September, Alleyn paid a shilling "for

ingrossing a particular of the lands *in capite* to shew the Lord Chancellor:" on the 13th and 26th of October he took " wine with Lord Chancellor's gentlemen," and thus the matter rested until the 14th of January, when he had another interview with the Lord Chancellor, but no result is stated. On the 26th of May he again saw the Attorney General, when Allen records, "after that I received my Patent once more of Mr. Attorney, who as before refused to accept any fee." On the next day he says, "I rode to Greenwich, and got the King's hand." On the 7th of June he "paid once more for the signet and privy seal" £5; on the 15th of July he waited upon the Lord Chancellor respecting the Great Seal, and on the next day, as has been already shown, Mathias Alleyn brought it to Dulwich. Such, with five shillings "paid to Tomsone for a box to keep the Great Seal in," is the history of the tedious process by which Alleyn at length accomplished his benevolent design. It seems more than probable that the impediments which so long stood in his way were removed by the kind instrumentality of the Duke (then Marquis) of Buckingham. *

---

* In Alleyn's Diary, under date of 26th May, 1620, we read as follows:—

" My wife and I acknowledge the fyne att the Comon Pleas barre of all my landes to the Colledge. Blessd be God that hath lent us lyffe to doe itt."

His wife Joane, there is every reason to suppose, was a willing party to the whole arrangement; at least Alleyn gives no hint to the contrary. The subsequent entries precede that above quoted:—

" May 15. Pd for inrowlling the College deed in the
    Chauncerie 2. 2. 0
Water to Westminster to acknowledge it in
    the Comon Pleas . . . 0. 0. 4
23. Pd my fyne being rated, all the landes att 65^{li},
    the Howses within Bishopsgate at 20^{li}, the
    Fortune att 20^{li}. I pd the xth per c. which
    came to . . . . 10. 10. 0."

The deed of foundation of "God's Gift College," which was enrolled on the 15th May, 1619, bears date on the 13th April preceding, and the Patent on the 21st June, though Alleyn did not get possession of it until the 16th July. The 13th September was a day of signal triumph to him, for then it was that the foundation and completion of the great work of charity and munificence were celebrated. The following entry is copied from his autograph Diary :—

"This daye was the fowndation off the Colledge finisht, and there were present, the Lord Chancellor; the Lo. of Arondell; Lo. Coronell Ciecell; Sir Jo. Howland, High Shreve; Sir Edward Bowyare; Sir Tho. Grymes; Sir Jo. Bodley; Sir Jo. Tunstall; Inigo Jones, the K. Surveyor; Jo. Finch, Councillor; Ric. Tayleboyce; Ric. Jones; Jo. Anthony. They first herde a Sermond, and after the Instrument of Creacion was by me read, and after an Anthem they went to dinner."

To this is appended a list of the viands, with their quantities and prices, the whole expense having been £20. 9s. 2d.* more than £100 of our money at its present value.

We thus see the founder in full possession of the manor of Dulwich and other lands for the endowment of his College, now nearly completed, and sanctioned by a royal Patent under the Great Seal of England. We may therefore take this opportunity of inserting a letter which throws a great deal of light upon the particular mode in which the manor of Dulwich devolved into Alleyn's hands. It is from Alleyn in reply to Sir Francis Calton, who, after he had parted with the estate, seems to have repented that he had sold it, and to have reproached Alleyn with some undue proceeding in obtaining it. Alleyn repels the imputation with becoming indignation. Our transcript is from Alleyn's rough copy, without date and much mutilated, but still enough can be

* The details of the banquet may be seen extracted at large, by such as have curiosity in matters of the kind, in Lysons' "Environs," i. 98. The reverend author also made other quotations from Alleyn's Diary, but with frequent errors of transcription.

made out to render the reply in most of its parts sufficiently intelligible, and to show how much the better Alleyn had of the argument, treating the subject as he does in his usual distinct, manly, and straightforward way, and without "much schollership." He asserts that Dulwich had cost him £5000, that he had purchased it when no other buyer could be found, and that he had been compelled to pay 800 marks for the patronage, which ought in fact to have gone with the rest.

Sir Francis Calton in his letters (which cannot be found) had taunted Alleyn, among other things, with having been originally a player, a point which the latter seems, in the first instance, to have intended to have passed over in silence; but he added a slip at the end, in which he makes a retort that could not have been very grateful to the feelings of the knight, who had evidently foolishly squandered the property left him by his father. The details of the transaction are not always clear for want of the epistles to which what follows is the answer; but Alleyn, as we learn from other sources, had exchanged some property at Kennington with Sir Francis Calton, in completing the bargain for Dulwich. This, too, it appears the knight afterwards sold, and complained that he had been deceived about its value. Mention is also made of a house at Greenwich with which Sir Francis Calton was not contented, no doubt referring to the assignment by Alleyn to the knight of the lease of a dwelling at Greenwich, "near the Park," on the 8th Feb. 1615, which lease Alleyn had purchased on the 26th May, 1608, as appears by original evidences.

"Sir Fr. I have received your strange letter. Itt beres no date, and therefore I can nott conjecture howe long you have bene in this mind; for as I take itt at our last parting all was [def. in MS.] at least on your side, for you reseivd your right, but I nott myne, which long er this I expected would have bene performed. Nowe to answer your severell rashe unfrendly letters for these 3 [def. in MS.] bear, though nott with so much schollership, for I have none at all, as you, yett with a great deal more

trewth, I thus begin. First you complayne of 15ˡⁱ [def. in MS.] in Keningtone as a great some, and thereby I knowe you have well studied the art of multiplication. I answer that my selfe hard you att our first meeting with [def. in MS.] Carey 1800ˡⁱ which you refusing, so it coust you 2050ˡⁱ and you would not [def. in MS.] fiftye. What after bargaine you made with hym I know nott: so iff you had [def. in MS.] itt, your loss had ben but 200ˡⁱ, but had you sould itt for 500ˡⁱ or given itt for nothing, what is this to me, no more then my giving awaye [def. in MS.] ing all Dull. as iff you had bene for lack of a good tytle. Unkind by lawe [def. in MS.] wear some thing [def. in MS.] and yett is that to me nothing, for I well remember and well [def. in MS.] any tyme be dep [def. in MS.] one first person about itt, you asked me of the tytle, and I answerd itt [def. in MS.] you disliking. I further said in theys wordes, Whie, Sir Fr. you have now asked me no further in the sute of Dull. for that which for my evidence I have but the Gr. Seal of England, and so have you for Kenington, and iff the state should be at any tyme pleased to returne all Abey landes to ther former use, I must lose Dull. for which I have paid now 5000ˡⁱ. So likewise iff all such leases made by queen Eliz. should by the king or prince be cald in and made frustrate, you must indure the losse of Kenington which you paid 2000ʰ [for]; to which you answered and said, In trewth all thinges in this world is uncertayn, and so you concluded to receave it most willingly without any pressing you to itt once, or proving itt on your show, for it wase your earnest desier. Nether was I so willing to leave itt as you suppose, for then I could have accepted the offer of 2 persones, which would have given me as much for itt as you paid.

"And whereas you touch on my disposition in the dedycating of that mite which god hath given me (and bleast itt with me) bringing example from Kanut, David and Selymus, all in despight and derogatory of my sincere and well meaning act, wherein I confess you have shewen much reading, and with all much envie. You say you forbere to make aplycation: you may very well, you have proved itt so playnly; but judge no man least you be judged. My hart in that action is best knowne to god that gave itt me. Yf I have don itt for worldly glorye or vayne ostentation, god knowes and will reward accordingly. All the sons off Adam are full off sin: ther is none that doth good, no nott one; and I confess my selfe to be the most sinfullest of all, and how then can I attribut to my selfe any action of goodnes? You demaund what hope I justly could have that god would blesse or prosper the purchase which I had procured by so unjust and so indirect meanes? I must withstand your murmur and harshe phrases, protesting I never intended to deal so unjustly with you, as you dyd by me in making me paye 800 markes more then I bargained for the patronage, then I should have

done, affirming untrewly it was sowld to Sir E. Duke and divers such like thinges which I cau call to memorie when tyme shall serve; and for the prosperity of the purchase, I thank god of his goodnes he hath blest itt better to me then eather to your father or your selfe; and, I give hym prayse, not only Dull. and Kennington, but all the thinges that ever I mett with all hath bene most prosperous and behoofefull unto me, where contrary wise all that ever you delt with all, so farre as my knowledge will goe, hath bene unfortunat to your great losse: for having Dull. you wear still at law with the tenauntes, in so much that your self towld me that you never sawe itt but with a heavie hart (wher, I thank god, I look uppon itt with joy). Your pencioners place you cowld nott kepe: Greenwich howes could nott content you; nor many other places. Kennington itt self had you kept [def. in MS.] Mr Alexsander had bene a bargayn good enough, but wher your [def. in MS.] ing of god is not all thinges turned to the worse, as gayne to losse, wisdome to folly, rest to contest, peace to discontent; and whilst a man thinkes to avoyd this fate by shifting many places, he doth but lyke the [def. in MS.] diseased, who hopes by changing beddes and chambers to leave his greef behind [def. in MS.] when he bears your envie in his brest.

"I wright nott theys thinges to greve you, but wishe you to look back upon your self before you judge another: nether will I any waye judge you, nor my self, but lett god be the judge between you and I. All this is but a short and rude answer to your discontent. More, lett me shewe you a little of my owne. First for the purchase of Dull. Sir, you made me pay more for itt then any other man should have done: witnes Sir Hugh Browninges own wordes, which many tymes he affirmed: next, when we had agreed, you towld me the patronage was gone to your brother Duke, and so gleand the Coll. of my bargayne; but when I towld you twas parte of your bargaine and a thing fitt for me, being allwayes belonging to Dull. then you wrested me to paye you 800 markes more, being in all above 1000^{li} more then any man would give for itt; for a skrivener in London towld me you offred him 40^{li} to gett you a chapman for it, being 7 year upon sale and refused by all men. Next, when I requierd to see your evidence, to shewe itt my councell, you towld me you had nothing but a greate seale and that the title was playne: your grand father bought itt of the K, your father had itt from hym, and you of your father; but before I could have and se the greate seale I was fayne to pay 1700^{li} for redemption out off mortgage, on which I disbursed to your sol^r. 300^{li} more, and made up the somme 2000^{li}. Then coming to councell you could not produce the manor evidence that showld derive the land to you, and your father being the yongest brother, and so nott heyr to your grand father,

the purchaser; which made my counceller saye, you went about to cheat me and wisht me nott to deal with itt at any termes, unless that wrighting weare brought forth. Therupon you stayd 6 months, and I resolved nott to deale with itt; but you continually importuned me to receave itt, saying you were utterly undon unless I went forward with itt. I offred you to pass itt to any other man, and to lett you have the use of my 2000li for nothing, but you replyd itt wase for no man if not for me. So in a maner you forst me to take itt, and for my better security 3000li showld rest in my handes 6 yeares tyll all fynes and reconizances were perfyted by lawe, you receaving annually for the forbearance 213li 6s. 8d which duly was performed on my parte.* But you, still discontented, as nowe you are, never willing to receave the paymentes according to the agreementes, but must have your quartredge before itt was due, and many tymes 2 qrs. to geather. Then I wase importuned to disburse parte of the principall for the purchase of Greenwich howse, and more to serve your occasions in building or otherwise, so the 1000li of the 3 was receaved and out of my handes longe before itt showld: the other 2000li in my handes wase still a great eye sore with you, so that continually I was importuned to lett you have that also, to which I answered that att your daye you showld have itt."

On a loose slip, marked with an asterisk:—

"* And where you tell me of my poore originall and of my quality as a Player. What is that? If I am richer then my auncesters, I hope I maye be able to doe more good with my riches then ever your auncesters did with their riches. You must now beare povertye and if you beare it more paciently then I, your desert wilbe the gretter. That I was a player I can not deny, and I am sure I will not. My meanes of living were honest, and with the poore abilytyes wherewith god blesst me I was able to doe something for my selfe, my relatives and my frendes, many of them nowe lyving at this daye will not refuse to owne what they owght me. Therfore am I not ashamed."

The whole letter is very difficult to be read; but it has few erasures, and it is written as an indorsement on a brief sheet, of what seems to have been originally intended by Alleyn as part of his will. At the back, and meant probably

* This passage refers to transactions as far back as the year 1606. A deed is preserved at Dulwich, thus indorsed by Alleyn: "Bargaine and sale of the Mannor of Dulwich, from Sir Fra. Calton and his Ladie to me, Ed. Alleyn."

as portion of the same letter, we read as follows, but there is no indication of the place where the passage ought to be inserted :—

"Howe so ever you handled the matter I know nott, but had I kept itt, still I would nott have lost one peny by itt; for I knowe the Prince, at the tyme my most excellent M^r., whose love to all his servantes wase suche, that I knowe he would have protected me in my right; and iff I had not gayned, yett he would nott have sene me sustayne losse in his servis."

It has been shewn, that Alleyn, long before he finally obtained his Patent for endowing Dulwich College with lands to the amount of £800 a year, had admitted and maintained various objects of charity. On Christmas Day, 1617, he and his wife "received and dined the poor people, and they did so again on the 4th January. On the 24th March, 1617-18, we meet with the following memoranda :—

"Pd Mr Young, my chapline and Schoolm^r., for his
 q^r. wages 5. 0. 0
Pd Mr Harrisone,* my chapline and Usher, for his
 q^r. wages . . . . . 3. 6. 8"

So that he had two chaplains, who were employed to teach the children whom he charitably maintained, considerably more than a year before he finally procured his Patent.

There is extant at Dulwich a long and formal letter, without date, from the Rev. Mr. Harrison, the chaplain and

---

* Under date of January 22, 1618-19, we read the subsequent memorandum :—

"Bought between me and Jo Harrison, my Chapline, Mr Minchawes dictionarie, being ij languages, the price was 22^s. whereof I gave . 0. 11. 0"

He does not, however, seem to have purchased many books. In different parts of his Diary we read of the following added to his stock :—"The general Practice of Physic;" "A book of the Bishop of Spalates;" "Fall of Shabot;" "A booke of Articles;" "Two bookes of Googes Husbandry;" "Rules of Lyfe;" "The Black Prince;" "An of Bullen;" "The Currant of News."

usher above mentioned, which has no address, but was doubtless sent to Alleyn. It contains an avowal by the writer, that he had secretly married Alleyn's niece, who lived in the College in the capacity of a servant. The rev. gentleman very elaborately argues the matter, presenting the case in all its bearings; and we may presume that he succeeded in reconciling the founder, as he left "the wife of John Harrison, clerk," a legacy in his will. It runs thus:—

"Wor^ll Sir. Not unfitlye is it spoken of the Poett, (Dicere quæ puduit, scribere jussit Amor) what shamefastnes forbids to speake, love commandes to write, like another alured about a match, not with Spaine but mine owne. Whereas, whether to your knowledge or without your knowledge, there hath bene affections bred and combined betwixt your kinswoman and me, and now united in a more sure maner then I presume yow know of: though many and sundry causes, and of them not a few, to me have seemed somewhat more serious then peradventure in other mens judgements they are, caused me to conceale this matter even from your self, to whom I confesse it ought to have bene first imparted, which though it come now a day after the faire, yet I hope not after the acceptance, nor after the desire of your best wishes upon it. To implead any mediate cause in this or that kinde were to be reputed rather like Eves defect, a crime then argument of this conclusion, and therefore not humane, much lesse schollerlike: onely, I appeale to the everliving god who (I do verily beleve) had an extraordinary hand in it, as is best knowne to my selfe by the passages thereof betwixt us, and I hope he hath ordeined it to both our good, to meward I verily beleve, if it please god to doe so much by me to herward. To satisfye then your self, whom I know none ought more to expect it then your self (settinge aside both our parents if extant) the conclusions were so hasty betwixt us (which I confesse argues want of judgement in me) that I did undergoe this concealed course for diverse reasons: vizt if the worlde had noted my supposed folly in so affectinge, it might happly have prevented my fortune (the question is better or worse)—2dly She was under the name of your servant. I know no other, and it would have bene thought unfitt in my poore judgement that a Ministers wife should have served tables, especially the wife of one (be it spoken without arrogancye) that hath taken the degree of M^r. of Artes. Yf concent on all sides had bene graunted, and the marriage more publicly celebrated, there might have bene more adooe then needed, and expences greater then I am sure there are, and I lesse contented, lovinge plainenes. 4^thly The nature of

this place moved me much to this silent course, by cause I am and was alwayes loath to be a prejudice to any future statute which I have conceived to have extended by yow, howsoever I thought it would be lesse offensive or prejudiciall to your self, whom in this case I confess I onely respect. Be it so, thes reasons may be reputed no reasons, blamed I may be, shamed I cannot be in this action because honest and godly. Other reasons I could alledge as likely consequences of the former. As in respect of the inconveniences which might have happened upon it, as appeared evidently at the not to be mentioned distast yow had of me not longe since, and other occasions in the like nature I could instance in. 2ly The now breedinge estate of your schole, which if it be intercepted before it come to a fuller growth, a greater inconvenience may happly arise then yow expect and others suggest unto yow, though I confess I not so worthy as I could wish. Other occasions in another nature which I leave to your mature judgement and consideration without my advise or declaration. If there be any other error (as far as I see) it is to my self, that I prepared myself like an Atlas, or an asse, to beare as questionlesse the worlde, so soone as it comes to light, may repute me, consideringe what matches I might have had, if carefull of my self, though now through my inconsideratenes I seeme to stand at the hazardes mouth: yet two thinges my comfort, my hope and love; the first to god an allsufficient father, who will not suffer me to fall, though I know some fat buls may thrust sore at me to make me fall, nor to want, seinge I have often prayed and in part learned to be content with what estate soever, knowinge that godlines is the onely true gaine: the second my love reciprocall betwixt her and me, in that truest conceut that (I protest) in respect of my assurance that god hath bestowed on me a virtuous and well disposed maide. I would not (I once againe protest) exchange, observing the course of the worlde, for the revenue of the best man in this parishe, (which for ought I know is your self) so much I esteme an honest and godly mind beyond riches; yea though I should not acquire one farthinge by her, yet I hope to be happy with her. You may impose rashnes by cause, not bitt with the worlde, I impute beleefe the basis of a lively hope. Thus (with many others) casting myself on your (I must confess) foretasted curtesye, I doubt not that you will thinke me unworthy of your kinswoman by cause the thinge hath proceded from the Lord who hath thought me worthy, nor my freeindes thinke me too worthy of one so well qualifyed; but with your favours and their furtherance we may love and live to gods glory, your good likinge, our freendes comfort and our own soules health and happines. And though I cannot add to your happines which (god be thanked) god hath so largely bestowed on yow, yet perad-

venture somewhat to your use, and I rather brave a free dismisse then be any prejudice, which I thinke cannot be Durante vita vestra, which I pray god longe to continue to your endles happines and the comfort of many to whom god hath made yow a fosterfather; or els, rather then I should admitt any disgrace, which may many wayes happen in respect of my self or my wife, I pray god direct yow aright herein to his farther glory and the mutuall love of yow and us. Thus daly prayinge for your welfare and your bedfellowes, I rest ever

"Yours not so much in tongue as affection
"Jo. HARRISON."

The commencement would lead us to suppose, that the letter was written while the match with the Infanta of Spain was on the tapis; but it is clear that Alleyn had not yet come to the resolution, afterwards embodied in one of his laws for the College, that none of the fellows should be married men.

CHAPTER XVI.

Alleyn's Diary continued — His Birth-day and Wedding-day celebrated — His Guests and Friends at Dulwich — Jack Wilson, the Singer — Marston's Play of Columbus — Mathew Roydon's Poverty — A Play performed by the Boys at Dulwich College — Alleyn's Fee at Court, and discharge of the Duties of his Office — Hymn in his hand-writing — Alleyn's health — Petition from Alleyn against Jacob Meade — Arbitration of their dispute.

THOSE objects of Alleyn's bounty and benevolence whom he called, in his Diary and elsewhere, "the poor brothers and sisters," were accustomed to dine with the founder and his wife and family on particular occasions. One of these was the birthday of Alleyn, and, on the 1st Sept. 1618, he made an entry in his Diary in the following terms:—

"1618 Sept. 1. This day the pore people dind with us, it being my birth daye and my 52 year ow'ld: blessed be the Lord God, the giver of liffe. Amen."

There is a similar note on the same day next year; and, on Sept. 1st, 1620, we have the additional information, that on that day " the 12 brothers and sisters had their gowns," for he furnished them with part of their clothing, as well as with food and lodging. In 1621 he " celebrated" his birthday, for some reason, on the 2d Sept.; and the last entry of the kind is Sept. 1st, 1622, which runs thus:—

> " Wee took the communion, feasted the pore, and gave the 12 ther newe gownes; and this being my birth day I am full 56 years owld: blessed be the Lord God, the giver of lyffe. Amen."

The Diary ends at Michaelmas, 1622, in the following manner:—

" This Booke contaynes the account of 5 years, viz from Michellmass 1617, to Michellmass 1622.

The generall disbursed for theys years is			.	8504.	04. 8¼
Wheroff in particuler as followeth.					
Howshowld charge	.	.	.	. 0917.	11. 2
The Colledge	.	.	.	. 1315.	04. 2
Rentes	.	.	.	. 1547.	19. 2
Debtes, building and reparing		.	.	. 3373.	17. 7
Lawe	.	.	.	. 0207.	8. 1½
Aparell	.	.	.	. 0078.	18. 8¼
Some of theys particulers	.	.	.	7440.	19. 0
Other Expenses	.	.	.	. 1063.	5. 8¼
In theys 5 years hath bene disbursed about building or reparing the Colledg		.	.	. 0802.	07. 9

" Praysed be the name off our good God, both now and ever, through Christ Jesus our Lord. Amen."

Thus it is evident, as the building and repairing of the College only cost £802 7s. 9d. in five years, that the greater part of the money expended upon the structure, &c. had been disbursed before Alleyn kept this book,* and was, doubtless, entered in one of a preceding date, which is un-

---

* Yet he enters various sums at different dates for alterations, additions, and improvements, as well as for ornaments. One of the most remarkable of the latter was the erection of a chimney-piece in " the great chamber," made out of the " upper part of the Queene's barge," which Alleyn bought

fortunately not now in existence. The latest entry in his extant Diary relates to money expended upon the College, &c. and it runs thus :—

"30 Sept. 1622. Disbursed for building this yeare, since the 1 of January 1621 to this 28 off September 1622, in repairing Baxtors howse about 8^{li}: the rest for the Colledg, as finishing the gates and walls off the cloysters, chymneyes and foundation, tilling the cloysters, the Mast. hows, the outer porch, the great Garden hows, and reparing all the other roofes and leaden spouts, with cestron and pipes, with cocks, paving the great kitchen, with other things 163li. 2s. 2d."

On the 13th of July, 1620, he says : " I laid the first brick of the fowndation of the Almes houses in Finsburie;" and on the 23d June 1621 he paid £4 " for five chaldron of coale for the 10 members in St. Giles Parish."

He mentions his wife on the 24th Sept. 1622, and she lived about nine months after the Diary closed. We have seen that, according to the memorandum in Henslowe's account-book, Alleyn was married to Joane Woodward on the 22d Oct. 1592. The twenty-fifth anniversary would, therefore, have fallen on the 22d Oct. 1617 ; but, in Alleyn's Diary, we meet with the subsequent note, dated the 19th Oct. :—

" Our wedding daye: there dind with us Doc. Nott, ould Best, his wife. Canterburie, his wiffe. Jo. Boane, Mr Harris and his frend Ro. Joace."

for £2. 2s. 6d. on 19th Dec. 1618. On the 16th July, 1619, he paid £1. 17s. 6d. for the joiner's work in putting it up; and, without the original cost of the materials, the whole expense was £2. 9s. 5d. This is no doubt the same " chimney-piece" which is now in the Library, and the columns there used probably originally supported the roof of the Queen's barge. Much praise cannot be given to the founder's taste in the affair: the paintings, we presume, were executed for him, and they are not certainly favourable specimens of the arts in his time. They were possibly by the same hand that furnished his fourteen heads of the Kings of England, which he bought on the 29th Sept. and 8th Oct. 1618, and his " 14 heads of Christ, our La. and the 12 Apostels," which he procured from Mr. Gibkin at " a noble a pece." In Aug. 1620 he paid £1. 4s. for carvings of the Four Seasons, which, on the 4th Sept., were put up as ornaments to chimney-pieces.

In the next year, Alleyn tells us that the 25th Oct. was his wedding-day, but possibly he kept it then instead of on the 22d Oct., because on that day he had to ride to London to meet Sir Francis Calton on business. No memorandum relating to it is found in 1619, but, in 1620, the celebration is noted under the date originally given by Henslowe:—

"Oct. 22. This daye was our weding daye, and ther dind with us Mr Knight, Mr Maund, and his wife, Mr Mylyor, Mr Jeffes, and 2 frendes with them, a precher and his frend, Mr Wilson the singer,* with others."

Therefore, there is no doubt that Henslowe was correct, though for some cause, not explained, Alleyn's wedding-day was twice kept on other days. The Diary is silent as to 1621, and it does not come down so low as Oct. 1622.

Much proof is given in the Diary of Alleyn's hospitality, especially to persons who continued in the profession of which he was formerly so great an ornament. The first name that we meet with among his guests of this description is that of William Cartwright, probably the father of him who in 1687 bequeathed to Dulwich College his books and pictures; and who, in his edition of Heywood's "Apology for Actors," (first printed in 1612) under the title of "The Actor's Vindication," (without date, but during the suppression of theatrical representations), thus speaks of Alleyn:—

"In his life time he erected a College at Dulwich for poor people, and for education of youth: when this College was finished this famous man was so equally mingled with humility and charity, that he became his own pensioner, humbly submitting himself to that proportion of diet and clothes which he had bestowed on others, and afterwards was interred in the same College."†

* It seems highly probable that this "Mr. Wilson, the singer," was no other than "Jacke Wilson," who personated Bathazar in "Much ado about Nothing," and whose name is inserted in the first folio of Shakespeare, instead of that of the character he represented. Malone's Shakespeare by Boswell, vii. 59.

† In the General Biographical Dictionary, it is absurdly enough stated that Heywood, writing in 1612, had given this eulogium upon Alleyn, who

Besides that of Cartwright we meet with the names of Lowin, Gunnell, Parr, Dunston, Juby, Massye, Taylor, Hobbs, Jeffes, Price, Borne, Grace, Hunt, and others, as having dined at Dulwich, sometimes with their wives, sons, and daughters; while entries, that "5 of the Fortune Company," "four of the Princes men," "the King of Bohemes men," were present on similar occasions, are not unfrequent.*

Considering that dramatic poets were so numerous about this period, and a little earlier, and that Alleyn must necessarily have been acquainted with many of them, we are surprised not to see such men as Jonson, Chapman, Dekker, Heywood, Webster, Marston,† Middleton, &c. among the persons occasionally entertained at Dulwich; but we find none such, and Alleyn does not seem, in this respect, to have kept up his connection with the stage. In one instance we

---

had not then built his College, and who died 14 years afterwards. The error arose from thinking Cartwright's re-publication of Heywood's "Apology for Actors" a mere reprint; whereas, he made several changes and additions, of which the passage above quoted is one.

* On the 26th October, 1619, Alleyn attended "the buriall of Mr. Benfield," who had been an actor, and was one of Alleyn's most intimate friends.

† The following undated note from Marston to Henslowe may not be unfitly introduced here: it refers to a play by Marston on the subject of Columbus, of which we hear on no other authority. It is one of the scraps of correspondence between Henslowe and the poets in his employ, existing at Dulwich College, of the major part of which Malone has given copies, but omitting the subsequent, which is certainly one of the most interesting of the whole collection.

"Mr. Hensloe, at the rose on the Bankside.

"If you like my play of Columbus, it is verie well and you shall give me noe more then twentie poundes for it, but If nott, lett mee have it by this Bearer againe, as I knowe the kinges Men will freelie give mee asmuch for it, and the profitts of the third daye moreover.

"Soe I rest yours
"JOHN MARSTON."

Marston had written for Henslowe in 1602.

read that "Goodman poet dind here," and a "Mr. Mondy" (perhaps Anthony Munday) was also received by Alleyn. With the date of 25th May, 1620, we read "Mr. Myddleton browght me a booke," for which Alleyn presented him with 5^s.; and on 12th December, 1618, he gave " Jo Taylor, the poett, for his jorney into Scotland," 4^d.; meaning, probably, that he purchased of Taylor a copy of the book containing a narrative of his journey; but, in general, Alleyn seems to have had little to do with authors of any class after his retirement to Dulwich. One of the earliest items in the book is, however, " 8^d. given to Mr. Roydon;" and in one of the last the same name again occurs :—" Aug. 16th, 1622, Given to Matthew Roydon, 6^d.;" which shews that it was no other than the poet, who wrote an elegy on Sir P. Sidney about 1586. Roydon must have been very old and very poor in 1622, when Alleyn relieved his wants by the gift of sixpence.

Alleyn appears to have frequented theatres very little, if at all, as places of amusement, after he became settled at Dulwich, or rather, after the date when his Diary commences. He visited the Red Bull, as has been already noticed, on October 3d, 1617, and he went "to the Fortune" on 9th April; but it is probable that it was for the purpose of collecting his rents, as he speaks at the same time of " the tenants."* On the 15th November, he gave a shilling " to the boyes of

* This opportunity may be taken for stating that if Alleyn at this date (April, 1618,) kept the Fortune Theatre in his own hands, he very soon afterwards let it to the Company there, consisting of Edward Jubye, William Birde (alias Bourne) Frank Grace, Richard Gunnell, Charles Massye, William Stratford, William Cartwright, Richard Price, William Parre, and Richard Fowler. The counterpart of the lease, subscribed by the players, is extant at Dulwich College. It bears date 31st October, 1618, and is for 31 years, at a rent of £200 per annum, and "two roundlets of wine, one of sack, and the other of claret," of the value of 10s. each, to be delivered every Christmas. The fire at the Fortune, of which we shall speak by-and-by, probably again brought the theatre into the possession of Alleyn.

Powles;" but the "Children of Pauls," as they were originally called, were not then actors. On the 6th January, 1621-2, twelfth day, he had some friends to supper, "Mr. Steele, Mr. Fowler, and their wives, and Tho. Allen and his wife;" and he adds, "the boyes play'd a playe," which is a solitary item of the kind. Most likely it was a dramatic entertainment acted by the poor boys taught in the school at Dulwich College.*

He received his fee from the Court, as Master of the King's Games, quarterly; and he usually enters it in the following form.

"Mar 20. 1617. Pd at rec. of my fee at Courte, *li s. d.*
beeing	. . . . .	5. 6. 4	}	
for the M^r. of the office	. .	2. 6	} 0. 4. 6."	
Given to the Clearks	. . .	1. 0	}	
The Chamberkeeper	. . .	1. 0	}	

He was naturally anxious to stand well with the Lord Chamberlain; and, on New-year's day, 1617-18, he made Lady Suffolk a present of a book (the contents of it are not stated) which cost him £15. He gives the items of this present thus:—

"Water to Suffolk House . . . 0. 1. 0
Given my La. with my silver booke
Pd for wrighting the verses . . 0. 10. 0
To Burkett for lyming it
To Mr. Bramheel for the glass work . 1. 2. 0
The whole valewe was 15^{li}."

On the 21st November, 1618, he gave Burkett 6s. "for paynting a smalle tytle to a booke, which I gave to my Ladye of Suffolke."

* It is difficult to explain the following entry, "Feby 6, 1617—18. Pd Mr. Pyd for my babe in the Counter at Lee sute—2s. 8d." "My babe" looks like some term of endearment bestowed upon a near friend, who had unluckily been arrested."

He continued to discharge the duties of his office, as far as we can now ascertain, to the very last, and some of the latest memoranda in his Diary refer to them. Thus, on 22d May, 1621, he says, "I bayted before the King at Greenwich:" again, on the 10th June, 1622, the following droll mixture of discordant topics is inserted, "Baighted before the King, and my man washd my shepe: pd 2^d. a skore." As we have already observed, he bestowed minute attention on rural affairs, and he himself sometimes bought or sold the produce and stock of his land. On the 24th June, 1622, he tells us, "I went to Croydon fayer, wher I sould my browne mare: sowlt to Ingram for 41s. and I bowght a baye mare of Tho. Denny of Kingston for 44s. And I bowght of Rych, the Constable of Eltham, 12 steres 4 year owld, and j of a year owled for 5li. 15s. 0d."

The accounts he gives, regarding his agricultural operations, the expenses of farming utensils, hay, straw, corn, &c. are extremely particular, but often hardly legible, from the small space into which he crowded his details. Every quarter terminates with a general summary, wound up with the words, " Blessed be the Lorde Gode everlasting, the gever of all. Amen," which he used, not as a mere form, but with unaffected piety. Among his scattered papers is the subsequent hymn, in his own hand-writing, and possibly of his own composition. It would seem to have been intended for the congregation of the College, and very likely was sung to the "pair of organes," which, on the 27th of April, 1618, he bought of "Mr. Gibbs of Powles," for £8. 2s., and which were put up in the chapel.*

---

* Alleyn had engaged an organist a month before he bought his organ, as the following memorandum proves.

"Memd. One Thursday the 26 off Marche (1617-18) Jo Hopkins the organist came to me.

A year afterwards Alleyn had " a diapason stop" put to the organ by a person of the name of Barett, and "other alterations" cost 5s. 10d.

O prayse the Lord, y_e servantes all,
  Prayse y^e his holly name;
Bless hym from East to West, henceforth
  For ever doe the same.

The Lord is great above all kings,
  Then Heven his glorie hier,
Who's like to hym? dwelling so highe
  Yett humbles his desier,

To see y^e things y^t ar in Heaven,
  And on the Earth be lowe;
Taking the pore and simple out
  Of dust and myre, we know;

That he may seat hym for to sitt
  W^t princes of the land,
Even w^t the princes of his people,
  His lawes to understand.

He make [s] a baren woman bear,
  And keep her House with joye;
To cheer her Hart he chilldren gives
  To gard hir from annoye.

All this and more our god doth send
  To us, y^t gid of peace:
For wch to prayse his holy name
  My Hart shall never seasse.

The chief recommendation of these stanzas is, certainly, their piety and simplicity. On the 16th of December, 1620, Alleyn registers that he had "bought five song bookes for the boyes" for fourpence.*

During the five years covered by his Diary Alleyn appears to have enjoyed excellent health, which is, perhaps, in part to be attributed to his temperate diet, and to the exercise he took on horseback: he usually rode to London, and that not unfre-

---

* On the 16th April, 1620, the subsequent entry occurs. "Easter daye. We received the Comunion with Mr Robinsone and his wife and all the pore. This daye the Chapple was furnished with basone and candellstickes: the children with 10 surplices, and the fellowes alsoe."

quently.* There are, however, two occasions on which he appears to have been unwell: one of them was on the 25th of April, 1618, when he says, "This morning, blessed be God, I sickend att my La Clarks. Water for Watt. Sent Doc. Lister my water." He was unable to return home, and next day "my wife came to me;" and on the 28th of April, he was visited by Dr. Lister, and paid him eleven shillings for his fee. Alleyn was not able to return to the college until the 9th of May:—"this day, blessed be God, I came home." The second instance of indisposition was in March, 1619, on the 13th of which month he sent his water to Dr. Gullson, and on the 27th of April "paid the Apothecaries bill for my last sicknes," amounting to only four shillings.

The autograph manuscript which has afforded us so much information, contains frequent mention of Jacob Meade, who had been taken into partnership by Henslowe in his shares of Paris Garden and the Hope theatre not very long before his death. How long after that event Alleyn and Meade proceeded harmoniously it is not possible to state; but it appears that they had disputes, and that Alleyn, who always disliked law, was willing to have the matters in difference settled by arbitration. On the 25th of April, 1619, he informs us, "I rode to London to meete with Jacob: spent at dinner with the arbytrators $0^{li}. 7^{s}. 0^{d}$. The following documents have no dates, but they seem to belong to this period, and the first refers to a petition which had been presented some time before by Alleyn to the Lord Chamberlain, while Lord Pembroke was attending King James in Scotland. It is at least likely that the points in question between Alleyn and Meade, which were arbitrated

* His journeys were generally confined to travelling from Dulwich to London, Windsor, Greenwich, or wherever the court might be; but, on one occasion, in August, 1617, he states that he went to Winchester, and slept at the house of a Mr. Allen, (perhaps some relation) on his way thither. He started on the 3rd of August, and was back again by the 10th; therefore he probably went upon business, and not for his health or pleasure.

in the spring of 1619, are contained in the subsequent petition:—

"To the right hble William Earle of Pembrooke, L. Chamberleine to the Kinges Matie, and one of his highnes right hble privie councell.

"The humble petition of Edward Allen, Esquire.

"Whereas there was a petition preferred to your Honor att Edenboroughe, in Scotland, one the behallfe of Jacobbe Meede, touchinge some interruptions by him pretended to be made by the petitioner, touchinge the baytinge of beares and bulls and the keepinge of that game, the which petition remaineth with your honors secretarie. The petitioner humblie desireth your honor to take consideration of his aunswer to the said petition, which is as followeth.

"First, the petitioner hath not made anie assignment of the pattent mentioned in the said Jacobbe Meedes petition, but onlie from tyme to tyme, as occasion serveth, doth make to him, or such as he shall appoynte, deputations of the said pattent, and that for no tyme certaine but duringe your petitioners pleasure.

"Secondlie, that he hath not since the tyme that the house and game, mentioned in the said Meedes petition, weare in his custodie received out of thexchequer, neither the wages and fees dewe by the Patent, nor the 4ˢ per diem for the Leopard and other beastes mentioned in the said Meedes petition.

"Thirdlie, the said Meede hath covenaunted with your petitioner, that if the wages and fees doe not amounte to 60ˡ per Ann, then the said Meede to allowe to your petitioner yerelie so much as the same want of 60ˡ per Ann.

"Fowerthlie, the said Meede doth not paye your petitioner the rent of 100ˡⁱ per Ann for the house, but refuseth to paye it, and combineth with those [who] oppose your petitioners title, to defeate your petitioner of the possession of the said house and his interest therein.

"Fifthlie, the said Jacobbe Meede, not payenge his rent nor performinge the articles made betweene your petitioner and the said Meede, your petitioner warnd the said Meede to forbeare to baite the said beares, but the said Meede continewed baytinge, notwithstandinge which the petitioner did not hinder."

It may be doubted whether this is the termination of the paper, as it concludes abruptly, but no more is extant. It is not in Alleyn's hand-writing, but it was wrapped up in the

annexed statement, which was written by the founder, and contains particularities of grievance in themselves curious.

"Imprim. 1 demaund the rentes dwe unto me since my mothers decease.

" 2 The stock of beares, bulls, doggs and other things apertayning to the personall estate of Phillip Henslowe, nott by hym bequeathed.

" 3 60^l per Ann^m for the use of my Comission for so longe as the said Jacob hath used the same [' 3 yeeres' in the margin.]

" The rentes accrew by 2 Leases, the one from Phill. Henslowe, the other from Annis Henslowe and my selfe: the rentes dwe by bothe these leases att mydsomer next is 200^l.

" Now Jacobs answer to this can be but that he paid the said rentes where he thought in his conscienc they were dwe; but the trueth is for to gayne to hym self a firme leas for 21 yeares, for that booth the other leases went with conditions and lymitations, and Jacob entred into on bond of 300^l for performance of the covenantes, and an other bond of 200^l to stand to an arbitrement.

" For the stock, that is playnly sett downe in a sedule which Jacob is to make good in his first lease, and when my mother lett hym the other moyety, we were about to frame a new sedule; but after considering that by the first lease and sedule he was charged with such a stock, and now in the second lease the whole state demised unto hym, we forbore to make any new sedull, the first being still in force. But some small cubbs which weare bread up betwixt my father and hym as a surplusage of the stock, I rec. mony for my mothers part, and so likewise of some hoggs.

" Nowe his answer wilbe for the stock that they wear all dead before my father dyed, or that he hath already paid for them or some such like.

" For the 60^l per Ann^m for my Comission he will saye ther is more then that owing me off the Court in fees and rewardes, according to his covenaunt.

" Lett that apere, and I shalbe satisfied allthough I never receive itt.

" But that allowances must amount to above 60^l per Ann, besides M^{rs} fee of 14^d per diem, in respeckt ther was 60^l allwayes paid and allowed for the Comission by the farmer theroff many years agoe, who never had any thing to doe with the fe 14^d per dyem."

Whether the preceding papers did or did not relate to the arbitration, referred to in Alleyn's Diary under date of 25th April, 1619, there is good reason to believe that the

M

points in difference were settled, though not till after the lapse of some months. On the 22nd September, 1619, Alleyn thus congratulated himself:—" I went to town to meet with Jacob. I dind with Jacob, Mr Adys and Mr Foster, and wee concluded our matters, both with him and Tho. Angell: blessed be the God of peac."*

CHAPTER XVII.

Alleyn's Accumulation of Property—His Purchase of the Manor of Lewisham — God's Gift College also a Boarding-school — Mrs. Henslowe's Death — Burning of the Fortune Theatre—Its Reconstruction; and the mode in which the Money for the purpose was raised — Alleyn's Leases of various Shares to his Tenants—Charles Massye's Counterpart — Date of the Completion of the New Theatre.

NOTWITHSTANDING Alleyn's heavy outlay for the College, he seems still to have gone on accumulating, and his purchases, whether leasehold or freehold, as he told Sir F. Calton, prospered in his hands. On the 21st April, 1621, he thus enumerates the rents he paid quarterly.

" The K's Matie for the Bancksyde . . .	13 17	5†
Mr Billson	1 0	0
Mr Luntley	3 10	0
Mr Travis	40 0	0
Mr Danson	2 10	0
Mr Cuxsone	7 10	0
The K's rent for Lewshame . . .	14 14	6
To Mr Watsons rent	9 17	6
Mr Sedley for Lewshame	75 0	0"

* Several entries respecting Jacob Meade, of a subsequent date, look as if Alleyne and he had been engaged in some common cause, defending their rights with respect to Paris Garden; but the expressions are general and ambiguous.

† This was the same amount of rent as he had paid on 22nd Oct., 1617. " Pd the Kings rent for the Bancke, 13^{li} 17^s. 5^d."—Diary.

It is to be remarked that we have no means of knowing what Alleyn received, only what he paid; so that we cannot tell to what advantage he sub-let any part of the property. Lewisham appears here for the first time, for he had completed the purchase of the manor and parsonage rather more than three months before. On the 11th December, 1620, he records, " I was in London with Sir Jo. Wildgosse about the maner of Lewishame ;" and on the 15th of the same month he says, " This daye I paid for the maner and parsonage of Lewisham £1000."* This was in itself a large sum, and we have just seen that he had besides to pay rent to the king to the extent of £58 18s. per annum for one part of the manor, and of £300 per annum to Mr. Sedley for another part. The rent of £160 per annum to Mr. Travis was for the Blackfriars, and no doubt he sub-let the theatre and other tenements at a considerably improved rent. Had the book of Alleyn's receipts, as well as of his payments, been recovered, we should have seen at once what proportion of his income was derived from these various sources. He makes a memorandum that, as lord of the manor, he " kept the first Court at Lewisham" on the 16th April, 1621. He had some copyhold property also in Lambeth Marsh, and for this he regularly enters the payment of quit-rent.† He also paid quit-rent and tithes for the Fortune, or for part of the ground on which it stood.‡

Besides the poor children who were gratuitously fed, taught,

---

* Among the miscellaneous papers at Dulwich is a list, dated 20th March, 1622, of persons to be fined for non-attendance upon juries, &c., in which Alleyn is termed " his Majesty's farmer of the maner of Lewisham."

† On October 2nd, 1621, the following memorandum was made by Alleyn. " This daye att a Court held in Kenington I was admitted tenaunt;" but of what he does not any where mention: probably of some copyhold houses or lands.

‡ In his will Alleyn mentions " all my lands in Yorkshire, *lately* purchased of George Cole." Of this acquisition we have no other notice.

and clothed, boys were also taken in to be boarded and educated; but whether the sums paid on this account went to the master and usher of the school, or to increase the general funds of the College, must be left to conjecture. On the 15th June, 1620, we read the following—" Mem: that Mr Rogers sent this daye his three sones att boord and scholing, for 12^{li} per Ann. a peece;" and on the 12th September of the same year occurs the subsequent entry: " This day Mr Woodwards sone came to sojorne and be taught here, at 20^{li} per Ann."

Agnes Henslowe, the mother of Alleyn's wife, having died shortly before the commencement of the Diary from which so many of the preceding particulars are taken, on the 6th February, 1617-18, Alleyn paid two shillings for " bringing in the inventorie of my mother," as he always called her. On the 28th June, 1618, he enters, " This daye was Judith Alleyn, the daughter of Mathias Alleyn, buried."

The statutes of the College evince the founder's partiality to the name of Alleyn, or Allen, since they require that the master and warden shall bear it; and he seems always to have given a preference to persons who were called Allen, whether they did or did not belong to his family. Thus on one occasion he invited an Irish preacher to dine with him because he was an Allen. He was also on terms of intimacy with Sheriff Allen, and " Allen the Goldsmith." On the 27th January, 1621-2, he makes the subsequent memorandum. " This day I took a pore fatherless child, Ed. Alleyn;" and, on the 22nd August, 1622, he states that another " Nedd Alleyn" came to reside at the College.

During the five years to which this record applies the founder was much invited out to the houses of the nobility and gentry. He dined with the Lord Treasurer, the Archbishop of Canterbury, the Bishops of London and Winchester, the Speaker of the House of Commons, the Master of the Rolls, Sir Richard Smith, Count Gondomar the Spanish Ambassador, Sir T. Grymes, the Countess of Kildare, the Dean of

St. Paul's, the Lord Mayor of London, &c. In the same way various persons of distinction came to partake of Alleyn's hospitality at his College.

When he went to London he not unfrequently dined, as he states, at Lady Clark's; but most commonly, when he was upon business, he resorted with his friends to houses of public entertainment. He was accustomed to go to Young's ordinary, and to Hart's ordinary near the Fortune; to the Bear, the Horn, the Mermaid, the Cardinal's Hat, the Bell (in Westminster), the Dancing Bears (near Paris Garden), the Paul's Head, the Bull's Head, the King's Arms, the Red Cross, the Three Tuns (in Southwark), the Hart (in Smithfield), and a place he calls "Dolls," which seems to have been near the Rose theatre.

By a letter from John Chamberlain to Sir Dudley Carleton we learn, that the Fortune Theatre was consumed by fire on the Sunday night preceding the 15th of December (Hist. of Engl. Dram. Poetry and the Stage, iii. 309); but Alleyn in his Diary furnishes the precise date of this calamity in the subsequent entry:—

" ☞ 1621. Dec. 9. Md. this night att 12 of the Clock the Fortune was burnt."

The loss to him must have been considerable, but he makes not the slightest observation in reference to it; and not long afterwards, as appears by other notes, he set about the reconstruction of the theatre. Thus we read, "Dinner at the Hart in Smithfeild, with the builders of the Fortune:" "I went to Westminster to meet the workmen of the Fortune:" "I met the workmen at Ric: Gunnells." &c. On the 13th May, 1622, he made the first payment of £25 upon it. On the 12th June he went to Lord Arundell's, and shewed him the ground-plot of the new edifice, which was a large round brick building, and not a square wooden house, as before. (Hist. of Engl. Dram. Poetry and the Stage, iii. 309.) On

the 19th July Allen informs us that he "sold the lease of the Fortune," by which he means that he sold the lease of a part of it before it was reconstructed; for, as we shall presently see, he divided it into twenty-four shares, and at various dates disposed of separate leases of each share to different parties. Thus he had many tenants, and a divided responsibility as to payment, which was a very prudent course for him to adopt. These leases were not all sold or sealed on 6th September, 1622, when Alleyn adds as follows to one of his memoranda:—"From thence to the Fortune, and dind with Mr Axell and gave his wife for Mr Houghton 20^s.* I gave his man 6^d and her mayd 6^d. So I sealled att Underwoods † the Fortune Leases, and so came home." This is the last we hear of the Fortune upon the same authority.

However, he left behind him quite as indisputable evidence to shew what he did with this property, and how he contrived to have it rebuilt without drawing on his own purse.

He divided it, as has been remarked, into twenty-four shares, letting each share upon a lease for fifty-one years, at a rent of £5 6s. 11d., requiring the tenant of every share to pay down, in the first instance, the sum of £41 13s. 4d. towards the rebuilding. Thus he raised a capital of £1000 for completing the new structure, and secured to himself an income of £128 6s. a year afterwards. These facts are esta-

* There was a player of the name of Robert Axell, or Axen, and this, no doubt, was he with whom Alleyn dined. Mr. Houghton was very likely the old play-poet, William Houghton, or Haughton, whose name often occurs in Henslowe's Diary. He was, perhaps, at this time old, and necessitous. There was also a " young Haughton."

† Henry Underwood was probably a scrivener, but there was an actor named John Underwood, of whom we first hear in 1601, when he was one of the children of the chapel. In 1620 he was one of the King's Servants, and so he seems to have continued in 1623; but, perhaps, he was also a speculator in the Fortune theatre on the recommencement of performances after the fire. Actors were often interested in the receipts of more than one playhouse.

blished by the existence at Dulwich College of the counterparts (or "counterpanes," as they are called in the indorsements) of two leases to Charles Massye* and Richard Price (both actors), which are exact copies of each other, and one of which is subjoined. It bears date on the 20th May, 1622, but it was, probably, one of those executed at Underwood's, on the 6th September, having been prepared ready for signature some time before.

"This Indenture made the twentith day of May Anno Dom. 1622, and in the yeeres of the raigne of our Soveraigne Lord James by the grace of god king of England, Scotland, Fraunce and Ireland, Defendor of the Faith &c. That is to say of England Fraunce and Ireland the twentith, and of Scotland the five and fiftith. Betweene Edward Alleyn of Dulwich in the County of Surrey, Esquire, of thone part, and Charles Massy of London, gent, of thother part. Witnesseth, that whereas the said Edward Alleyn the day of the date of these presentes is seized in his desmeane as of fee of and in all that part or parcell of ground upon part whereof lately stood a Playhouse or building, called the Fortune, with a Taphouse belonging to the same, a tenement in the occupation of Marke Briggum, one other tenement heretofore demised to one John Russell, one other tenement in the occupation of William Bird, alias Bourne, and one other tenement in the occupation of John Parson, conteyning in breadth from East to West one hundred and thirty foote, and in length one hundred and thirty one foote and eight inches or thereabout, abutting on the East West North and South as is specified in a plottforme. And is also seized of and in one other messuage or tenement contayning a shopp, a chamber and a garrett towards the streete, and two roomes and a garrett behinde the same, and

* Alleyn seems to have been very kind to Massye, and possibly the loan to him of £50, solicited in a letter already inserted, enabled him afterwards to save money enough to pay down £41 13s. 4d. towards the reconstruction of the Fortune, and to yield Alleyn a yearly rent of £5 6s. 11d. An item in the founder's Diary, dated 19th November, 1622, would seem to shew that Massye had then taken a benefit at the Fortune theatre, and that Alleyn had presented him with 5s. : it is, "Given Charles Massye at his playe 0. 5. 0," and it is the only entry of the kind. This was about three weeks before the Fortune was consumed, at which date it was in possession of the company called "The Palsgrave's Servants," who, as has been shewn, were formerly the players of Prince Henry.

one yard thereto belonging, late in the tenure of William Garrell, and now in the occupation of Henry Smith, scituate on the North side of the way leading to the said Playhouse, all scituate lying and being betweene Whitecrosse streete and Golding lane, in the parish of S^t. Giles without Cripplegate in the county of Midd. upon part of which said ground there is intended to be erected and sett upp a new Playhouse. Now this Indenture witnesseth, that the said Edward Alleyn, as well for and in consideration of the rentes hereunder reserved, as also for that the said Charles Massy is to pay or cause to be paid unto Anthony Jarman and Thomas Wigpitt for the new building and erecting of a Playhouse in Golding lane aforesaid, according to the plottforme by them allready drawne, for his part the somme of forty one pounds thirteene shillings and fourpence, proportionally according to the foure and twentith part thereof, and according to such dayes and tymes as in one paire of indentures of Articles of Agreement, indented bearing date with these presentes, made betweene Thomas Wigpitt Cittizen and Bricklayer of London and Anthony Jarman Cittizen and Carpinter of London of thone part, and Thomas Sparkes, Cittizen and Merchanttaylor of London, William Gwalter Cittizen and Innholder of London, Richard Gunnell of London, gent, Charles Massy of London, gent, Richard Price of London, gent, Adam Islipp of London, Stationer, John Fisher of London, Barber Chirurgeon, Edward Jackson of London, gent, and Frauncis Juby of Southwark in the County of Surrey widowe of thother part, him, the said Edward Alleyn hereunto especially moving, hath demised graunted and to ferme letten, and by these presentes doth demise graunt and to ferme lett unto the said Charles Massy one part of the said ground and premisses, in foure and twenty equall partes to be devided, with all easements wayes and passages, proffits and commodities thereunto belonging or in any wise appertayning, to have and to hold the said one part of the said ground and premisses, in foure and twenty equall partes to be devided as is aforesaid, with all and every thappurtenances, unto the said Charles Massy his executors administrators and assignes, from the feast day of the Nativity of S^t. John Baptist next ensuing the date hereof unto the full end and tearme of fiftie and one yeares from thence next ensuing and fully to be compleate and ended, yeilding and paying therefore, yeerely and every yeere during the said terme, unto the said Edward Alleyn his heires or assignes, five pounds six shillings and eleaven pence of lawfull English money at foure most usuall feastes or termes in the yeere, that is to say S^t. Michaell tharchangell, the Birth of our Lord god, thannunciation of our blessed Lady S^t. Mary the virgin, and the Nativity of S^t. John Baptist, by even and equall portions at or in the College called Godsgifte in Dulwich aforesaid. And the said Charles

Massy for him his executors administrators and assignes doth covenant promise and graunt to and with the said Edward Alleyn his heires and assignes by these presentes, that he the said Charles Massy his executors administrators and assignes, the said one part of the said ground and premisses, in foure and twenty equall partes to be devided, and likewise one part of foure and twenty equall partes to be devided of all buildings and edifices which shall hereafter be erected and sett upp upon the said plott of ground or upon any part or parcell thereof, or of any the premisses, in by and with all manner of needful and necessary reparations whatsoever well and sufficiently for and concernyng the said foure and twentith part, shall repayre, uphold, susteyne, fence, maintaine and keepe, and the pavementes, wayes and passages leading to the said plott of ground and premisses shall well and sufficiently pave, repayre, amend, rateably according to the foure and twentith part thereof as is aforesaid, from tyme to tyme when and as often as neede shall require during the said terme. And in the end of the said terme, or other sooner determination of this present lease, the said foure and twentith part of ground and premisses so demised as aforesaid and the buildings thereupon to be erected as aforesaid, soe well and sufficiently repayred upholden, susteyned maintayned kept paved and amended, shall leave surrender and yeild up unto the said Edward Alleyn his heires or assignes. And further, that it shall and may be lawfull to and for the said Edward Alleyn his heires and assignes, with workemen and others at his and their willes and pleasures, twice in every yeere yeerely or oftener during the said terme, at convenient tymes to enter and come into all the said buildings and premisses, there to view search and see the state of the reparations of the same, and if any default or want of reparations then and there be upon any such view found thereof to give or leave notice or warneing in writing to or for the said Charles Massy or to his executors administrators or assignes to repayre and amend all and every such decayes, defaultes, or wantes of reparations according to the rateable proportion of the foure and twentith part thereof as is aforesaid, within sixe monthes next ensueing such warneing given. And further, the said Charles Massy for him his executors administrators and assignes doth covenant promise and graunt to and with the said Edward Alleyn his heires and assignes by these presentes, that he the said Charles Massy his executors administrators or assignes shall not at any tyme hereafter devide part, alter, transport or otherwise convert the said one part of the said ground and premisses, in foure and twenty equall partes to be devided, or any the edifices and buildings that now are or shalbe hereafter erected and sett upp as is aforesaid, to any other use or uses then as a Playhouse for recreation of his Majesty's subjectes his heires and successors. Provided alwayes, and it is covenanted

condiscented, concluded and fully agreed upon by and betweene the said parties to these presentes, that if it shall happen the said yeerely rent of five poundes sixe shillings and eleaven pence, or any part or parcell thereof, to be behinde and unpaide by the space of eight and twenty dayes next after any feaste or terme of payment thereof in which the same ought to be paid at the place aforesaid, or if the said Charles Massy, his executors administrators or assignes, doe not for his and their partes pay or cause to be paid unto the aforesaid Anthony Jarman and Thomas Wigpitt severally such sommes of money, for their part and proportion of the said Playhouse according to the lymitation of the aforesaid Articles of Agreement, or if the said reparations be not well and sufficiently done within the tyme and lymitation above said, and all and every other the covenantes, promises, and agreementes abovesaid, which on the part and behalfe of the said Charles Massy his executors, administrators and assignes are and ought to be performed and kept, be not well and sufficiently observed, performed, fulfilled and kept according to the intent and true meaning of these presentes, that then and at all tymes after, it shall and may be lawfull to and for the said Edward Alleyn his heires and assignes into all and singular the said demised premisses wholly to reenter, and the same to have againe, repossesse and enjoy as in his and their former estate, and the occupiers thereof from thence utterly to expell, putt out and amove, anything herein contayned to the contrary hereof in any wise notwithstanding. In witnes whereof the parties first above named to these present Indentures their seales, either to other, interchangably have putt. Yeoven the day and yeere first above written.

" CHARLES MASSYE.

" Sealed and delivered in the presence of

" HENR. UNDERWOOD.
" MATHIAS ALLEYN."

How long it occupied to build the new theatre we have no precise information, Alleyn's Diary not coming down to so late a date; but it was certainly finished by the 29th January, 1623, because on that day Alleyn granted a lease to Margaret Gray of two twenty-fourth (or one twelfth, as it is called in the instrument) shares of the Fortune, at a yearly rent of £10 13s. 10d., with the same covenants as in the lease to Massye, with a difference in the description of the property, inasmuch as it is stated in Margaret Gray's lease that the edifice was " one new Play-house or building

called the Fortune, with a Tap-house belonging to the same, being a tenement now in the occupation of one Robert Hart." On the 20th February following, Alleyn granted a similar lease of a twenty-fourth share to George Bosgrave, which is likewise extant. At this date, therefore, the house was finished, and ready for the performance of dramatic entertainments. We have the evidence of Thomas Heywood, whose " English Traveller" was printed in 1633, having been acted, in all probability, at the Fortune after its reconstruction, that " the picture of Dame Fortune" was exposed on the outside of the house as its sign. No doubt such had been the case from the period when it was first opened by Henslowe and Alleyn in the very commencement of the seventeenth century.

CHAPTER XVIII.

Death of Alleyn's first Wife — Her Character — Alleyn's Courtship of his second Wife — Alleyn's Letter to Dr. Donne after having married his Daughter—Alleyn's desire to obtain a Knighthood—Letter to him from Henry Gibb upon the subject—Alleyn's acquaintance with Sir W. Alexander—Original Stanzas addressed by the latter to the former.

THE inscription on the flat stone over the grave in the chapel in Dulwich College states that Alleyn's first wife, Joane Woodward, whom he had married in October, 1592, died on the 28th of June, 1623. This was only about nine months after the close of Alleyn's autograph diary or account-book at Michaelmas, 1622, and she seems to have enjoyed good health during the whole of the five years to which that MS. relates. Her husband never hints at any indisposition on her part, and there is not a single entry of any payment for medicine or attendance for her. They seem to have lived together for more than thirty years in uninterrupted comfort and harmony: Alleyn was a man of a quiet and contented temper, and his

wife most likely possessed an amiable and complying disposition, looking up with respect and admiration to her husband, and happy to second his plans and purposes. When he went out to visit his friends she usually accompanied him, and one of the very latest entries is of this kind:—"Sep. 24 [1622] I and my wife dined at Sir Tho. Grymes;" and there is not a syllable in any of the papers at Dulwich to show that they ever had the slightest disagreement.

The taking of a second wife has been held by some a tribute to the first, or, at all events, to the matrimonial state: if so, Alleyn appears to have paid that tribute early; since we have it upon his own admission, that on the 23rd of October, 1623, less than four months after the death of his wife Joane, he was in treaty with the father of his second wife, whose christian name appears to have been Constance. What was her surname has been questioned: the General Biographical Dictionary asserts broadly that it was Kinchtoe, and that Alleyn married her "about two years" after the death of his first wife. This is clearly an error, and the documents preserved at Dulwich strongly support the tradition that she was a daughter of Dr. Donne. Alleyn's Diary shows that he was acquainted with Donne, for he records under date of the 23rd of May, 1620, " Mr. Donne preached here," meaning in the College Chapel; and on the 20th of July, in the following year, it appears that Dr. Donne visited Alleyn. The memorandum is this: "I herd Dr. Done at Camberwell, and after dind with Sir Thomas Grymes. They and Mr. Angell came to Dull. in the after none." Now, Sir Thomas Grymes appears to have been a person very much concerned in the negotiation for the marriage of Alleyn with his second wife Constance, and we find, under Alleyn's own hand, that his father-in-law was of a "reverend calling." This fact, and other particulars of a highly interesting nature in relation to the biographies both of Alleyn and Donne, are contained in the copy of a letter found at Dulwich, which has no date, but must have been written

after the 24th of January, 1624-5, because it is scribbled very illegibly by Alleyn on the spare spaces of a letter to him of that date from William Becher the elder, recommending a poor man for reception into the College. Alleyn was then married, and he enters into a variety of curious details respecting the whole affair, alleging that the union had been hastened by Dr. Donne's illness, and showing that serious disputes had subsequently arisen between him and Dr. Donne on the subject of money, in the course of which the latter had even gone so far as to give the lie to the former. Here, also, we find it distinctly stated by Alleyn, that a portion of his property was "the playhouse" in the Blackfriars, which was worth £120 a year, exclusive, we suppose, of the other tenements. This is the interest which in a former part of the present memoir it has been conjectured he purchased from Shakespeare. The whole of what follows will be read with great curiosity: as already mentioned, it is from the original in Alleyn's handwriting, and in some places it is penned so illegibly as to be deciphered with considerable difficulty.

"Sir. Your unkind, unexpected and undeserved deniall off the common curtesie afforded to a frend asking the loane off unusefull money, which yourselfe som few dayes before, I making you acquainted with all my proceedings, did then so lovingly grant unto, besides voluntary offer of 500^{li} more then I entreated, and your after repetition off it to Sir Tho. Grymes, made me wonder what so strangely altered your mind at the very pointe of my occasion: and trewly, Sir, I can nott dwell in quiett till I bee in som sort resolved herin, and to that end I have examined my selfe, in all my proceedinges towching you and yours, to see if I cowld find any such cawse of offenc in me to move you to this bad dealing; and surly I can find none. Yet it seems you conceive it wholy to bee in me, but I hope I shall allwayes be able before god and the world well and trewly to cleer my selfe off the least breach of any jott of that promise I first made, and for your better remembranc, I pray you, look backe and revert to the whole process off the business, which as farre as I can remember I will here trewly sett downe.

"Then thus: after motion made by Sir Tho. Grymes on both sides, I was envited to your house the 21 of october 1623, wher after dinner in your parlor you declard your intention to bestow with your daughter Con. all

the benefitt of your pryme Leet which, as you said, you knew would shortly be received, and that you were assured iff I stayd till michaellmass next to bee worth 500ᵘ att the least, and when so ever it showld rise to more it showld wholy be hirs. My offer was to doe as much for her as your selfe, and add to that at my death 500ᵘ more, and so her estat should be a 1000ᵘ. This gave you content ; and Sir Tho. perswaded me to doe some what more which I did, and promis'd to leave her at my death 2000 markes. This was accepted and security demanded. I then towld you all my landes were stated on the Coll. 3 leases I had, one of them was given to the Coll. the other 2 being the manor and recktory of Lewsham worth 120ᵘ a year, and divers tenementes in the Black-friars, as the plaie howse theare, worth 120ᵘ the year, booth which cost me 2500ᵘ: iff nowe my statute or recognisance would serve, those 2 leases should be past over to some persone in trust that after my death, shee surviving, should be leaft 2000 markes. This was accepted on all sides, and your selfe being calld away by the coming of some Ladyes, you tooke your leave of Sir Tho., and referd the accomplishing of these businesses to his direction.

"I presently returned to Peekham, and coming then to Con. towld her what had past; and more, to show my love to her, off my owne voluntary, I towld her before Sir Tho. I would make it upp 1500ᵘ, which was then by your selfe and Sir Tho. extraordinary contented with. All this while there was no 200ˡ a yeere spoken off nor any other joynter, but so muche mony at my death : tis trew itt wase thought more convenient for her to have 200ᵘ a yeere then 1500ʰ in money, and as I sayd divers tymes iff god enabled me, 1 shalbe more willing to doe itt, and soe it was a desire rather then a promise.* Thus past itt on till the begining of your sicknesse, and then you desire our maryag should be performd with as much speed as might bee; for as you sayd the world tooke surer knowledge of itt, and for what wase promisd on your part, iff god lent you lyfe should be really performd.† I directly went on, urging you to nothing, but rested wholy on your bare word (which I then thowght 10 tymes the valew could not make you breake). Itt is now allmoste 3 quarters sinc our maryag: I have all this tyme loved her, kept her and maynteyned her, and never thought to have so great a cause off discontent as your selfe now gave.

* In his will Alleyn left his wife £1500, secured upon his property in Southwark, consisting of the "capital messuage and Inn" called the Unicorn, and three other houses with the signs of the Barge, the Bell, and the Cock. He also gave her £100 in money for "present use." Sir Nicholas Carew of Beddington, and Sir Thomas Grymes of Peckham, were trustees for Mrs. Alleyn under the will.

† It is known that Dr. Donne had so severe an illness about this period, that his life was considered in danger.

" Thus I may safly take god and the world to witness I have with trew love and affection performd all that ought to be don on my part to you and yours. My conscience knowing made me angred att your soudeyn deniall of that which before you had graunted, and delever those passionat wordes you tooke so hanously, seeing thereby I must be branded either for a foole or a knave in the business I had undergone; but itt seems itt wase your desire to drive me into that defenc, els you would never continew me in hope till very late, and then forste me uppon all termes; but the Lord judge this caus beetwen you and me, and so the Lord deale with me, either in mercie or judgment, as I had a trew intention to doe good to those pore men, and no wrong to you nor yours. My language you tooke so harsh was this — that I now perceived you esteemd 500^{li} befor my honesty, yea, my reputation, or your daughters good. You presently being enflamd sayd, that it was false, and a lye, wordes in my mynd fitting you 30 years ago, when you might be questiond for them, then now under so revereut a calling as you are. But as fals as you suppos them, I wish they prove not all trew, for some off them, I am to well assurd off before this violenc brake forth. You calld me a playn man: I desire alwayes so to be, for I thank god I never could deceive in my lyfe, and I am to owld now to turne [and] wear it off, the cursedst felow in Christendom. My hart and tong must goe to gather, and allthough this be thought great folly in the world, yett I hope [it] will easely forgive the fault, iff it be one. Therefore, sinc I am willing to be so as your knowledg long held of me, I pray you pardon such faultes as my hart in its playness committes.

" And now in playne termes give me leave to enquire what faultes of myne hath caused so manie unkind passages in you? as first after our mariage, before Sir Tho. Grymes upon your recovery, the people all giving joy, you then promised to send my wyfe her mothers embroiderd lynnen for new years guift. After that my wyfe had a great desire to a little nagg off yours, for her owne selfe to use for her health to take the ayre, and hearing you many tymes saye it did you no servis, caused her brother George to move you for itt on her be half, which she making no doubt of was very much hurt in, but to prevent her of the comfort, the nagg was suddeynly sent away to Oxenford. Again, she having but 2 dyamond ringes you wisht me to tell her you were importund for your owne, and if she would send you itt, you would return her the ring with the stone you received in lew thereof. I brought you your owne, but the other you have still. Again; one tyme you towld me in the great Chamber you had 9^{cli} for the Leet, but Con. should have but 500^{li}, when as you allways promised the uttermost valew. Agayn, you were very fond to wish me to [be] as bowld in your house as in my owne, and to take a lodging at any tyme when I pleasd; but when I towld you this term my occasion would have me in town, and

that I was willing to accept your former loving offer, you aunswerd, moe with favour, and so I took itt. Many tymes have I moved you for matters of indifference belonging to your place, but they were eather put by to circumstance, or flattly denyed.

"All these backward favors, was it for some fault in me or your judgement? but you can not find itt, unless it be to much commodyty to trust wordes in sted off deedes. For my wyfe's mony I should receave, you may conceave I desire itt owt of covetousness: itt is coveting that to make itt better for her, and iff you can imploy itt more for her good then I intend, of your own discretion: for the enlarging of my own estate I never desired itt, for I thank my good god I have enough for my selfe and others, but my care in this was onely for her, which, I thank you, you now took from me.

"In this little tyme of our so nere aquaintanc iff ever you had found me as a man alltogether unfitt to receave any frendly curtesie off your handes, for I here you profess it largly to severall persons, then for a conclusion lett me entreat you, as I find you no waye willing to my furtheranc, so be not any ways a meane of my hindranc; and as your daughter Luce is good companie for my wife, so your ability is better able to bear her charge then myn. And thus, beeing a playn man, I hope you will pardon me in delivering my mind in playn termes, yet ever ready with my best love to your daughter, and my best servis to you, I —— &c."

The whole contents of this singular and valuable relic serve to illustrate very forcibly the character which we have seen Alleyn from the first so consistently sustain.

Alleyn's second marriage had taken place "almost three-quarters" of a year before the preceding letter was written. In July 1624, Alleyn entertained some ambitious views with regard to rank, not hinted at by any of his biographers. He was lord of the manors of Dulwich and Lewisham, the owner of much land and several houses in those manors, the chief proprietor, as far as we can now learn, of the Blackfriars Theatre, and the sole owner of the Fortune, besides having lands in Yorkshire, estates in Bishopgate, and in the parish of Lambeth. The former possessor of much of the property which had devolved into his hands, as well as the holder of the office he filled, had been knighted, and Alleyn seems to have entertained the hope of himself enjoying the

same distinction. Such is the interpretation which, we apprehend, must be put upon the following letter, obviously written by some Scotch gentleman about the person of the king, to whom Alleyn had resorted for advice and assistance, in return, perhaps, for having received a poor boy upon his charitable foundation at Dulwich.

> "To my much respected and loveinge friend, Mr Alleyn, at his hous at Dulwith, thes dd.
>
> "Sir
> "I receavd your letter wherby I understand that you have now receavd the boy I wrett unto you for, and of your cair towardes him, wherof I doubt not, and for the which I kyndly thank yow. I understand by it also your desire to have sum further dignetie conferd uppon you, according to the qualetie of the place wherin you serve, wherof I should be very glad, and will not only advise, but assist with all willingnes. But for the present I can not satisfie yow so weill as I wold, in regaird yow know that now we ar in prograsse and still staieinge; but if yow will be pleased, my opinion is that yow defer a litell, untill sutch tyme as the K be cumminge homward nere Windsor forrest, against when I shall speik with all these men that Mr Holliburton speiks of, and see how I find them affected towards him; and do all I can for your advantage, always reservinge to my self who the party is: and shall not faill to send you adverteisment by a lyne or twoo, what I shall learne. And in the meane tyme if I can any way, ather in that or to any other of your desirs, be usfull, latt me butt know, and gif your self the assurance that non shall be reddier to satisfie them, then
> "Your loveinge freind in what I cane,
> "Westminster this   "HENRY GIBB.
> 23d of July 1624."

If the inference we have drawn from the preceding communication be correct, it supplies an incident not by any means in keeping with the general tenor of Alleyn's tranquil and retiring character. It is very possible that his second wife had induced him to make the application, and that he rather sought to gratify her wishes than his own. James I. had rendered knighthood cheap, in every sense of the word, and if money alone had been necessary, Alleyn could have found no difficulty in accomplishing the object; but it is very likely

that his origin and early occupation stood materially in his way, and we certainly have no evidence that his friend Gibb was ever able to obtain what was desired. The expressions in the preceding letter of " some further dignity," " according to the quality of the place wherein you serve," may be said to be a little equivocal, but the communication does not read as if Alleyn's wish were merely to procure some higher situation at court.

At about this period, and earlier, Alleyn appears to have been upon terms of friendship with Sir William Alexander, the distinguished poet, (afterwards Earl of Stirling,) now high in favour with King James. We do not find that he was in any way applied to to forward Alleyn's design in procuring " some further dignity;" and among the miscellaneous papers at Dulwich are four stanzas, addressed by Sir William Alexander to Alleyn, which are not of a complexion to lead us to suppose that he suspected any such ambitious disposition in the founder of Dulwich College. The lines were probably written some years anterior to the date to which we are now adverting; and they sufficiently intelligibly allude to the profession to which Alleyn had been bred, and in which " he far exceeded both ancients and moderns:" they also notice the " better state" to which Alleyn had risen, but justly speak of his great work of charity, as if he had had no worldly purpose in commencing and completing it. We may take this opportunity of inserting them as an addition to the poetical remains of so distinguished an author.

"To his deservedlie honored frend Mr. Edward Allane, the first founder and Master of the Colleige of God's Gift.

"Some greate by birth or chance, whom fortune blindes,
 Where (if it were) trew vertue wold burst forth,
 They, since not haveing, can afford no worth,
 And by their meanes doe but condemne their myndes.
  To honour such I should disgrace my penne,
  Who might prove more, I count them lesse then men.

"But thee to praise I dare be bould indeade,
By fortunes strictnesse whilst at first suppress'd,
Who at the height of that which thou profess'd
Both ancients, moderns, all didst farr exceede;
  Thus vertue many ways may use hir pow'r;
  The Bees draw honnie out of evrie flow'r.

"And when they state was to a better chang'd,
That thou enabled wast for doing goode,
To clothe the naked, give the hungrie foode,
As one that was from avarice estrang'd:
  Then what was fitt thou scorn'd to seeke for more,
  Whilst bent to doe what was design'd before.

"Then prosecute this noble course of thyne
As prince or priest for state, in charge though none,
For acting this brave part, when thou art gone,
Thy fame more bright then somes' more high shall shyne.
  Since thou turnd great, who this worlds stage doe trace,
  With whom it seemes thou hast exchangd thy place.
                        "W. ALEXANDER."

CHAPTER XIX.

Alleyn only twice married—His Will and Last Illness—George Coles' Letter to Alleyn—The Day of Alleyn's Death—Alms-houses built by him in Cripplegate, and ordered by his Will in St. Botolph and St. Saviour—Fragments of a former Will—Plays in which Alleyn was particularly concerned—Second Letter to him from T. Dekker—Conclusion.

WE are now rapidly drawing towards the close of the most useful, honourable, and benevolent career of Edward Alleyn. He adds one more proof to the many already existing, that life is generally much shortened, when a man, considerably past the prime and strength of his years, marries a comparatively young woman. How much younger the second Mrs. Alleyn was than her husband we have no means of deciding, as we know

not when Constance Donne (as we suppose her to have been) was born; but, in 1624, when their union took place, Alleyn was in his fifty-eighth year. There is a tradition in Dulwich College, and it has been mentioned by some of the biographers of Alleyn, that he was married three times; but not a particle of evidence to support it has been discovered. He lived with Joane Woodward (to whom he was united in 1592) until 1623, and then married Constance, who survived him, as appears by his will. It is true, he might have been a widower in 1592; but no hint of the kind is given in any of the extant papers, and we may therefore conclude, pretty confidently, that he was only twice married.

His will, which bears date 13th November, 1626, states that he was then "sick in body," and how long he had been ill before he made this final disposition of his property can only be conjectured: it appears that he had executed former wills, which were revoked by that which was proved by his executors, Thomas and Mathias Alleyn, whom the testator calls his "kinsmen," without mentioning the degree of their relationship. One letter is extant at Dulwich, which seems to shew that Alleyn was in his usual health in the middle of February, preceding his death in November; for it speaks of his coming to London upon business, and other matters, as if there were no infirmity to prevent him. It also mentions the claims of two persons of the name of Wright and Boyer, one for £50, and the other for £20, which Alleyn, for some unexplained cause, had not settled. Of course it could not arise from want of money, for Alleyn was affluent. The writer, Mr. George Cole, who had sold Alleyn some "lands in Yorkshire," was probably a barrister, and Alleyn's legal adviser upon a case which he had drawn, and upon which he had given his opinion. The nature of it does not appear; but we gather from it that Alleyn, almost to the last, was annoyed by the necessity of proceedings at law. He had evidently a strong dislike of contention, especially when it involved him in suits

and actions; and on one occasion, when stating in his Diary his quarterly expenses he put down a sum for "law," he added to the entry that it was the "worst of all" his charges. Cole's letter runs thus:

"To the wo⌞. his very loving frind, Edward Allen Esq, give thease att Dulledge.

"Sir, the bearer hearof, Mr. Henry Wright, hath ben with me for the 50ˡ due unto him, and saith that he was comming to you about it. I have therfore made a reconing with him, and given him satisfaction for the intrest till the end of Micaelmas terme last; and so there wilbe about 20ˢ for you to pay unto him, besides the 50ˡ uppon the vacating of the recognizance, which shalbe don when you come to London.

"I do entrete you to send Mr Allen to Mr Boyer in the Poultry, to give him content for his 20ˡ; and of the use we shal speake at your comming to London.

"I have drawne your Case, and set downe myne owne opinion, and you may have it written againe, and see the variety of opinions, if any be, uppon your Case, and then resolve what course you will take uppon them.

"Thus in hast, remembring my love to your wife, and referring divers conferences till your comming to London, I rest

"Your very lov. frind
"16 Febr. 1625."   "Geo Cole.

This is the latest extant document, with a date, we have been able to find at Dulwich: "16 Febr. 1625," was, of course, (according to the then mode of calculating the beginning of the year from Lady-day,) 16th Febr. 1626. Alleyn died on Saturday the 25th November following.

The precise day has hitherto been doubted, or mis-stated. Aubrey (as quoted in Lysons' "Environs," i. 96,) gives it "the twenty-first day of November 1626;" and an existing inscription on the flat stone in the chapel of the College, where he was buried, states that "the worthy founder departed this life Nov. 26 A.D. 1626, Ætat. 61." Both are wrong; and Aubrey probably misread "twenty-first" for "twenty-fift," as it was then commonly spelt; for, as we have said, the correct date is Saturday the twenty-fifth of November 1626. Before

the death of the founder, Thomas Alleyn became Master, and Mathias Alleyn Warden of the College, and it was the business of the latter to keep the accounts of the institution: his original book preserved at Dulwich commences thus, and ascertains the point in dispute beyond contradiction.

"The accompt of Mr Mathias Alleyn, Warden of the College of Godsguift, in Dulwich in the Countie of Surrey, from the death of the Fownder of the said College, viz the xxvth of November 1626, being Satterday, to Satterday the third day of November 1627."

The error in this particular has arisen, as in many other cases, from not consulting original and authentic documents. Alleyn's burial took place, as appears by the College Register, on the Monday immediately subsequent to his decease; and he especially charged his executors that his funeral should be plain and unostentatious, and that he should be buried in "Christ's Chapel," the name which the religious edifice, forming part of the College, had received at its consecration.

One of the provisions in Alleyn's will was, that his executors, Thomas and Mathias Alleyn, should build twenty Alms-houses, ten in the parish of St. Botolph, Bishopgate, and ten more in the parish of St. Saviour, Southwark. From his autograph Diary we have learned that he had himself superintended the construction of Alms-houses in the Liberty of Finsbury, near the Fortune Theatre, having "laid the first brick" on the 13th July, 1620. On the 29th April following, he placed "three men and seven women" in them; and on the 23d June, he paid £4 for five chaldrons of coals for the inhabitants of them. Therefore, as far as the parish of Cripplegate was concerned, the charitable work was accomplished in Alleyn's life-time; but he left it to his executors to fulfil the injunctions of his will in the parishes of St. Botolph and St. Saviour. At Dulwich is preserved a single sheet of what was obviously a former, and therefore a revoked will by Alleyn: his last will consisted of two sheets, but this

is clearly only a fragment, and injury to the paper has rendered it in some places illegible: it probably was the middle sheet of three, and the two outside sheets have been lost, or have perished; but it is in Alleyn's hand—is written in a very large clear character, and was signed by him at the conclusion. It was prepared before he had built the Almshouses in Finsbury, for in it he states his desire that such accommodation for the poor should be provided at the expence of his estate in three parishes; whereas, in his last will he names only two. As a particular declaration of his wishes and intentions, before the year 1620, it is worth preserving, and it begins abruptly as follows:—

"in theyr upper coates and capps, which I will shalbe black and off the same prisse and goodenes as the brothers and sisters are. And I will my Cosen Thomas Allen, barber surgion of London aforesayd, and his sone Edward Alleyn, my godson, and the survivor off them, in consideration off the legacie before given them, to be during theyr lyfe surgions to the Colledge, or to find and alowe a sufficient and skilfull persone for the performance theroff. And further more, for that I see the number of pore daly to encrease in and about the Cittye off London, being in theyr youth brought up to a faculty [def. in MS.] theyr age nott able to labore, receving pensions of ther parishe which will scarce find them bread, sitting att great rentes and nott able to pay, according to that tallent which god hath lent me I am desirus to resarve [def. in MS.] in the most needfull things viz House rent, fuell [def. in MS.] Therfor my will is to have in the 3 parishes in or nere London [def. in MS.] Almes Howses built; vid^u 10 in each parish, contayning one roome apece, and on such wast grownd as the said parishes will alowe for that purpose, which said howses [def. in MS.] 30 of the most aged and porest pencioners off the said parishes, and to those 30 persones I give unto everie one of them a gowne off the same goodnes, and att the same tyme the brothers and sisters shall receave theyrs, being one in 2 years, and on the 1 daye of September, and more I give to the said 30 persons on the same daye yearly to each off them, halfe a challdron off sea Coales, and tenn shillings a piece in money, to be paid and delevered unto each of them eather quarterly, or yearly upon the said first daye of September for ever: which 30 persones aforesaid shalbe taken and reputed as members of gods guift Colledge aforesaid for ever, and upon the death or departuer off any brother or sister off——

"E. ALLEYN."

There can be no doubt that this will was cancelled by Alleyn some time before his death, as he used the back of the sheet for the rough draft of his letter to Sir Francis Calton, already inserted. The subsequent is a document of a similar kind, also in the hand-writing of the founder: it is at the back of a deed, which precedes the Statutes of the College, and it refers to his "will," but in all probability to a former will, revoked by that of the 13th November, 1626 :—

"Item I ordeyn and for ever establish, that wheras I have given in my will to the Churchwardens off the parishe of s^t butolphe without beshopps gate London, and to theyr successors for ever, a tenement in Dullwich called the blew Howse, with the purtenances ther unto beelonging, now in the tenur of Edm. Kipping, for the only benefitt of the pore of the sd parish, shalbe thus disposed on and distrybuted, in maner and form following and no otherwise; that is to say, every year yearly for ever, on the first sonday in September after morning prayer, the whol years rent shalby sd Churchwardens [be] given to the most nedest pore off the sd parishe, 12^d apece, wherof the 10 members in the sd parish shalbe first payd 12^d apece, and after to as many more as the sd rent will rech unto."

Having corrected the date of the day of Alleyn's death, it may be necessary to give his age with exactness. The inscription on the stone over his tomb is, that he was " Ætat. 61." As he was born on September 1st, 1566, he was precisely sixty years, two months, and twenty-five days old when he died on the 25th November, 1626. There can be no possible doubt upon this point, because, as we have seen, Alleyn records his age very distinctly in his autograph Diary several times over.

There is one point of Alleyn's character upon which we have not touched in the course of the present memoir. It might be supposed, from certain memoranda in Henslowe's account-book, that Alleyn was an author: in August, 1602, he received £4 for " two books," " Philip of Spain," and " Longshanks;" in October of the same year he was paid

forty shillings for "his booke of Tambercame;" and on another occasion he was similarly remunerated for "a book" called "Machomett." Nevertheless, it is not to be supposed that he was concerned in the writing, though he very likely was instrumental in the getting up of those pieces, the unnamed poets having entrusted their productions to him in consequence of his interest in the theatre. "The plott of the first parte of Tamar Cam" was formerly preserved at Dulwich, and is printed in Malone's Shakespeare by Boswell, iii., 356. What was the precise nature of this species of performance we can only conjecture, but much of it appears to have consisted of dumb shew, accompanied by an explanatory chorus. Alleyn was an actor in it, and doubtless lent his assistance in preparing it for the stage; and in this way, possibly, he entitled himself to the forty shillings paid to him by Henslowe "at the appointment of the company." He might, however, only receive it in trust for those who were engaged with him in bringing it before the public.

Another production of the same description is "the Plott of Frederick and Basilea," in which the prologue and epilogue were spoken by Richard Alleyn, whom Steevens confounded with Edward Alleyn, observing that "as manager he took both prologue and epilogue to his own share." Edward Alleyn is throughout the piece called "Mr. Allen;" and Richard Alleyn, who delivered the prologue and epilogue, we know, entered the company on 25th March, 1598, as "a hired servant" to Henslowe. (Hist. Engl. Dram. Poetry and the Stage, iii., 431.) He might be some relation to Edward Alleyn, or he might be retained by Alleyn's influence merely on account of his name; for throughout life the founder of Dulwich College was fond of collecting round him persons who bore the same appellation. Of this various proofs have been already adduced, and the subsequent undated letter from Thomas Dekker to Alleyn, existing among the hitherto unnoticed papers at Dulwich, may be added to them.

"Sr.

"I give you thanks for the last remembrance of your love. I write nowe, not poetically, but as an orrator, not by waye of declamation, but by petition, that you would be pleased, upon my lovinge lynes, to receave a yong man (sonn to a worthie yeoman of Kent here prisoner) able by his owne meanes to mayntayne himselfe, whose fortunes will answere itt. Hee is a yonge man lovinge you, beinge of your name, and desires no greater happines than to depend upon [you] You shall doe mee much honor if you thinke him fitt to serve you as a servant, and him much love, because of your name, to receave. The yonge man is of good parts, both of bodie and mynd. I knowe you respect such a one, and I would not (upon that reputation I hold with you) offer a servant to bee unworthie of your attendance. If you please to receave him upon my commendation and your owne tryall, I shall thinck my selfe beholden to you, and you, as I hope, no waye repent the receavinge of such a servant of your owne name. Soe I rest

"Your lovinge freind,
"Tho. Dekker."

The emphasis with which Dekker repeatedly dwells upon the circumstance, that the party he recommended was of Alleyn's name, of itself seems to shew that any body possessing it had a prior and peculiar claim to the founder's favour. The letter above quoted is remarkable on other accounts. When Dekker before made an appeal to Alleyn's known liberality (see p. 131), and sent him some laudatory verses, Dekker was in confinement in the King's Bench, and we see that he was again a prisoner when he introduced a young man to Alleyn's notice as a servant: the expression, "I give you thanks for the last remembrance of your love," warrants the conclusion that Alleyn had sent pecuniary assistance to Dekker on more than one previous occasion. Respecting the date of the letter we can give no information, and the back of the sheet having been torn off, the address has been lost; but, considering its contents, and the place where it was found, we cannot entertain a doubt that it was sent to the benevolent man who had devoted all the later portion of his life to deeds of disinterested kindness and charity,

and, besides amply providing for his wife and for other relations, had built "God's Gift College," had endowed it to the extent of £800 a year, and had provided thirty almshouses for the poor, in the three parishes of St. Giles, Cripplegate, St. Botolph, Bishopgate, and St. Saviour, Southwark.

It deserves notice, in conclusion, that, notwithstanding his disputes with Sir Francis Calton, and the abuse he had received from the knight, Alleyn left him £100 as a legacy, besides forgiving him £20 which had been long owing. The will makes no mention of his wife's father, whom we have supposed to be Dr. Donne, and who survived Alleyn several years. It is somewhat remarkable, also, that Izaac Walton, in his Life of Donne, does not allude to an incident so important as the marriage of his daughter to the founder of Dulwich College. This fact ought, perhaps, to induce caution in receiving the tradition upon the point, even supported as it is by various confirmatory circumstances noticed in the preceding pages.

NOTES AND CORRECTIONS.

Page 5, line 15. By a deed, preserved at Dulwich College, (discovered since the passage relating to the building of the Rose Theatre was written) it appears that in the 6th Edw. VI. Thomasin Symondes of London, widow, late wife of Raphe Symondes, citizen and fishmonger, solde " her messuage or tenement, called the Little Rose, with two gardens to the same adjoining," in the parish of St. Saviour, Southwark, to Ambrose Nicholas and others. On the 17th Nov., 17th Eliz., Nicholas and others let the same to William Griffin, citizen and vintner, for thirty-one years at £7 per annum. This lease was assigned, on 11th Dec. 1579, to Robert Withens. On 24th March, 1584, Withens assigned his right in the same premises, " in consideration of a certain competent sum of lawful money," to Philip Hinchley, citizen and dyer, of London.

Thus we see exactly in what way, and at what date, Henslowe (or Hinchley, as his name was often spelt) came into possession of a lease of the Rose. From another deed (also existing at Dulwich) between Philip Hinshley, citizen and dyer, of the one part, and John Cholmley, citizen and grocer, of the other part, we learn that Henslowe and Cholmley agreed to enter into partnership for eight years and three months, in " all that parcel of ground or garden plot, containing in length and breadth square every way four score and fourteen foot of assize, little more or less, as also to and of the havings takings and receivage of all the benefit, sums of money, profits and advantage of a play-house now in framing, and shortly to be erected and set up, upon the same ground or garden plot." Cholmley was to have half the receipts, in consideration of the sum of £816, to be paid quarterly, at the rate of £25 per quarter, for the eight years and three months. Cholmley was also to be allowed to " hold and occupy

a small tenement or dwelling house in Maiden Lane and Rose Alley," at the end of the ground, for the purpose of keeping " victualling in, or to put to any other use." Henslowe, on his part, covenanted to complete the playhouse by the aid of John Grigges, a carpenter, with all convenient speed. Cholmley and Henslowe were " jointly to appoint and permit such person and persons, players, to use, exercise and play in the said play house:" and Henslowe undertook to keep the premises in repair, together with " all the bridges and wharfs, belonging to the said parcel of ground." Further, Henslowe covenanted not to permit any other person but Cholmley, or those by him appointed, " to utter sell or put to sale, in or about the said parcel of ground play house or garden," &c. " any bread or drink, other than such as shall be sold to and for the use and behoof of the said John Cholmley."

Page 15, line 26. The parsonage of Firle, in Sussex, has not been " before mentioned."

Page 17, line 9. These particulars are not inserted in the Appendix, but among the Notes and Corrections.

Page 38, line 10. The documents at Dulwich do not elucidate the following additional extract from Henslowe's Diary. No names are subscribed to it, and, perhaps, the money was not paid. The entry is in a strange hand, most likely that of some scrivener.

"Md. that the xxixth daye of September 1596, being Michaelmas daye, the some of one hundered and xxvj^{li} was tendered and redye to be payd yn the house of Mr Phillippe Henslowe, the daye and year aforesayd, which sayd some was to be payd by Edward Allene, as aforesayd, before the settinge of the sunne of the same daye, yn the presentes of those whose names are herunder wryten unto Arthure Langworthe gent."

Page 46, line 33. In the last number of the " New Monthly Magazine" for Jan. 1841, is a very interesting letter from W. J. Thoms, Esq., F.S.A., to Thomas Amyot, Esq., Treasurer S. A., on the subject of the performance of English actors in Germany early in the seventeenth century. Is it possible that the journey of Lodge and Sewell " into the Arch Dukes Country" had any connection with this enterprise?

Page 50, line 29. For " recontre" read *rencontre*.

Page 51, line 19. For " Heglowe" read *Henslowe*.

Page 52, line 8. This statement requires some qualification, because it is not at all certain that " the Comedy of Humours" (or, as it is spelt in Henslowe's Diary, " the comodey of Umers"), was the same as Ben Jonson's " Every man in his Humour," more particularly as that play was certainly acted by the Lord Chamberlain's servants in 1598. It may have been first played by the Lord Admiral's servants, and Ben Jonson may have taken it away from them to the association playing at the Globe and at the Blackfriars. Possibly this gave offence to Henslowe, and he might, therefore, in the letter of the 26th September, 1598, call Ben Jonson " bricklayer" in derision.

Page 59, line 16. At the back of Streete's agreement for building the Fortune, dated the 8th January, 1599, are entered receipts of money, by Streete, for the work as it proceeded. The last of these is dated 11th June, 1600. How nearly finished the building then was is not stated.

Page 60, line 23. For " the date of the Patent to Bowes bears date," &c., read, *the Patent to Bowes bears date*, &c.

Page 82, line 22. The oldest document in Dulwich College, respecting the purchase of the manor by Alleyn, is dated 3d October, 1605. It is indorsed " Sir Fran. Calton's livery. The extent and value of the land," and runs as follows :

" Md it is agreed betweene S^r. Francis Calton, knight, and Edward Alleyn, gent. this third daie of October 1605, That the said S^r. Frauncis Calton shall bargaine, sell, and assure to the said Edward Alleyn and his heires the Mannor of Dulwich in the Countie of Surrey, with all the Roialties and appurtenances thereof, all his landes in the parishe of Camberwell, except onelie the Advowson of the vicaridge of Camberwell, and shall passe the same as the learned Councell of the said Edward Alleyn shall reasonablie devise, with warrantie against the said Sr Frauncis and his heirs, and all that shall clayme by, frome, or under his father or his grandfather, and with warrantie that the said Mannor with the appurtenances is worth, as it is nowe letten, the cleare yearlie value of Cv^{li} at the leist, besides all chardges and reprises, and besides the wooddes and woodlandes, which are noe parcell of the demeanes. And that the said Sr Frauncis shall procure the Ladie Dorothie, his wife, to joyne with him in a fine, for the better conveyance of the said estate. All which assurances are to be doen and perfected before thend of the next tearme, with a sta-

tute of viij M^li frome Sr Frauncis for performance of the bargaine. In consideration of which bargaine and conveyance the said Edward Alleyn ys to paie to the said Sr Frauncis Calton the some of fower thowsand and nyne hundred poundes in this manner; viz, uppon thensealinge of the Indenture of bargaine and sale, one thowsand and eight hundred poundes, and uppon the acknowledginge of the fine one hundred poundes, and uppon thensealinge of the said Indenture of bargaine and sale the said Edward Alleyn shall enter into statute to the said Sr Frauncis in the some of v M^li, that either he shall paie to Sr Frauncis twoe thowsand poundes att thend of vj monethes next after the date of the said Indenture, or ells paie the said Sr Frauncis vij C^li att thend of the same sixe monethes, and Cxx^li by yeare for forbearance of the xiij C^li for iij yeares then following; and then att thend of the same three yeares to paie the said Sr Frauncis the said xiij C^li in money, or ells in satisfaction thereof to assure to Sr Frauncis Calton the Lease of the parsonadge of Firles in the Countie of Sussex, with such landes theare which the said Edward Allen latelie purchased, att the choice and election of the said Sr Frauncis. Soe as six monethes before thend of the said three yeares the said Sir Frauncis Calton geve to the said Edward Alleyn direct notice which he will accept. And alsoe the said Edward Alleyn by the said statute shall stande bound for paiement of the other thowsand poundes residue of the purchase, att thend of one yeare and a half next after the date of the said Indenture. Of which some of iiij M ix C^li the said Edward Allen hath paid to the said S^r. Frauncis in earnest of the bargaine the some of v^li which is to be accepted as in parte of the first payment. In witnes whereof the said parties have hereunto sett their handes.

"Fran: Calton
"Ed. Alleyn"

Page 83, line 36. Mathias Alleyn was *warden* of the College, and Thomas Alleyn master, in 1619, seven years before the death of Alleyn, as he himself records in the Register.

Page 95, line 16. This point is made clear by a subsequent letter from Alleyn, by which it appears that part of the purchase money of Dulwich was to remain in Alleyn's hands for a certain time, he allowing Sir F. Calton interest for it.

Page 95, line 25. Malone, (Shaksp. by Boswell, iii., 222) expressed his belief that Alleyn did not quit the stage until 1616, and on the next page in a note asserts, on the authority of Lord Bacon's Letter to the Marquis of Buckingham, that Alleyn quitted the stage in 1618. It is quite clear that neither date is the correct one. (Vide

Hist. of Engl. Dram. Poetry and the Stage, iii., 312) and that Alleyn ceased to be connected with theatres as an actor much earlier.

Page 98, line 4. In vol. xxi., p. 416, of Malone's Shakespeare by Boswell, will be found certain "Articles of grievance against Mr. Henchlowe," which, probably, were found at Dulwich College, though not now extant there. They must have come into Alleyn's hands, when the players appealed to him on some occasion against the "oppression" of Henslowe.

Page 99, line 5. Alleyn's connection with the Bear Garden no doubt brought the following curious document into his hands. He probably bought the lion, which Morris and Grove sold to Peadle. It is indorsed by Alleyn, "Sale of a Lyon to Pedle."

"Be it knowen unto all men by these presentes, that we Thomas Morris of London, gentleman, and William Grove of London, fustian dresser, for and in consideration of the somme of twelve poundes of lawfull monny of England to us in hand, att or before thensealling and delivery of these presentes by William Peadle of London, citizen and armorer, truly paid, whereof and wherewith we doe acknowledge our selves fully satisfied and paid, and thereof and of every part and parcell thereof we doe clearly acquite and dischardge the said William Peadle, his executors and administrators and every of them by these presentes, have bargained, sold and delivered, and by these presentes doe fully clearly and absolutely bargaine, sell and deliver unto the said William Peadle one male Lyon, to have, holde, use, possess and enjoye the said Lyon unto the said William Peadle, his executors, administrators and assignes, to his and their owne proper use and behouff, and as his and their owne proper goodes and cattalls for ever. And we the said Thomas Morris and William Grove, for us and eyther of us, our executors and administrators, doe covenaunte and graunte to and with the said William Peadle, his executors administrators and assignes, by these presentes to warrante and defende the sale of the said Lyon against all people for ever by these presentes. In witnesse whereof we have hereunto sett our handes and seales. Dated the thirteenth daye of Aprill in the tenth yeere of the raigne of our Soveraigne Lord James, by the grace of God, Kinge of England Fraunce and Ireland, defender of the Faith &c. And of Scotland the fyve and fortith. 1612.

"THOMAS MORRYS (L S)
"per me WILLIAM GROVE (L S)

"Sigillat. et deliberat. in prtia mei
"HENRICI DOUGHTY
"et ROGERI DOUGHTY."

Page 104, line 9. Yet in a note on p. 135, it appears that Alleyn was said to be "of the parish of St. Saviour's Southwark," when he might have no residence there in 1607. It is, however, very doubtful whether at this early date he did not still occupy a house near that of Henslowe. The time of his final and entire removal to Dulwich is quite uncertain.

Page 107, line 33. The entry respecting the receipts on this occasion at the Red Bull Theatre is quoted by Malone. (Shakesp. by Boswell, iii., 223). In Tatham's "Fancies Theatre," 1640, is " a Prologue on the removing of the late Fortune Players to the Bull," but this must have been considerably after Alleyn's death. The same performers might be interested in both houses, and remove to the Bull, because it was in a more populous vicinity, or because the theatre was better liked. Tatham informs us that the appointments at the Bull were superior to those at the Fortune; at least, they had a silk curtain at the former, and only a worsted one at the latter.

Page 110, line 12. Charles Massye did not long survive Alleyn; and in Dulwich College account books, kept by Mathias Alleyn, "the widow Massye" is entered as the tenant paying rent for her share of the Fortune. "Old Massye" is also introduced as another tenant at the same time.

Page 117, line 11. It may be worth while to insert the following though of a somewhat earlier date, than that at which we have now arrived. The precise degree of relationship between Thomas Calton and Sir Francis Calton does not appear.

"Md. that Thomas Calton, gent, hath bargained, this present ixth of Novembr 1611, to convey to Edwd. Alleyn Esquier all that nowe dwelling house of the said Tho. Calton in Dulwich with the appurtenances, and all theis landes there, viz the three acres next the house, Addingtons meadowes, Carters hall, and great Brownings, as by the Councell of the said Ed. Alleyn shalbe advised, in consideration of fyve hundred poundes for the full purchase thereof; and hereupon yt is agreed that three hundred poundes of this money shall remayne in Mr Allens handes untill Mr Caltons wief do levy a fyne of this land, and in the mean tyme Mr Alleyn is to have for the mony partely disbursed after the rate of the purchase, and Mr Calton is to hold his house and land untill Michmas next rent free, and Mrs Calton is to have x^{li} given at the delivery of the fyne as above.

"Thomas Calton.   Ed. Alleyn.

"Teste me Johannes Ewen.

"Rd this 15th of november bye me Thomas Calton of Edward Allen, in parte payement of the concideration above sayde, the sum of 116ˡ of good and lawfull mony of Ingland, in wittnesse where of I the sayd Thomas have sett too my hand.

"By me THOMAS CALTON

"Rd more this xxixth of november xxijˡˡ"

Page 121, line 15. Many of the notes are without dates, and may have been written subsequent to 31st December, 1613, but that is the latest paper marked with the day, month, and year.

Page 147, line 32. Could the "Fall of Shabot," here mentioned, be an earlier edition of Chapman's and Shirley's play of "Chabot, Admiral of France," which, as far as we now know, was first printed in 1639? It was licensed in 1635; but that might possibly have been its second appearance before the Master of the Revels. Perhaps the "Fall of Shabot" was a tract or narrative, which Chapman and Shirley subsequently used in the composition of their tragedy.

Page 153, line 28. The statement of Cartwright, that Alleyn "submitted himself to that proportion of diet and clothes" which he bestowed on others, hardly seems borne out by Alleyn's Diary, from which we find that he was somewhat particular as to his dress. Thus we meet with the following memoranda there.

"Pd Booth for dressing my bever hatt . . . 0. 2. 6
Lyning itt with Taffata in the head . . . 0. 1. 6
Mʳˢ Fludd sent me a night cap and my wife a pair of rich
    gloves—given 0. 2. 0
Bought a sattin embroydered hatt band . . . 0. 3. 0
Orang tawney silke for a night cap . . . 0. 0. 4
Mʳ Calton sent a pair of gloves of cordivaunt for me, and
    a pair of rich furd for my wife" . . . .

At the end of the book is the following:

"A noat of silk stockins which hath beene knitt for me.
  A pʳ of watshed
  A pʳ of rose collerd
  A pʳ of popingay
      ashe colord
      decoy
      Se water green."

The founder's portrait in Dulwich College is not that of a man who appeared to be inattentive to dress.

Page 155, line 5. Taylor's "Pennyless Pilgrimage" from London to Edinburgh was printed in 1618.

Page 182, line 19. Alleyn himself commenced the Register of the College, in 1616, in the following terms, whence it is certain that the chapel was consecrated by Archbishop Abbott.

"A Register book for this Colledge of Gods guift in Dullwich in the Countie off Surrey, wherin is contayned first of all the names of the Colledgiautes. Then all Christenings Burialls or mariages, which hath bene since the Chapple of the sd Colledge wase consecrated, and dedicated to the Honor off Christ, by the most Reverent father in god, George Abbot Archbishopp of Canterbury his grace, on Sundaye the first of September, and in the yeare off our Lord 1616."

APPENDIX.

No. I.

The WILL of EDWARD ALLEYN, Senior.

In the name of God amen. The xth daye of September in the yeare of our Lord god 1570. I Edward Allen, Cittizen and Inholder of London, and of the parishe of St. Botolphe without Bushoppes gate of London, sicke in body but in good and perfect remembrance, I hartely thanke Allmightie god therefore, do make my laste will and testament in manner and forme followinge &c. Fyrst and principally I gyve and commend my soule to Allmightie god my only Creator, Saviour, redemer and sanctifier, and I will my body to be buried at the discretion of my Executrix and Overseer herunder named, and gyve all my landes and tenementes to my welbeloved wife Margaret, to have and to enjoye all the same duringe her lyfe tyme only, and after her decease I gyve all the same landes and tenementes to all my children and theire heires, equally to be devided amonge them. And as touchinge all my goodes, leases and redy mony (my funerall charges and debtes, and also this my will proved and paied) I will to be devided into two partes, thone parte my said wife to have, and the other parte I will to be devided amonge my children by even porcions, parte and parte like. And of this my laste will and testament I do appoynte and make the said Margaret, my said wife, my sole Executrix, and I hartely desire my neighbour and fellowe to be overseer of this the same my laste will and testament, whose name is Hewgh Walker of the same parishe, brasier, whome I will my Executrix honestly to content and paye for his paines. Theis persons followinge beinge witnesses Peter Maria, John Buffin, the minister, and Willm Reave the clerke of the same parishe, Margaret Hopkins, Rose Somers, and Margaret Hardee and others. Per me Johem

Buffum ministrum dictæ ecclesiæ. Hugh Walkers marke . this marke is Margaret Hardee . this marke is Peter Maria . By me William Reve parishe clarke . this marke is Rose Somers.

No. II.

Agreement between ALLEYN and R. JONES.

Be it knowen unto all men by theis presentes that I Richard Jones of London, yoman, for and in consideration of the somme of Thirtie Seaven poundes and Tenne shillinges of lawfull mony of Englande to me by Edward Allen of London, gent, well and trulie paid, have bargayned, and solde, and in playne and open market, within the citie of London, have delivered to the said Edwarde Allen all and singular suche share, parte and portion of playing apparalles, playe bookes, Instrumentes, and other commodities whatsoever belonginge to the same, as I the said Richard Jones nowe have or of right ought to have, joyntly with the said Edward Allen, John Allen, citizen and Inholder, of London, and Robert Browne, yoman. To have and enjoye all and singular my said share of playinge apparell, playe bookes, instrumentes and other commodities whatsoever, above bargained and solde to the said Edward Allen, his executors administrators and assignes, as his and theire owne goodes, freelie, peaceablee and quyetlie for evermore, without let, clayme or disturbaunce of me the said Richard Jones, my executors, administrators, or assignes or any of us, or of any other person or persons by our meanes consent or procurement. In witnes whereof I the said Richard Jones to this my present writinge have set my hande and seale, the thirde daie of Januarye aº dni 1588 And in the one and thirtiethe yeare of the raigne of our soveraigne Ladie Elizabeth, by the grace of god Quene of England, Fraunce and Irelande, defender of the Faithe &c.

      By me RICHARD JONES   L. S.

Sigillat. et delebat. in presentia mei JOHANNIS HARNEY apprentic. THO. WRIGHTSON Scr.

No. III.

ALLEYN's Part in R. GREENE's "Orlando Furioso."

    *   *   *   *   gloriouse waine
  *   *   *   viewe of Daphnes excellence;

* * * morn, faire bewty of the even,
* * * Orlando languishing in love
* * * groves, wheare the nimphes
* * pleasance laugh to see the Satyres playe,
* * Orlandos faith unto his love
* she thes lawndes, sweet flora, bost thy flowers
seek she for shade, spred cedars for her sake.
Kinde Flora, make her couch fair cristall springes:
washe you her Roses, yf she long to drink.
oh thought my heaven, oh heaven y^t knowes my thought!
Smyle joy in hir that my content hath wrought.
———————————————— dwell.
Orlando, what contrarious thoughts are those
that flock with doutfull motion in thy minde?
heavens smile, thes trees doe boast ther somer pride;
Venus hath graven hir triumphes here beside.
———————————————— shall ensewe.
Angelica! ah, sweet and blessed name
life to my life, an essence to my ioye!
this gordyon knott together counites
ah medor, partner in hir peerlesse love.
unkind, and will she bend hir thoughts to chaunge?
hir name, hir writing! foolishe and unkind!
no name of hirs, unlesse the brokes relent
to hear hir name, and Rhodanus vouchsafe
to rayse his moystened lockes from out the Reedes,
and flowe with calme along his turning bowndes.
no name of hirs, unlesse the zephire blowe
hir dignityes along the desert woodes
of Arden, wher the world for wonders waightes.
and yet hir name! for why, Angelica?
but mixt with Medor, then not Angelica.
only by me was loved Angelica;
only for me must live Angelica.
I fynd hir drift; perhappes the modest pledg
of my content hath wth a privy thought,
and sweet disguise, restrayned hir fancy thus,

shadowing Orlando under Medors name:
fyne drift, faire nymphe, Orlando hopes no lesse.
yet more! are muses maskine in these trees,
forming ther dittyes in conceited lynes,
making a goddesse in despight of me,
that have no goddess but Angelica?
———————————— sorowes dwell.
dare Medor court my venus? can hir eyes
bayte any lookes but suche as must admyre?
      *   *   * what may Orlando deeme?
Etna, forsake the bowndes of Sicelye,
for why, in me thy restlesse flames appere.
refusd, contemd, disdaynd, what not, then thus.
    *   *   *   * angry brest.

Argalio. ———————————— my Lord.
come hether, Argalio: vilayne, behold these lynes;
see all these trees carved wth true love knottes,
wherin are figurd Medor and Angelica.
what thinkst thou of it?————————
———————————————— is a woeman
and what then? ———————————— some newes.
what messenger hath Ate sent abrode
wth Idle lookes to listen my lament?
Sirha, who wronged happy nature thus,
to spoyle thes trees wth this Angelica?
yet in hir name, Orlando, they are blest.
———————————————— folow love.
As follow love! darest thou disprayse my heaven?
offer disgrace, and preiudice hir name?
is not Angelica the queene of love,
deckt wth the compound wreath of Adons flowers?
she is: then speak, thou pesant, what he is
that dare attempt, or court my quene of love,
or I will send thy soule to Charons charge.
————————————————and Medors love.
Nought but Angelica, and Medors love!
shall Medor, then, possesse Orlandos love?

APPENDIX.

danty and gladsome beames of my delight,
why feast your gleames on others lustfull thoughtes?
delicious browes, why smile your heaven for those,
that woundring you prove poor Orlandos foes?
Lend me your playntes, you sweet Arcadian nimphes,
that wont to sing your late departed loves.
thou weeping floud, leave Orpheus wayle for me.
proude Titans neces, gather all in one
those fluent springes of your lamenting eyes,
and let them streame along my faintfull lookes.
——————————————— of S [def. in MS.]
Argalio, seek me out Medor, seek out that same,
that dare inchase him with Angelica.
——————————————— be [def. in MS.]

 O feminile ingegno, di tutti mali sede,
 come ti vuolgi et muti facilmente
 contrario oggetto proprio de la fede
 O inf * * * * credi
 * * portune super * * *
 prive di amor, di fede, et di Consiglio;
 temerarie, crudeli, inique, ingrate,
 per pestilenza eterna all mundo natae.

———————————————————————————
———————————————————————————

vilayne, Argalio, whers medor? medor is, medor a knave; what,
  lyes he here,
and braves me to my face? by heaven, Ile tear
[*dragges him in*]
him pecemeale in dispight of these.
[*enters with a mans legg*]
villayns, provide me straight a lions skynne.
——————————————— on his neck.
for I, thou seest, am mighty Hercules.
see whers my massy clubb upon my neck.
I must to hell to fight wth Cerberus,
and find out Medor ther, you vilaynes, or Ile dye.
——————————————— shall I doe?

ah, ah, ah, Sirha, Argalio!
Ile weare the speare framd out of • • •
• • • • • • • •
• • • • • • • •

ORLANDO.

Solus. ——————————————————————

Woodes, trees, leaves, leaves, trees, woodes: tria sequuntur tria, ergo optimus vir non est optimus magistratus. a peny for a pott of beer and sixe pence for a peec of beife? wounds! what am I the worse? o minerva! salve; god morrow; how doe you to day? sweet goddesse, now I see thou lovest thy ulisses. lovely Minerva, tell thy ulisses, will Jove send Mercury to Calipso to lett me goe?

Here he harkens.] will he? why then he is a good fellow; nay more, he is a gentleman, every haire of the head of him. tell him I have bread and beife for him: lett him put his arme into my bag thus deep, yf he will eate. goddesse, he shall have it. thre blew beans [def. in MS.] a blewe bladder, rattle bladder [def. in MS.] Lantorne and candle light; child [def. in MS.] children, a god when———

He walketh up and downe] but soft you, minerva, whats a clock? [def. in MS.] hye tree.

He singes.] I am Orlando [def. in MS.] so bragg. [def. in MS.] who • • Jupiters brayne when you were

He whistles for him.] begotten. Argalio, Argalio! farewell, good Minerva; have me recommended to vulcan, and tell him I would fayne see him dance a galyard.
———————————————————— my lord.

I pray the, tell me one thing: dost thou not know wherfore I cald the • • •?
———————————————————— neither.

Why knowest thou not? nay nothing, thou mayst be gone. stay, stay, villayne, I tell thee, Angelica is dead, nay she is in deed.
———————————————————— lord.

but my Angelica is dead.
———————————————————— my lord.

APPENDIX.

He beats] and canst thou not weepe
——————————————Lord.
  Why then begin, but first lett me geve
  [def. in MS.]
A begins to weepe] your watchword, Argalio.
  Argalio, stay.

  •   •   •   •
  •   •   •   •

  That the belydes. youle fetch me hir, sir.
  spare no cost, run me to Charlemagne,
  and say Orlando sent for Angelica. away, villayne!
——————————————— your humor.
  Oh, oh! as though y^t Sagitar in all his pride
  could take faire Leda from stout Jupiter;
  and yet, forsooth, Medor durst enterprise
  to reave Orlando of Angelica.
  syrha, you that are the messenger to Jove,
  you that can sweep it through the milke white pathe
  that leades unto the synode howse of Mars,
  fetch me my helme, tempred of azure steele,
  my sheild, forged by the ciclopps for Anchises sonne,
  and see yf I dare combat for Angelica.
  heaven, and hell, godes and devylls! whers Argalio?
——————————————— Angelica.
  Ah, my dear Angelica!
  syrha, fetch me the harping starr from heaven,
  Lyra, the pleasant mynstrell of the spheares,
  that I may dance a galyard wth. Angelica.
  ride me to Pan; bidd all his waternimphes
  come wth. ther bagpypes and ther tamberins.
——————————————— for a woeman.
  howe fares my sweet Angelica?
——————————————— for his honesty.
  art thou not fayre Angelica,
  wth. browes as faire as faire Ibythia,
  that darks Canopus wth. her silver hewe?
——————————————— art Angelica.
  Why are not these those ruddy coulered cheekes,

Wher both the lillye and the blushing rose
syttes equall suted with a natyve redd.
———————————————— a ballad.
Are not, my sweet, thes eyes, these sparkling lampes,
Wherout proud Phebus flasheth fourth his lights?
———————————————— wth. an othe.
but tell me, false Angelica,
strumpett, worse then the whorish love of Mars,
traytresse, surpassing trothlese Cresida,
that so inchast his name wthin that grove,
wheres medor? say me for truth wher medor is.
yf Jupiter hath shutt him wth young Ganymede,
by heaven, Ile fetch him from the heles of Jove.
inconstant, base, injurious and untrue!
such strumpetts shall not scape away wth. life.
———————————————— god be wth. you.
[def. in MS.] wher are my souldiours? whers all
the campe, the captayns, leutenantes, sargeantes,
[def. in MS.] of the band, corporalles, and, ancpresades,
gentlemen and mercenaries? seest thou not, medor
standes braving me at the gates of Rome?
———————————————— to much wages.
follow me! I may goe seek my captaynes out,
that Medor may not have Angelica.
Exit.]

ENTER.

Sirha, is she not like those purple coulered swannes,
y^t gallopp by the coache of Cinthya?
her face silvered like to the milkwhite shape
y^t Jove came dauncing in to Semele?
tell me, Argalio, what sayes Charlemagne?
his nephew Orlando, palantyne of fraunce,
is poet laureat for geometry.

———————————————————————————

ORLANDO.
———————————————— in the w [def. in MS.]
base mynded traytors! yf you dare but say
Thetis is fayrer then Angelica,

APPENDIX.

Ile place a peal of rysing rivers in your throates
[def. in MS.] Virgill, Lucian, Ovide, Ennius,
Sirha, were not these poettes? ——— yes, my lord.
Then Jove, trotting upon proud Eolus,
shall not gaynesay, but maugre all his boultes
Ile try wth vulcane cracking of a launce,
Yf any of the godes mislikes my rondelayes.
Argalio, these be the lockes Apollo turnd to bowes,
when crimson daphne ran away for love.
love! whats love, vilayne, but the bastard of Mars,
the poyson of penns, and yet thou seest I wear
badges of a poet laureat ———— the world.
Clyme up the cloudes to Galaxsy straight,
And tell Apollo that orlando sittes
making of verses for Angelica.
Yf he denye to send me downe the shirt
that Deianyra sent to Hercules,
to make me brave upon my wedding day,
Ile up the Alpes and post to Meroe, the
watry lakishe hill, and pull the harper
from out the ministrills handes and pawne.
[def. in MS.] to lovely Proserpine, y^t she
may fetch me fayre Angelica.
vilayne, will he not send me it?
——————————— no answerr.
So, Orlando must become a poet.
No, the palatyne is sent champion unto ye warrs.
take the Laurell, Latonas bastard sonne:
I will to flora, sirha, downe upon the ground,
for I must talke in secrett to the starres.
————————— doth lye.
when Jove rent all the welkin wth. a crake.
fye, fye! tis a false verse. ——— penylesse.
how, fellow, wher is the Artick bear, late baighted
from his poel? scurvy poetry! a litell to long.
————————— by force.
Oh, my sweet Angelica, braver then Juno was.
but, vilayne, she converst with Medor.

———————————————————— I give.
drownd be Canopus child in those arcadyan twins.
is not that sweet, Argalio?
———————————————————— confesse it.
stabb the old whore, and send her soule to the divell.
Lende me the nett that vulcan trapt for Mars.
[def. in MS.] felows, vilaynes, whats there adoe?
the court is cald, an nere a Senatur.
Argalio, geve me the chayre; I will be judg
my selfe ——————————————— souldioures.
So, sirs, what sayes Cassius? why stabbd he Cæsar
in the senate howse?
———————————————————— his furye.
Why speakes not, vilayne, thou peasaunt!
Yf thou beest a wandring knight, say who
hath crackt a Launce with the? ——————— to him.
what sayest? Is it for the armour of
Achilles thou doest strive? yf be Ajax
shall trott away to troy, geve me thy
hand ulisses, it is thine. ——————— Armorer.
And you, fair virgin, what say you?
Argalio, make her confesse all ———————

ORLANDO.

———————————————————— have relet.
[def. in MS.] the flowes of Ilium.
Fear not Achilles, overmadding boy:
Pyrrhus shall not. Argalio, why sufferest
this olde trott to come so nere me.
away with thes rages!
fetch me the Robe that proud Apollo wears,
that I may Jett it in the capytoll.
Argalio, is Medor here? say whiche of
these is he. courage! for why, the palatyne
of fraunce straight will make slaughter
of these daring foes. *currunt.*

APPENDIX.

are all the troyans fledd? then geve me
some drynke, some drink.———— my lord.
els will I sett my mouth to Tigris streames,
and drink up overflowing Euphrates.
———————————————— my lord.
This is the gesey shepherdes bottle, that Darius
quaft. so, so, so, oh so. ————
Inchaunt]
What heavenly sightes of pleasaunce filles my eyes,
that feed the pride with view of such regard?
[def. in MS.] admyres to se the slombring dreams.
skyes are fullfild wth lampes of lasting joye,
that boste the pride of haught Latonas sonne,
who lightneth all the candells of the night.
nemosene had kist the kingly Jove,
and entertayn a feast wth in my braynes,
making her daughters solace on my browes.
Methinkes I feel how Cinthias tyms conceipts
of sad repent, and meloweth those desires
that frenzy scarse had ripened in my braynes.
Ate, Ile kise thy restlesse cheek awhile,
and suffer fruitlesse passion byde controle.
Recumbit] ————————————————
What sightes, what shapes, what strange conceipted dreams!
more dreadfull then apperd to Hecuba,
when fall of troy was figured in her sleeps.
Juno, methought, sent from the heaven by Jove,
cam sweeping swiftly thorow the glomye ayre,
and calling Iris, sent her straight abrode
to sommon fawnes, the satires and the nimphes,
the dryades and all the demygodes
to secret consayle, [def. in MS.] parle past,
she gave them [def. in MS.] full of heavenly dew.
with that, mounted upon hir party coulered coach,
she slipt with Iris to the sphear of Jove.
what thoughts arise upon this fearfull showe!
wher? in what woodes? what uncouth grove is this?
how thus disguysd? where is Argalio? Argalio!

———————————————— mad humores.
say me, sir boy, how cam I thus disguysd,
like mad Orestes quaintly thus attyred?
———————————————— you are.
As I am! villayne, termest me lunaticke?
tell me what furye hath inchaunted me?

what art thou some sibill, or some godes,
or what? frely say on.

ORLANDO.

———————————————— batt [def. in MS.]
Hath then the [def. in MS.] of Alcumenas child
ledd fourth my thoughts, wch. for more egar rage
then wrastled in the brayne of Phillips sonne,
when madd wth. wyne he practised Clytus fall.
break from the cloudes, yon burning brandes of Ire,
that styrr wthin the thunderers wrathfull fistes,
and fixe your hideous fyers on Sacrapant.
from out your fatall tresoryes of wrath,
you wastfull furyes, draw those eben bowles,
that bosted lukewarme bloud at Centaures feast,
to choak with bloud the thirsty Sacrapant,
thorough whom my Clymene and hebe fell,
thorow whom my sprittes wth fury wer supprest.
my fancyes, post you unto Pindus topp:
ther midst the sacred troupes of nimphes inquire,
seek for my Venus nere Erycinne,
or in the vale of [def. in MS.] yf she sleep.
tell her Orlando [def. in MS.] second Mars,
hath robd the burning hill of Cicelye
of all the Ciclops treasurs ther bestowed,
to venge hir wronges. and stoupe those haught conceiptes,
that sought my Jelowsye and hir disgrace.
Ride, Nemesis, upon this angry steel
that thretneth those that hate Angelica,
who is the sonne of glory that consumes
Orlando, even the phenix of affect.   [*Exit.*

——————————————————————— slave as he.
Prynces, for shame! unto your royall campes.
base not your selves to combatt such a dogg.
follow the chase, mount on your coursers strong;
manage your spears, and lett your slaughtering swordes
be taynted with the bloud of them that flee.
from him passe ye; he shalbe combated.
——————————————————— withine.
I am, thou seest, a cuntry servile swayne,
homely attired, but of so hawty thoughtes
as nought can serve to quench the aspiring flames,
that scorch as doe the fiers of Cicelye,
unlesse I win that princly diademe
that semes so ill upon thy cowardes head.
————————————————————————— a king.
Then mayst thou deme some second mars from heaven
is sent, as was Amphitrios foster sonne,
to vale thy plumes and heave the from a crowne.
prove what thou art, I wreke not of thy gree:
as Lampethusas brother from his coach,
prauncing and visor open, went his course
and tombled from Apollo's chariott,
so shall thy fortunes and thy honor fall.
to prove it, Ile have the guerdon of my sword
wch. is the glory of thy diademe.
————————————————thy name?
first thine. ———————

ORLANDO.

——————————————— Sacrapant.
Then lett me at thy dying day intreat,
by that same sphear wherin thy soule shall rest,
yf Joue deny not passage to thy ghost,
then tell me, yf thou wrongst Angelica or no?
——————————————— thy name.
Extinguish, proud tesyphone, those brandes:
fetch dark Alecto from black phlegeton,

P

or Lethe water to appease those flames,
that wrathfull Nemesis hath sett on fire.
dead is the fatall author of my yll.
vassall! base vilayne! worthlesse of a crowne,
knowe that the man that stabd the dismall stroke
is Orlando, the palatyne of fraunce,
whom fortune sent to quittance all thy wrong.
thou foyld and slaine, it now behoves me, dogg,
to hye me fast to massacre thy men—*exit*
——————————————————— hir love.
French man, for so thy quaint aray importes,
beest thou a peer, or beest thou Charlemayne,
or hadst thou hectors or Achilles hartes,
or never daunted thoughtes of hercules,
the infusd metemsichosis of them all,
I tell the, sir, thou liest wth in thy throate,
the gretest brave Cis alpine fraunce can brook,
in saing y^t sacred Angelica
did offer wrong unto the palatyne.
I am a slavishe Indian mercenary,
yet for I see the princesse is abusd
by newcome straglers from an uncooth coast,
I dare the proudest of the westerne Lordes
to crack a blade in tryall of hir right.
——————————————————— foyld.
Twelve peres of fraunce, twelve divylles, whats y^t?
what I have spoke, ther I pawne my sword
to seale it on the helme of him that dare,
Malgrado of his honor, combatt me.
——————————————————— Lords of India.
You that so proudly bid him fight,
out wth your blade, for why, your turne is next.
tis not this champion can discorage me.

Pugnant M. victus]
You, sir, that braved your heraldry,
wher is the honor of the howse of fraunce?

APPENDIX.

———————————————————— to doe.
faire princesse, what I may belonges to the:
wittnes, I well have hanseled yet my sword.
now, sir, you that will chastyce when you meet,
bestirr you, french man, for Ile taske you hard.
Oliver victus] ————————————————
Provide you, lordes; determyne who is next:
pick out the stoutest champion of you all.
they wer but striplinges: call you those the peers?
Hold, madam, and yf my life but last it out,
Ile gard your person with the peires of fraunce.
  by my side. ————————————
So, sir, you have made a godly oracion,
but use your sword better, lest I well
beswinge you.
Pugnant] ——————————————————
by my faith, you have done pretily well; but
sirha, french man, thinck you to breath? come,
fall to this geer close: dispatch, for we must
have no parle. ————————————————
O. victus] ———————————————— Orlando.
Ogier, sweet cuss, geve me thy hand, my lord,
and say thast found the county Palatyne.
———————————————————— Lunacye.
So was I, Lordes; but geve me leave a while,
humbly as mars did to his paramour
when as his god head wrongd hir wth suspect,
so to submitt to faire Angelica,
upon whose lovly Roseat cheekes, me semes,
the cristall of hir morne more clerly spredes,
then doth ye dew upon Adonis flower.
faire nimphe, about whose browes sittes floras pride,
Elisian bewty trappes about thy lookes,
pardon thy Lord, who, perst wth. Jelowsie,
darkned thy vertues wth a great ecclipse.
pardon thy Lord, faire saynt Angelica,
whose love, stealing by steppes into extremes,

grew by suspition to causlesse Lunacye.
———————————————— in his.
Thankes, sweet Angelica.
but why standes the prince of Africa,
and Mandrycard, the King of mexico,
so deep in dumpes, when all rejoyse besides?
———————————————— Palatyne.
And that, my leig, durandall hath averd
agaynst my kinsmen and the peires of fraunce,
next know, my lord, I slaughtered Sacrapant.
I am the man y^t did the slave to death,
who falsely wrongd Angelica and me;
for when I stabd the traytor to the hart,
and he lay breathing in his latest gaspe,
he frankly made confession at his death
that he ingravd the Rondelays on the trees,
and hung the scedule of poor Medors love,
entending by suspect to bred debate
deeply twixt me and fair Angelica.
his hope had happ, but we had all the harme.
and now revendg, leaping from out the seat
of him that can commaund sterne Nemesis,
hath heapd his treasons justly on his head.
———————————————— honor the.
Thankes, Angelica, for her.
but nowe, my Lordes of fraunce, frolick, my frendes,
and welcome to the courts of Africa.
courage, companyons, y^t have past the seas
furrowing the playnes of neptune wth your keles
to seeke your frend the county Palatyne.
you thre, my Lordes, I welcome with my sword,
the rest, brave gentlemen, my hart and hand.
what welth wthin the clime of Africa,
what pleasure longst the costes of mexico,
Lordinges commaund, I dare be bold so far
with Mandrycard and prince Marsilius.
the pretious shrubbles, the * * of mirh,

the founts as riche as Eden did aford,
whatso ever is faire and pleasing, Lordinges, use,
and welcome to the county Palatyne.
——————————— or none.
Thankes, Affrike vicroye, for the Lordes of fraunce.
and, fellow mates, be merry, we will home
as sone as pleaseth King Marsilius
to lett his doughter passe wth us to fraunce.
meane while wele richly rigg up all our fleet
more brave then wer the [def. in MS.] keles.

No. IV.

HENSLOWE and the Mastership of the Games.

Elizabeth, by the grace of God Queene of England, France and Ireland Defendor of the Faith &c. To all to whome their presents shall come greetinge. Wee lett youwitt that wee, of our speciall grace, certen knowledge and meere motion uppon surrender to us of a former Patent or Comission heretofore by us   and graunted to our welbeloved servant Raphe Bowes Esquire, have geven and graunted, to and by theis presents doe geve and graunte, unto our welbeloved servante Phillipp Hensley, for and in consideration of his faithfull service heretofore doen unto us, the roome or office of Cheife Mr., Overseer and Ruler of all and singular our games pastymes and sportes, that is to saye, of all and everie our Beares, Bulls and Mastiff Dogges meete for that purpose, and the same Phillipp Hensley, cheif Mr, Ruler and Overseer of all and every our games sportes and pastymes aforesaid, wee doe make, ordaine and constitute by theis presentes. To have and to hould the same roome or office to the said Phillipp Hensley, by himselfe or his sufficient Deputie or Deputies, for and duringe his naturall liefe with all and al manner rewardes, preheminence, liberties, proffitts, comodities and advantages whatsoever to the same office or roome in any wise belonging or apperteyning, in as large and ample manner and form as Cuthbert Vaughan or Sir Richard Longe, knighte, deceased, or the said Raphe Bowes, or any other havinge and exercising the same office att any tyme in his or their lief or lyves, ever had, used, perceaved and enjoyed in, for, and by reson of the same roome or office.

And of our further speciall grace wee doe geve and graunt by theis presentes unto the said Phillipp Hensley, and to his said Deputie or Deputies, duering his said lief, full power, comission and authoretie, not onelie to take upp and lead for our service, pastyme and sporte any Mastiff Dogg or Dogges and Mastiff Bitches, Beares, Bulls and other lyke, meete and convenient for our said service and pastyme, any of them beeinge within this our Realme, or other our domynions, att and for suche reasonable price and prizes as our said servant can agree with the owner or owners for the same Beares and Bulls; but alsoe to staie, or cause to be staied, att his discretion, all and every or any suche Mastiff dogges or bitches as the said Phillipp Hensley or his assignes shall fortune at any tyme hereafter to take and finde goinge, passinge or conveighinge, or to be conveyed in any wise unto any parte of beyond the seas, without our speciall lycense warrant and comission for conveighinge of the same. Willinge, and streightlie charginge and comandinge by theis presentes, that as well all our officers, Mynisters and subjectes and everie of them, from henceforth from time to time, to aide, assiste, strengthen and helpe the said Phillipp Hensley in exercisinge of his said office and other the said premisses, but alsoe other our officers and mynisters in any wise apperteyninge to our said games shall dilligentlie obeie and bee attendinge, and doe every thing and things reasonable that the said Phillipp, as Mr. and cheef Ruler of our said games, shall commaunde for our better service therein. And alsoe of our further speciall grace, for the consideration aforesaid, wee doe geve and graunt full power and authoretie by theis presentes to the said Phillipp Hensley to bayte or cause to be bayted our said Beares and others, beinge of our said games, in all and everie convenient place and places, and att any tymes and att his discretion, and that noe other officer or under officer belonginge or in any manner apperteyninge to our said Beares and [illegible] for the tyme beeinge, ne any of them, shall from henceforth bayte or cause to be bayted any of our said Beares or others of our games aforesaid, in any yarde or other place or places, without the speciall lycence and appointment of the said Phillipp; nor that any of them shall from henceforth take upp any beare or beares, or any other apperteyninge to our said games, or for our service and comoditie without the [illegible] appointment of our said servant as is aforesaid.

Any manner of graunte or lycense, heretofore made or hereafter to be made to any of them for the same, to the contrarie hereof in any wise notwithstandinge. In witnes &c.

[The above seems to have been drawn up by Henslowe's orders, when he had some expectation of obtaining the office to which it refers before the death of Elizabeth. The copy from which it is taken was subsequently altered by him in his own hand, to suit the reign of James I., when Henslowe hoped to be made Master of the King's Games, in preference, probably, to Sir John Dorington.]

No. V.

The Building of Dulwich College.

This Indenture, made the seaventeenth day of May, 1613, and in the yeres of the raigne of our soveraigne Lorde James, by the grace of God, Kinge of England, Fraunce and Ireland, defender of the faethe &c the eleventh, and of Scotland the sixe and forteth, Betweene Edward Alleyn of Dulwich in the parishe of Camerwell in the County of Surrey, Esquier, on th'one partye, and John Benson of Westminster in the County of Midd, bricklayer, on th'other party. Witnessethe, that it is covenanted, graunted, concluded, condescended and agreed by and betwene the saide partees to thees presentes, and the said John Benson for him selfe covenanteth and graunteth to and with the saide Edward Alleyn his executors and assignes by thees presentes in manner and forme as hereunder from article to article is expressed, that is to say; That the saide John Benson or his assignes shall and will (for the consideration hereunder written and specified) builde erect and sett up, upon a certen parcell of ground appoynted and layde out for that purpose upon Dulwich Greene in the parishe of Camerwell aforesaide, the trench for the foundation to be digged and made fitt by the saide Edward Alleyn, his executors or assignes, a certaine buildinge of brick, of and with such brickes, lyme, sand, or other stuff belonginge to brickeworke, as shalbe provided and delivered to him att the place aforesaide by the saide Edward Alleyn his executors or assignes, which buildinge shalbe for a Chappell, a Schoole howse, and twelve Almeshowses,

proportionably accordinge to a plott thereof made and drawen by the saide John Benson and subscribed by the saide parties; the saide Chappell and Schoolehowse tobe in lengthe from east to west fowerskore and fyfteene foote of assize, and in bredthe from out side to out side twenty and nyne foote of assize, and in height from the upper parte of the foundation even from the grounde to the raysinge peece thertye foote of assize, and upon the head or topp of the same height sixe foote of assize of finishinge worke. And in the middle of the forefront of the said Chappell shall erect and build one faire porche, to conteyne in length eighteene foote of assize and in bredthe from the other buildinge forward nyne foote of assize, the same porche to be bewtifyed and fynished as hereunder is mentioned. And behinde on the backe parte of the saide buildinge, directly against the saide porche, shall erect and sett upp one Tower of bricke to be eighteene foote of assize square from out to outside, and in height to be threeskore foote of assize, with decent and comely fyneshinge, and at each corner of the same Tower one pynacle of brick: and in the midest of the same Chappell and scholehowse, for a partition betweene them, shall make one partition wall to be in thecknes one brick and a halfe. To sett out the rome appoynted for the parlor of the saide Schole-howse backward by way of inlargement ten foote of assize, and under the same parlor and rome before the same appoynted for an entree and staire case, shall make one cellar of brick to be in bredthe thirteene foote of assize and in lengthe thirty fower foote of assize, and seven foote of assize deepe. And in the same Scholehowse shall make and erect sixe chimneyes sufficiently and substancially to be made and wrought, with arched mantle trees of brick, and to carry and avoide smoke cleane thorough the tonnels of the same chimneyes; that is to say, one chimney in the parlor, one in the chamber over the parlor, one in the chamber or garrett over the same parlor chamber, one in the kitchen, one in the chamber over the kitchen, and one in the chamber over the Scholehowse. The foundation of the Chappell walls within the grounde to be in thicknes sixe brickes, and so racled of untill at the upper parte of the grounde it be brought to fower brickes in thicknes; and from the grounde to the watertable to be three brickes and a halfe in thicknes; and from the watertable to the raysinge peece the walls to be three brickes in thicknes. The foun-

dation of the Tower and the walls thereof to be of the same thicknes as the Chappell is within the grounde, and the walls from the grounde uppward to the covering of the same Tower to be three brickes in thicknes, and even with the ridge of the Chappell the same Tower to have a decent watertable, and from the watertable upward the same Tower to have forward twoe pillasters, and suche other bewtifyinge and fynishinge as the forfront of the saide porch is to have, as hereunder is mentioned. And that the forefront of the said Chappell and Scholehowse shalbe bewtifyed with sixe Dorick pillasters with pettystalls, bases, capitalls and cornishe, to reach from the lowest part of the foundation within the grounde unto the raysinge peece, and twoe pillasters to bewtifie the same porche, and the saide sixe foote of fynishinge worke on the hedd or topp before mentioned, to rise and be made with a small pillaster on the heade of every greate pillaster, with three kinde of tafferells on the forefront; that is to say, one over the porche, and on either side of the porch one; and in the same forefront fower halfe roundes for the bewtefyinge, and betweene every tafferrell and halfe rounde one piramides. And in the forefront of the same Chappell, Scholehowse and porche shall make fowerteene windowes, viz; in the Chappell sixe, in the Scholehowse sixe, and over the saide porch twoe, every windowe to have fower lightes with a transsam, each light to be arched or turned over with brick, and every light to be twoe foote wide, besides the monyon, which monion is to be nyne ynches thick. And att the east end of the saide Chappell shall make one faire windowe, wherein shalbe ten arched lightes with a transam in the middle thereof, all the lightes and monyons thereof to be of the proportion of the saide former windowes, and on the back parte of the saide Chappell, towardes the south, shall make one dore rome and butteres and sixe arched windowes in the same Chappell, proportionable to the windowes in the forefront. The walls of the Scholehowse, and romes thereunto appoynted as aforesaide, to be in thicknes as hereafter followeth, viz; from the lowest parte of the foundation within the grounde to the watertable twoe brickes and a halfe in thicknes; from the watertable to the first story twoe brickes in thicknes, and from the first story to the topp a brick and a halfe in thicknes, with sufficient windowes in every of the saide romes, as the same romes and storyes will conveniently beare and

require. And in the kitchen chimney of the same Scholehowse shall make twoe meete and sufficient ovens; one greater and th'other lesser. And that sixe of the saide Almes'howses shalbe made and erected from the east corner of the saide Chappell northwardes, and th'other sixe Almeshowses from the west corner of the saide Scholehowse northwardes, as by the said plott is prescribed and prefigured, every of the same Almeshowses to be twelve foote square within the walls: and in the same Almeshowses shall make twelve severall chimneyes viz; to each Almeshowse one, the mantle trees of the same chimneyes to be arched or turned over with brick, and to be made to carry and avoid smoke cleane through the tonnells of the same: and in every of the same Almeshowses shall make one windowe with twoe lightes, and under the eves of the same Almeshouses small make a slight cornishe, and to each Almeshowse one dore rome to be arched or turned over with brick. And at the north end of eache of the same rankes of Almeshowses shall erect one howse of office, to conteyne ten foote one way and twelve foote another, with a vault to each howse of office of brick, eight foote deepe, and a vent out of each howse of office in the manner of a chimney above the ridge of the same Almes howses: and also shall erect one wall of brick thwart from end to end of the saide Almes howses to enclose the courte, eight foote high, and in the midest of the same wall one faire gate rome to be fynished in the best and most decent manner with pillasters, freze, cornishe and piramides: the saide wall to be a brick and a halfe in thicknes. All the pillasters, freezes, cornishe and windowes and fawmes of the saide buildinge to be fairely and cleanely fynished white, as is accustomed in buildings of like nature. And all the same worke before prescribed, and all other bricklayers worke to the same buildinge apperteyninge, shall well, workemanlike and sufficiently worke make and fynishe in all thinges to the trade of a bricklayer belonginge. And shall and will begin the same worke on or before the last day of this instant moneth of May, and shall and will contynue at the same worke and fynishe the same with as much convenient speede as possibly may be, and as the saide Edward Alleyn his executors or assignes shall require the same, shall provide stuffe for doeinge thereof. For and in consideration of which worke and covenantes, in forme aforesaide to be done and performed, the said Edward Alleyn, for him, his executors and

administrators, covenanteth and graunteth to and with the saide John Benson, his executors and assignes, by these presentes in manner and forme followinge; that is to say, That he the said Edward Alleyn, his executors or assignes, shall finde and allowe sufficient scaffolding boards, cordes and nailes for the buildinge aforesaid. And also upon the fyneshinge of every five rodd square of the saide buildinge, every rodd conteyninge sixteene foote and a half of assize, shall pay or cause to be paide to the said John Benson the sume of seaven poundes ten shillinges of lawfull mony of England, the same to be measured one with another, and runninge measure, which is thirty shillinges for every rodd. And upon the full fynishinge and endinge of the saide worke and buildinge for every rodd the same shalbe measured into, one with another after the measure aforesaide ten shillinges more, which in all is after the rate of forty shillinges a rodd, without fraud or covyn. In witnes whereof the said parties to theis present Indentures interchangeably have sett their handes and seales. Yeoven the day and yeres first above written.

JOHN BENSON

Sealed and delivered in presence of me
    THOMAS BOLTON Scr.
    ANTHONY WILLIAMS
        Servant to the said THO. BOLTON.

THE END.

LONDON:
F. SHOBERL, JUN., 51, RUPERT STREET, HAYMARKET,
PRINTER TO H. R. H. PRINCE ALBERT.

PROSPECTUS

OF

THE SHAKESPEARE SOCIETY.

It is remarkable that all that has hitherto been done for the illustration of Shakespeare has been accomplished by individuals, and that no Literary Association has yet been formed for the purpose of collecting materials, or of circulating information, by which he may be thoroughly understood and fully appreciated.

To supply this deficiency THE SHAKESPEARE SOCIETY has been established; and it is hoped that, when once its purpose is generally known, it will produce a spirit of inquiry and examination, the result of which may be the discovery of much curious and valuable information, in private hands and among family papers, of the very existence of which the possessors are not at present aware. Every thing, whether derived from manuscript or printed sources, that will throw light on our early Dramatic Literature and Stage, will come within the design of the Society. The cabinets of collectors and our public libraries contain much that will contribute to this end.

Some of the productions of our Dramatists prior to the Restoration have never yet been published, and the printed copies of many Old Plays have the rarity of manuscripts. The best of these will be edited under the sanction of the Society, accompanied by biographical sketches and notes.

The Tracts by such prolific authors as Nash, Greene, Harvey, Dekker, Breton, Munday, Rowlands, Rich, Taylor, Jordan, &c., are known to comprise matter of great interest and curiosity, in connexion, either immediate or remote, with our early Stage and its Poetry; and to the republication of these the attention of the Society will also be directed. In time complete sets may thus be afforded of the scattered productions of distinguished and once popular Writers.

The Works of Northbrooke, Gosson, Lodge, Rankins, Whetstone, Stubbes, Heywood, and others, who wrote for or against theatrical representations in their comparative infancy, are important in the History of our Drama, and these (most of which are of the rarest possible occurrence), it is intended to reprint in a connected series.

The Society is limited to one thousand Subscribers, and, until this limit is attained, Members are admitted on the introduction of one of the Council, or by application to the Secretary or Treasurer.

Communications relative to the Society may be addressed to the Secretary, 186, Fleet Street, or any other Member of the Council, or to Mr. RODD, Bookseller, 2, Newport Street, Long Acre. Subscriptions of Members received at the Metropolitan Bank, 4, Pall Mall East.

LAWS OF THE SHAKESPEARE SOCIETY.

I. The Society shall be called "The Shakespeare Society."

II. The chief object of the Society shall be to afford every species of illustration to the Plays of Shakespeare and his Contemporaries, by the publication or reprinting of works connected with the origin and progress of English Dramatic Poetry and the Stage, anterior to the Restoration. Attention will also be directed to the general Literature of the period, in relation, either immediate or remote, to dramatic representations, and to the lives, characters, and opinions of such as have in any way been concerned in them.

III. The Society shall consist of One Thousand Subscribers of £1 annually; such subscription to be paid in advance, on or before the 1st day of January in every year.

IV. The controlling power of the Society shall be vested in the general body of the Members, who, at their General Meetings, shall elect the Council, and make regulations affecting the Society.

V. The management of the affairs of the Society, and the election of Officers, shall be vested in a Council composed of Twenty-one Members, exclusive of a President and four Vice-Presidents.

VI. Five Members of the Council shall be a quorum.

VII. The present Council shall continue in office until the 25th of April, 1842; and thenceforward the Council shall be elected annually.

VIII. Five Members of the Council shall retire in each year, and not be re-eligible for the ensuing year.

IX. If any Member of the Council shall resign, or a vacancy be otherwise occasioned, the remaining Members of the Council may fill up such vacancy.

X. The Council shall, from amongst their own body, elect a Director, who shall act as Chairman of the Council in the absence of the President and Vice-Presidents.

XI. A General Meeting of the Members shall be held on the 25th of April, 1842, and on each succeeding 25th of April, unless it fall on a Sunday, and in that case on the following day.

XII. The accompts of the Receipts and Expenditure of the Society shall be audited annually by three Auditors, to be elected at the General Meetings, and the Report of the Auditors, with an abstract of the accompts, shall be printed.

XIII. No Member shall be entitled to vote at any General Meeting whose Subscription is in arrear.

XIV. The Chairman of the Council for the time being shall have a Second Vote in case of equality of numbers.

XV. Every Member not in arrear of his Annual Subscription shall be entitled to one copy of every work printed by the Society during that year.

XVI. The Members shall be invited to contribute Works for publication.

XVII. The Editors of Works printed by the Society shall be entitled to twelve copies of the Works they edit.

XVIII. Any Member of the Society may at any time compound for his future annual subscriptions by payment of £10 over and above his subscription for the current year.

XIX. Every Member of the Society who shall not pay his subscription for the current year within three months after his election, or after such subscription shall have become due, shall thereupon cease to be a Member of the Society.

XX. The Council may appoint Local Secretaries in such places and with such authorities as shall be deemed expedient: every Local Secretary being a Member of the Society.

XXI. The Works issued by the Society not to be sold by the Society.

XXII. After the 25th of April, 1842, no alteration shall be made in these Laws, except at a General Meeting, nor then, unless one month's notice of any alteration intended to be proposed at such Meeting shall have been given in writing to the Secretary. Until the 25th of April, 1842, the Council shall have power to amend or add to the above Laws.

ALREADY PRINTED.

1. MEMOIRS OF EDWARD ALLEYN, the Actor, Founder of Dulwich College, from original sources, with new information respecting Shakespeare, Ben Jonson, Lodge, Dekker, Marston, and other contemporary Dramatists and Actors. By J. PAYNE COLLIER, Esq., F.S.A.

WORKS IN THE PRESS.

2. THE SCHOOL OF ABUSE: containing a pleasant Invective against Poets, Pipers, Players, Jesters, &c. By STEPHEN GOSSON. From the edition of 1579, compared with the impression of 1587.

3. The DIARY AND ACCOUNT BOOK OF PHILIP HENSLOWE, between the years 1590 and 1610, in which he entered his various Transactions relating to Plays, Players, and Dramatic Authors, (parts only of which were imperfectly printed by Malone), from the original MS. at Dulwich College. By permission of the Master, Warden, and Fellows.

4. A COLLECTION OF ALL THE DOCUMENTS which have reference to the Events of Shakespeare's Life. The Will edited by SIR FREDERICK MADDEN, F.R.S., F.S.A., Keeper of the MSS. in the British Museum, with Fac-similes of the Signatures. The Marriage Licence, transcripts from the Registers at Stratford-upon-Avon, and all the other Documents, edited by JOHN BRUCE, Esq., F.S.A.

5. THE DEBATE BETWEEN PRIDE AND LOWLINESS, pleaded in an Issue of Assize, &c. by FRANCIS THYNNE. Imprinted at London by John Charlwood, &c. n.d. B.L. 8vo. This work is in verse, and is the original from which Robert Greene, the Dramatist, took his "Quip for an Upstart Courtier," 1592, 4to.

WORKS SUGGESTED FOR PUBLICATION.

6. SIR THOMAS MORE: an unprinted Historical Play, on the Life and Death of that great Statesman and Lawyer: written and licensed for the Stage about the year 1590, and preserved in the original manuscript in the British Museum.

7. FOUR EARLY GERMAN PLAYS, thought to be translations of English Dramas not now known to be extant, but from which Shakespeare derived the plots of four of his Plays. To be edited, with an English translation, by WILLIAM J. THOMS, Esq., F.S.A.

8. AN ACCOUNT of, and extracts from some of the OLD PLAYS, (many of them *unique*) in the Library of the Right. Hon. Lord Francis Egerton, M.P.: accompanied by remarks historical, bibliographical, critical, and biographical, illustrative of our early Stage and Dramatic Poetry. By J. PAYNE COLLIER, Esq., F.S.A.

9. AN ANSWER TO STEPHEN GOSSON'S SCHOOL OF ABUSE. By THOMAS LODGE. This work was printed about the year 1580; but, as the writer informs us, it was "suppressed by authority," and the only copies known are both without title-pages.

10. AN APOLOGY FOR ACTORS, &c. By THOMAS HEYWOOD. From the edition by Nicholas Okes in 1612, compared with Cartwright's edition printed during the Civil Wars.

11. LUDUS COVENTRIÆ: A COLLECTION OF MIRACLE PLAYS, formerly represented at Coventry on the Feast of Corpus Christi. From a MS. in the British Museum of the Reign of Edward IV. To be edited by JAMES ORCHARD HALLIWELL, Esq., F.R.S., F.S.A., &c.

12. TARLTON'S NEWS OUT OF PURGATORY: only such a Jest as his Jig, fit for Gentlemen to laugh at an hour, &c.; published by an old companion of his, Robin Goodfellow. From the earliest edition, printed by Edward White about 1590, compared with the impression of 1630.

13. PIERCE PENNYLESS, HIS SUPPLICATION TO THE DEVIL. By THOMAS NASH. To be printed from the first edition of 1592, compared with the two other impressions in the same year.

14. THE PLEASANT COMEDY OF PATIENT GRISSELL. By THOMAS DEKKER, HENRY CHETTLE, and WILLIAM HAUGHTON. 1603. With an introduction on the origin of the story, and its application to the Stage in various countries of Europe.

15. A volume of the Names, Lives, and Characters of the Actors in the Plays of MARLOWE, GREENE, PEELE, SHAKESPEARE, LODGE, BEN JONSON, CHAPMAN, MASSINGER, FORD, WEBSTER, MIDDLETON, DEKKER, HEYWOOD, &c., alphabetically arranged, and embracing various particulars hitherto unknown.

16. HONOUR TRIUMPHANT, OR THE PEER'S CHALLENGE, BY ARMS DEFENSIBLE AT TILT, TURNEY, AND BARRIERS, &c. Also, THE MONARCH'S MEETING, OR THE KING OF DENMARK'S WELCOME INTO ENGLAND. By JOHN FORD. 1606. A totally unnoticed production, in prose and verse, by the celebrated Dramatic Poet.

17. A ROYAL ARBOUR OF LOYAL POESIE, consisting of Poems and Songs. By THOMAS JORDAN. 1664. It contains various Dramatic Ballads, particularly those founded upon Shakespeare's Much Ado about Nothing, Winter's Tale, Merchant of Venice, &c.

18. PASQUIL'S JESTS, mixed with Mother Bunch's Merriments. Whereunto is added a dozen of Gulls. Pretty and pleasant to drive away the tediousness of a Winter's Evening. From the earliest edition of 1604, compared with later impressions.

19. A NEST OF NINNIES, SIMPLY WITHOUT COMPOUNDS. By ROBERT ARMIN. From the only known edition of 1608. It contains an account, in verse and prose, of various celebrated Fools and Jesters, theatrical and private.

20. A COLLECTION OF BROADSIDES AND MANUSCRIPT PIECES, in prose and verse, principally relating to Authors, Plays, Actors, and Theatres, during the Reigns of Elizabeth, James I., and Charles I.

THE
ALLEYN PAPERS.

A COLLECTION OF

ORIGINAL DOCUMENTS

ILLUSTRATIVE OF THE LIFE AND TIMES OF

EDWARD ALLEYN,

AND OF

THE EARLY ENGLISH STAGE AND DRAMA.

WITH AN INTRODUCTION BY

J. PAYNE COLLIER, ESQ., F.S.A.

LONDON:
PRINTED FOR THE SHAKESPEARE SOCIETY.

1843.

LONDON:
F. SHOBERL, JUN., 51, RUPERT STREET, HAYMARKET,
PRINTER TO H.R.H. PRINCE ALBERT.

COUNCIL

OF

THE SHAKESPEARE SOCIETY.

President.

THE MOST NOBLE THE MARQUESS OF CONYNGHAM.

Vice-Presidents.

RT. HON. LORD BRAYBROOKE, F.S.A.
RT. HON. LORD FRANCIS EGERTON, M.P.
RT. HON. THE EARL OF GLENGALL.
RT. HON. EARL HOWE.
RT. HON. LORD LEIGH.
RT. HON. THE EARL OF POWIS.

AMYOT, THOMAS, ESQ., F.R.S., TREAS. S.A.
AYRTON, WILLIAM, ESQ., F.R.S., F.S.A.
BOTFIELD, BERIAH, ESQ., M.P., F.R.S., F.S.A.
BRUCE, JOHN, ESQ., F.S.A.
CLERKE, MAJOR T. H. SHADWELL, K.H., F.R.S.
COLLIER, J. PAYNE, ESQ., F.S.A., DIRECTOR.
COOPER, C. PURTON, ESQ., Q.C., F.R.S., F.S.A.
CORNEY, BOLTON, ESQ.
CUNNINGHAM, PETER, ESQ., TREASURER.
DICKENS, CHARLES, ESQ.
DYCE, REV. ALEXANDER.
FIELD, BARRON, ESQ.
HALLAM, HENRY, ESQ., F.R.S., V.P.S.A.
HALLIWELL, J. O., ESQ., F.R.S., F.S.A.
PETTIGREW, T. J., ESQ., F.R.S. F.S.A.
PLANCHÉ, J. R., ESQ., F.S.A.
SHARPE, THE REV. LANCELOT, M.A., F.S.A.
THOMS, WILLIAM J., ESQ., F.S.A.
TOMLINS, F. GUEST, ESQ., SECRETARY.
WATSON, SIR FREDERICK BEILBY, K.C.H., F.R.S.
WRIGHT, THOMAS, ESQ., M.A., F.S.A.

The Council of the Shakespeare Society desire it to be understood that they are not answerable for any opinions or observations that may appear in the Society's publications; the Editors of the several works being alone responsible for the same.

INTRODUCTION.

By permission of the Master, Warden, and Fellows of Dulwich College, the Shakespeare Society is enabled to make some curious and interesting additions to its publication, the "Memoirs of Edward Alleyn." These additions chiefly consist of documents relating to the life and times of the Founder of Dulwich College, preserved in that institution, with some others, the property of J. O. Halliwell, Esq., which in all probability formerly came out of the same depository, and copies of which he unhesitatingly furnished, in order to render the present publication complete. In the last century, little attention was paid to the custody of these papers: their value was not understood, excepting by a few individuals, and they seem to have been removed without restraint. Malone had the custody of many of them for a long period; and at his death, although the greater part were restored, not a few were dispersed, and found their way into other hands. Of some no intelligence has since been obtained; and it is likely, if they have not been destroyed, that

they belong to individuals who are not even aware that they have possession of such relics.

Edward Alleyn was an actor of great and merited celebrity: he was the rival of Richard Burbage, (who seems to have performed most of the leading characters in Shakespeare's dramas) and it is probable that he left behind him copies of nearly all the parts he represented, as delivered out to him at the theatre to which he belonged, for the purpose of getting them by heart and studying them. One of these (Orlando, in R. Greene's "Orlando Furioso," 1594) is still extant at Dulwich College: but it is the only one; and as this has been handed down to us among the papers of the Founder, we cannot help thinking that they must originally have been much more numerous: if Alleyn kept one, why should he not have kept others?—and had they been now forthcoming, how much they would have contributed to the illustration of our drama and stage is evident from the single specimen which has been preserved, and which is printed entire in the Appendix to the "Memoirs," p. 198. We know that Alleyn was the representative of Faustus, in Marlowe's tragedy of that name, from the subsequent lines by one of his cotemporaries:—

> The Gull gets on a surplis,
>   With a crosse upon his brest,
> Like *Allen playing Faustus;*
>   In that manner was he drest.
>
>   S. Rowland's *Knave of Clubs.* 4to. 1600.

Marlowe's drama was not printed until ten years after we first hear of the performance of it; and, as in the

case of Greene's "Orlando Furioso," had Alleyn's part in it, written out by the copyist of the theatre, been extant, we have no doubt that important additions and variations would have been found in it.

On a different authority we learn that another of Alleyn's famous characters was Cutlack. A play with this title, (derived no doubt from the hero of it) according to Henslowe's Diary, was performed in May, 1594; but no fragment of it has come down to our day. Alleyn's performance of it, with the peculiar "gait" he assumed in the part, it thus mentioned in that very scarce collection of epigrams and satires entitled "Skialetheia, or the Shadow of Truth," 1598, which we know, on the authority of "England's Parnassus," 1600, was the authorship of Edward Guilpin:—

> Clodius, me thinkes, lookes passing big of late,
> With Dunstan's browes and *Alleyn's Cutlack's gate*.
> What humours have possess'd him so I wonder:
> His eyes are lightning, and his words are thunder. Sig. B. 2 b.

It would have been highly interesting to have found at Dulwich even such portions of lost plays as Alleyn was concerned in in his capacity of an actor. If he did not take part in any of Shakespeare's works, there is good reason for believing that he did perform in some of the pre-existing dramas on the same subjects, such as the old "Hamlet," the old "Merchant of Venice," the old "Pericles," &c.; and it would have been most interesting to have recovered any fragment of these pieces, by which we might have seen, in some degree, the nature and extent of our great dramatist's obligations to his

predecessors: however, they have probably irretrievably perished, and no doubt had done so long before the time of Malone, or he could hardly have failed to advert to them, although the MS. portion of Greene's "Orlando Furioso" escaped his attention.

The ensuing documents will illustrate, still farther than the facts detailed in the "Memoirs of Edward Alleyn," his gradual and steady acquisition of wealth, which enabled him, even before the commencement of the seventeenth century, to make considerable purchases of land and houses. There is a remarkable passage in the comedy of "The Return from Parnassus," not printed until 1606, but clearly written before the demise of Elizabeth, which must, we think, refer either to Shakespeare or Alleyn, but has yet never been distinctly applied to either: it relates to the manner in which some person, who had been an actor, was able, by means of his profitable profession, to become the owner of estates, and to obtain the title of esquire. Our readers will be aware that the usual style given to actors of old was merely that of "gentleman;" and it is to the advance of such a person to the rank of an esquire that the anonymous writer of "The Return from Parnassus" adverts. We hear of no other performers of the time, who attained to comparative wealth and consequence, but Shakespeare and Alleyn; and our reasons for thinking that the following quotation relates to Alleyn are, that our great dramatist could hardly be considered sufficiently wealthy, anterior to the death of Elizabeth, to excite observation; and that the person referred to is not spoken of as an author, as well as an

actor, which in all probability Shakespeare would have been, considering his success and popularity as a dramatist, and the inferior place we may suppose that he held as a player:—

> Vile world, that lifts them up to high degree,
> And treads us down in grovelling misery!
> England affords these glorious vagabonds,
> That carried erst their fardles on their backs,
> Coursers to ride on through the gazing streets,
> Sweeping it in their glaring satin suits,
> And pages to attend their masterships:
> With mouthing words, that better wits have framed,
> They purchase lands, and now esquires are made.

The manner in which actors formerly walked about the town, in gaudy and expensive dresses, is alluded to by Gosson, and by various other contemporaneous authorities. This was during their prosperity, and in the metropolis; but at times, when they were obliged to travel round the country, they did not always journey even "each actor on his ass," but sometimes were obliged to go on foot and to carry packs of apparel, &c., on their backs. In the old "Taming of a Shrew," 1594, we have an exact representation of this state of their affairs in the following stage-direction:—

Enter two of the Players, *with packs on their backs*, and a boy.

The "boy" was generally the performer of female characters, was commonly apprenticed to some leading member of the company, and possibly now and then officiated in London in the capacity of a page, attending upon his "mastership."

In connection with the quotation from "The Return from Parnassus," we may remark that what is said in the two last lines is contained, in much the same words, in the rare tract, "Ratseis Ghost, or the Second Part of his Madde Prankes and Robberies," (without date, but published, as is reasonably supposed, prior to 1606) where the highwayman-hero, Gamaliel Ratsey, is giving advice to a country player who had acted before him. In " The Hist. of Engl. Dram. Poetry and the Stage," i., 332, it is conjectured that the expressions may apply to Shakespeare, but on reflection it seems more probable that they were intended for Alleyn. Ratsey recommends the player to try his fortune in London:—

> There (says he) thou shalt learn to be frugal, (for players were never so thrifty as they are now about London) and feed upon all men; to let none feed upon thee; to make thy hand a stranger to thy pocket, thy heart slow to perform thy tongue's promise; and when thou feelest thy purse well lined, *buy thee some place of lordship in the country*, that, growing weary of playing, thy money may there bring thee to dignity and reputation: then, thou needest care for no man; no, not for them that before made thee proud with speaking their words on the stage.

It will be recollected, that it was just about the year when the tract from which we have quoted came out, that Alleyn bought his "place of lordship" at Dulwich of Sir Francis Calton, by which he became a lord of the manor. However, the concluding words of the paragraph seem more applicable to Shakespeare than to Alleyn, inasmuch as Alleyn was born in London, and had not, like Shakespeare, come to the metropolis "very meanly:"—" I have heard indeed of some (replied the

player to Ratsey) who have gone to London very meanly, and have come in time to be exceeding wealthy."

Whether the whole passage relate to Shakespeare, or to Alleyn, or to neither, but to some other actor, not now known to have been rich, who had in fact made a fortune by his profession, it is unquestionably very curious, and certainly was meant to have an individual and personal application.

On the subject of Alleyn's property, some additional information has come to light since the collection of the materials for the " Memoirs" of the founder of Dulwich College. It consists of a memorandum-book, kept by Alleyn himself in considerable detail, giving an account of the times at which, the circumstances under which he obtained, and the sums he gave for most of the land, houses, &c. he died possessed of. It is singular, however, that he omits all notice of purchases he made in the Blackfriars in the year 1612, although his Diary contains entries of frequent payments of rent by him, especially to a person of the name of Traves. This deficiency may, perhaps, be explained by the fact that although there is one notice in Alleyn's pocket-book regarding the purchase of " the Blue House" at Dulwich in 1614, and another in 1613, respecting money paid for 17 acres of land in the same neighbourhood, the memoranda regarding other property do not come down to a later date than 1610. We may infer from hence, that whatever might be the precise nature of his property in the Blackfriars, (and there is little doubt that it was leasehold, and none that it was theatrical) he did not acquire it until after 1610. Alleyn's pocket-book is also,

for the same reason, silent on the subject of his "lands in Yorkshire," mentioned in his will as having been "lately purchased of George Cole, Esq." A letter from Cole to Alleyn, dated 16th Feb. 1625, is inserted in the "Memoirs," p. 181, which may refer to some part of this transaction. It is to be observed that Malone saw this autograph record-book, and made an extract from it relating to the cost of the Fortune Theatre; but it was afterwards mislaid for many years, and was only recently discovered in the old "Treasury Chest of God's Gift College," as it is called in the carving on the lid.[1]

We will first insert the details with which we are thus furnished, (leaving out only the useless titles of deeds and "evidences," as Alleyn calls them) and then follow them by a few explanatory remarks. One item cannot fail to strike the reader immediately: it shews that Edward Alleyn (at what precise date does not appear) was in possession of an inn called "The Boar's Head," which had formerly been kept by his elder brother, John Alleyn. No locality is stated; but it would be very singular if it were the very Boar's Head in Eastcheap, which existed in the time of Shakespeare, and which he has made so famous. It was, however, not an uncommon sign in London; and the inn which John Alleyn at one time kept in Bishopsgate, and which he inherited from his father, may have been so called.

[1] The writer of this "Introduction," not then contemplating the present Supplement to the "Memoirs of Edward Alleyn," as few of the materials for it had reached his hands, published a summary of the contents of the pocket-book in a literary journal, soon after he had found it.—See the "Athenæum," August 28th, 1841.

INTRODUCTION.

We give the following, *verbatim et literatim*, as they stand in Edward Alleyn's handwriting in the pocket-book, a small 8vo. of considerable thickness, upon many of the leaves of which nothing is entered.

EXTRACTS FROM A MEMORANDUM-BOOK IN ALLEYN'S HANDWRITING.

What the Bear garden cost for my owne part in December, 1594.

First to Mr Burnabye	200^l
Then for the Patten[t]	250
Some is	450
I held it 16 year, and Rd 60^l per annum, which is .	960^l
Sould itt to my father, Hinchloe, in Februarie, 1610, for .	580^l

What the Parsnage of Firlls coste me (in all) of redy money or other wayes.

	l.	s.	d.
First to Ar. Langth [Langworth] . . .	1066	13	4
3 years daye forberaunc . . .			
The last payment lost, which he should have payd .	66	13	4
I gave hym at last parting . . .	070^l		
With 2 bonds of	30^l		
My charges for conveyances and law . .	10^l		
Which is in all, without allowaunc for 3 year forberaunc, ...	1273	6	8
So in all it cost .	1323	6	8

What I reseved of itt

	s.	s.	d.
5 payments from Ar. Langworth a 100 marks			
A payment half yearly	333	vj	8
For j years of Crop to Page declare . .	100^l		
For 4 years of Mr Roots declare . .	440^l		
Some 873 vj 8 (l. s. d.)			
Sowld this parsnage to Mr Homden and Mr Bunc about Christ., 1605, for . . .	1300^l		

What the Fortune cost me, Novemb., 1599.

First for the leas to Brew	240^l
Then for the building the playhouse	520^l
For other privat buildings of myn owne	120^l
So in all it hath cost me for the leasse	880^l
Bought the inheritance of the land of the Gills of the Ile of Man, which is the Fortune, and all the howses in Whight crosstrett and Gowlding lane, in June, 1610, for the some of	340^l
Bought in John Garretts lease in revertion from the Gills, for 21 yeares, for	100^l

So in all itt cost me 1320^l.
Blessed be the Lord God everlasting.

What the Manore of Kenington cost me, Novemb., 1604.

First to Mr Skevingtonn for the lease in possession	660^l
Then to Tho. Webber for the lease being in revertion	405^l

So in all, 1065^l.

Sowld this mannor of Kenington to Sir Fr. Calton, Knight, the 1st of Septemb., 1609, for . . . . 2000^l.

In no. do. Amen. An. 1605.

Bought the lordshipp of Dulwich of Sr Francis Calton, Knight, this 20 of October, for . . . . . 5000^l.

Wher of 2000^l is payd in hand.

The other 3000^l at the end of 6 years, with consideration yearly for forberaunce of the 3000^l, the some of 213^l 6^s 8^d per ann.

Pd S^r Fr. the said some of 3000^l att severall payments, and the last on the 25 of October, 1613.

[This is followed by a list headed "The Evidences belonging to the same," containing the substance of the writings Alleyn received from Sir Francis Calton. They are 32 in number, besides some cancelled indentures, statutes, bonds, &c., between Sir Francis Calton and "Sir Ro. Lee, Mayor."]

j of June, in Trinitie Terme, 1606.

Bought of Mr Tho. Emerson a howse and 5 acers of lande in Dulwich, price 230^l, of free hould sockage tenure.

[Sixteen "Evidences belonging to the same" follow here.]

In Trinitie Terme, 1606, *the 3rd of July*.

In Dullwich, bought of Mr Tho. Calton, Hethersalls howse and land, viz. 16 acers cald North Croftes, 12 acres calde great Bornes, 4 acers about the howse, in all 32 acres.

Price 300^l. Tenure in Capitie.

[Here follow 4 "Evidences of the lands that were Tho. Caltons."]

The 16 *of October,* 1606.

In Dullwich, bought of John Berrey his howse and land, conteyning 13 acres, being coppie howld of the same mannore, price 231^l.

["The wrightings belonging to the same" follow.]

Candelmass Tearm, 1606.

Bought of John Ewine Bodgers Howse and land, which he howldeth by lease, vidz. j. tenement and 9 acers of land for the some of 80^l.

Bought in the lease which Ewin had in revertion of the same howse and land from me for 21 years, and for the same lease payd the same John Ewin, the 25 of Aprill, 1608, the some of 12^l.

["The Evidences of the lands wear Jo. Ewins," 12 in number, follow.]

Cundellmass Terme, 1606.

Bought of Thomas Turner his howse and land in Dullwich, calde Perrie Feeld, contayning 13 acers, for the some of . 226^l 13^s 4^d

Given Ewin for procuration, and making the bargayne 5^l

["The Evidences of the lands that wear Tho. Turners," 21 in number, follow.]

The j of June, 1607.

Bought of Tho. Calton and his wyfe, Henrie Farr and his wyfe, the corner howse in Dullwich, and 16 acres of land.

[Eight "Evidences belonging to the same" follow.]

The 22nd of October, 1607.

Bought of Elice Parrei all his landes in Dullwich, as well free as

coppie howld, vidz. Ambls howse and land, Anthonie Kichins howse and land, and Jo Lewes howse and grownd, for 400^l.

[Twelve "Evidences belonging to the same" follow.]

The 29th off october, 1608, bought of Tho. Calton 2 percells of land in the occupation of Jo Fering, caled Little Brownings and Carters garden, beeing 5 akers more or less, which landes wear past in the conveighanc of the landes I bought of Jo. Ewine in Hilarie Terme, 1606, and nowe pd to the same Tho. Calton for the sayd landes the sume of 50^l.

The Evidenc for the same is Calton's release as afore, as itt is sett downe before in Ewins evydences.

The 13th *off December*, 1608.

Bought of S^r. Ed. Bowyar all ther lands in Dullwich, and Tenimentes both free and coppie howld, being about 70 akers, and 8 or 9 Howses, for the sume of . . . . 1650^l.

And as this 13 of December I kept Court at Dullwich, and they surendred their coppiehold.

[Numerous "Evidences" follow.]

Bought the Inheritannc off the Fortune the 30th off maye, 1610, and allso the lease in reversion of Jo Garrett the same tyme, for the sume of . . . . 440^l.

[Forty "Evidences for the same" follow.]

[This is succeeded, after two or three blank pages, by "More wrightings concerning the Lordshipp of Dullwich," which are very numerous.]

Bought of Tho. Calton and his wyfe Ann ther dwelling howse and Hethersalls howse, with theys percells of grownd following.

3 acres behynde Tho. Caltons howse.

4 acres, caled Carters Hall, belonging to Hethersall howse.

7 acres, calde great Brownings.

12 acres, caled Addingtons meadowes.

Theys percelles for 510^l, the 25 off November, 1611, and R. Jacobus the 9th.

[Eighteen "Evidences belonging to the same" follow.]

Bought of S^r. E. Duke, Knight, the 2 of November, 1613, 17 acres off land, lying betwene Blanch Downes and the highe waye towards the north, for the some of . . . . 160^l.

[Six "Evidences for the same" follow.]

A generall note of all my writings, deedes or evidences, bondes or bills, belonging to me,

E. ALLEYN.

[Among these are the following.]

My deeds for the wharfe in the Close.

Lo. Mountagues lease to West.

Young West to Robert Bromfeeld. Indentur Ro. Bromfeeld to me by pole dede.

Itt cost me 115^l.

The deedes of my howses in Bushopsgate Street.

An indentur of sale from Cornelius [Parker] to my father.

My fathers will.

A releas from my mother and Brown to John and me, in Lattin.

[The following are crossed out.]

Of the Bores Head.

A leas from Julyan Cropwell to John Alen.

His pol dede to me.

A bond on the same.

My howse on the Banck.

The leas to Curtis.

Roberts his sale to me.

[Then follows a list of a variety of deeds, &c., under the general heading of,]

The Wrightings of the Bear Garden.

[Among them these.]

Ballards lease to Pope.

Morgin Pope to Edward Boes.

Rafe Boes and Edward Boes to Morgin Pope.

Rafe Boes and Edward Boes to Burnabie.
Burnabie to Edward Alleyn.
Edward Alleyn to Phelop Henslow.
Jacobe Meades lease.

Bonds.

A bond of Wisloes for covenants of 200^{li}.
Pope to Hayes in 200^{li}.
Napton to Pope a 100 markes.
Burnabie to Alleyn in 40 pounds.
Burnabie to Alleyn in 100 pounds.
Burnabie to Alleyn in 200 pounds.
Burnabie to Alleyn in 300 pounds.
Henslow to Alleyn in 500 pounds.
Henslow to Alleyn in 500 pounds.
Jacob Meade in 300 pounds.

The wrightings of Firles.

The church lease to Mathew Marsh and Peter Marsh for 250 years.

A conveyance from Peter Marsh and Mathewe to M^r. Wattes, Aldermann.

Frome John Chapman to Wattes.
Frome Earl to Wattes.
Frome Wattes to Buckhurst.
Frome Lo. Buckhurst to his sonn.
Frome M^r Ro. Sackvile to A. Langworth.
From A. Langworth to E. Allin.
From E Allin to Jo. Langworth.
From Jo. Langworth to E. Allin.
A releas from A. Langworth.
2 bondes of 2 thousand pound.
Richard Earles Letter of Attorney to Chapman.

Bought the j. daye of June, 1614, an^o. R. Jacobus, the 12th, of Marie Shillingford and Francis Shillingford, off Aylesford, in Kent, mother and sone, all theyr 3d partes, part and parcell of a Tenement

in Dulwich, called the Blew House, and tooke it in the names of Phillip Henslowe, Esq., Will. Austen, Esq., Jo. Bingham, Esq., George Payne, cittisone and grocer of London, Rich. Yarwoode, cittizen and grocer off London, Roger Cole, Robert Bromefeeld, Edw. Bromefeeld, Jo. Marshall, and Drew Stapley, in trust to such uses as I, E. A. shall in my last will and testament, or other deed under hand and seale declare. The some pd. wase 16^{li}

[Eight " Evidences belonging to the same" follow.]

Thus we see that Alleyn bought his share of Paris Garden as early as 1594, and that he sold it to Henslowe (the husband of his wife's mother) in 1610 for £120 more than he had given for it, and after he had derived £60 a-year from it for sixteen years. He did nearly as well with the parsonage of Firle, in Sussex, which he bought (the date is not inserted) for £1323, and sold again in 1605 for £1300, after receiving £873 from it in the interval. The Fortune Theatre cost him £1320: from 1599 to 1610 he paid rent for the ground on which it stood, but in the latter year he was able to purchase the inheritance from the Gills, as well as a reversionary interest possessed by a person of the name of John Garrett. In 1604 Alleyn bought the Manor of Kennington for £1065, and after holding it for five years, and no doubt reaping considerable advantage from it, he sold it to Sir Francis Calton for nearly £1000 more than he had paid for it. The year after he became possessed of the Manor of Kennington, Alleyn paid down £2000 for the Manor of Dulwich, and agreed to give £3000 more in six years, paying interest upon it; but the last payment was not, in fact, made until 1613. Possibly the delay was occasioned by the

expenditure of Alleyn from time to time in the accumulation of other landed property in Dulwich which belonged to various parties: in the whole Alleyn gave no less a sum than £8870 for his estate at Dulwich, which would be equal to more than £40,000 of our present money. Well, therefore, might the author of "Ratsey's Ghost" say (if the allusion be to Alleyn) that he "had come in time to be exceeding wealthy."

These particulars, it will be evident, are of importance with reference to Shakespeare, and to the property he acquired during his professional life. If Alleyn could attain to such wealth, being merely an actor, it renders it more likely that Shakespeare, when he retired to Stratford-upon-Avon, had realised at least a comfortable and easy independence.

In the "Memoirs," pp. 179 and 187, the marriage of Edward Alleyn with his second (or possibly third) wife Constance is mentioned, and some doubt is stated whether she were or were not the daughter of Dr. Donne. The Editor was not then aware of the fact, since brought to his knowledge, that the Parish Register of Camberwell Old Church contains the following record of Alleyn's union with Constance Donne, within six months after the death of his wife Joan, whose maiden name was Woodward. We copy it from a communication made to "The Gentleman's Magazine" in 1834 by that excellent antiquary, Mr. G. Steinman Steinman:—

Married December 3[d], 1623, Edward Alleyn, Esq. to Mrs. Constance Donn.

Of course this extract puts an end to all question upon the point, and gives much additional interest to the

letter of Alleyn to his father-in-law, preserved at Dulwich, and printed in the "Memoirs," p. 173. It throws much new and curious light on the character and conduct of Dr. Donne. Constance Alleyn, as Mr. Steinman Steinman correctly states, afterwards married Samuel Harvey, Esq., of Abury Hatch, Essex, at whose house Dr. Donne was seized with his last illness.

It will be seen, by Alleyn's will, (a copy of which we subjoin) that he left his wife two sums of £1500 and £100, and all her jewels and other ornaments. This was more than he had undertaken before marriage, as is evident from the letter of Alleyn to Donne just referred to; and in addition she retained what she had brought her husband, which, according to the same authority, appears to have been £500. Alleyn's will, which we believe has never till now been printed, is in the following terms; and we learn from it that Mathias Alleyn, afterwards Master of Dulwich College, was "cousin" to Edward Alleyn, but what degree of relationship the latter meant to indicate by that word does not appear. It may be considered singular that he does not name in his will any of his early friends and associates, although not a few of them must have been then living, and although he kept up his intercourse with some of them to a late date.

EXTRACTED FROM THE REGISTRY OF THE PREROGATIVE COURT OF CANTERBURY.

In the name of God, Amen, the thirteenth day of November, Anno Dom., 1626, and in the second year of the reign of our Sovereign Lord King Charles, &c., I, Edward Alleyn, of Dulwich, in the

county of Surrey, Esquire, being sick in body, but of perfect mind and memory, thanks be given to Almighty God, do make and ordain this my presente testament, declaring herein my last will in manner and form following: that is to say, first and principally I commend my soul to Almighty God, my merciful Creator, and to Jesus Christ, my most loving Saviour and Redeemer, in whom and by whose merits I only trust to be saved, and made partaker of everlasting life: and my body I will to the earth, from whence it came, without any vain funeral pomp, or show, to be interred in the quire of that chapel, which God of his goodness hath caused me to erect, and dedicate to the honor of my Saviour, by the name of Christ's Chappell, in God's Gift College, heretofore by me founded in Dulwich aforesaid.

Item, my mind and will is, that all such debts and duties, which of right or in confidence I do owe and stand truly indebted in unto any person or persons whatsoever, shall be truly paid and satisfied after my decease, so shortly and conveniently as may be.

And whereas, I, the said Edward Alleyn, and one Matthias Allen, he being a person by me put in trust, for and in performance and assurance of one thousand and five hundred pounds, to and for my dear and loving wife Constance Alleyn, after my decease have by two several deeds of demise, grant, and assignment, bearing date the nine and twentieth day of June, last past, before the date of these presents, granted, assigned, and set over, unto Sr Nicholas Carew, of Beddington, and Sr Thomas Grymes, of Peckham, in the county of Surrey, knights, their executors and assigns, one capital messuage and tenement, or inn, called the Unicorn, in Saint Saviours parish, in the borough of Southwark, in the county of Surrey, and all other messuages and tenements there, &c.

And also, I, the said Edward Alleyn, and Matthias Alleyn, by the other of the said deeds, have likewise granted, assigned, and set over, unto the said Sir Nicholas Carew and Sr Thomas Grymes, their executors, and assigns, certain capital messuages and tenements, called the Barge, the Bell, and the Cock, situate and lying on the bank side, in the parish of Saint Saviours aforesaid. And whereas, likewise for further assurance of the said one thousand five hundred pounds, for my said wife as aforesaid, I, the said Edward Alleyn, have acknowledged a statute of two thousand pounds, bearing the

said date of the nine and twentieth day of June last, unto the said Sir Nicholas Carew, and Sr Thomas Grimes.

And whereas, by a pair of indentures of defeazance, dated the said nine and twentieth day of June last, between me, the said Edward Alleyn, and the said Sr Nicholas Carew, and Sr Thomas Grimes, knights, wherein the said two knights have covenanted, that, if my said wife (in case she survive me) shall by me, and out of my estate, be left the said sum of one thousand five hundred pounds, in ready money, and that then my executor, or executors, shall, within three months after my decease, pay to her, the said Constance, the said sum of one thousand five hundred pounds, that then, and not otherwise, the said statute of two thousand pounds, to be void and of none effect, together with the two deeds of assignment, or to resign them to such person or persons, as I, the said Edward, shall nominate and appoint.

Now in full performance of the aforesaid assurance, and to shew my full desire to have it really accomplished, I will and require my executors hereunder named, that, first and principally, my loving wife Constance, (in case she survive me) be, according to my agreement, fully satisfied in the best manner that may be; and then I desire the said two knights to resign and set over the said two knights' leases unto my executors.

Item, I give and bequeath unto my said loving wife, Constance Alleyn, in testimony of my further love to her, and for her present use and benefit, one hundred pounds more, of lawfull money of England, which I have already, vidt., on the six and twentieth day of September last, in the presence of Mathew Sweeteser, Edward Alleyn, John Sayford, and John Casinghurst, delivered to and for her use, unto the hands and custody of the said Sr Thomas Grimes; and moreover I give unto my said wife all her jewels and other ornaments she is now possessed withall.

Item, I give and bequeath to the Corporation of God's-Gift College aforesaid, these goods and implements following, that is to say: first my seal ring with my arms, to be worn by the Master and his successors. Next I appoint that a common seal shall be made for the said College, at the charge of my executors, which said two seals shall be repaired by the College as often as need shall require.

Also all the wainscots, hangings, pictures, carpets, presses, tables, chairs, fforms, and stools, in the said College, with all shelves, desks, and seats, also my books and instruments, and likewise all the furniture in the twelve poor schollars chamber, that is to say, six bed-steads, six matts, sixe mattresses, six feather beds, six feather bolsters, twelve pair of sheets, twelve blankets, twelve rugs, three dozen of bedstaves, and six pewter chamber potts; also I give unto the said College, of my linen, twelve table cloaths, six dozen of napkins, and six towels, whereof one sort or suit shall be of damask, and other of diaper; likewise two dozen of pewter vessell, with all other brass and iron vessell of ffurniture, which shall be in use of the said College, at the hour of my death, in any room of the said College whatsoever; also all implements and tools of husbandry, together with two furnished teams, the one with five horses, and the other with six oxen, and my mind is, that all these goods by me given to the said College, shall be by my executors presently by inventory delivered unto them to be continually by the said College kept in good repair.

Also, I will and require my executors, hereafter named, within two years after my decease, to build ten almshouses, in the parish of Saint *Buttolphe*, without Bishopgate, London, for ten poor people of that parish, to be members of the aforesaid College. And likewise ten other houses in St Saviours parish aforesaid, for other ten poor people of the said parish, to be likewise members of the said College, which said twenty poor people being placed in their several houses, shall have such relief and maintenance as in the statutes of the aforesaid College is set down.

Item, I give to Thomas Alleyn, the son of John Alleyn, late of Willen, in the county of Bucks, being my cousin and next heir at the common law, the sum of fifty pounds.

Item, I give to Edward Alleyn, junior, of Newport, the sum of twenty pounds; and to his two sisters, Elizabeth Newman and Anne Ashpoole, twenty pounds a-piece; and I give unto my Aunt Jane Waldock, of Water-Eaton, the sum of ten pounds.

Item, I give to Anne Alleyn, the now wife of John Harrison, clerk, the sum of twenty pounds.

Item, I will my copyhold lands in Lambeth Marshes to Edward

Alleyn, my godson, and his heirs male, (which I hope the custom there will allow); and, for want of such issue, to John Alleyn, the son of Mathias Alleyn, and his heirs for ever.

Item, I give to Sir Francis Calton, knight, the sum of one hundred pounds, and hereby forgive him twenty pounds he owes me on his lre due long since.

Item, I give to Elizabeth Cutler, my late wife's god-daughter, the sum of ten pounds.

Item, I give to Hanna Pickerley the sum of ten pounds.

Item, I give to Elizabeth Fassell, a young girl that is now in my house, ten pounds.

Item, I give to all the rest of my household servants that are in my service at the time of my death, so many pounds a-piece as they severally have been and continued years in my service, besides their wages then due.

Item, I will and bequeath to the churchwardens of Saint Buttolphes without Bishopgate, London, and their successors, for ever, a tenement in Dulwich, with the appurtenances, called the Blew House, now in the tenure of Edward Kipping, to and for the only use of the poor of their said parish, to be by them employed and disposed of in such manner and form as in the statute of God's-Gift College aforesaid is set down, and not otherwise.

And my Will is, and I do hereby declare that, after the said fifteen hundred pounds, and all and every the legacies herein above bequeathed shall be respectively paid, that the said two leases so assigned as aforesaid to the said Sir Nicholas Carew and Sir Thomas Grimes shall be and remain to the said corporation of God's-Gift College as an augmentation unto them, during the terms thereof, over and above what I have already assigned and assured unto them, to be employed current according to the intent of the statutes of the said college.

And I give and bequeath (after my legacies paid) to my two executors herein to be named, all my lands in Yorkshire, by what name or names, or title soever called or known, which I lately purchased of George Cole, Esq., in their two names, to hold to them and their two heirs and assigns jointly for ever.

And I do by these presents give and bequeath all the rest and

residue of my goods, chattles, cattle, and ready money whatsoever, after my funerals are discharged and my debts paid, with all the legacies of this my Will performed, unto Thomas Alleyn and Mathias Alleyn, my kinsmen, whom of this my last Will and Testament I make my sole executors, charging them, as they will answer it before the face of Almighty God, at the dreadful day of judgement, that they truly and punctually in every particular (so far fourth as they possibly may) perform this my last Will and Testament.

And I do hereby revoke all former Will and Wills by me at any time heretofore made; and in witness of this my last Will, containing two sheets of paper, I have to the bottom of each sheet subscribed my name, and, being both sheets joined together, at the foot thereof set to my seal, the day and year first above written.

E. ALLEYN.

Sealed, Delivered, and Published as his last Will and Testament, in the presence of us, Joseph Reading | = | Matthew Sweeteser | = | Henry Dell | = | John Casinghurst | = | Geo. Brome.

Probatum apud London, 13 Dec. 1626. Coram Magro Thoma Ryves Legum Doctore surrogato juramentis Thome Alleyn et Mathie Alleyn executorum cui, &c. debe, &c. Jurat.

Some of the most valuable papers in the ensuing pages, especially in relation to the history and state of our Stage in the time of Shakespeare, were copied for Malone, and are inserted in vol. xxi. of the edition of the works of our great dramatist, edited by Boswell in 1821. We say that they were copied for Malone, because we can hardly believe that he would have himself been guilty of so many errors and oversights: he must have employed some person to transcribe them who could not read any old writing with facility,

and, least of all, some of the hasty scraps of Daborne and others in Henslowe's pay, who were constantly pressing him for money in advance upon compositions then in hand. From this, and other testimony derived from the old manager's diary, we find that it was the frequent custom for the urgent wants of dramatists to be thus supplied, and hardly one of those who wrote for Henslowe's company, from Ben Jonson downwards, finished a new play without making some claims of the kind. Whether such was the case at other theatres is a question we have no means of deciding beyond inference; but there is good reason to suppose that Shakespeare, excepting perhaps very early in his career, was able to avoid making such demands. Judging from what we know of Henslowe's practice, we may conclude that the purchasers of new plays usually paid a stipulated sum to the authors, and took the risk upon themselves. An agreement on the part of a dramatist to accept a contingent advantage, depending upon the receipts of a particular night or nights, seems to have been an exception to the rule, and we hear of it of old only in the case of Daborne.

The mistakes and omissions committed by Malone's scribe sometimes affect importantly the whole sense of a passage; at others, one name is substituted for another, as William Haughton, the dramatist, for a person known as "Will Hunt, the pedlar," (p. 24): wrong dates and sums are here and there given, and, in one instance, lines from some lost play, in the handwriting of John Day, the celebrated dramatist, were wholly overlooked at the back of a note from Samuel Rowley, relating to a drama

called "The Six Yeomen of the West," (p. 23). These defects and deficiencies it was obviously necessary to correct and supply, and such original papers of the kind as remain at Dulwich we have carefully collated. One of them contains the signatures of the different members of the company under Alleyn, just before the death of Shakespeare, and these we have given in fac-simile (p. 87) as a remarkable relic of the period. Henslowe's Diary furnishes others of an earlier date, which will be contained in the forthcoming impression of that unique and most valuable manuscript.

As we have assigned a title to each separate document, and introduced it by such information as seemed necessary, or could be procured, in order to render the subject intelligible, we need not here say more of their particular import. The Shakespeare Society is again obliged (as in the case of the "Memoirs of Edward Alleyn") to the Master, Warden, and Fellows of Dulwich College, for the unrestricted use of the archives of that Institution. The collection of the materials for this small work was commenced in the time of the late learned, liberal, and accomplished Master, John Allen, to whom many of our literary associations are more or less indebted: it has been continued under the sanction of the present Master; and the labours of the editor have not only been encouraged, but readily assisted by the Rev. Charles Howes, who has now the custody of the library and manuscripts, and upon whose time and patience frequent encroachments were necessarily made. If a Shakespeare Society had existed fifty years ago, and the same liberal spirit, which the editor has invari-

ably experienced, had then prevailed among the heads of the establishment, we have no doubt that much new and valuable light, now obscured or extinguished, might have been thrown upon the condition of our stage and drama during the whole of the period when Shakespeare was an actor or an author. We have done our best both to preserve and to perpetuate what remains of the large mass of papers which must formerly have been in the possession of " The College of God's Gift." Some of these may, possibly, be considered of trifling moment; but there are few which do not, either directly or indirectly, illustrate the more immediate objects of the Shakespeare Society, and the state of society and manners at the end of the reign of Elizabeth, and in the beginning of that of her successor.

J. P. C.

Kensington, September, 1843.

NOTES TO THE INTRODUCTION.

Page vi. line 6. Richard Burbage, who seems to have performed most of the leading characters in Shakespeare's dramas.] This fact, hitherto depending upon conjecture, is ascertained, from the MS. Epitaph upon Burbage, sold among the books of the late Mr. Heber, a copy of which is contained in "New Particulars regarding the Works of Shakespeare," 8vo. 1836. Hence we find that Burbage was the original Hamlet, Romeo, Prince Henry, Henry the Fifth, Richard the Third, Macbeth, Brutus, Coriolanus, Shylock, Lear, Pericles, and Othello. These parts are all distinctly mentioned as having been sustained by Burbage, and on the same authority we know that he played Jeronimo in Kyd's "Spanish Tragedy," Antonio in Marston's "Antonio and Mellida," Frankford in Heywood's "Woman Killed with Kindness," Philaster, Amintas, &c.

Page vi. line 28. S. Rowland's Knave of Clubs.] This tract, with two others, belonging to the same amusing class in literature, has recently been reprinted by the Percy Society, under the editorial care of Mr. Rimbault, in the state in which it came from the press in the edition of 1611. We highly approve of these reprints in their entire shape, since nothing can well be more mistaken than to suppose that what may seem indecorous to our more refined ears (the difference being only in the increased susceptibility of those organs, and certainly not in any greater sensibility of heart or purity of manners) was so considered by our ancestors, or ought, in truth, to be so estimated by ourselves.

Page vii. line 4. Important additions would have been found in it.] There is, however, no reason to think that "Faustus" was originally printed as imperfectly as some others of Marlowe's dramas—"The Massacre at Paris," for instance, (by E. White, without date) which obviously consists only of fragments of the old manuscript. That it was so we have positive proof beyond internal evidence; and in the last edition of "Dodsley's Old Plays," viii. 244, is inserted a small portion of the tragedy derived from a manuscript of the time, which contains considerably more than the printed copy. We may take this opportunity of pointing out the absurdity of imputing to Marlowe the play of "Lust's Dominion," after the direct proof afforded (D. O. P. last edit. ii. 311), that he could not have written one line of it. Nevertheless, whenever "Lust's Dominion" has been since spoken of, it has still been attributed to Marlowe. It is doubtless the same piece as is called "The Spanish Moor's Tragedy" in Henslowe's Diary, which Malone strangely misread "The Spanish Morris." It was written by Dekker, Haughton, and Day. See Hist. Engl. Dram. Poetry and the Stage, iii. 96.

Page vii. line 7. Derived, no doubt, from the hero of it.] The "Biographia Dramatica" not very happily suggests that for "Cutlack" we ought to read "Good lack," as the title of the drama.

Page vii. line 15. This circumstance was first pointed out in "Reasons for a new Edition of Shakespeare's Works," 8vo. 1841. A beautiful but very restricted reprint of "Skialetheia" has recently been made by Edw. V. Utterson, Esq. It consists, we believe, of 15 impressions, but of the original edition only three copies appear to be known.

Page ix. line 22. The old "Taming of a Shrew," 1594.] The Shakespeare Society is about to reprint this valuable relic, of which only a single copy of that date remains. It is in the collection of the Duke of Devonshire, who has most liberally placed it at the disposal of Mr. Amyot for the purpose. His Grace has also the impression of 1607, which Steevens used; and a unique copy, dated 1596, is in the library of Lord Francis Egerton. All three will be collated by Mr. Amyot, in order to render his edition as perfect as possible.

THE ALLEYN PAPERS.

RELEASE TO JOHN ALLEYN.

[John Alleyn, or Allen, as the name is spelt in the following document, was the elder brother of Edward, the founder of Dulwich College. From a similar instrument dated 18 November, 1580, it appears that John Alleyn was at that date one of the theatrical servants to Lord Sheffield. See "Memoirs of Edward Alleyn," p. 3.]

Be yt knowen unto all men by theis presentes that I, Richard Johnson of the parishe of St. Gyles, without Creeplegate, London, carter, have remysed, released, and for me, myne heres, executors, and administrators perpetually, quite claymed to John Allen of London, yeoman, all and all manner of actions, as well reall as personall suites, quarrells, trespasses, executions, somes of money, debtes, duties, and demaundes whatsoever, which I the said Richard Johnson now have, ever hadde, or of right ought to have had, against the said John Allen, for any cause, matter or thinge whatsoever, from the begynnynge of the worlde untill the day of the date hereof. In witnes whereof I, the said Richard Johnson, have hereunto sett my hand and

seale the second day of December Anno Regni dnæ nostræ Reginæ Elizabeth nunc xxiij°.

(Seal, but no name nor mark.)

Signed, sealed, and delivered
in the presence of us—
    HENRY WRYGHT
    THOMAS CURTES
    THOMAS MADOCKS.

ANOTHER RELEASE TO JOHN ALLEYN.

[A document of the same kind as that which precedes. What claims either Johnson or Cox had upon John Alleyn (here called Inn-holder) is no where stated. A Robert Cox, at a considerably later date, was connected with the stage, as a writer or compounder of Drolls acted at fairs, &c.]

Be it knowne unto all men by these presentes that I, Roberte Cox, of Bemyster, in the countie of Dorset, yeoman, have remised, released, and alwayes for me my heres, executors and administrators, for evermore have quite claymed to John Allen, Citizen and Inholder of London, all and all maner of actions, as well reall as personall, sutes, quarrelles, debtes, debates, somes of money, recknings, accomptes, and demaundes whatsoever, wch againste the same John ever I had, have, or by any wayes or meanes hereafter may have, for any maner of matter, reason, cause, or thing, whatsoever it be, from the begynnynge of the world untyll the day of the date hereof; and also all bondes, writinges, covenauntes, and all other matters whatsoever. In witness wherof I have here unto set my hande and seale, the eighte and twenteth day of November, 1586, and in the nyne and twenteth yeare of the raigne of our soveraigne Lady Elizabethe, by the grace of God Quene of England, Fraunce, and Ireland, defendour of the fayth, &c.

                              ROBT. COX. (L. S.)

Sigillat. et delibat. in presentia mei Johnis
   Harvey, apprenticius Tho. Wrightson
   Scr. &c. curialis London.

INVENTORY OF FURNITURE, &c.

[The subsequent Inventory exhibits John Alleyn in 1587 as creditor and administrator to a person of the name of Richard Browne: Browne was probably some relation to the stepfather of John, Edward, and William Alleyn, their mother, Margaret, after the death of their father having married a haberdasher of that name.]

Thinuentarie indented of all and singuler the goods, chattels, and debtes, which late were belonging and appertayning unto Richard Browne, Shipwrighte, late of the parish of Alhallowes in Lomberstrete, deceassed, which were renounced by Margery Browne his wife, praysed the eight day of Januarye, Anno Regni Elizabeth Reginæ tricesimo, by us Phillipp Browne gent. and James Tunstall yeoman as followeth—

	s.	d.
Imprimis an old bedsted, a bed, a bolster, a blanckett, and a coverlett	xvj	
Item a cupbord, a settle bedstede, a little table, ij old chestes and fye stooles	viij	iiij
Item an old chest and iiij old chayres	ij	vj
Item old brasse	vj	
Item certayne peices of pewter, wayeng about xx pound wait	vj	viij
Item ij payr of old sheetes, three old napkins, ij old table clothes, and ij hand towells	v	
Item a payre of andyrons, a payre of tongues, a fierr shovell, and a payr of pothookes	xviij	

Summa Totalis hujus Inventarij xlvj

Extum fecit &c., 23º die Januarij Aº dom. juxta &c. 1587 p Johem Allen creditorem et Administratorem pro pleno &c.

THO. REDMAN, deputatus
JO. INCENT REGRARII &c.

LETTER OF RECOMMENDATION.

[A singular document, by which it was intended to influence the decision of a suit in favour of the servant of the writer. That servant was John Alleyn, and the nobleman who was thus to interpose was the Earl of Nottingham, to whose company of actors John Alleyn at this time belonged. It is merely the draft of a letter, and the probability is that it was never sent, the object having been accomplished without it.]

After my very harty commendōns. Whereas my Lls. of her Ma^{tes} Privie Counsell did in July last direct their letters to the now Lo. M. of the cytty of London, All. Byllyngsly and others, for the endyng of a controversye between this bearer, my servant, and one Docter Marten, who by indirect meanes, as their lordshipps have beene gyven to understand, seekethe to mak; for that a lease of a certayn tenement with a garden, demised by John Royse to the suppliants father, mother, and hym sellfe, as by ther sayd letters may at large appear: for asmuch as the sayd Lo. M. and the rest have commytted the decyding of the variance to Mr. Sallter and Mr. Woodcock, as arbytrators, and your sellfe as umpire in the cawse, becawse they dowtted not by reason of your suffyciencie and experience in such matters, but by the meanes the same showld be ordered accordyng to all indyfferencie and equyte. Wherefore I have thought good (for that my sayd L^{ds} of the cownsayll do incline to favour the goodness of my sayd servantes suyte) very ernestly to desyre yow, that by your discretion and approved good consyderation, all possyble justyce may be aforded unto hym, and that he may injoy the bennefyte of the sayd leas and demyse, according to the contents of ther L^{ps} sayd letters wherin, allthoughe I mystrust not of your integrety and uprightnes, without any shew of partiallyte to thadvers part, to the prejudice of my servaunt, yet did I judge it not impertinent to the cawse to crave your frendship and favour hearin; for that hearby yow shall take occasyon to demaund a greater curtesye at my handes hereafter, and shall deserve great commendation for the travayll yow

shall sustayn in compowndyng of the difference, which as well my sellfe as my said servant shall indeuour to reqwytt. And thus referryng the determynation of the hole to your grave consyderation, I wyshe you very hartely well to fare. From the cowrtt at Rychemond thes   of decemb. 1589.

Y^r very loveing Freind.

LETTER FROM THE PRIVY COUNCIL TO THE LORD MAYOR, &c.

[This is a curious original document (referred to in the preceding) shewing in what way the privy council of that day interfered in behalf of a favoured suitor, who was under the protection of a powerful nobleman. A course of this kind might possibly be necessary to secure justice to John Alleyn, because the Lord Mayor and Corporation were at all times adverse to actors. See "Hist. of Engl. Dram. Poetry and the Stage," i. 272, for documents which show that in this very year, 1589, Harte, the Lord Mayor, had evinced his strong hostility to theatres and to those engaged in them. What follows also establishes that Mrs. Browne, the mother of John, Edward, and William Alleyn, was dead in 1589.]

To our lovinge freinds Mr. Allderman Harte, Mr. Allderman Bellingsley, Thomas Hunte, and Humfrey Huntley, or to any three or two of them.

After our hartie commendations. This enclosed petition hath been exhibited unto us by John Allen, servaunte to me the Lo. Admyrall, wherein he informeth us of verie hard and extreame dealing used against him by one Doctor Martin, who seeketh by indirecte meanes to make frustrate a lease of a certen tenement and garden demised by one John Roise to the suppliants father, mother, and himselfe, for divers years yet unexpired, uppon some sleight surmises of breach of covenauntes by the suppliant, clayminge certaine right and tytle thereunto as executor unto the said Roise, notwithstandinge the expresse

mind and will of the testator was that the leases by him made should not be violated. Forasmuch as his said mother, (as he allegeth) did before her decease expend in building uppon the premisses the summe of 300 markes, and now, uppon some straight construction of doubtful wordes conteyned in his said lease, the said Doctor Martin seeketh to defeate and defraude him of the bennefytt and commodityes which should redound to the suppliant by vertue of the said Lease. We have thought good therefore, and because the said D. Martin detayning in his custody the said lease taken from him by craftie meanes (as we are given to understand) the suppliant could not so well observe the tenour therof, and the covenauntes which he was enjoyned by vertue of the same to performe, not knowing the contentes and strict interpretation therof, which he pretendeth for defaults therof to be now called in question, to pray and require you by vertue hereof to call before yow the said Martin, and to take such order for the reliefe of the Suppliant that he may not be by anie indirecte course oppressed, but, according to the purport of his lease, enjoy the bennefytt of his said graunt and lease, according to equity and conscience: and to certifie us with convenient speede what effecte your travell shall have taken in this behalfe. So we bid yow hartely farewell. From the Court at Nonesuche, the 14^h of Julie 1589.

Your loving freindes,

EDWARD DYER.   C. HOWARD.
J. HUNSDON.
        COBHAM.   T. BUCKHURST.
    FRA. WALSINGHAM.   JAMES CROFT.

ALDERMAN HARTE.
ALDERMAN BILLINGSLEY.
THO. HUNTE.
HUMFREY HUNTLEY.

ARBITRATION BOND.

[The bond by which Dr. Martin engaged, under a penalty of £100, to submit to the award of the arbitrators, or umpire. John Allen, as we have seen, was an "Inholder" as well as an actor, and his inn-yard was probably the theatre where performances were represented.]

Noverent universi, &c. decimo quarto die Novembr. Anno Dom. 1589.

The condition of this obligation is suche, that yf the above bounden Thomas Martyn do for his parte in all thinges observe, performe, fulfill, and kepe the awarde, arbitrament, order, rule, judgment, and fynall determynation of William Sallter, grocer, and Hughe Woodcock, salter, arbitrators indifferently named, appoynted, elected, and chosen, as well on the parte and behalfe of the above bounden Thomas Martyn, as also on the parte and behalfe of the above named John Allen, to arbitrate, awarde, order, rule, judge, and fynallye determyne of, for, and concerninge all and all manner of actions, aswell reall as personalle, suytes, quarrells, debtes, accomptes, recconinges, trespasses, and demaundes whatsoever, had, made, moved, stirred, or dependinge in variance betwene the said parties at any tyme from the beginninge of the worlde untyll the daye of the date hereof: so as theire said awarde, arbitrament, order, rule, judgment, and fynall determynation, of and uppon the premysses betwene the said parties, be made and given uppe in writinge before the Twelth daye of December next ensewinge the date of theis presentes. And yf the said arbitrators cannot agre nor none awarde do make of and uppon the premysses betwene the parties within the said tyme before to them limmitted, then yf the above bounden Thomas Martyn do for his parte in all thinges observe, performe, fulfill, and kepe the awarde, arbitrament, order, rule, judgment, and finall determynation of William Drewry, doctor of the civill lawe, umpire of and uppon the premysses betwene the said parties indifferently

named, appoynted, elected, and chosen, so as his said award or umpirement, of and uppon the premysses betwene the said parties, be made and given uppe in writing before the one and twenteth daye of the said moneth of December, that then this obligation to be voyde and of none effecte, or ells to stande in full force, strength, and vertue.

By me, THO. MARTYN. (L. S.)

Sigill. et del. in presentia mei
JOHIS STODDARDE serv. cum
JACOBO SMYTHE de London generosus.

THEATRICAL DIALOGUE, IN VERSE.

[In the original MS. this dramatic dialogue in verse is written as prose, on one side of a sheet of paper, at the back of which, in a more modern hand, is the name "Kitt Marlowe." What connection, if any, he may have had with it, it is impossible to determine, but it was obviously worthy of preservation, as a curious stage-relic of an early date, and unlike any thing else of the kind that has come down to us. In consequence of haste, or ignorance on the part of the writer of the manuscript, it has been necessary to supply some portions, which are printed within brackets. There are also some obvious errors in the distribution of the dialogue, which it was not easy to correct. The probability is that, when performed, it was accompanied with music.]

Jack.   Seest thou not yon farmers sonn?
        He hath stolne my love from me, alas!
  What shall I doe? I am undonn;
        My hart will neer be as it was.
  Oh, but he gives her gay gold rings,
        And tufted gloves [for] holly day,
  And many other goodly thinges,
        That hath stolne my love away.

Frend.   Let him give her gaie gold rings,
        Or tufted gloves; weere they nere so [gay;]

   Or were her lovers lords or kings,
    They should not carry the wench away.
   But a' daunces wonders well,
    And with his daunces stole her love from me.
   Yett she wont to saie I bore the bell
    For daunsing and for courtesie.

Jack. Fie, lusty younker! what doe you heer,
    Not daunsing on the greene to-day?
   For Perce, the farmer's sonn, I feare,
    Is like to carry your wench away.
   Good Dick, bid them all come hether,
    And tell Perce from me, beside,
   That if he think to have the wench,
    Here he stands shall lie with the bride.

W. Fre. Fy, Nan! why use thy old lover soe
    For any other newcome guest?
   Thou long time his love did know;
    Why shouldst thou not use him best?
   Bonny Dick, I will not forsake
    My bonny Rowland for any gold;
   If he can daunce as well as Perce,
    He shall have my hart in hold.

Per. Why, then, my harts, letts to this geer,
    And by daunsing I may wonn
   My Nan, whose love I hold soe deere
    As any realme under the sonn.

Frend. Then, gentles, ere I speed from hence,
    I will be so bold to daunce
   A turne or two, without offence;
    For, as I was walking along by chaunce,
   I was told you did agree.

'Tis true, good sir, and this is she
   Hopes your worship comes not to crave her,
For she hath lovers two or three,
   And he that daunces best must have her.

Gen. How say you, sweet, will you daunce with me?
   And you [shall] haue both land and [hill;]
My love shall want nor gold nor fee.
   I thank you, sir, for your good will;
But one of these my love must be.
   I'm but a homly countrie maide,
And farre unfitt for your degree.
   [To daunce with you I am afraide.]

Fre. Take her, good sir, by the hande,
   As she is fairest: were she fairer,
By this daunce you shall understand
   He that can win her is like to ware her.

Foole. And saw you not [my] Nan to-day,
   My mother's maide haue you not seene?
My prety Nan is gone away
   To seeke her love upon the greene.
[I cannot see her mong so many.]
She shall haue me, if she haue any.

Wen. Welcome, sweet hart, and welcome heer,
   Welcom my [true] love now to me;
This is my love, [and my darling dear,]
   And that my husband [soon] must be.
And, boy, when thou comst home thou'lt see
Thou art as welcome home as he.

Gen. Why, how now, sweet Nan, I hope you jest.

Wen. No, by my troth, I love the foole the best.

And if you be jelous, god giue you good night;
I feare you're a gelding, you caper so light.

Gen. I thought she had jested and ment but a fable,
But now doe I see she hath play[d] with his bable.
I wishe all my frends by me to take heede,
That a foole com not neere you when you mene to speede.

SALE OF A CLOAK AND ROBE.

[An agreement for the sale by Isaac Burgess to John Alleyn, "citizen and inholder," of a cloak and robe, no doubt for the purpose of being worn on the stage. The price, £16, seems very high, recollecting the great difference in the value of money then and now: it affords another proof of how much was expended at this date upon theatrical apparel.]

Be yt knowen unto all men by theise presentes, that I, Isaacke Burges, of Cliffordes Inne, London, gent., for and in consideration of the somme of sixtene poundes of good and lawfull money of Englande, to me before hand payde by John Allene, Cytizen and Inholder of London, have bargainde and solde, and by theise presentes doe fully, clearelie, and absolutely bargaine, sell, and deliver unto the sayd John Allene, in playne and open market of or within the Cytty of London, one cloke of velvett, with a cape imbrothered with gold, pearles, and redd stones, and one roabe of cloth of golde: to have and to holde the sayd cloke and roabe, with thappurtenances, unto the sayde John Allene, his executors and assignes for ever, to the onely use and behoofe of the sayde John Allene, his executers or assignes for ever, as his and theire owne propper goodes and chattels. And I, the sayd Isaake Burges, the sayd cloke and roabe againste all men shall and will warrante and defende for ever, by theise presentes. In witnes whereof, I have hereunto putt

my hande and seale the xxiijth daye of November, in the xxxiijth yere of the reigne of our sovereigne lady Quene Elizabeth, &c., 1590.

p me, ISAACUS BURGES.

Sealed and delivered in the presence
 of me, JOHN DEANE, Scr.
JAMES TONSTALL.

THEATRICAL APPAREL.

[Here we see the brothers John and Edward Alleyn buying a single cloak for no less a sum than £20 10s. 0d. At this date they were, no doubt, partners in some theatrical speculation. James Tonstall, or Tunstall, (for he spells his name both ways) was an actor, and, we may infer, was a member of the same company.]

Be yt knowen unto all men by theis presentes, that I, John Clyffe, of Ingatestone, in the countie of Essex, gentleman, for and in consideration of the somme of twentye poundes and Tenne shillynges of lawfull money of Englande, to me in hande before thenscaylinge hereof, by John Allen, Cytizen and Inholder of London, and Edwarde Allen, of London, gentleman, well and truly payed, whereof and wherewith I doe acknowledge me satisfied and pleased, haue bargayned and solde, and by theis presentes do bargayne and sell unto the sayde John Allen and Edwarde Allen, their executors and assignes, one blacke velvet cloake, with sleves ymbrodered all with silver and golde, lyned with blacke satten stryped with golde. To haue and to holde the sayde prebargayned premisses, and euery parte and parcell thereof, unto the sayde John Allen and Edwarde Allen, and to either of them, their executors and assigns, from henceforth for evermore. And I, the sayde John Clyffe, for me, my executors and administrators, covenante and graunte to and with the sayde John Allen and Edwarde Allen, and either of them, their executors, administrators, and assigns, by theis presentes, that I, the sayde John Clyffe, my executors and admi-

nistrators, shall and will warrant and defende the sayde pre-bargayned premisses and euery parte thereof unto the sayde John Allen and Edwarde Allen, and either of them, their executors, administrators, and assignes, for ever by theis presentes. In witnes whereof hereunto I have set my seale. Yoven the sixte daye of Maye, 1591, and in the xxxiijth yere of the reign of our sovereign Ladye Queene Elizabeth, &c.

By me, JOHN CLYFF. (L. S.)

Sealed, subscribed, and delivered
  in the presence of me,
    GODFREY RYNES, Scr.
By me, JAMES TUNSTALL.

THE DEFENCE OF TAILORS.

[It is difficult to account for the ensuing verses, unless we suppose them to have been penned in return for some attack made upon tailors and their trade upon the stage; perhaps at a theatre with which Alleyn was connected. Possibly they were spoken by some clown of the company in the dress of a tailor, and are much such lines as Richard Tarlton would have composed on the sudden and blurted out on a similar occasion. They exist on a separate sheet of paper, are written in an ignorant hand, and are clearly of an early date.]

    You pevish fooles of poetrey
      That seek for to disgrace
    The tayler and the taylers lades
      That were within this place;

    But now, prowd fooles, 'tis knowne full well
      They have confuted you,
    And made you geve them that is fitt
      Unto theyr prayses dew.

    Your popery was for to playe
      That taylors were no men,
    But now I see your acte is torned
      More true than it was then.

In deed it is ageynst theyr willes,
   As trewly you may saye,
A prentice once being bownden fast,
   Then needes he must obay.

So is it now with you, prowd fooles,
   That all men here may see;
For you are penny taylers geuefes;
   You thanke them on your kne.

And thus I hope I have not yett
   Offended aney here,
But onley those prowd begging fooles
   That now doe bend for feare.

And this at last to let you know
   Our persones doe not feare
To send this token unto you all
   To weare within your heare.

ACKNOWLEDGMENT OF DEBT.

[The following paper does not look as if, in July, 1591, John and Edward Alleyn (less than three months after they had given £20 10s. for a cloak) were in very flourishing circumstances: they required more than two months' credit for the payment of only fifteen shillings. The debt was, doubtless, incurred in connection with the theatre, or company of players, to which they belonged. John Alleyn is called "citizen and innholder," and Edward Alleyn, as before, "gentleman," a rank which players were allowed to assume. John Webster, the dramatic poet, was a member of the Merchant-tailors' Company; perhaps the John Webster mentioned below was his father.]

All men shall know by these presents that we, John Allein, cytysen and Inholder, of London, and Edward Allein, of London, gentleman, do owe and ar indebted unto John Webster,

cytysen and merchauntayler of London, the somme of fyftene shyllynges of lawfull money of England, to be payed to the sayd John Webster, or his assygnes, on the last day of September next insewinge the date hereof, wherto wee binde us, our heyres and assygnes, by these presentes. Subscrybed this xxvth day of July, 1591, and in the xxxiii of her Maties raygne.

JOHN ALLEIN.
ED. ALLEYN.

PROPOSAL OF MARRIAGE.

[The following is a very singular letter from John Alleyn to a person of the name of Burne (possibly Bourne the actor), proposing for his daughter. It is written in a very ignorant manner, but in a high-flown style, and no doubt the writer obtained his knowledge of Paris and Helen, and of Ajax (which name he writes *Achakes*) from plays in which he had performed. No year is given, but John Alleyn dates from the Bear-garden, where he was, doubtless, then employed. The original is the property of Mr. Halliwell.]

Mr. Burne, my hartye commendats to you and to you wyefe, hoping in God that you and all youre is in as good helfe as I and my frends are att this tyme. The caues is why I write to you one thes haes his to let you understand, that I have hernest besnes to you conserning your dather, and that is this, gife you be ples with the mater. I ame to let you understand that I bare good will to your dater, as a man should doe to get kredett by her; and nowe to the fulle I woulld crave your datter in marrige, iff you be so plesd; why I ryette to you first is as ouer London fashenges to in trete you that I may haue your good will and your wiefe, for gif we geate the father good will first, then may we bolle speke to the dather; for my possebelte is abel to mantayne her when I should that I should haue all my ounkell welthe to lef her, where itt so profite I should playe as Parres did by Hellene, dye for her. Rather

had take my forteune with that small posshene that itt is, which is abell to mantayne a good wommann lovingly, but rather had I take hear with what ples God, then with some thousantes if you stane in nead of any thing I can put you in good securaty, and this to make her gointer of 24^{li} a yere. If you should denie my sheute, which is but new begonne, I should play as Achakes did, kill him sealfe with his one sord. I did hope that you would prove a good father to her and to me, iff you thinke your datter well bestode one me, so then doe I find comford, as the dew of hevene dothe comford the thinges one the earth, so will your letter comford me. Tell I here your ansere I shall be like the Temes, which dueth ebe and flow twies in 24 oweres, never stanne still. Itt may be youe bete me gite her good will first, and then I should haue yours; butt I had rather you should doe as ould Tobias did by his sone, when he was blind, that was his blesing one his sone and his new betrothe wiefe. I do besheech you that you would stane a father to me, which has none. Some of your kinsmen, some of them that well stand by me, did incurrich me to rite to you thus bolld. Hopping you will stane my good father, as I hope you well be to me, I doe commite you to the hanes of the all-mithe God, which I do pray to bles you and all your in Harford and in Londone. Thus in has I bed you far weill from the bare garden, thes 11 daye of June.

Your to command to his pore,
while liefe dothe last, your
sone that wod be
JOHN ALLEYN.

Mr. Burne, remember your sone John of the whelpe which he did promes me, so hoping he his in good helfe which I praye for.

THE GILLS AND THE FORTUNE PLAYHOUSE.

[The ensuing copy of a letter, no doubt, relates in some way to the ground on which the Fortune playhouse was built, which Edward Alleyn bought of a family of the name of Gill. Patrick Brewe was also concerned in the bargain, as Alleyn gave him £240 for a lease of the property. The writer of this letter was a clergyman in the Isle of Man, and is called "Sir William Crowe" in the indorsement, in the same way as he speaks of "Sir Daniel" in his letter. "Sir" was a title at that date usually given to clergymen, as well as to knights.]

[Addressed]

To my approved good cossene, M. Patricke Brewe, goldsmythe, and citizene off London, dwellinge in Lombard Streat, at the sygne off the Eagle and Child, geve thesse.

(Vera Copiæ.)

Havinge had perfect intelligence off your prosperite in your layte letter sent by younge Gyll, wch I praye to the Almightie longe to contenewe to your contentatione, and the expectatione off your wellwyllers and poore kynsmen, off whosse nomber I protest unfayngnedly to be on, and I humblie thanke your goodnes ffor your lovinge commendations, &c.

Where you wryte unto me your mynd concerninge Gyll his matter in his lyvinge at Londone to be indifferent, and to drawe all parties to suche unitie as Lawers might not have the correctione of theyr pursstes, so yt is for mine none parte that I would have justyce, who geveth his owne to everey man, to procead: I ought to remember our mortall stayte, and not be oblivious of our immortalitie. The truth ys that ould Gyll dyd demysse, and by all sufficient covenauntes that could be devysed, or might be by promysse, unto his sonne Sr. Daniell, and to the issues off his bodye, the whooll lyvinge after his and his wyves deceasse, as appeareth by wryttynges; and to confirme the same gave seasone and possessione by you unto his said

sonne, to the intente his demysse might be more surely accomplished.

And now wheare conscience and good meaninge wylleth that no man should be defrawded of his bargane, I find in ould Gyll a great desyre that the poore orphanes should not have, nor posses that lyvinge accordinge to his promysse; but pretendeth a righte therof to his other childrene, wch I cane not lyke well off, bayth for that yt is contrarye to bargane, as also agaynst the poore orphanes of a spirituall man, whiche poore childrene havinge there guyfte of that livinge, may prefere some kinsman off yours and my best beloved. Therffore, I wold crave off you to be cayrefull herein, and to geve possessione and seassone unto the childrene as hearetoffore you have geven unto there ffather, which I take to be conscience and indifferencie, and prejudiciall in lawe to no partie, seyinge they are executrixes to there ffather, S^r. Daniell, and the wyll proved. Where objectione ys mayd agaynst there mother concerninge the dead of guyfte and other devysses, I knowe yt is all donne ffor the childrens welth: she intendeth naturally to deall, and ys nowe marryed to a better lyveynge. For the present tyme thus much off that matter, earnestly cravynge once agayne off you, consyderinge my intention to be more then indyfferent, (viz.) to prefere your owne rather then a straunger, and nothinge donne amysse nor contrarye to justyce, ffor he mayd yt to the poore childrene. As for an acquyttance to be had for your last rent payd to Mr. Ellys, the Archdeacone ys in England, and Mr. Ellys ys at London: get you an acquyttance from Mr. Ellys, and I wyll procure on from the Archdeacon. Thus with a thowsand blessynges and comendations to you and your bedfellowe, and all other our dear ffrendes, I ceasse this xijth of January, 1592.

    Your lovinge Cossene to usse in that he may,

          W^m. CROWE,
           persone:

ENGLISH PLAYERS ABROAD.

[The following is a curious letter: the writer, it appears, belonged to a company of English actors who were going to perform abroad, thus adding to the imperfect information we already possess upon the point from Heywood's "Apology for Actors." See the Reprint by this Society, p. 58, and a few other sources. Malone (Shaksp. by Boswell, xxi., 396) was in possession of a copy of this letter, but it does not seem that he was aware of its importance in connection with the history of our early stage. Several persons of the name of Jones were connected with the stage at the end of the sixteenth and beginning of the seventeenth centuries, but we have here no clue to a date. "Mr. Browne" might be some connection of Alleyn.]

Mr Allen, I commend my love and humble duty to you, geving you thankes for yor great bounty bestoed upon me in my sicknes, when I was in great want: god blese you for it. Sir, this it is, I am to go over beyond the seeas w^t Mr Browne and the company, but not by his meanes, for he is put to half a shaer, and to stay hear, for they ar all against his going: now, good Sir, as you have ever byne my worthie frend, so helpe me nowe. I have a sute of clothes and a cloke at pane fo^r three pound, and if it shall pleas you to lend me so much to release them, I shall be bound to pray fo^r you so longe as I leve; for if I go over, and have no clothes, I shall not be esteemd of; and, by gods help, the first mony that I gett I will send it over unto you, for hear I get nothinge: some tymes I have a shillinge a day, and some tymes nothinge, so that I leve in great poverty hear, and so humbly take my leave, prainge to god, I and my wiffe, for yor health and mistris Allene's, which god continew.

Yo^r poor frend to command,
RICHARD JONES.

THREAT TO ALLEYN.

[It appears from what follows, that the writers, Wheeler, Lowe, and Handcock, had sustained some disappointment by Alleyn's means, and that he was at that time (no date is furnished) in want of a considerable sum of money. The Lord Keeper mentioned in the letter, to whom the parties threatened to complain, was of course Sir Thomas Egerton, afterwards created Lord Ellesmere, Lord Chancellor to James I.]

[Addressed] To M^r. Edward Alleyn, Esq.

S^r.

If you forsake us in such distastfull fassion now we have most need of you, you will absolutly overthroughe the busines to the great losse and prejudice of a many creditors. It is not unknowne to you that we bergened with you, and relyed upon your former promisse till the last day, by which means our unconscionable adversarye hath obtayned a great deale of advantage, which we doe not know how to opposse without your promised assistance; in which you diverse tymes profest much charetye, which we should be glad to find, and which cannot any way be to your prejudice, if you please rightly to consider thereof. Well, we hope farther yett of you, but if there be none, then we all shall have cause to say, and that verie justly, that your suspending the tyme is cause of all the ruine that is like to fall upon this busines. If you want the 1000^{li} at present, you may have it now upon reasonable securitye. If you will not go forwards with us, we must lett my lord Keeper know tomorrow how, and by your meanes, we are crossed in this busines; and so god keepe you.

Y^{rs}, AMB. WHEELER.
GEORGE LOWE.
GEORGE HANDCOCK.

If you will take it from the Alderman, we will redeeme ytt for you in 3, six monthes, or els you shall have ytt for what you have offred.

LOVE VERSES.

[It is evident that what follows is a copy of love-verses, much corrupted in the transcription by some ignorant hand, who sadly mangled most of the lines. We do not recollect any printed work in which they are found, and they were perhaps incorrectly copied from some original manuscript by an author of that day.]

Can she excuse my wronges with vertuous cloke?
   Shall I call her good, when she proves so unkinde?
Shall those cleare fires vanish into smoke?
   Shall I praise the leafes wher no frut I find?
No, no; wher shadowes do for bodyes stande,
   Thou mayes be deseved yf thy lite be dime.
Could love is like to words written in sand,
   Or to bubbels which upon the water swime.
Wilt thou be thus deluded still,
   Seinge that she will right thee never?
Yf thou canst not overcom her will,
   Thy love wilbe but frutles ever.

Was I so base that I might not aspire
   Unto those high joyes which she holds so from me?
As they ar hy, so hy is my desire.
   Yf she this deny, what may graunted be?
Or yf that she will graunt to that which reson is,
   It is resons will that trewe love should be just.
Deare, make me happi, then, by graunting this,
   Or cut of my days, yf so be dy I must.
Better a thousand times to dy, then for to live thus still tormented.
Deare, but remember it was I that for thy love did dy contented.

FINIS. 1596.

LETTER TO EDWARD ALLEYN.

[In the "Memoirs of Edward Alleyn," p. 50, is printed a letter dated 26 September, 1598, directed to Alleyn at the Brill (or Broyle), in Sussex, which probably soon brought him to London: the following, from John Langworth, (who was most likely the son of Arthur Langworth, with whom Alleyn and his wife had been staying) was written to Alleyn in London in the February following, and it shows not only that Alleyn was about to purchase property in Sussex, but that he had advanced so much money to young Langworth, that the latter was more willing to grant an annuity upon it, than to pay it off. The original, like several others, is among Mr. Halliwell's MSS.]

[Addressed]
    To my verye good frend, M^r. Edward Aleyne,
     at London, geve these.

M. Aleyne, by meanes of a mischaunce that I caught, which kepte me within doores, and a speciall man that I desyred to talke with beinge from home since I could goe, I have done little in the busynes you desyred, but only this: I understand that it is worth by the yeare, yf corne beare any good price, fowre score pounds, but the perticulars of the state of the thinge I will send you worde of by the nexte convenient messanger I can have, yf it require hast.

I would gladly knowe whether you would be willinge to take a yearely annuetie of me for the money I have of yours, or not? for I had rather paye you a yearely rent, either for certaine yeares, or duringe youre lyfe, hopinge you will be reasonable, then to paye the money at this tyme; for that I would gladly prepare myselfe, with all the speede I could, to goe to house keepinge. Yf you lyke to deale this waye, I will not be longe ere I come to you to take order about it: yf not, I will tarrye untill the tyme of your payment, and bringe your money with me. Thus desyringe youre answere, with oure hartye com. to youre selfe and your wyfe, I leave you to the Allmightye. From the Broyle, this 21 Februari, 1598.

    Youre assured frend,
     JOHN LANGWORTH.

THE CONQUEST OF THE WEST INDIES.

[The following note and the next relate to a play called " The Conquest of the West Indies," which, according to Henslowe's Diary, was written by William Haughton, John Day, and Wentworth Smith. Samuel Rowley had perhaps been commissioned by Henslowe to hear it and report upon it.]

M^r. hinchloe, I have harde fyve sheetes of a playe of the Conquest of the Indes, and I dow not doute but it will be a verye good playe: tharefore, I praye ye delyver them fortye shyllynges In earneste of it, and take the papers into y^r one hands, and on easter eve thaye promyse to make an ende of all the reste.

SAMUEL ROWLEY.

lent the 4 of Ap^{r}ell, 1601—xxxx^s.

M^r. Hynchlye, I praye ye dow so muche for us, if Ihon Daye and wyll haughton have reseved but thre pounde ten shyllynges, as to delyver them thurtye shyllynges more, and take thare papers.

yo^rs to comande,
SAMUELL ROWLYE.

THE SIX YEOMEN OF THE WEST.

[This play belongs to the year 1601, and we do not find that any other authors were engaged upon it but Haughton and Day. Day, in the annexed note, desires that his share of the money should be given to " Will Hunt, the pedlar," and not to " Will Haughton," as it stands misprinted in Malone's Shakspeare by Boswell, xxi., 392.]

M^r. Henchlowe, I pray ye delyver the Reste of the Monye to John daye and wyll hawton, dew to them of the syx yemen of the weste.

SAMUELL ROWLYE.

[The above note was written on a scrap of paper, which at the back of it has the following lines in the handwriting of John Day; no doubt a part of some play then in hand. Malone took no notice of them.]

Brother, they would be rulers of our state,
Yet both infected with a strange disease
And mortall sicknes, proud abylitie
Which being vast, and almost measureless
Had they not been prevented, might have provde
Fatall and dangerous. Then, since their death
Hath, like a skilfull artist, cur'd that feare
Which might have prov'd so hurtfull to our selves,
Lets to the Court instead, and after send
Their wretched wifes —— their bodies to the grave;
For the dead Percy had a gallant band,
And glad has my pursuers left behinde.

I have occasion to be absent about the plott of the Indyes, therefore pray delyver it to Will Hunt, the Pedler ....

by me, JOHN DAYE.

BEN JONSON'S "RICHARD THE THIRD."

[With the date of 22d of June, 1602, Malone inserts a memorandum by Henslowe, showing that Ben Jonson was then engaged on a play called "Richard Crook-back." Shaw's note to Henslowe, inserted below, does not seem to refer to this play; but the memorandum at the back of it obviously relates to a sketch of five scenes of one of the acts of a drama on the story of Richard the Third, which very possibly was that which Ben Jonson had undertaken to write. It was printed in Mal. Shaksp. by Boswell, xxi. 393, but most inaccurately and imperfectly.]

Mr. Henslowe, we have heard their booke, and lyke yt: their price is eight pounds, wch I pray pay now to M^r. Wilson according to our promysse. I would have come my selfe, but that I am trobled with a scytation.

Yo^{rs} ROBT. SHAA.

[On the back of this paper]

1. Sce. Wm Wor. and Ansell, and to them the plowghmen.

2. Sce. Richard and Q Eliza. Catesbie, Lovell, Rice ap Tho. Blunt, Banester.

3. Sce. Ansell, Denys, Hen. Oxf. Courtney, Bourchier, and Grace. To them Rice ap Tho. and his Soldiers.

4. Sce. Milton. Ban. his wyfe and children.

5. Sce. K. Rich. Catesb. Lovell, Norf. Northumb. Percye.

JOHN OF GAUNT.

[Entries in Henslowe's Diary show that the full title of this play was "The Conquest of Spain by John of Gaunt," and that it was the joint authorship of Richard Hathway, John Day, and William Haughton. It belongs to the spring of 1601.]

M^r. hynchlo, I pray ye let M^r. hathwaye have his papars a gayne of the playe of John a gante, and for the repayemente of the monye back a gayne he ys contente to gyve ye a byll of his hande to be payde at some cartayne tyme, as yn yor dyscressyon yow shall thinke good; wch done ye may crose it oute of yor boouke and keepe the byll, or else wele stande so muche indetted to you, and keepe the byll o^r selves.

SAMUELL ROWLYE.

TOO GOOD TO BE TRUE.

This play (also called in Henslowe's Diary "The Poor Northern Man") must have been founded upon the old ballad reprinted by the Percy Society, in 1841. Henry Chettle, Richard Hathway, and Wentworth Smith were the writers of the play.]

I pray you, M^r. Henshlowe, deliver in behalfe of the Company, unto the fifty Shillings wch they receaved the other day, three pounds and tenn shillings more, in full payment of six pounds, the pryce of their play called to good to be true.

Yo^{rs} ROBT. SHAA.

FAIR CONSTANCE OF ROME.

[This play was by Robert Wilson, as well as by Munday, Hathway, Drayton, and Dekker, to whom Malone assigned it, under date of June, 1600. Hence we find that the price paid by Henslowe for a new play, at this date, was £6. In a previous note, p. 24, we have seen that £8 were required for some unnamed drama.]

I pray you, Mr Hinchlow, deliver unto the bringer hereof the some of fyve and fifty shillings, to make the 3^1 fyve shillings, wch they receaved before, full six pounds, in full payment of their booke called the fayre Constance of Roome; whereof, I praye you, reserve for me Mr. Willsons whole share, wch is xi^s, wch I, to supply his neede, delivered him yesternight.

Yo^r Lovinge ffreind
ROBT. SHAA.

COMMISSION FOR THE BEAR GARDEN.

[The subsequent receipt proves that in January, 1601-2, Henslowe and Alleyn paid £40 per annum to Doryngton, then Master of the King's Games of Bulls, Bears, &c., for a commission to them as his deputies at Paris Garden. Malone thought that the rent of the Bear Garden was £40 a year; but this sum was paid, not as rent to the owner of the property, but for the permission of Doryngton to employ it for the purposes to which it was then, and had been for so many years, devoted. We hear of Paris Garden, as a place where bears were baited, in 1526.]

Rd of M^r. Henslowe and M^r. Alleyn the 1 day of Janewary, 1601, for 1 quarters rent, dewe unto my M^r., Mr. Doryngton, for the commission for the Beargarden, the somme of tenne pounds, by me, Richard Lefwicke, I say R. x^{li}.

RICHARD ✕ LEFWICKES marck.

ALLEYN'S INCREASING PROSPERITY.

[This letter, and the answer to it on the same sheet, establish the increasing wealth of Edward Alleyn. He was the landlord of the person he addresses at Croxted; and perhaps this was the property he contemplated purchasing in February, 1589-9. Hence we also find that he was in treaty for other property, consisting of land, for which he was to pay £1300, a sum equal to more than £6000 of our present money. At this date, 1602, the Fortune Theatre had been recently opened, and no doubt the speculation was found very profitable. The original belongs to Mr. Halliwell.]

[Addressed]
>To my loving Frend, M^r. Page, at Croxted, geve this.

[Re-addressed]
>To his loving good Frynd, M^r. Edward Alleyn, thes be delyvered.

Wheras I thought to see you agayne in a fortnight, I know not as yett how my bussines will fall out, but yett go forward with that we talk of, although since I have heard itt hath been long upon the sale, the thing to be very baren, and no better then a hard penyworth is to be look for; but, howe soever, what you have donn, and how you think of itt, I praye you send me word. Thus with my harty salutations I committ you to god. London, this 15 of July, 1602.

>Yo^r loving Frend and Landlord,
>>ED. ALLEYN.

M^r. Alleyn and my good Landlord, thes ar to answer your leter. I have delt with M^r. Sherley, accordyng as I promysed you, and have the forsakynge of the land for xiiij dayes for 1300^{li}., and I thinke it wort the mony and a good penworth, for I think the land will be worth lxxx^{li}. a yere, and it is manor, and the wod worth 200 markes. This must be presently answared. I woulld a byn glad to a sene you and my landladye at my house. This, with my hertie comendasyon, I comyt you

to god. From Croxstedes, this xvijth of Juley. Yours to commaund to his power,

JOHN PAGE.

For want of paper I ham forsed to anwar you in your owne leter.

ALLEYN'S PROJECTED PURCHASE IN SUSSEX.

[The ensuing letter is misdated 1640, instead of 1604, and it is from Alleyn's tenant, John Page, and relates, as far as we can judge, to the same property referred to in the preceding letter. We here find that it was a manor called Riches in the letter, near to Firle, the living of which Alleyn at one time was the owner.]

[Addressed]

>To his verye good Frend, M^r. Edward Allene, thes be delyvered, nere to Sanctuaris stayres.

Landlord, my loving comendasyons unto you remembred. Thes ar to let you under stand that I have talked with Sr John Sherley for you, tuching the purchsing of the manar of Riches. If it be so that you purpose to by it, I praye you let me heare from you, for I think it will be sould to M^r. Warnat, if you have it not. It lyeth well to the personage of Fyrles. You wryt to me that you would have it: if you plese you may. Ther is a tenement, and iij barns, and 300 acars of land ther aboutes: the wod is wort 200 markes at the lest. It is a manor, and there is viij or ix tenantes payeth heryates and relefe. This is as much as I can geve you to understand of. If you do dele for it, ther muste be paid 200^{li}. this terme. I praye you writ unto me your mynd her in by this Bearer; and so I commit you to god. From Croxstedes, this xxviijth of Januarye, 1640 (i.e., 1604). Yours to his pour,

JOHN PAGE.

A MUSICAL DIALOGUE.

[The subsequent dialogue between a man and a boy is probably a theatrical relic, which was formerly set to music and sung. It has been evidently much corrupted in the transcript, which was made by some very ignorant person. Judging from such scraps as have come down to us, the copyists of our old theatres must have been generally very incompetent to the duty, and miserably mangled the manuscripts of authors. We are not sure that we have not met with something like this poem in one of the miscellanies of the time.]

Man. It fell upon a sollem holledaye,
Boye. Woe me, that the day should be termed holey.
Man. When idell wittes had gotten leave to play.
Boye. Such play ill please the mind that's wean'd from folly.

Man. The lettell god that hyght the mighty man,
Boye. Woe me, such a god should be termed mighty.
Man. Sweet love, that all in all things only can,
Boye. That all is naught but thinges regarded lightly.

Man. In royall state, in all his mother's pryde,
Boye. Woe me, foles pryde should be termed royall.
Man. Thus in the ayre methought I saw him ryde.
Boye. Ayre to unkind to beare a god disloyall.

Man. White was the steed the jolly lad rode on ;
Boye. Woe me, such a lad should have cullers pure.
Man. Droppinges of grene and stars of gould among ;
Boye. Dim stars are those that will with love indure.

Man. Upon his head a flowry garland stode,
Boye. Woe me, suche a god should weare daintie flowres.
Man. Woven with cowslips, pinkes, and lillies good:
Boye. Good judgement them behight for princes bowres.

Man. Silver his haire, in curls, and curled rounde,
Boye. Woe me silver should be loved so derely.
Man. And at his back two pecockes traines were bound.
Boye. Pide cullers show that love is wittles merely.

Man. And in his cheekes two lovely roses sprang;
Boye. Woe me, roses should in love be springing.
Man. On either side an ivory quiver hang;
Boye. From thens the springes of toyes had their beginning.

Man. His arme was armed with a bowe of steele;
Boye. Woe me that he wants parfett skill to use it.
[*Man.*] And knightly spurs fast buckled to his heele.
[*Boye.*] A good thing is bad, if such a god abuse it.

[*Man.*] And as he rode, before him flew amayne
[*Boye.*] Woe me, if good things were by him oretaken.
[*Man.*] Millions of hartes that his steele bowe had slayne.
[*Boye.*] Well they deserve death that by him ar beaten.

[*Man.*] Thicker then hayle he lett his arrows flye,
[*Boye.*] Woe me, if such stormes should be ever showring.
[*Man.*] Till gazing long one light within mine eie.
[*Boye.*] Fond fool, that couldst not scape that balefull scowring.

[*Man.*] Yet though I greve, this toye doth heale my wounde.
[*Boye.*] Woe me, what toye can there be in anguish.
[*Man.*] More fooles then wyse ones yerely are to be founde.
[*Boye.*] Fooles all that liste in love to live and languish.

Finis.

ANNE POYNTZ TO ALLEYN.

[In the "Memoirs of Edward Alleyn," p. 77, is inserted a letter from John Poyntz, of Woodhatch, dated March 6, 1605. It is very probable that the writer of what follows was some relation to him, in poor circumstances: he might even be her husband, of whom she complains, desiring Alleyn's advice upon the subject. He seems always to have been a kind neighbour and a good friend.]

[Addressed]
     To her very loving frend, Edward Allin, es-
      quyer, geve thes w. speed.

Good Mr. Allin. I have ever found you my good kind frend hetherto, and which makes me the boulder with you in my adversity to request so much loving kindenes att your hands to lende me v pounds untyl our lady day next, and then, as I am an honyst pore woman, I will trewly pay you: farther more, I desier you to com to me, that I may speak with you conserning my unkind husband. This being in hast, I rest and ever remayne
     Your pore frend,
      ANNE POYNTZ.

I pray comend me to good M^{rs}. Allin,
 and my love to all that loves you.

BULLS FOR PARIS GARDEN.

[An undated letter, showing the nature of Alleyn's transactions in the country, in order to obtain bulls for baiting at Paris Garden, (spelt by the writer Palles Garden) which we learn from the same authority had "lofts" above the baiting-yard, as well as "grates" to protect the spectators. The letter, which is the property of Mr. Halliwell, is a remarkable specimen of rustic writing, orthography, and phraseology.]

[Addressed]
     To mey Verey Loving frend, Mr. Allin, at
     the Palles Garden at London, give thes.

Mr. Allin, mey love remembered. I understoode bey a man which came with too Beares from the gardeyne, that you have

a deseyre to bey one of mey Boles. I have three westorne boles at thes tyme, but I have had verey ell loeck with them, for one of them hath lost his horne to the queyck, that I think that hee will never bee able to feyght agayne; that is mey ould star of the west: hee was a verey esey bol; and my Bol, Bevis, he hath lost one of hes eyes, but I think if you hed him hee would do you more hurt then good, for I protest I think hee would other throo up your dodges in to the loftes, or eles ding out theare braynes ageanst the grates, so that I think hee is not for your turne. Besydes, I esteeme him verey hey, for my lord of Rutlandes man bad mee for him xx marckes. I have a bol which came out of the west, which standes mee in twentey nobles. If you so did leyck him, you shall have him of mey: faith, hee is a marvailous good Boole, and shuch a on as I think you have had but few shuch, for I aseure you that I hould him as good a doble bole as that which you had amee last a single, and one that I have played therty or fourty courses before he hath bene tacken from the stacke, with the best dodges which halfe a dosen freyghtes had. If you send a man unto mee he shall see aney of mey boles playe, and you shall have aney of them (def. in MS.) refor, if the will plesoure you. Thus biding you hartely farewell, I end,

Your louing friend,

WILLIAM FAWNTE.

GATHERERS AT THEATRES.

[The writer of this note had been an actor before the close of the sixteenth century: it has no date, but it was probably written before Alleyn had quitted the profession. It is unique in its kind, and lets us very curiously behind the curtain in the management of our old companies. We hear on no other authority of John Russell, either as gatherer, actor, or in any other capacity. The original is in the possession of Mr. Halliwell.]

Sir,

There is one Jhon Russell, that by youre apoyntment was made a gatherer with vs, but my fellowes finding [him

often] falce to vs, haue many tymes warnd him from taking the box; and he as often, with moste damnable othes, hath vowde neuer to touch: yet, notwithstanding his execrable othes, he hath taken the box, and many tymes moste vnconsionablye gatherd, for which we haue resolud he shall neuer more come to the doore. Yet, for your sake, he shall haue his wages, to be a nessessary atendaunt on the stage, and if he will pleasure himself and vs to mend our garments, when he hath leysure, weele pay him for that to. I pray send vs word if this motion will satisfye you; for him, his dishonestye is such we knowe it will not.

Thus yealding ourselues in that and a farr greater matter to be comaunded by you, I committ you to God.

Your loving frend to comaund,
W. BIRDE.

To his loving frend, Mr. Allin, giue these.

W. BIRDE'S NECESSITIES.

[We might, perhaps, assign an earlier date to the following urgent claim for a loan from Henslowe to the same performer. The note at the foot, signifying that Henslowe had paid the money to Birde's servant, is in a different handwriting.]

Mr. Hinchlowe, I pray let me intreate you to lende me forty shillings till the next weeke, and Ile then paye it you agayne by the grace of God. I pray, as you love me, fayle me not: here is one at home must receave it presently. If you will doe me this favour, you shall comaunde me in a greater matter.

Yours,
WILL. BIRDE.

Feched by William Felle, his man.

SEIZURE OF A BEAR.

[It should appear, by what follows, that Henslowe and Alleyn had taken possession of a bear belonging to a person of the name of Ashmore: perhaps he had employed it for bear-baiting to the injury of Henslowe and Alleyn, who claimed some exclusive rights as Deputy Masters of the King's Games of Bulls, Bears, &c. Henry Middleton was perhaps one of the sons of Sir Thomas Middleton.

[Addressed]

To the wo[ll] and my verie good Frend Mr. Edward Allen Esq. be these dd.

Mr. Allen. Wheras yow have taken a Beare from the bearer hereof, Henrie Ashmore, my frend, I pray you lett him have his beare againe at my request, till you be further satisfied from S[r] Tho. Middleton, who is now in Wales. And I shall rest beholding to yow for your kindnes. This 9th of March, 1608.

Your loving Frend
HENRY MIDDLETON.

Beleave this to be trew by the same token
I mett yow lately in Lothbury, and
saluted you.

GROUND-RENT OF THE FORTUNE.

[This letter relates to some dispute respecting the ground on which the Fortune Theatre had been erected. We have before seen (p. 17) that differences had arisen between adverse claimants. The writer was Vicar-General of the Isle of Man.]

[Addressed]

To our very lovinge ffrende Mr. Edward Alleyne esquyer at London geve these.

Mr. Allane, as unaquanted wee commend us unto yow, &c. Wheras wee are credably enformed that you hould certen landes

att London, wherof the one halfe is due to our children, and the halfe of the rent is due unto us, duringe the lyfe of my wyffe, as itt may appeere by our evidences: wee are therfore to desyre yow to doe so muche for us as to paye our halfe rent into the handes of our Cozin, Mr. Patricke Brewe, whome we have auctorized to receave and to geue acquittance for the same; and further wee request you nott to delyver our said rent into the handes of no maner person or persons, but to us or our lawful attourney; for wee are not willing to receave our rent att the handes of noe man ells but from yourselfe who doith hould the land by our leasse; and if our said rent should passe your handes, and from hande to hande, wherby wee or our children may come to trouble for our owne, itt may bee an occation for us to put those landes with their evidences into their handes that will deale more stricklier then we meane or intende to do; butt if you please to deale well with us and to delyver our rentes to our attourneys, if the children bee at any tyme willinge to so sell or sett to anie manne, you may haue an offer before any other. The bearer herof cann certifye you how that lande standeth, and for your better understandinge we haue sent to you a copie of an awarde ordered for the children concerning those landes. And thus hopinge you will accomplishe this our requestes, wee comitt you to Godes tuition. From Douglas, in the Isle of Manne, this first of June in Ao. Dm̃., 1608.

    Your lovinge frendes in that
     they maye to their powers.
    WILLM. NOREIS,
     Vic. geñall.
    ELIZABETHE NOREIS,
     her marke ✗.

BREW TO ALLEYN.

[Another letter connected with the same subject. No year is given after the day of the month, but the next letter ascertains it to have been written in December, 1608. Brew was at this date living in the Isle of Man.

[Addressed]

To my very good Frend, Mr. Edwarde Allen, esquyere gyve this in London.

Mr. Allen, youre healthe wished et c^a. I dyd sende to youe bye my wyffe those wrytinges I promysed youe: I pray youe kepe them saffe. It is reported here that youe or Mr. Garrett have payde the rent of Gylles land, dwe in Maye laste, into the Chekker. I praye youe lett me knowe from youe by this bearer howe the matter standes for the rente. It is also reported that Garrett hath offredd thre hundrethe poundes for the lande. The yong women and the reste are willinge to sell, nowe that there mother is deade. The eldeste of Gylles sonns was att Chester, intending to go for London at halantyde, and hearinge of the sicknes camm home agayne, butt I thinke he will go agayne at the springe. Thus, with my verye hartye commendatyons to youre selfe and to good mystris Allen, do commytt youe to God. Douglas, this 8 of December.

Youre lovinge Frende,
PATRICKE BREWE.

DISPUTES BETWEEN THE GILLS.

[At this date Alleyn seems to have entertained the design of buying the freehold of the ground on which the Fortune Theatre stood from the Gills, who had family disputes regarding the property.]

[Addressed]

To Mr. Edwarde Allen, esquyre, gyve this, nere unto pallace garden, withe spede.

Mr. Allen youre healthe wished. I have written to youe in december laste, but whether my letter cam to youre handes or

no I am uncertayne. This is to certefye youe that the Gylles, and the dawghters of Gill deseased, cannott agree uppon the sayle as yett, and yett theye would sell, and yett theye strayne curtesye who shall begynn. I would have sente to you the writings whiche I dyd promys to sende to youe, but I can nott meete with a trustye messenger to sende them bye; as also to write unto youe sum other thinges whiche I dare nott put to writtinge, except I knewe him very well, and to be verye trustye too, for they are thinges youe littell thinke of; but eyther I wilbe messenger my selfe or sum other trustye and spetyall frende, for oure letters are commonlye opened commynge or goinge: butt assure youre selfe that you shall have them God willinge. Thus with my verye hartye comendatyons to your selfe and to good Mrs. Allen, with many thankes for all kyndnes, do committ youe to the tuytyon of the most hyghest, who ever kepe you, amen. This 6 of aprill, 1609. Youre verye lovinge frende to his power,

PATRICKE BREWE.

THE VICAR-GENERAL OF MAN.

[On p. 34 is a letter from William Norris, Vicar-General of the Isle of Man: his wife died in July, 1609, leaving her husband entitled to a share of the ground-rent of the Fortune. Patrick Brew here requests Alleyn to pay it on behalf of the widower.]

[Addressed]

To my approved good Frende, Mr. Edwarde Allen, esquyer, gyve this withe spede.

Mr. Allen, your healthe wished, these are to lett youe understand that god hath called to his mercye my cozin Norris his wyffe, and she was buryed the xxvth of Julye last past. The rente is dwe unto her husbande for this laste yeere, dwe at may laste, prainge youe of all frendshippe to paye unto the bearer here of, John More, the sayde summ of vj^{li}, and youe

shall receyve an aquytance from my Cozin Norrys for it. I am a wyttnes unto the saide aquyttance, my selffe praing youe of all frendship to paye this monye, as my spetyall truste is in youe. I have sente youe accordinge to my promys, and my wyffe will tell youe other thinges which I spare from writinge. Thus with my verye hartye commendatyons to your selffe and to good Mrs. Allen, do comytt youe to god. Dowglas, this 3 of Auguste, 1609. Youre lovinge Frende, to his power,

PATRICKE BREWE.

Poste Scriptum. I praye you se the bearer hereof payde, for he hathe payde the monye here in the contrye to my Cozin Norris. Youres ever,

PATRICKE BREWE.

ACROSTIC UPON HENSLOWE.

[Of the author of the ensuing acrostic upon Philip Henslowe (or Hinslie, as the writer spells the name) we know nothing, and the style of his verses, as well as the form in which they appear, would show that he was not calculated to reach any very lofty height in the regions of poetry.]

The name of Phillip Hinslie, Gentelman, litterallie set downe in verse uppon those three especiall poyntes, his love to God, his Prince and countrie.

To God.
P rovident cheifelie gods worde to imbrace,
H opinge by the same salvation to obtayne;
I ndowed plentifullye with all giftes of grace,
L ove, zeale, and charitie, in his harte remayne,
L ikewise resolved man's meritts to be vayne;
I esus Christe, his savior, he trewlie doth love,
P ure in faithe, whiche no stormes can remove.

H e is moste carefull his roiall Princes to sarve
I n love and dutie, as he thereunto is bounde;

N ever from allegiance hathe he sought to swarve,
S o faithefull and constante he hathe bene founde,
L oiallie provinge in all poyntes a member moste sounde;
I njuriose villaynes and traytors he hathe disdayned,
E ver charie of credditt, whose name was never stayned.

G even and preste to pleasure his countrie like case,
E ver willinge for the same his derest bloode to spende:
N ot quarrellinge nor contentiose, but peace imbrace,
T hat to his power still is prest the same to defende,
E ver sekinge by industrie contentions to ende.
L ovinge, gentle, and affable, both to ritche and pore,
M oste willinge his counsell and comforte to bestowe—
A nd God with his grace duilie blesseth his store:
N one better then this cittie his dealings doth knowe,
Sit sola laus deo.

A prayer for your selfe and your godlie and vertuose wife, speakinge in the terms of a gardiner.

Plante, lorde, in them the tree of godlie life,
Hedge them aboute with thie stronge fence of faith,
And, if it thee please, use eke thy proinynge knife;
Leaste that (O lorde), as a good gardiner saithe,
If suckers drawe the sappe from bowes on hie,
The toppe of tree in tyme perhapps maye die:
Lett, lorde, this tree be sett within thy garden wall
Of parradise, where growes no one ill sprigg at all.

FINIS.

Your affectionate and hertie well willer,
RICHARDE WILLIAMS.

ALLEYN'S BILL IN CHANCERY.

[In the "Memoirs of Edward Alleyn," p. 82, it is shown that the founder of Dulwich College was Lord of the Manor of Dulwich, in 1606, by purchase from Sir Francis Calton. On p. 94 of the same work is inserted a letter from Calton to Alleyn, proving that they were on good terms up to the 9th of May, 1611, Alleyn having made many pecuniary advances to Calton. The following bill was filed in Chancery on the 27th May, 1611, from which it is evident that a quarrel had taken place between the 9th and the 27th May. Alleyn then apprehended that Calton was taking secret measures to re-obtain possession of the Manor of Dulwich. The document establishes in what way the property came into the hands of the Calton family, and that Alleyn, according to his estimate, had paid dearly for it. The signature at the end was of course that of the party who drew the bill.]

[Indorsed]

Allen, con. Calton miles.

[And by Alleyn in his own hand]

A bill of complaynt in ye Chawncerie against Sr Francis Calton, knight, dat. ye 27 of May, 1611:

To the Right Honourable Thomas Lord Ellesmere, Lord high Chancellour of England.

In most humble wise complayninge showeth unto your good Lordshipp your daylie Orator, Edward Allen, Esquire: That whereas one Thomas Calton, cittizen and goldsmith of London, purchased of the late Kinge of famous memorie, kinge Henrye the Eight, all that the mannor of Dulwich with the appurtenances, and dyvers other landes, meddowes, pastures, woodes, and underwoodes, scituate, lyinge, and beinge in the parrish of Camberwell in the Countye of Surrey, to him, the said Thomas Calton, and Margaret, his then wife, and to the heires of their

bodyes begotten, and for default of such issue to the right heires of the said Thomas Calton.

Afterwardes they, the said Thomas Calton and Margaret his wife had yssue, William and Nicholas Calton, and dyvers other sonnes. Shortlye afterwardes the said Thomas Calton died thereof so seized, and the said Margarett him survived and soe was seized of the said mannor and premisses in her demesne as of fee tayle, the remaynder in reversion over unto the said William Calton, sonne and heire of the said Thomas Calton, deceased. And the said Margarett so beinge seased, the remaynder or reversion to William as aforesaid, shortly afterwardes she, the said Margarett, and the said William, by theire writinge bearinge date about the fower and twentieth day of Januarie, in the twelveth yere of the raigne of our late soveraigne ladye Queene Elizabeth, made betweene the said Margarett and the said William Calton, her eldest sonne, on the one partie, and Giles Pawlett, alias Lord Gyles Pawlett, and William Chiball, draper, on the other partie, (the certen date whereof, for want of the same, your Orator knoweth not,) did covenant and grant, before our ladie daie then next followinge, to levye a fyne of the premisses par recognizance de droit, &c., to theis uses followinge, that is to saie, to the vse of the said Margarett for the terme of her owne life without ympeachment of anie manner of waste, and after her decease to the use of the said Nicholas Calton, the second sonne of the said Thomas Calton and Margarett, and to the heires of his boddie lawfully to be begotten; and for default of such yssue the remaynder over to divers other uses in the same Indenture conteyned, with the remaynder to the right heires of the said Margarett or to the right heires of the said Thomas Calton her husband.

Afterwardes shee, the said Margarett, beinge so seized, dyed thereof so seized, by and after whose decease, and by vertue of the statute of conveyinge uses into possession, the said Nicholas Calton entered into all and singular the said Mannor and

premisses with thappurtenances, and thereof was seized in fee, or fee tayle, by vertue of the said fyne and conveyance as aforesaid. And shortlie afterwarde hee, the said Nicholas Calton, beinge so seized, tooke to wife Joan, and they had issue betweene them lawfullye begotten, Sir Frauncis Calton, Knight, now livinge, and dyvers other sonnes. And then, shortlie after, the said Nicholas Calton died of the said Mannor and premisses seased as aforesaid, by and after whose decease the same descended and came as of right the same ought to descend and come, unto the said Sir Frauncis Calton, knight, as eldest sonne and heire of the said Nicholas Calton, deceased, lawfullye begotten, who likewise entered into the said Mannor and premisses, and thereof was seized likewise in fee, or fee taile, by vertue of the said conveyance as aforesaid.

And hee, the said S^r. Frauncis Calton, beinge so seized, afterwardes, that is to saye in or about the fowerth yere of the raigne of our soveraigne Lord the Kinges Matie, that now ys, of England, France, and Ireland, and of Scotland, the fortith, for and in consideration of a great some of money, unto the said Sir Frauncis Calton in hand paied by your Lordshipp's said Orator, did by good and lawfull conveyances in the lawe convey and assure the said Mannor with thappurtenances and dyvers other landes in the parish of Camberwell, in the said Countye of Surrey, unto your Lordshipp's said Orator and to his heires; by vertue of which said conveyance your Lordshipp's said Orator hath byne and still is of the said Mannor and premisses with thappurtenances lawfully seized in his demesne as of fee to him and his heires.

And likewise the said Sr Francis Calton, knight, by his said conveyance made to your Lordshipps said Orator, as aforesaid, did bargaine and sell unto your said Orator all and all manner of deedes, evidences, wrytinges, escriptes and mynymentes touchinge or any waies concerninge the said Mannor and premisses. But now so it is, and it maie please your good Lordship, that by casuall meanes unto the said Orator unknowen,

dyvers of the evidences and ancient writinges touchinge and concerninge the said Mannor and premisses are of late come into the handes, custodie, and possession of the said Sʳ Frauncis Calton, knight, or into the custodie or possession of some other person or persons by his meanes, deliverye, consent, or privitie, either from the said Thomas Calton, grandfather to the said Sir Frauncis, or from Margarett Calton, grandmother of the said Sʳ Francis Calton, as also some deede or conveyance made by the said Margarett, alone or jointlie with the said William Calton, eldest sonne of the said Thomas Calton, unto dyvers persons of trust, unto the use of the said Margarett Calton for the terme of her owne life, and then to the use of the said Nicholas Calton, one of the youngest sonnes of the said Thomas Calton and Margarett, and to the heires of the boddie of the said Nicholas Calton, with dyvers remaynders over, as by the same deede or conveyance, whereunto reference beinge had, more at large it doth and maie appeare; which said deede or writinge, with the other evidences and conveyances touchinge and concerninge the said Mannor and premisses with thappurtenances, he, the said Sir Francis Calton, havinge in his custodye or possession, or in the custody and possession of some other, by his deliverie, consent, or privitie, hath endevored, and still doth endeavor, to the uttermost of his power, to conceale and suppresse the said deede or writinge, and other the evidences touchinge the said Mannor and premisses. And hee, the said Sʳ Frauncis Calton, well knowinge in whose handes and possession the said deedes be, yet notwithstandinge he unconscionably concealeth the same from your Lordshipps said Orator, and refuseth to delyver them.

And hee, the said Sir Frauncis Calton, well knowinge that there was such a deede made by the said Margarett and William Calton, theldest sonne of the said Thomas Calton, the purchaser to the said Lord Pawlett or to some other, and to such uses as aforesaid, yet notwithstandinge, contrarye to his owne knowledge, hee, the said Sʳ Frauncis Calton, doth conceale and

detayne the same from your Lordshipps said Orator, confederatynge and combyninge himselfe together with the heires of the said William Calton, the eldest sonne of the said Thomas Calton (to whome the inheritance of the said Mannor and premisses was and should have discended, if the said deede or conveyance had not beene made and executed), to defeate your Lordshipps said Orator of the inheritance of the said Mannor and premisses, with thappurtenances.

As also he, the said Sr Frauncis Calton, knight, hath made and contryved, or hath caused to be made and contryved, dyvers secret estates of and in the said Mannor and premisses, or of some part thereof, to dyvers persons to your Lordshipps said Orator unknowen, thereby unconscionablie intending hereafter to defraude your said orator and his heires of the said Mannor and premisses; or hee doth knowe of some secret or former estates to be made of the premisses, or of some part thereof, whereby hee should not be liable to convey the same to your Orator, according to the true meaning of his said sale so made unto your said Orator, contrarie to all right, equitie, and good conscience, your Lordshipps said Orator having paied verie dearely for the said Mannor and premisses unto the said Sir Frauncis Calton, being well assured that the said Margarett Calton, and the said William Calton, her eldest sonne, did joyne in a conveyance made of the said Mannor and of the premisses to dyvers persons, as by the office found after the death of the said Thomas Calton, it doth and maye appeare, and to such use and uses as in the said office is expressed and found. In tender consideration whereof, and for as much as your Lordshipps said Orator hath no remedie at or by the strict course of the common lawes of this realme to compell him, the said Sir Francis Calton, knight, to shew fourth the said deede and other the writinges and evidences touchinge the said Mannor and premisses, and the same to cause to delyver unto your said Orator for the preservation of his lawfull inheritance in and to the said Mannor and premisses.

As also to compell him, the said S^r. Francis Calton, truelye and directlie to aunsweare and sett fourth what secret estates or conveyances hee hath made and contryved of the said Mannor and premisses, or of anie part or parcell thereof, and to whome the same is soe made; or whether he knowe of anie secret conveyance thereof made by anie other, but onlie by the due course and order of this hōble Court. And for asmuch also as your Lo. said Orator knoweth not the certaine dates or nomber of the said deedes, evidences, or writinges, and other the secret conveyances made by the said S^r. Frauncis Calton or anie other touchinge the said Mannor and premisses, nor whether the same be in bagge, chest, or box, sealed, locked, or unlocked, or in whose handes the same be; and for asmuch also as he, the said Sir Frauncis Calton, doth goe about and indeavour to suppresse and conceale the said deede and evidences concerninge the said Mannor and premisses, confederatinge with the heires of the said William Calton to defeat and defraude your Lordshipps said Orator of the said Mannor and premisses, your said Orator having truelie paied unto the said S^r. Frauncis Calton a great summe of money for the same, maie it therefore please your good Lordshipp, the premisses considered, to graunt unto your said Orator his Maties most gracious writt of subpena to be unto the said S^r. Frauncis Calton, knight, directed, commaunding him thereby at a certeine daie, and under a certeine paine therein to be limitted, to be and personallye to appeere before your good Lordshipp in his Maties high Court of Chancery, then and there, upon his corporal oath, truelie, plainlie, and directlye to aunsweare to all and sundrie the premisses.

And that he, the said S^r. Frauncis Calton, maie truelie sett fourth uppon his oathe what secrett estates hee hath contryved or caused to be made, or knoweth by anie other to be made or contryved of the said Mannor and premisses, or of anie part thereof, and to what person or persons the same was so made. As also to sett fourth what estate hee, the said Sir Frauncis, had and stood seized of in the said Mannor and premisses at

the time of the sale thereof unto your Lordshipps said Orator. As also to sett fourth what deedes, evidences, or writinges touchinge or concerninge the said Mannor and premisses hee, the said Sir Frauncis, hath or had in his handes or custodie, or in the handes and custodie of any other person or persons by his deliverie, knowledge, consent, or privitie; as to aunsweare, uppon his oath, whether there were not such a deede or conveyance made by the said Margarett and William Calton to such uses as aforesaid, or to what uses it was made. And to shewe in whose handes the same is and remayneth, and what thestates are conteyned in the said deede.

And further, that your Lo. would be pleased to grant unto your said Orator his Maties writt of duces tecum, to be unto him, the said S^r. Frauncis Calton, knight, directed, commandinge him thereby to bring unto your hōble Court the said deede or deedes so made by the said Margarett and William Calton, as aforesaid; as all such other deedes, evidences, and writinges remayning in his handes and custodie, or in the handes and custodie of any other person or persons by his delivery, knowledge, consent, or privitie, or otherwise, touchinge or anie waies concerning the said Mannor and premisses with thappurtenances.

And further, to stand to and abide such order and decree in the premisses, as to your good Lordshipp and this hōble Court shall seeme meete to agree with right equitie and good conscience. And your Orator, accordinge to his bounden duty, shall dailie praie unto God for the preservation of your Lordshipp with longe life and increase of honor.

JOHN HARRYES.

A MYSTERIOUS LETTER.

[A somewhat mysterious epistle, which the writer obviously intended should only be intelligible to Alleyn. The Countess of Dorset, mentioned in it, was the widow of Thomas Sackville, Lord Buckhurst, and Earl of Dorset, the author of the two last acts of the tragedy of "Gorboduc" (afterwards called "Ferrex and Porrex"), 8vo. 1565, and of the "Induction" to the "Mirror for Magistrates." Mr. Hallam, in his "Introd. to the Lit. of Europe," ii. 167, inclines to Warton's opinion that Sackville was concerned in the three first acts of "Gorboduc;" but the oldest edition states expressly that "the two last acts" only were by Sackville, and the three first by Norton. The first edition of "Gorboduc" is a great literary curiosity, which Warton had probably not seen. Lord Montagu was Antony Brown, Baron Montagu, who died in 1629.]

[Addressed]

To his loving frend Mr Edward Allen, Esquire, these bee dd with speed.

Mr. Allinge, I have receved your letter by your lade, wher in I do beleve you in all you wryte unto me in the sayd letter: and with all Mr. Boltonne did tell me that if ther wer erneste haste made of the mony, ther sholde be good bandes geven for it, which ther shalbe now no such nede: for so it is, that aboute some fortnyght hinch, my lorde Montegewe dothe com to London; and as he commeth to loge at my howse, nowe the countys of Dorset is come to London, he lyeth not at Horsly; so, with Godes helpe, I will atend him to London, and that day you shall have word wher you shall find his logginge the morow, and then will I tell you the party that told me the newes I did writ you, and I pray kepe my sekertes about the matter I write unto you. So in haste I take my leve of you this fyrste of November, 1611, your lovinge frind

RICHARD FORKENCH.

NAT FIELD AND HENSLOWE.

[Upon what play Field and Daborne were at this time engaged is nowhere stated. No date is mentioned; but Field was a very young man when his "Woman is a Weathercock" was published in 1612. That excellent comedy has been reprinted in the supplemental volume to the last edition of "Dodsley's Old Plays."]

Mr Hinchlow,

Mr Dawborne and I have spent a great deale of time in conference about this plott, wch will make as beneficiall a play as hath come these seaven yeares. It is out of his love he detained it for us; onely xl. is desir'd in hand, for wch we will be bound to bring you in the play finish'd upon the first day of August: wee would not loose it, wee have so assured a hope of it, and, on my knowledge, Mr Dawborne may have his request of another Companie. Pray, let us have speedie answere, and effectuall; you know, the last money you disburst was justly pay'd in, and wee are now in a way to pay you all so, unlesse yor selfe, for want of small supplie, will put us out of it againe. Pray, let us know when wee shall speake with you; till when, and ever, I rest

Yo^r loving and obedient Son,
NAT. FIELD.

A TENANT FOR ALLEYN.

[A proposal from John Hibborne, who held some minor office about the Court, to become tenant to Alleyn of a house at Dulwich. It does not appear from the superscription where Alleyn at this date resided, but probably on his manor of Dulwich.]

[Addressed]

To my verie loving frind Mr. Edward Alleyn
deliver these.

M^r. Alleyn, the last tyme I spoke with you, I remember you told me that now you could fit me conveniently at Dulage with

a little habitation. I am now likewise willing to deale with you: yf you will take the paynes to-morrow or on Sunday to come to my lodging at Whithall, we shall confer about it. I wold come unto you, but that an ill disposition of bodie hath caused me to keep my chamber this foure or five dayes: you shall doe me a curtesie to come unto me, and I will be readie to goe much further for you. So wishing you health, I rest

Your well-wishing frind,
JOHN HEBBORNE.

Whithall, this 3 of Januarie, 1611.

Postscript. I am affrayd I shall on Tewsday attend his Matie to Royston; wherfor I desire to confer with you before my goinge.

THE UPPER PIKE-GARDEN.

[An ordinary arbitration-bond, (with a penalty of £100) in consequence of disputes between Henslowe and a person of the name of Abraham Wall, respecting the right to a piece of ground called the Upper Pike-Garden, on the Bank-side, Southwark. It should seem that Henslowe's residence was in or near the spot in question.]

Noverint universi, &c. 16: Feby. 9 James I.

The condition of this present obligation is such, that where controversies and suites in lawe are dependinge betweene the above bounden Abraham Wall, on the one partie, and the above-named Phillip Henslo on the other partie, for and concerninge the possession, right, and tytle of certaine lands and tenementes, with goods and implements of howshold, at the upper pyke garden, on the banke syde in Southwarke aforesayd: Now, yf the sayd Abraham Wall shall well and trewly observe, performe, fulfyll, and kepe all and singular such orders, arbitrementes, judgements, and awards as by William Symons and John Wood, clerks, William Richardson, gent, and George Payne, citizen and grocer of London, elected indifferently by both the said parties shalbe awarded, and adjudged to be per-

formed and kept by the said Abraham Wall, without fraud or coven, so that the sayd award be published in writing under the handes of the said arbitrators within one moneth next after the date of this present obligation, that then this same obligation is to be voyd and of none effecte, or els to stand and abyde in his full strength and vertue.

p me, ABRAHAM WALL.

Sealed and delivered in the presence of
  ROBERT NODDINGE.
  THOMAS SEDGWICK.
  GREGORY MARTON.

SUPPLY OF PARIS GARDEN.

[The subsequent letter, we may presume, related to the furnishing Alleyn and Henslowe with some bulls or dogs for the sports at Paris Garden. It has no date of the year, but at this time, probably, Alleyn had the chief management of the business.]

  [Addressed]

To Mr Allen at Dulledge, dd with spead. In his absence to his father-in-law, Paris Garden.

Sturmester, 24 of Auguste.

Sir, my comm. rem. yt wilbe the beginge of the next weeke or that I begiñe my jorney, and yt wilbe five dayes jorney. I rec. directions frome your man allso about the busines, and you shalbe so well provided as ever you were in your lyffe, and to that I will engage you my creditt. For the reason of my stay here so longe I omitt to speake of for want of tyme, and so I comitt you to God.

Your frind to use,
THOMAS YONGE.

ROSE, AN ACTOR, AND HIS WIFE.

[The writer of the following letter may have been some connection of Alleyn, as his mother had married a person of the name of Browne. Of Rose, an actor, this is the first time we hear; and, as his name is not included in any list of the theatrical servants of Prince Charles, we may presume that he did not attain any great distinction in the profession. The letter also affords evidence that the wives of performers sometimes officiated as " gatherers."]

[Addressed]
               To his assured Frend, Mr. Edward Alleyne,
               Esquier, geve thes.

M^r. Alleyn, I commend me hartely unto yow. I understand that M^r. Rose is entertayned amongst the Princes men, and meanes to stay and settell him selfe in that company, and to sett up his rest, and to do his best endevors onely in that company. His money is but small, but he hopes so to carry himselfe amongst them, that in time he will so beare him selfe that but according to his deserts they will use him. In the mene time, he hath requested me to be solicitus for him to yow (who he knowes can strike a greter stroke amongst them then this) as to procure him but a gathering place for his wife; for he hath had many crosses, and it wilbe some comfort and help to them both: and he makes no dout but she shall so carry her selfe in that place, as they shall think it well bestowed, by reason of her upright dealing in that nature. Now, sir, if for my sake you will procure it, I will not one[ly] acknowledge my selfe greatly beholding to yow, but he also shall have reason to pray for your health and happy proceedings. He hath been an old servant of mine, allwayes honest, trusty, and trew, and I would, if I could, do him aney good I can; and now he meanes to apply him selfe onely in this cowrse. Thus, hoping yow will show him what favor you may, I cease prayeng for your helth as for mine owne. Clarkenwell, this 11 of April, 1612.

               Your loving Frend,
                  ROBT. BROWNE.

ANOTHER OF ALLEYN'S TENANTS.

[The maiden name of Alleyn's mother was Towneley, and she is supposed to have been one of the distinguished family of the Towneleys of Lancashire. Had the writer of the following letter, who was one of Alleyn's tenants, been a kinsman, he would probably have urged his relationship in favour of his request. As no address is given with the letter, we cannot now ascertain where the house he held of Alleyn was situated.]

{Addressed]

To the worshipfull and his loving frind, Edward Allen, Esq.

Gentle Landlord, lett me intreat you to helpe us to a little timber or poles, to finish that wee have in hand, and also to mend thother howse before I part with my carpenter; for it will be verie difficult to get a carpenter, that is againe, especially to doe only jobes of woorke. Commend me to my Landladie with many thanckes: in hast,

Your freind, loving and assured,

T. TOWNLEY.

10 Nov., 1612.

A BAD TENANT.

[Robert Pallant was an actor of considerable eminence in the reign of James I. Whether what follows relates to him may be a question, but he certainly was a member of the company with which Alleyn and Henslowe were connected. His conduct does not appear to have been very creditable in this instance; and it is very possible that the "Mr. Pallent" mentioned below was not Robert Pallant, the actor: perhaps he was one of Alleyn's tenants.]

A true note how M^r. Pallent is charged for rent and other chardges.

Imprimis, he entred into the said tenement one our Ladie daye in Lent, in the xxxixth yeare of our late soveraigne ladie

the queene, deceased, and was to paie yearlie vj^{li}. by xxx^s. a quarter.

He remayned there vij yeares and a hallf, and for the first three quarters of the yeare he paied his rent orderlie: then he would everye yeare leave unpaid either a quarter or hallf yeares rent; so that in five yeares rent there was two yeares rent behind, which was xij^{li}., and all the acquitances went, received &c., in part of paiment of a farther some, beinge all of his owne hand writing, such was the trust at that tyme reposed in him; and a yeare and a hallf before his going from the said tenement he paid not any thinge: soe there remaineth for that ix^{li}.; soe there is in all due for rent, xxj^{li}.

He also promised to leave the said tenement in as good repaire as he found it, which he did not, but made great wast and spoile, so that the repairinge thereof commeth to xx^{tie} nobles at the least, as wilbe proved by mani witnesses.

The chardges susteined in lawe, in prosecutinge the said M^r. Pallent by way of ejectment, to get the possession, commeth to iiij^{li}.

At the carrienge away of his stuffe, he garded it so that none durst attempt the aresting it for feare of murther, such was his desperatnes and others his associates; and duringe the tyme he abode in the said tenement, no man could come in to distrain, by reason he kept his dores locked.

> The whole some for rent, repaire, and chardges in lawe, commethe to xxxj^{li}. xiij^s. 4^d., which money goeth to tamend the maintenaunce of thre poore schollers in Cambridge, &c. the which M^r. Phillip Henslowe hath disbursed allredie.

ALLEYN'S KINSWOMAN.

[This letter, from a kinswoman of Alleyn, shows that up to 1612 he still had a residence on the Bankside—perhaps at or near the Bear Garden. John Alleyn, Edward's elder brother, it should seem, had lived in the family of the Earl of Nottingham, probably, from the terms used, in some domestic capacity, and not merely as one of his theatrical servants. "Wardon," or "Warden," from whence the letter is dated, was most likely Saffron Walden, in Essex.]

[Addressed]

To the worpp. and her very lovinge Cozen, M^r. Edward Allen, dwellinge at the Banckeside, give these.

This ys to be delivered by Edwarde Mannynge, the Powlter of Warden.

After my moste harty comendations remembred unto you, very lovinge Cozen, hopinge in God that you are in good healthe, as I was at the makinge hereof. I woulde bee very glade to here of you; naye, muche more to see you in the countery at my poore dwellinge howse. I would intreat you to send me worde in wrytinge, wheather your Tenaunte, Thomas Clemente, did deliver unto you any letter from me aboute three or fower yeares agoe. And I have sente you by this bearer a small remembraunce, a littell cheise. And when your brother, my lovinge Cozen, John Allen, dwelt with my very good lord, Charles Heawarde, hee did then, when hee cam unto the countery, lye att my Fathers howse, Goorde Everytt, in Tuddington parishe, when as I did never see your selfe. And thus prayinge to God for your longe lyfe, with my very good cozen your wife, I cease. From Wardon this Two and Twentethe daye of September, 1612.

Your lovinge cozen untell death,

ELIZABETH SOCKLEN.

ALLEYN'S DEBT TO CALTON.

[The following is from Mr. Halliwell's MSS., and would seem to prove that Alleyn and Sir Francis Calton had had money transactions subsequent to the filing of the bill in Chancery, 27th May, 1611. It is not unlikely that Calton had sold Alleyn some further property, and that at this date part of the purchase-money was yet unpaid.]

Maye the 12, 1612.

Recd since the sixte daye of december last paste, the full som of one hundred and seventye poundes, togither with the consideration of 300^{ll}. which M^r. Allen then oughte me, beinge xx^{ll}. xiiij^s., so that all reckonings made even to this daye, he nowe remayneth indebted unto me the juste some of 200 poundes. In witnes whereof, I have subscribed my name the day and yeare above wrytten.

p me,

FRAN. CALTON.

Witnes,

MOYSES BOWLER.

SIR F. CALTON'S NECESSITIES.

[This note, and the appended receipt, (also from Mr. Halliwell's MSS.) show that in 1612-13 Sir Francis Calton was in want of so small a sum as £5, for which he was under the necessity of applying to Alleyn.]

M^r. Allen, I praye yow send me fyve poundes by this bearer, w^{ch}, to tell yow the very truthe, muste be the moytie of a brybe I am in expectation to bestowe upon one this daye, yf matters succeede accordinglye; and so in haste I bydd yow farewell.

Your lovinge frend,

FRAN. CALTON.

Rec. this xviijth of March, 1612, by me, John Cockin, to the vse of my M^r., S^r. Frauncis Calton, the some of five pounde, acording to the tenor of this note. I say Rec. .... } v^{ll}.

JOHN COCKIN.

FARTHER CLAIMS BY CALTON.

[To the same effect as the preceding, and from the original, belonging to Mr. Halliwell. It does not appear whether the sum of £70, here requested, was the whole of Sir F. Calton's demand upon Alleyn.]

M^r. Allen, my man will tell yow the cause of my not cominge; howbeit, I pray you pay him the reste of the monye, which is 70 pound, with the speedieste dispatche that yow convenientlye maye, and these presentes shall testyfie the receit of 95^{li}. since our laste reckoninge.

I have sent, accordinge to your desyre and my promis, my letters to M^r. Knighte, with others also to M^r. Vicker, for the deliverye therof, and to receave an acquittance in such forme as I have sett downe.

Your very frend,
FRAN. CALTON.

Rec. this viijth of Aprill, 1612, by me, John Cockin, to the use of my M^r., S^r. Fran. Carlton, the some of } lxx^{li}.

JOHN COCKIN.

MACHIAVELL AND THE DEVIL.

[Of this play we have no other information than in this and the following papers: it perhaps related to Machiavelli's novel of Belphegor, in which the Devil plays so principal a part, and which is called, in the enumeration of the author's minor productions, *Unà dilettevole novella del Demonio che pigliò moglie*. It does not appear that Daborne had any assistance from other dramatists. The price of a new play at this date had risen to £20.]

Memorandum: 'tis agreed between Phillip Hinchlow, Esqr and Robert Daborn, gent., y^t ye s^d Robert shall before ye end of this Easter Term deliver in his Tragoedy, cald Matchavill and ye Divill, into the hands of ye sd Phillip, for ye summ of xxty pounds, six pounds whearof ye sd Robert aknowledgeth to hav receaved in earnest of ye sayd play this 17th of Aprill,

and must hav other fowr pound upon delivery in of 3 acts. and other ten pound upon delivery in of ye last scean p̃fited. In witnes hearof the s^d Robert Daborn hearunto hath set his hand this 17th of Aprill, 1613.

P^r me, ROB. DABORNE.

Mem. I have receaved of Mr Hinchlow the full somm of sixteen pounds, in part of twenty pounds due to me, Robert Daborne, for my tragoedy of Matchavill and the Divell: I say receaved sixteen pounds, this 19th of May as aforesaid. In witnes whearof I hereunto hav set my hand, 1613.

ROBT. DABORNE.

This play to be deliverd in to
Mr Hinchlow with all speed.
JOHN ALLEYN.

HENSLOWE'S LOAN TO DABORNE.

[Daborne was a man of some property and family, who had lawsuits upon his hands. Out of those grew part of his necessities. The witness to the payment of the 20s. here borrowed was Hugh Attwell, a celebrated actor, who died Sept. 25, 1621. See "Hist. Engl. Dram. Poetry and the Stage," i. 423, for an Epitaph upon him by William Rowley.]

Good Mr Hinchlow, I am upon ye sodeyn put to great extremyty in bayling my man, comitted to Newgate upon taking a possession for me, and I took less mony of my kinsman, a lawier y^t was with me, then servd my turn. I am thearfor to beseech y^u to spare me xxs., which will doe me so great pleasure y^t y^u shall find me thankfull, and performing more then ever I promisd or am tyed to: so, bold upon so great an occation to truble y^u, I crave y^r favorable interpretation, and rest

ever at y^r comaund,
ROB. DABORNE.

28 Aprill, 1613.

Lente Mr Daborne this money.
wittness, HUGH ATTWELL.

THE ARRAIGNMENT OF LONDON.

[The ensuing note refers to two plays, upon one of them Daborne being engaged alone, while, in the other, " The Arraignment of London," he was to be assisted by Cyril Tourneur, a well-known dramatist of the time. R. Greene and T. Lodge wrote a play (printed in 1594), called "A Looking-glass for London and England;" and perhaps Daborne's and Tourneur's drama was intended to be of the same moral and satirical character.]

M Hinchlow, the company told me y^u wear expected thear yesterday, to conclude about thear comming over, or goinge to Oxford. I have not only labord my own play, which shall be ready before they come over, but given Cyrill Tourneur an act of ye Arreignment of London to write, y^t we may have y^t likewise ready for them. I wish y^u had spoken with them to know thear resolution, for they depend upon y^r purpose. I hav sent y^u 2 sheets more, fayr written: upon my ffayth, s^r, they shall not stay one howr for me; whearfor I beseech y^u, as heatherto, so y^u would now spare me 40s., which stands me upon to send over to my counsell in a matter concerns my whole estate, and wher I deale otherways then to y^r content, may I and myne want ffryndship in distress! so, relying one y^r favor, which shall never reap loss by me, I rest

at y^r commaund,
ROB. DABORNE.

5º June, 1613.

Receved by me, Garred Leniaghe, xx$s$.

DABORNE'S LAWSUIT.

[Either Daborne's "Term business," as he calls it, occasioned him a heavy disbursement, or he made use of it as a means of obtaining money from Henslowe. The play he alludes to was no doubt that mentioned in his note five days before.]

S^r, I expected y^u one munday. I perceav y^u misdoubt my readynes: s^r, I would not be hyred to break my ffayth with

yu. Before god, they shall not stay one hour for me; for I can this week diliver in ye last word, and will yt night they play thear new play read this; whearof I have sent yu a sheet and more fayr written: yu may easyly know thear is not much behind, and I intend no other thing, god is my judge, till this be finisht. The necessity of term busines exacts me beyond my custom to be trublesom unto yu; whearfore I pray send me the other 20s. I desyred, and then when I read next week I will take ye 40s. yt remaynes, and doubt not yu shall receav thanks in doing me this curtesy. so presuming one yr favor, I rest

Yrs to commaund,
ROB. DABORNE.

10 June, 1613.

DABORNE'S SUIT TO HENSLOWE.

[A note of similar import to the last: we may also gather from it that Henslowe sometimes employed Daborne to read the "books," or plays, of other dramatists.]

Mr Hinchlow, I am inforced to make bold with yu for one 20s. more of ye xl., and one Fryday night I will deliver in ye 3 acts fayr written, and then receav ye other 40s.; and if yu please to have some papers now, yu shall; but my promise shall be as good as bond to yu, and if yu will let me have perusall of any other book of yrs, I will after Fryday intend it speedyly, and doubt not to giv yu full content; so with my best remembranc I rest

at yr commaund,
ROBT. DABORNE.

3 May, 1613.

R. the some of xxs. of Mr Hinchley, to the use of Mr. Daborne, the 3 of Maye, 1613, by me,

THOMAS MORE.

ALLEYN'S JUDGMENT IN PLAYS.

[Here, and in other letters, we see that Alleyn was in the habit of hearing plays read, before his wife's stepfather thought fit to buy them.]

Mr Hinchlow, my trubles drawing to some end, have forced me to be trublesom to y^u beyond my purpose, bycause I would be free at any rate. some papers I have sent y^u, though not so fayr written all as I could wish. I will now wholy intend to finishe my promise, which, though it come not within compass of this Term, shall come upon ye neck of this new play they ar now studyinge: my request is, the xl. might be made up, whear of I have had 9l.; if y^u please to appoynt any houer to read to Mr Allin, I will not fayle, nor after this day loose any time till it be concluded. My best rememberance to y^u, I rest

yo^rs, ROBT. DABORNE.

8 May, 1613.

R. the some of xx$s$. of Mr Hinchlowe, to the use of Mr Daborne, 8° May, pd . . } xx$s$.

THOS. MORE.

DABORNE'S LAW-TROUBLES.

[Daborne's disputes at law had in some way produced a separation between him and his wife, who, it appears by this letter, had now returned to him.]

Mr. Hinchlow, y^r tried curtesy hath so far ingaged me y^t howsoever this term hath much hindred my busines, y^u shall see one Tuesday night I have not bin Idle. I thank god moste of my trubles ar ended, upon cleering whearof I have taken home my wife agayne; soe y^t I will now, after munday, intend y^r busines carefully, y^t the company shall aknowledg themselfs bound to you I doubt not. One Tuesday night, if y^u will ap-

poynt, I will meet y^u and Mr Allin, and read some, for I am unwilling to read to ye generall company till all be finisht; which upon my credit shall be to play it this next term, with ye first. S^r, my occasions of expenc have bin soe great and soe many, I am ashamed to think how much I am forct to press y^u, whearin I pray let me finde y^r favorablest construction, and ad one xx*s.* more to ye mony I have receaved, which makes xi*l.*, and y^u shall one Tuesday see I will deserve, to my best ability, y^r love, which I valew more in it self then ye best companies in ye town. So myself and labors resting at y^r service, I commit y^u to god.

y^rs to command,
ROBT. DABORNE.

16 May, 1613.

Receved by me, GARRET LENIAGE, xx*s.*

MASSINGER AND DABORNE.

[Daborne here puts himself in comparison with Massinger as a dramatist; and we may infer that the latter had on some occasion received more for a play than the former. The two extant plays by Daborne do not show that he was entitled to hold the rank he would assume.]

S^r. I did thinke I deservd as much mony as Mr Messenger, although knowinge y^r great disbursments I forbour to urdge y^u beyond y^r own pleasure; but my occations press me so neerly, y^t I cannot but expect this reasonable curtesy, consydering I pay y^u half my earnings in the play besyds my continuall labor and chardge imployd only for y^u; which if it prove not profitable now, y^u shall see I will giv y^u honnest satisfaction for the utmost farthinge I owe yow, and take another course. Whearfore this being my last, I beseech y^u way my great occation this once, and make up my mony even with Mr Messengers, which is to let me have x*s.* more. I am sure I shall

deserv it, and y^u can never doe me a tymelyer curtesy, resting at y^r commaund

         ROBT. DABORNE.

I pray S^r let the boy giv order this night to the stage-keeper to set up bills ag^st munday for Eastward hoe, and one wenesday, the new play.

DABORNE'S RAPIDITY.

[Hence we may gather that Daborne, before he had completed one play, had commenced another, but sent that which was nearest finished (only wanting a scene) to Henslowe, as a means of obtaining a fresh supply of money.]

S^r if y^u doe not like this play when it is read, y^u shall have the other, which shall be finished with all expedition; for, before god, this is a good one, and will giv y^u content: howsoever, y^u shall never loose a farthing by me, whearfor I pray you misdoubt me not; but as y^u hav bin kynd to me, so continew it till I deserv the contrary; and I pray send me ten shillings, and take these papers, which want but one short scean of the whole play, so I rest

      y^rs at commaund,
        ROBT. DABORNE.

pd unto you^r Daughter, the 11th of Marche, 1613 . . . . x_s.

DABORNE'S URGENCY.

[Daborne seems seldom to have applied to Henslowe in vain, and hence the repetition of his demands. He does not name the play he and others were at this date at work upon.]

Mr Hinchlow, of all ffryndship let me beholding to y^u for one xx_s. which shall be the last I will request till the play be

fully by us ended. Upon my honnest ffayth with y\u, which I will never break, I will request no more, and soe much will be due to me then. S\r this is my last request of y\r trouble, which my speedy occation presses me to; soe I rely upon y\r lov hearin, for which y\u shall ever

comand me,
ROB. DARBORNE.

16 July, 1613.

dd this xxs. the 16th July, 1613.

SALE OF DABORNE'S ESTATE.

[At this date, it seems that Daborne was endeavouring to sell his estate in order to relieve his necessities: he again resorts to Henslowe for assistance. The Mr. Griffin spoken of in the following letter was perhaps the same person mentioned more than once in the "Memoirs of Edward Alleyn." He was a tradesman who carried on business near the house in which Henslowe resided.]

M\r Hinchlow, I wrote a leter to M\r Griffyn requestinge thearin y\r awnswer, and end to those businesses and debts betwixt us, but I cannot hear from him. My desyre was y\t eather y\u would be my paymaster for another play, or take xl. of y\t mony we hav had into y\r hands agayne, and security for the rest. S\r, it is not unknown to y\u y\t I could and had good certeynty of means before I wrote unto y\u, which upon hopes of y\r love I forsooke, and must now, if y\u and I had ended, return to them agayne; for my occations, untill I have made sale of y\t estate I have, ar soe urgent, y\t I can forbear no longer, whearfor I pray, S\r, of y\r much ffryndship, doe me one curtesy more till Thursday, when we deliver in o\r play to y\u, as to lend me twenty shillings, and upon my ffayth and Christianyty I will then or giv y\u content, or secure y\u to the utmost farthing y\u can desyre of me. S\r, I pray of all y\r gentlenes deny not this curtesy to me; and if y\u fynd me not most just and hon-

nest to y^u, may I want a ffrynd in my extremyty. It is but till thursday I request y^u hearin, and so rest

at y^r commaund,
Rob. Daborne.

S^r, y^u hav a receipt of myne for twenty shillings, which I sent y^u by the waterman at the cardinalls hatt: that or this shall sufficiently giv y^u assurance.

witnes Moyses Bowler.

30 July, 1613.

THE ARRAIGNMENT OF LONDON.

[This play has been introduced before, (p. 58) although the title of it is here abbreviated. "The common place bar" is of course the bar of the Court of Common Pleas.]

S^r, I sat up last night till past 12 to write out this sheet; and had not necessity inforct me to ye common place bar this morning to acknowledge a ffynall recovery, I would this day hav deliverd in all. I hav bin heartofor of ye receaving hand; y^u shall now find return to y^r content and y^t speedyly. I pray, S^r, let me have 40s. in earnest of ye Arreighnment, and one munday night I will meet y^u at ye new play, and conclud further, to y^r content I doubt not, resting my self and whole indevors

wholy at y^r Service,
Rob. Daborne.

18 June, 1613.

A NEW TRAGEDY BY DABORNE.

[From the ensuing note, we learn that Daborne had a tragedy in progress, as well as "The Arraignment of London," which perhaps was a comedy, and in which he was assisted by Tourneur. The price of £25 is higher than any sum hitherto mentioned for a new play.]

Mr Hinchlow, I perceave y^u think I will be behind with my Tragoedy; if soe, y^u might worthely account me dishonest:

indeed, for thear good and myne own I have took extraodynary payns with the end, and alterd one other scean in the third act, which they have now in parts. For ye Arreighnment, if y^u will please to be my paym^r, as for the other, they shall have it; if not, try my Tragoedy first, and as y^t proves so deal with me: in the mean, my necessity is such y^t I must use other means to be furnisht upon it. Before god, I can have £25 for it, as some of ye company know; but such is my much debt to y^u, y^t so long as my labors may pleasure them, and y^u say ye word, I am wholy yours to be

ever commaunded,
ROB. DABORNE.

I pray, S^r, if y^u resolv to do this curtesy
   for ye company, let me hav 40s. more tell
we seale.

25 June, 1613.   pade to Mr Daborne xx*s*.

NAT. FIELD IMPRISONED.

[Field, having been taken in execution for £30 and in confinement, applies to Henslowe, whom he considers in the light of a father, in his extremity. He was doubtless an actor in Henslowe's company at the time, so that his liberation was a matter of some importance to the old manager.]

Father Hinchlow,

I am unluckily taken on an execution of 30*l*. I can be discharg'd for xx*l*. x*l*. I have from a frend: if now, in my extremity, you will venture x*l*. more for my liberty, I will never share penny till you have it againe, and make any satisfaction, by writing or otherwise, y^t you can devise. I am loath to importune, because I know yor disbursments are great; nor must any know I send to you, for then my creditor will not free me but for the whole some. I pray, speedily consider my occasion, for if I be putt to use other meanes, I hope all men and yor

selfe will excuse me if (inforcedly) I cannot proove so honest, as towards you I ever resolv'd to be.

Yo^r loving son,

NAT. FIELD.

THE BELLMAN OF LONDON.

[This was probably a different play to "The Arraignment of London," previously introduced. The mode of payment is here varied: it was to be £12, and what was taken at the doors over and above a certain amount, deducting perhaps for the expenses of the house. Here we see the origin of the modern practice (though even now somewhat obsolete) of giving dramatic authors the receipts of particular nights, deducting the charges, &c. Daborne had reduced his price for a new play to £12, with the contingent advantage of " the overplus of the second day."]

Mr. Hinchlow, I hav ever since I saw y^u kept my bed, being so lame that I cannot stand. I pray, S^r, goe forward with that reasonable bargayn for the Bellman; we will hav but twelv pownds and the overplus of the second day, whearof I hav had ten shillings, and desyre but twenty shillings more, till y^u hav 3 sheets of my papers. Good S^r, consyder how for y^r sake I hav put my self out of the assured way to get mony, and from twenty pounds a play am come to twelv; thearfor in my extremyty forsake me not, as y^u shall ever command me. My wif can aquaynt y^u how infinite great my occation is, and this shall be sufficient for the receipt, till I come to set my hand to your booke.

yor at comand,

ROB. DABORNE.

Aug. 3, 1613.

Lent Mr Daborne upon this not the 32 of
   Auguste in earnest of a playe called
   the bellman of London, xx^s.

RIVAL COMPANIES.

[Daborne here threatens Henslowe with selling a new play to the king's men, *i. e.*, the company to which Shakespeare had belonged, and from which he probably had retired. At this time there seems to have been great competition in theatricals. We may conclude, from what is said, here and elsewhere, that Daborne was Henslowe's tenant.]

S^r, I hav bin twise to speak with y^u both for the sheet I told y^u off, as also to know y^r determination for the company, wheather y^u purpose they shall have the play or noe. They rale upon me, I hear, bycause the kingsmen hav given out they shall hav it: if y^u please, I will make y^u full amends for thear wrong to y^u in my last play, before they get this; for I know it is this play must doe them good, if y^u purpose any to them. I hav sent y^u 2 sheets more, so y^t y^u hav x sheets, and I desyre y^u to send me 30s. more, which is just eight pound, besyds my rent, which I will fully satisfy y^u, eather by them or the king's men, as y^u please. Good s^r, let me know y^r mynd, for I desyre to make y^u part of amends for y^r great fryndship to me, wishing my labor or service could deserv y^u: so trusting one y^r gentlenes, which cannot long be without satisfaction, now I rest

ever at y^r commaund,
Rob. Daborne.

Lent Mr Daborne upon this bille more,
the 29 of october, 1613 . . xx$s$.

BEN JONSON'S PLAY.

[The play by Jonson, mentioned in the following note, was probably, as Malone suggests, his "Bartholemew Fair," which was acted at Paris Garden early in 1614. Daborne again reminds Henslowe of the earnestness of the king's players to obtain a play of him, even at the cost of returning Henslowe the money he had advanced, and 30s. to boot.]

S^r., y^r man was with me, whoe found me wrighting the last scean, which I had thought to have brought y^u to-night, but it

will be late ear I can doe it; and being satterday night, my occation urges me to request y^u spare me xs. more, and for y^r mony, if y^u please not to stay till Johnson's play be playd, the king's men hav bin very earnest with me to pay y^u in y^r mony for y^r curtesy, whearin y^u shall have 30s. proffit with many thanks. Purposing to-morow night, if you call not upon me, to com and shew y^u *fynis*, I pray, S^r, supply this my last occation, which crowns ye rest of y^r curtesies, to which I will now giv speedy requitall, resting,

ever at y^r commaund,
ROB. DABORNE.

Nov. 13, 1613.

DABORNE'S PREFERMENT.

[This seems to be the latest letter with a date from Daborne. Possibly Lord Willoughby was the means of obtaining preferment for Daborne in the church, as he soon afterwards took orders, and a sermon by him is extant which was preached at Waterford in 1618.]

S^r, if ever my service may do y^u so much pleasure, or my ability make y^u payment for it, let me receav now this curtesy from yow, being but xs.: by god, had it not bin sunday, I would not have for twise so much wrote to y^u in this manner, but my Lord Willoughby hath sent for me to goe to him to-morow morning, by six a clocke, and I know not how proffitable it may be to me; and without y^r kindnes hearin I cannot goe: he goes away with the kinge to morow morning; whearfor I must be thear by tymes. Making this last tryall of y^r love and favor, I rest

y^{rs} to command,
ROB. DABORNE.

Lent upon this bille the 2 of Aguste, 1614.

HENSLOWE'S AGENCY.

[It is not at all clear that Henslowe did not derive part of his profits from being a medium between authors and actors: he, having money at command, supplied the wants of authors, who placed their dramas in his hands at such a price as they could obtain, and Henslowe sold them again to the company. The following letter looks as if such had sometimes been the course of dealing.]

Mr Hinchlow, I builded upon y^r promyse to my wife, neather did I aquaint the company with any mony I had of yow, bicause they should seek to y^u, as I know they will, and giv you any terms y^u can desyre: if they doe not, I will bring y^u y^r mony for the papers and many thanks: neather will I fayle to bring in the whole play next week; whearfor I pray S^r, of all ffryndship, disburse one 40s., and this note shall suffice to acknowledg my self indebted to y^u with my q^{r}ter's rent, 8l., for which y^u shall eather have the whole companye's bonds to pay y^u the first day of my play being playd, or the king's men shall pay it y^u and take my papers. S^r, my credit is as deer to me now as ever, and I will be as carefull of it as heartofore, or may I never prosper nor myne: so, desyring this may satisfy y^u till y^u appoynt a tyme when I shall bring y^u the companie's bond, I rest expecting y^r no more defering me,

ever at y^r command,
Rob. Daborne.

Witnes,   Moyses Bowler.

october xiiij, 1613.

MODE OF COMPOSITION.

[Some of our old dramatists must have written so much and so rapidly that we can hardly suppose them to have had time to copy their compositions out fair. Nevertheless, such was evidently the case with Daborne, as we find by the following letter which relates to an unnamed play.]

Mr Hinchlow, y^u accuse me with the breach of promise. Trew it is, I promysd to bring y^u the last scean, which that y^u

may see finished, I send y^u the foule sheet, and ye fayr I was wrighting, as y^r man can testify; which, if great busnies had not prevented, I had this night fynished. S^r, y^u meat me by ye common measuer of poets: if I could not liv by it and be honest, I would giv it over: for rather then I would be unthankfull to y^u, I would famish, thearfor accuse me not till y^u hav cause. if y^u pleas to p̄form my request, I shall think myself beholding to y^u for it: howsoever, I will not fayle to write this fayr and perfit the book, which shall not ly one y^r hands.

y^rs to commaund,
Rob. Daborne.

Lent at this tyme v*s*., the 13 of November, 1613.

ANOTHER LOAN TO DABORNE.

[It is to be hoped that all the poets in the employ of Henslowe did not give him as much trouble as Daborne. Had they made as many applications for money, probably more of their letters would have been preserved at Dulwich.]

S^r, I have sent to y^u to request y^u to send me the twenty shillings I soe earnstly desyred y^u to lend me last night; for which, as all the rest of y^r mony, I will give yow that honnest and just satisfaction one Tuesday next, if y^u please to come or send to me, as I told y^u, that y^u shall never repent y^r many curtesyes to me; which ty me so far to perform the faythfull part of an honnest man, that I shall never trewly rest contented till I manyfest myself worthy y^r great favor, which ever I will aknowledge in all servic

to be commanded,
Rob. Daborne.

27 Nov., 1613.

Wittnes, Moyses Bowler, dd. xx*s*.

BOOK BORROWED BY DABORNE.

[What kind of "book" was borrowed by Daborne from Henslowe we can only conjecture: a play was then often called "a book," and possibly Daborne wished to inspect the production of some of his fellow-dramatists. Perhaps it was some book out of the story of which he was to form a drama; and this seems the more probable from what is said on p. 73.]

S^r, out of the great love I have felt from y^u, I am to request y^u to my great occation and present necessety, which with less mony will be unsupplied, to send me xx$s$. I pray, s^r, accoumpt me not amongst the number of those y^t wholy serv thear own turns, for, god knows, it is not mony could hyre me to be dishonest to so worthy a ffrynd as y^u ar: whearfor sinc thear remayns so small a somm, I pray part with it to my good, which xs. will not I protest doe. You know it is term tyme, and a litle mony wanting will much hynder me; whearfor, good S^r, let me fynd y^u put some trust in me, which, when I deceav, god forsake me and myne. One munday I will be with y^u; so, desyring y^u to send me the book y^u promysd, and no less than 20s., I rest

ever at y^r commaund,

R. DABORNE.

Nov., 1613.

Witnes, MOYSES BOWLER.

IMPORTUNITY OF DABORNE.

[Certainly, for a man who was destined ere long to go into the church, Daborne, in his letters to Henslowe, was not scrupulous in his asseverations and imprecations. He is especially emphatic in the following.]

Mr Hinchlow, I acquaynted you with my necessity, which I know you did in part supply, but if y^u doe not help me to tenn shillings by this bearer, by the living god I am utterly disgract. one ffryday night I will bring you papers to the valew of three

said Phillip Hinchlow shall approove, alowe, and accept of, that then and from hence foorth this present obligacōn to bee voyde and of non effect, or else to remayne in full power, strength, and virtue.

ROBERT DABORNE.

Signed Sealed and Delv^r ed in the presence of
  Edwarde Griffin, Walter Hopkinss, Geo. Hales.

DABORNE'S BOND TO HENSLOWE.

[Notwithstanding the advance of £7 upon "The Owl" on the 24th December, 1613, Daborne was again in extreme want of money on the 31st December, and accordingly obtained 10s. more from the old manager.]

S^r, I yeeld y^u many thanks for y^r last kindnes, which did me infinite pleasure. I hav bin very ill this week of an extream cold, ells I had come this night unto you. I will request no farther curtesy at y^r hands upon any occation till y^u hav papers in full and to y^r content, only the other tenn shillings which I requested agst this day, being a tyme y^t requires me beyond my present means. S^r, think not y^r curtesy can loose by me. I will be any thing rather then ingratefull to so much love as I hav receaved from y^u; as y^u hav donn what I can desyre in doing this, so now look for my honnest care to dischardge my Bond. I will not truble y^u with many words. God send y^u many hapy new years, and me no otherwise then I approv myself honnest to y^u.

y^{rs} ever at commaund,

31° December, 1613.   ROB. DABORNE.

One munday I will come to y^u, and appoynt for the reading the old book and bryng in the new.

    pd upon this bille toward the Owle, xs.

DAWES, THE PLAYER'S, ARTICLES.

[This is the oldest specimen of theatrical "articles" (as they are still called) between managers and players. It is very curious and minute in its details and provisions; but as the original, which must have been in a very much injured state, is not now to be found in Dulwich College, it is necessarily given as Boswell printed it, vol. xxi. p. 413. Henslowe and Meade were at this time in partnership. Meade and Alleyn were connected in business, at least after the death of Henslowe, in January, 1616, and had violent disputes. See "Memoirs of Edward Alleyn," p. 159.]

Articles of Agreement] made, concluded, and agreed uppon, and wch are to be kept and performed by Robert Dawes, of London, Gent, unto and with Phillipp Henslowe, Esqre, and Jacob [Meade, Waterman], in manner and forme following, that is to say—

Imprimis. the said Robert Dawes for him, his executors, and administrators, doth covenante, promise, and graunt, to and with the said Phillipp Henslowe, and Jacob Meade, their executors, administrators, and assynes in manner and formme followinge, that is to saie—that he the said Robert Dawes shall and will plaie with such company as the said Phillipp Henslowe and Jacob Meade shall appoynte, for and during the tyme and space of three yeares from the date hereof, for and at the rate of one whole Share, according to the custome of players; and that he the said Robert Dawes shall and will at all tymes during the said terme duly attend all suche rehearsall, which shall the night before the rehearsall be given publickly out; and if that he the saide Robert Dawes shall at any tyme faile to come at the hower appoynted, then he shall and will pay to the said Phillipp Henslowe and Jacob Meade, their excutors or assignes, Twelve pence; and if he come not before the saide rehearsall is ended, then the said Robert Dawes is contented to pay twoe shillings; and further, that if the said Robert Dawes shall not every daie whereon any play is or ought to be played be ready apparrelled and —— to begyn the play at the

hower of three of the clock in the afternoone unles by sixe of the same Company he shall be lycenced to the contrary, that then he the said Robert Dawes shall and will pay unto the said Phillipp and Jacob, or their assignes, three [shillings]; and if that he the saide Robert Dawes happen to be overcome with drinck at the tyme when he [ought to] play, by the Judgment of ffower of the said company, he shall and will pay Tenne shillings; and if he [the said Robert Dawes] shall [faile to come] during any plaie having no lycence or just excuse of sicknes he is contented to pay Twenty shillings; and further, the said Robert Dawes, for him, his executors and administrators, doth covenant and graunt to and with the said Phillipp Henslowe and Jacob Meade, their executors, adminstrators, and asignes by these presents, that it shall and may be lawfull unto and for the said Phillipp Henslowe and Jacob Meade, their executors or assignes, during the terme aforesaid, to receave and take back to their own proper use the part of him the said Robert Dawes of and in one moyetie or halfe part of all suche moneyes as shal be receaved at the Galleres and tyring howse of such house or howses wherein he the saide Robert Dawes shall play; for and in consideration of the use of the same howse and howses, and likewis shall and may take and receave his other moyetie . . . .
the moneys receaved at the galleries and tiring howse dues towards the pa[ying] to them the saide Phillip Henslowe and Jacob Meade of the some of one hundred twenty and fower pounds [being the value of the stock of apparell furnished by the saide company by the said Phillip Henslowe and Jacob Meade . . . . . the one part of him the saide Robert Dawes or any other somes . . . .
to them for any apparell hereafter newly to be bought by the [said Phillip Henslowe and Jacob Meade until the saide Phillip Henslowe and Jacob Meade] shall therby be fully satisfied, contented, and paid. And further, the said Robert Dawes doth covenant, [promise, and graunt to and with the said Phillip

Henslowe and Jacob Meade, that if he the said Robert Dawes] shall at any time after the play is ended depart or goe out of the [howse] with any [of their] apparell on his body, or if the said Robert Dawes [shall carry away any propertie] belonging to the said Company, or shal be consentinge [or privy to any other of the said company going out of the howse with any of their apparell on his or their bodies, he the said] Robert Dawes shall and will forfeit and pay unto the said Phillip and Jacob or their administrators or assignes the some of ffortie pounds of lawfull [money of England] . . . . and the said Robert Dawes, for him, his executors, and administrators doth [covenant, promise, and graunt to with the said] Phillip Henslowe and Jacob Meade, their Executors and Administrators, [and assigns]

that it shall and may be lawfull to and for the said Phillip Henslowe and Jacob Meade, their executors and assignes, to have and use the playhows so appoynted [for the said company   one day of] every fower daies, the said daie to be chosen by the said Phillip and [Jacob]

monday in any week on which day it shalbe lawful for the said Phillip [and Jacob their administrators] and assignes to bait their bears and bulls ther, and to use their accustomed sport and [games]

and take to their owne use all suche somes of money as thereby shall arise and be receaved

And the saide Robert Dawes, his executors, administrators, and assignes [doth hereby covenant, promise, and graunt to and with the saide Phillip and Jacob,] allowing to the saide company for every such daye the some of ffortie shillings money of England . . . . [In testimony] whereof I the saide Robert Dawes have hereunto sett my hand and seal this [sev]enth daie of April, 1614, in the twelfth yeare [of the reign of our sovereign lord, &c.]

            ROBERT DAWES.

HENSLOWE'S DISPUTE WITH HIS COMPANY.

[The subsequent paper is also not now found at Dulwich, but Malone printed it from some original once existing there: it is entitled "Articles of Grievance against Mr. Henchlowe." It is followed by "Articles of Oppression against Mr. Hinchlowe," and both throw a great deal of light upon the obscure history of theatricals at the time.]

Imprimis in march, 1612, uppon M^r. Hinchlowes joyning companes with M^r. Rossiter, the companie borrowed 80^{li} of one M^r. Griffin, and the same was put into M^r. Hinchlowe's debt, which made it sixteen score pounds, who after the receipt of the same or the most parte thereof, in march, 1613, hee broke the said companies againe and ceazed all the stocke under culler to satisfie what remayned due to him; yet perswaded M^r. Griffyne afterwards to arest the companie for his 80^{li} who are still in daunger for the same. Soe nowe there was in equitie due to the companie . . . . 80^{li}

Item, Mr. Hinchlowe having lent one Taylor 30^{li} and 20^{li} to one Baxter, fellowes of the companie, cunninglie put theire said privat debts into the general accompt, by which meanes hee is in conscience to allow them . . . . 50^{li}

Item, havinge the stock of Apparell in his hands to secure his debt, he sould tenn pounds worth of ould apparell out of the same, without accomptinge or abatinge for the same. heare grows due to the Companie . . . . 10^{li}

Alsoe upon the departure of one Eglestone a fellowe of the companie, he recovered of him 14^{li} towards his debt, which is in conscience likewise to bee allowed to the companie . . . 14^{li}

In march, 1613, hee makes up a Companie and buies apparell of one Rosseter to the value of 63^{li}: and valued the ould stocke that remayned in his hands at 63^{li}, likewise then uppon his word acceptinge the same at that rate, which beinge prized by Mr Daborne justli, betweene his partner Meade and him came but to 40^{li} so here growes due to the Companie . . . 23^{li}

Item, he agrees with the same companie that they should enter bond to plaie with him for three yeares at such house and houses as hee shall appointe, and to allowe him halfe galleries for the said house and houses, and the other halfe galleries towards his debt of 126ˡⁱ and other such moneys as hee should laie out for playe apparel duringe the space of the said three yeares agreeinge with them, in consideracõn wheareof to seale each of them a bond of 200ˡⁱ to find them a convenient house and houses and to laie out such monies as fower of the sharers should think fitt for theire use in apparrell, which at the three yeares beinge paid for to be delivered to the Sharers; whoe accordinglie entered the said bonds, but Mʳ. Henslowe and Mʳ Mead deferred the same, and in conclusion utterly denied to seale at all.

Item, Mʳ Hinchlowe having promised in consideracõn of the companies lying still one daie in forteene for his baytinge, to give them 50ˡⁱ hee having denied to bee bound as aforesaid, gave them onlie 40ˡⁱ, and for that Mʳ Field would not consent thereunto, hee gave him soe much as his share out of 50ˡⁱ would have come unto, by which meanes hee is dulie indebted to the companie. . . . . xˡⁱ

In June followinge the said agreement, hee brought in Mʳ. Pallant and shortlie after Mʳ Dawes into the said Companie, promising one 12ˢ a weeke out of his part of the galleries, and the other 6ˢ a weeke out of his part of the galleries, and likewise Mʳ Field was thought not to be drawne thereunto; hee promissed him six shillinges weeklie alsoe, which in one moneth after unwilling to beare so greate a charge, he called the Companie together, and told them that this 24ˢ was to be charged upon them; threatninge those which would not consent thereunto to breake the Companie and make up a newe without them. Wheareuppon knowinge hee was not bound, the three quarters sharers advauncing them selves to whole sharers consented thereunto, by which meanes they are out of

purse 30ᵘ and his parte of the galleries bettred twise as much 30ᵘ

Item, having 9 gatherers more than his due, itt comes to this yeare from the Companie 10ᵘ

Item, the Companie paid for Arras and other properties 40ᵘ which Mʳ Henchlowe deteyneth 40ᵘ

In februarie last, 1614, perceivinge the Companie drew out of his debt and called uppon him for his accompts, hee brooke the Companie againe by withdrawinge the hired men from them, and sells theire stocke in his hands for 400ᵘ givinge under his owne hand that he had receaved towards his debt 300ᵘ

Which with the juste and conscionable allowances before named made to the Companie, which comes to 267ᵘ makes 567ᵘ

ARTICLES OF OPPRESSION AGAINST MR. HINCHLOWE.

He chargeth the stocke with 600ᵘ and odd pounds, towards which hee hath receaved as aforesaid 567ᵘ of us, yet sells the stocke to strangers for fower hundred pounds, and makes us no satisfaction.

Hee hath taken all bonds of our hired men in his own name, whose wages though wee have truly paid, yet att his pleasure hee hath taken them awaye, and turned them over to others to the breckinge of our Companie.

For lendinge of viᵘ to pay them their wages, hee made us enter and to give him the profitt of a warrant of tenn pounds due to us at court.

Also hee hath taken right gould and silver lace of divers garments to his owne use without accompt to us or abatement.

Uppon every breach of the Companie hee takes new bonds for his stocke, and our securitie for playinge with him; soe that hee hath in his hands bonds of ours to the value of 5000ᵘ and his stocke to, which he denies to deliver, and threatens to oppresse us with.

Alsoe havinge appointed a man to the seeinge of his accompts

in byinge of clothes, hee beinge to have vi[s] a weeke, he takes the meanes away and turnes the men out.

The reason of his often breakinge with us hee gave in these words: Should these fellowes come out of my debt, I should have noe rule with them.

Alsoe wee have paid him for plaie-books 200[li] or thereabouts, and yet he denies to give us the coppies of any one of them.

Also within 3 yeares hee hath broken and dismembered five Companies.

BOND OF HENSLOWE'S DEPUTY.

[A bond given by Thomas Radford, one of Henslowe and Alleyn's deputies, as Masters of the King's Games, in reference to his deputation and conduct regarding it. The latter portion of the instrument relates to the complaint of a person of the name of Penkett against James Starkey, who had probably seized a dog or a bull belonging to the former, under pretence that it was for the king's use. Starkey is one of the witnesses, as well as Jacob Mede, or Meade, who was one of Henslowe's partners.]

Noverint Universi, &c.

7 June, 1613.

The condition of this obligation ys suche, That whereas the above named Phillipe Henslowe did heretofore of late deliver unto the above bounde Thomas Radforde his Ma[ts] letters pattents or commission, that he, the saide Thomas, as deputie to the said Phillipe Henslow, and to one Edwarde Allen, Esquire, sholde by vertue of the saide Patent take upp for his Ma[ties] use bulls, beares, and dogges, according to the intent and effect of the saide letters patents or commission. Yf therefore the saide Thomas Radforde have well and justlye performed and executed the trust therein committed to him, soe that the saide Phillipe Henslowe and Edwarde Allen, or either of them, be not hereafter at any tyme or tymes molested, hindered, ympeached, menaced, scandalized, defamed, or damni-

fyed by any person or persons whatsoever for any matter, cause, or thinge which the saide Thomas Radforde hathe either done or procured to be done, or hereafter shall doe or speake, other by worde or deed, concerninge the same letters patents or the trust committed to him, the saide Thomas Radforde, and that the quarrell, debate, or controversie of late had or moved betwene one Richarde Penkett, of Penkett, within the Countie of Lancaster, gentleman, and one James Starkey, gent, did not growe or concerne any thinge or thinges, cause or matter, concerninge the saide letters patents, or commission, or deputation aforesaid, that then this obligation to be voide and of none effect, or els to stande, remaine, and be in full power, strength, and vertue.

     Thomas T. R. Radfords marke.

Sealed and delivered in the presence of
  James Starky.
  Jacob Mede.
  Edwarde Griffin.

THE SHE SAINT.

[Daborne here assumes a somewhat different tone, and talks about engaging a play with some other company. "Mr. Pallant" was, of course, Pallant the actor, who, in 1623, had become one of the king's servants.]

Mr Hinchlow, y^u hav now a full play. I desyr y^u should disburse but 12l. a play til they be playd. I mean to urdge y^u no farther; for if y^u like not this, y^u shall hav another to y^r content. Befor god, y^u shall hav the full play now; and I desyr but 20s. to serv my ordynary turn, till I have finished one, that y^u may hav y^r choyse, for I would hav y^u know I can hav mony for papers, though I hav cast myself upon y^u with a purpose to deserv y^r love. As for Mr Pallant is much discontented with your neglect of him: I would I knew y^r mynd to giv him awnswer. S^r, if y^u deny me this reasonable kyndnes,

it will forc me to ingage a play which y^u will miss: so desyring y^r awnswer I rest,

y^rs at comand,
R. Dab.

28 March, 1613.

pd unto Mr Daborne the 2 of Aprell, 1614, in earnest of the Shee Saynte, at his owne howsse, the some of .. viii*s*.	Lent of this bille the 29 of Marche, in full payment of his new playe laste written, the some of .... x*s*.

ALLEYN'S PROPERTY IN BLACKFRIARS.

[The following is a copy of one of the receipts which Alleyn gave quarterly for the rent of a house in the Blackfriars, and which was, in all probability, in some way connected with the Theatre there.]

Rd. this 7th of January, 1616, of Mr Edward Allen, for a quarters rent of a house latly in the hands of Robert Jones, being in Blackfryers, due at Christid last past, I say Rocd. the some of three pounds tenn shillings for my master, Edmond Traves: I say Rd. the some of .... } 3*l*. 10*s*.

p me, Reynold Sotherne.

A GRATEFUL RETURN.

[A tribute, in verse, from Richard Meridall, who had been educated at Dulwich College. It seems to have been addressed to Mrs. Alleyn, and does not say much for the proficiency of the writer as a verse-maker: he was not deficient in gratitude, and his scholarship was no doubt enough for his station in life, although nature never destined him to undergo the misfortune of being a poet.]

Right Wor^ll,

Itt were needlesse to commend the worth of vertue to a vertuous and understanding disposition, and especially to one that

is, as it were, the Patrones of vertue and understandinge. Never the lesse, I have presumed, though not worthy your acceptation, to dedicate theis few lynes to your curteous viewe for the binifitts I have all readye received from your gratious hands:—

> Loe heare shee dwells, whome vertue doeth embrace,
> And keepes foule vice from this most heavenly place:
> To those shee seemes a star most shining bright,
> Whome fortune makes to seeme more darke then night,
> As maye appeare by those twelve orphants poore,
> Whome shee releeves at charrityes blest dore.
> I was one of them that can witnes well
> Shee doeth in love [and] charritye excell,
> For which wee all are joyntly bound to pray
> God to preserve you both night and daye:
> And to conclude, your virtues such are found,
> That none cann equall them one earthly ground.
>
> Your worshipps humble servant,
> ever to commaunde tell death,
> RICH. MERIDALL.

ALLEYN'S PURCHASES.

[Relating to Alleyn's pecuniary transactions: the £30 may have been either for a purchase, or for a loan. The mention of Minsheu, as a teacher of languages, is interesting: in "The Memoirs of Edward Alleyn," p. 147, it is stated, on the authority of an entry in his diary, that, in conjunction with the Rev. John Harrison, his chaplain, Alleyn had bought a copy of Minsheu's Dictionary, for which they gave 22s., on January 22, 1618-19.]

[Addressed]

To the worl my good freind Mr Allyn, at his house on the Banks side.

Sr, if it please you to lay downe xxx^{li}, either your desire shalbe effected, or the mony restored within a month or two.

For security you shall have my bond, or if you please a Citizens of good worth. Mr Joanes I heare not yet of. If you send not answer by this bearer, I pray send your man hether with the soonest, that I may know your mind. If you know where I might find Mynshew, or any other Italian or Spanish teacher, you may do me a favour to signify it in your letters. So I rest

Yours in all love,
R. REDMER.

Lambeth, Mai 27.

REDMER'S NECESSITIES.

[A note of much the same purport as the last, and, like it, without date. The similarity of the sum would show that it related to the same transaction. It elsewhere appears that Redmer lived in a house belonging to Alleyn, in Lambeth.]

[Addressed]
To the wor^{ll} my good freind Mr. Allyn.

S^r,—Upon answer returned on Friday last, I appointed a payment of xx^{li} to be made as to march, but missing your messenger to day at one a clock, and not able to furnish my self so sodainely, I would intreat you either this night (for my quieter sleeping) to send that x^{li}, or to be sure of it to morrow by 6 or 7 a clock in the morning. If you please to deliver to this bearer, my man, this shall be sufficient discharge, together with a note of his hand to testify his receipt. So I desire to be excused, and rest,

Y^{rs} in all love to com.
R. REDMER.

This Sunday at 5 a clock.

ADDRESS TO ALLEYN FROM HIS COMPANY.

[The following interesting document has no date, but we may, perhaps, conclude that it was subsequent to Henslowe's death, in January, 1615-16. It is the original, and contains the signatures of the different players, which we give in fac-simile as a very curious relic of the time. Most of the names will be familiar to those who are acquainted with the history of our early stage: that of Robert Hampton is, in fact, the only new one. William Rowley was an author as well as an actor, and is not to be confounded with Samuel Rowley, to whom he was perhaps related, and who was also an author and an actor. Joseph Taylor has been supposed, on the authority of Wright's *Historia Histrionica*, 1699, to have been the original Hamlet; but this is now known to be a mistake, the part having been played by R. Burbage until his death in 1619. Alleyn had had a quarrel with Jacob Meade, of whom the actors complained, and possibly the address grew out of this proceeding. We may conjecture that the company had been performing at Paris Garden, when it was alternately playhouse and bear-garden, until they were turned out by Meade, and compelled to seek a settlement on the Middlesex side of the water. In this dilemma they applied to Alleyn for a temporary advance, but it does not appear whether he did or did not comply with their wishes: he probably did, as appeals of the kind were seldom made to him in vain.]

M^r. Allen commends,

S^r. I hope you mistake not o^r remooval from the bank's side. wee stood the intemperate weather, till more intemperatr M^r. Meade thrust us over, taking the day from us wch by course was owrs; though by the time we can yet claime none, and that power hee exacted on us, for the prosecution of our further suite in a house: wee entreate you to fore-think well of the place, (though it crave a speedie resolution) lest wee make a second fruitless paines, and as wee purpose to dedicate all our paines, powers, and frends all referent to yor uses: so wee entreate you, in the meane time, to look toward our necessityes, leaving you ever a certaine forme of satisfaction. Wee have neede of some monie (indeed urdgent necessitie,) wch wee rather wish you did heare in conference then by report in writing:

wee have to receive from the court (wch after shrovetide wee meane to pursue with best speede) a great summe of monie; meane while, if you'le but furnish us with the least halfe, wch will be fourtie pounds, it shall be all confirm'd to you, till your satisfaction of the fourty. What we can do for yor availe or purpose wee profess our readiest furtherance, and you shall command it, for wch wee entreate this kindness from you still resting

  In your emploimentes,

    friendes to their best powers,

[signatures: Robt. Pallant, William Rowley, Joseph Taylor, John Newton, Robt. Hamlen, ... Howell, ... Smyth]

[Indorsed]
  To our worthy and much respected Frend, Mr. Allen, these bee ded.

LORD OF THE MANOR OF KENNINGTON.

[The ensuing receipt seems to prove that up to the 30th of September, 1619, Alleyn remained Lord of the Manor of Kennington, as well as Lord of the Manor of Lewisham.]

Kenington, Surry. The last day of September, 1619.

Receved of Edward Allinn, gen., one shilling and eight pence, for one hole yeares quitt Rente, due at St Michael last past, for all his landes, and Ten^{ts} in the mannor aforesaide, I say Rec to the use of the princes heighnesse the some of . . . .   li s d
00. 01. 8

p me, THO. CHEYNIE,
Bayliffe.

PRAYER AND POEM.

[The following prayer is in a female handwriting, and perhaps was penned by one of Alleyn's wives, probably the daughter of Dr. Donne: it may be more than doubted whether his first wife, Joan Woodward, could write. The well-known lines upon sack are on the margin of the paper, accompanied by various scribblings of no interest. The whole is on the back of the rough draft of the appointment of John Wickender to be Alleyn's deputy for the collection of rents, &c., in the parish of Cowden, part of the Manor of Lewisham.]

Allmighty god, thy name be blessed for presarving me this day: grant mee thy grace to pass all my days in thy feere, and in the love of my husband.
AMEN.

Sacke will make the mery mind be sade,
Soo will it make the mallincolly glad:
If mearth and sadenes dooth in sake remaine,
When I am sade Ile drinke sum sake againe.

ALLEYN'S KINDNESS TO HIS NAMESAKE.

[The writer was Warden of Dulwich College at the death of the founder, and subsequently became Master. He resided in the country (it is not stated where, nor at what date) at the time when he sent the following letter, which shows how kind Edward Alleyn had already been to him. It does not distinctly appear whether Mathias Alleyn was any, or what relation to Edward Alleyn.]

[Addressed]
>To the woorshipfull my very good M^r, Mr Edw. Alleyn, at the bancke sid, geive these.

My dutie remembred unto your woŏp, and unto my mistr. with my humble and hartie thankes for all your loving kindnes shewed unto me, and for your laste kindnes that I received at your handes in every respecte, when I was with you laste. And nowe at this time, as my dutifull love dooth binde me, I wryte unto your woŏp leaste that you shoulde thinke that I had forgotten my selfe of that which is my dutie to dooe in regard of your kindnes towardes mee: and further I intreate your good will and your furderance concerninge my comminge to London to settell; as your kinde speeches was at my laste departure from you that I should have your good will and your faver in that or in anie thinge for my good, and I hope it would be for my good; but three thinges I dooe especially desire: the firste is God's mercifull blessinge and your love and kind furderance, and that I might have but woorke to keepe 3 or 4 at woorke, &c. Yt nowe fallethe out that there is a howse, that if it please you soe to directe me that I might have as my freind the bringer of this unto you will more at large sertifye you of it, better then I can nowe wryte of it, because I never it [yet] did see it, but by my freindes letter have harde of it, but I will com to see it shortly, if please you to direct me at [sic] to take it alsoe; but I desire your opinion in thease courses, and alsoe your kind answer soe

shortly as it maye please you, &c. And in remembrance of my love and dutie, I have sente you and my mistris a cople of fatt henns. I praye except of that, and thus, as my cristian dutie dooth bynde me, I praye and will dooe that the lord will blese and preserve you booth in soule, in body, and mind, to his glory and your everlastinge joye. The x of marche.

Your servante to command,

MATHIAS ALLEYN.

My freind's name, the bearer or bringer heereof, is William Scotte.

ALLEYN A TENANT OF BANKSIDE PROPERTY.

[The writer of this letter was at the time confined in the White Lion Prison in Southwark, (see Stowe's Survey, by Thoms, p. 153) and probably parted with his property in consequence of pecuniary difficulties. It does not appear what the "certain tenements on the Bankside" were which Alleyn held of Luntley. The Rose theatre, in which Henslowe and Alleyn had been interested, must at this date have been pulled down.]

M^r. Allen, my love remembred unto you. Whereas you hold a lease of me of certeine Ten^{ts} on the bancke side for a certeine terme yett to come. Soe it is, I have made them over for twoe yeares to one M^r. John Freebody, whoe is to receave of you the rent you paie me, which is xiiij^{li} a yeare. He is to receave of you this quarters rente, iij^{li} x^s, which I pray you paie unto him, and the rest as it shall growe due; whereof I thought good to certefye you under my hand, notwithstandinge the deede, which I would have done soner, but expectinge to have seene you. And soe for present I take my leave.

Your lovinge freind,

JOHN LUNTLEY.

From the White Lyon in Southwarkth, is
   viijth of January, 1623.

RECEIPT FOR THE RENT.

[This is the receipt given to Alleyn by Freebody, in consequence of the payment of the rent mentioned in the foregoing letter.]

The xvth day of January, 1623.

Receaved by me, John Freebody, of Edward Allen, Esquire, the some of three poundes and tenn shillinges, for a quarters rent due att Christmas last past, for certeyne ten^{ts} on the Bankes side, which are assigned over unto me by Mr John Luntley. I say R. .... } iij^{li} x^s

Jo. FREEBODY.

INTRODUCTION TO THE STATUTES OF DULWICH COLLEGE.

[The subsequent draft of an introduction to the statutes of Dulwich College must have been prepared under Alleyn's inspection very late in his life, which terminated 25th November, 1626. He was born two years after Shakespeare, and outlived him by about ten years. It is on a blank space of this draft that Alleyn wrote, with his own hand, that clause in his Will which is printed in his "Memoirs," p. 184. The document inserted below, which must have been prepared by a lawyer, is evidently incomplete, as none of the statutes of the College of God's Gift are appended.]

In the name of God, amen. To all Christian people to whom this present writinge quadrupartite shall come. I, Edward Allen, of Dulwich, in the countie of Surrey, Esquire, sende greetings in oure Lorde God everlastinge. Whereas, our late sovcraigne lord Kinge James of famous memorie, late King of England, Scotland, Fraunce, and Ireland, deceased, by his highnes letters patentes under the Great Seale of England, bearinge date at Westminster the one and twentieth daye of

June, in the yeare of his raigne of England the seventeenth, and of Scotland the two and fiftieth, did of his speciall grace, certaine knowledge, and mere motion, for him, his heires, and successors, amongst other thinges, graunt and geve license to me, the sayde Edward Allen, that I, or after my death, my heires, executors, or assignes, or everie or anie of them, for and towardes the reliefe, sustenaunce, and mayntenaunce of poore men, women, and children, and for the instruction of the sayde poore children, to be enabled and to have full power and libertie, at mine owne and my heires, executors, and assignes will and pleasure, to make, found, and erect, create and stablish, one Colledge in Dullwich aforesayde, in the sayde Countie of Surrye, which should endure and remaine for ever, and should consist of one maister, one warden, fower fellowes, sixe poor brethren, six poore sisters, and twelve poore schollers, to be maintayned, susteyned, educated, guided, governed, and ruled, according to sutch ordinances, statutes, and foundation, as shall be made, sett downe, stablished, and ordeyned, by me, the sayde Edward Allen, in my liffe tyme, or by anie other person or persons after my decease, sutche as shalbe especiallie nominated, deputed, and appoynted theareunto by me, the sayde Edward Allen, in my lyfe tyme, under my hand and seale in writinge, for the mainteynaunce, sustenaunce, education, instruction, guidinge, government, and rule of the sayde maister, warden, fower fellowes, six poore brethren, six poore sisters, and twelve poore schollers.

And whereas our sayde late soveraigne lord Kinge James, by the sayde letters patentes, of his more ample and aboundant grace, certayne knowledge, and mere motion, did graunte and geve license for him, his heires and successors, to me, the sayde Edward Allen, as longe as I shall live, and after my death to such person or persons as I, the sayde Edward Allen, shall in my liffe tyme nominate, depute, and appoynt, under my hand and seale, in writinge, and to everie or anie of them, from tyme to tyme, and as often as neede shall require, to make,

ordayne, constitute, and establish, statutes, ordinances, constitutions, and rules, for the good and better mayntenaunce, sustenaunce, relieffe, education, government, and orderinge, as well of the sayde Colledge so to be created, erected, founded, and established, as aforesayde, as of the sayde maister, warden, fower fellowes, six poore brethren, six poore sisters, and twelve poore schollers, and their successors, for ever, and also of all and everie the manor, messuages, landes, tenementes, heredittamentes, in the sayde letters pattentes mentioned, and the rentes, issues, revenewes, and profittes of the same. And that the sayde statutes, ordinances, constitutions, and rules, so by me, the sayde Edward Alleyne, in my liffe tyme, or by the sayde other persons, or anie of them, after my decease, to be made, ordeyned, or constituted, shall for ever and in all succeeding tymes stande, be, and remaine inviolable, and in full force and strength in lawe, to all constructions, intentes, and purposes, the same beinge not repugnant to the prerogative royall of our soveraigne Lorde the Kinges Matie, nor contrarie to the lawes and statutes of this his highness realme of England, nor anie the ecclesiasticall lawes or constitutions of the church of England, which then shouldbe in force, as by the sayde letters patentes, whereunto reference beinge had, amongst other thinges, more at large itt dothe and may appeare.

And whereas I, the sayde Edward Allen, by my deede quadrupartite bearinge date the thirteenth day of September, in the sayde seventeenth yeare of the raigne of our sayde late soveraigne lord Kinge James, for the better mainteynaunce, education, relieffe, and sustenaunce of poore, needie people, men women, and children, of the several parishes of St. Botolphes without Bishopps gate, London, of St. Saviours in Southwarke, and of that part of the parish of St. Giles without Cripplegate, Londen, which is in the countie of Middx, and of the parish of Camerwell, in the countie of Surrey, by vertewe and force of the sayde letters pattentes, and by the power and authoritie

thereby to me graunted and given by our sayde late soveraigne lorde Kinge James, did, by the sayde writinge quadrupartite, make, founde, erect, create, and establish one Colledge in Dullwich aforesayde, in the sayde countie of Surrey, which shall continewe and remaine for ever, and shall consist of one maister, one warden, fower fellowes, sixe poore brethren, six poore sisters, and twelve poore schollers, and that the same Colledge shall for ever be called and named the Colledge of Gods Guift in Dulwich, in the countie of Surrey, as in and by the sayde writinge quadrupartite, whereunto reference beinge had, amongst other thinges, more at lardge itt doth and may appeare. Now know ye that I, the sayde Edward Allen, to the honour and glorie of Almightie God, and in thankfull remembraunce of his guifts and blessinges bestowed uppon me, and for the better mainteynaunce, relieffe, sustenaunce, education, government, and orderinge, as well of the sayde Colledge, as of the sayde maister, warden, fower fellowes, six poore brethren, six poore sisters, and twelve poore schollers, by vertewe and force of the said letters patentes, and by the power and authoritie thereby to me graunted and geven, do ordeyne, make, constitute, and founde ordinaunces, constitutions, provisions, rules and statutes for the good and orderlie rule and government, as well of the sayde Colledge, as of the sayde maister, warden, fower fellowes, six poore brethren, six poore sisters, and twelve poore schollers, and also of the sayde manors, messuages, landes, tenementes, and hereditamentes, in the sayde letters patentes, mentioned, in manner and forme as itt foloweth written in these English wordes, viz.

NON-PAYMENT OF RENT BY THE FORTUNE TENANTS.

[The succeeding document is important in connection with the history of the Fortune Theatre, and the property belonging to it, only about ten years after the death of its owner. The tenants had fallen into arrear, and the matter had been thrown into Chancery. The whole annual rent was £128 5*s.* 4*d.*, and the Master, Warden, Fellows, and Court of Assistants certify that they had been compelled to take money up at interest to supply the deficiency. At this date the rent of the Fortune, &c., formed an important part of the property of the College, but it soon became of little or no pecuniary value, and the improvement in the worth of land at Dulwich and its vicinity rendered the loss comparatively little felt. There is no doubt that about this date the Fortune began to be disused as a place for dramatic representation, and before 1640 the company, which played in it, had removed to the Red Bull.]

4to Septembris, 1637.

At a Court of Assistantes held at Goddes guifte Colledge in Dulwich, the daie and yeare aforesaid, it appeared that the Tenauntes of the Fortune betweene Whitecrossestreet and Golding Lane, in the parish of St Giles, Creplegate, London, are in arrere and behind in rent at this present the summe of 132^{li} 12^{s} 11^{d}. And there wilbe a quarters rent more at Michas next, which is doubted wilbe also unpaid, amounting to 32^{li} 1^{s} 4^{d}, which will make in toto due at Michas, 1637, 164^{li} 14^{s} 3¾. And in respect the rentes come not in as aforesaid, the said Colledge is compelled to take moneys up at interest to supplie their wantes, and relief of the poore of the said Colledge.

Mathias Alleyn, M^{r}
Thomas Alleyn, Ward.
Simon Mace
Samuel Porter
William Sutton
William Holmes
} fellows.

Fran. Grove
Thomas Haward
Will Fulchine
Rob. Sandarson
Joseph Arment
Nicholis N. I. Ive
} Assistantes.

THE TENANTS OF THE FORTUNE.

[This petition to Lord Keeper Littleton proves that the College had again had trouble in collecting the rents of the Fortune property, and we now hear of two new names in connection with it — Edward Jackson and John Beale.]

[Indorsed]

Petition to the Lord Keeper, 1640.

To the right hon^{ble} Sir Edward Littleton, Knight, Lord Keeper of the Greate Seale of England.

The humble petition of Mathias Alleyn, the Master, Thomas Alleyn, the Warden, 4 fellowes, 6 poore brethren, 6 poore sisters, and 12 poore schollers of the Colledge called Gods Guift Colledge, in Dulwich, founded by Edward Alleyn, esq., deceased.

Humbly sheweth,

That your Petitioners did heretofore exhibit their Bill of Complaint in this ho^{ble} Court against the Tennauntes of the Fortune Playhowse for rent, which they unjustly detayned from your Petitioners upon pretence of a restraint from playing.

That, upon a full hearinge of the said cause the 26 of January, in the 14 yeare of our gracious King Charles, his Lordship did order that the said Tennants should pay all their rent in arreare without any abatement, which accordingly they did either compound for and pay for a certaine tyme.

That, since the making of the said order, one John Beale bought a lease of a parte of the said Playhouse, which lease was heretofore demised by the aforesaid Edward Alleyn to Edward Jacson, under the yearely rent of 10^{li} 13^s 10^d, for which rent the said Beale is now in arreare 42^{li} 15^s 1^d.

That the said John Beale combining with the rest of the

Tennants have detayned their rent from the Colledge, whereupon your Petitioners did exhioitt their bill of complaint the second time in this ho^ble Court in Michalmas terme in the 15th yeare of our gracious King Charles; and the Tennants being served with subpenas to answer to the said bill, every of the said Tennants, except the said John Beale, pretended payment of their rent, and did pay, but since doe detaine their rent, to the great prejudice of the pore people of the said Colledge.

That the said John Beale did delay your petitioners in putting in his Answer, insomuch that three attachments issued out against the said Beale before he would put in his answer.

That the said Bill and Answer haveing had their due proceeding in this Court, and publication being now past this Hillary terme, the said Tennants are runn in arreare with your Petitioners the sume of 104^li 14^s 5^d due at Christmas last past, insomuch that your petitioners, to maintaine their poore of the said Colledge, are compelled to take moneys at interest to supply their wants. Now, in tender consideration of your Petitioners great necessity herein,

> Your Petitioners humbly pray your Honour to be pleased, according to the aforesaid order hereunto annexed, that all the Tennants which are behinde with their rent may be ordered to pay their rentes to the Colledge; or otherwise to bee pleased to set downe a day of hearing the said cause sometime this vacation before your Honour, that your Petitioners may not be delayed any longer by the said John Beale and the rest of the aforesaid Tennants. All which your Petitioners doth submitt to your Honours grave wisdome and charitable consideration. And shall pray for your happines, &c.

The above said order of the 26 of January, and the certificate for publication are hereunto annexed.

If this cause be ready for hearing, lett it be sett downe for

the fourth seale after the Terme, so as proces be timely served on the adverse parties.

(Cop.)   Ed. Littleton, C. S.

9 Feb. 1640.

Ex. Vera Copia,
  Geo. Brome.

SURVEYOR'S REPORT ON THE FORTUNE.

[What follows affords a very exact and minute account of the state of the Fortune Theatre, and of the adjoining property, in the summer of 1656, little more than 30 years after it had been rebuilt of brick. The report also contains a project for constructing twenty-three tenements on the ground, the College being put to no expense in the erection of them.]

To all to whom theise presentes may conceirne, wee, whose names are heerto subscribed, being desired by the Mr. and Warden of Dulwich College to vew the ground and building of the late playhouse called the Fortune, scituate betweene Whitecrosse streete and Goulding lane, in the County of Middlesex, after consideration had in each particular, doe humbly certefy as followeth, viz.

That the late playhouse, and tapphouse belonging to the same, standeth upon a peece of ground, conteyninge in length, from East to West, one hundred twenty and seven feete and a halfe, a little more or lesse; and in breadth, from North to South, one hundred twenty and nine feete, a little more or les: and that by reason the lead hath bin taken from the said building, the tyling not secured, and the foundation of the said playhouse not kept in good repaire, great part of the said playhouse is fallen to the ground, the tymber thereof much decayed and rotten, and the brickworke so rent and torne that the whole structure is in no condition capable of repaire, but in great danger of falling, to the hazzard of passengers' lives. And further, that the said building did in our opinions cost building

about twoo thousand pound; yet, in as much as greate part of the tymber is rotten, the tyles much broaken and decayed, and the brick walls much shaken, and the charge for demollishing the same will be chargeable and dangerous, uppon these considerations, our opinion is that the said materials may not bee more worth then eighty pound.

And secondly, in as much as we fynd there are severall tenements, northward of the gateway next Whitecrosse streete, belonging to the said hospitall, which are out of lease, and other in Goulding lane, which are neere out of lease, that our opinion is, it will bee most convenient and profitable for the sayd hospitall to cutte a streete of twenty fower feete wyde from Whitecrosse streete to Goulding lane, and that there may bee fowerteene tenementes erected betweene the said streete and lane, on the north syde thereof, besydes the tenementes on the streete syde; each of which tenementes may conteyne in front, from East to West, about eighteene feete; and in depth, from North to South, fifty feete or thereabouts: also that there may bee nyne tenementes erected betweene the said streete and lane, on the South side thereof, each of which sayd tenements may conteyne in front, from East to West, eighteene feete or thereabouts; and in depth, from North to South, fifty feete or thereabouts: and that the ground on which the said twenty-three tenements may bee erected will or may yeeld to the said hospitall about three shillings each foote, in front; and that the said two fronts doe conteyne in length, from East to West, fower hundred and fifteene feete or thereabouts; and that each foote of the said front may bee worth the some [of] three shillings, soe that the whole fower hundred and fifteene feete may amount unto the sum of sixty and two pound, five shillings, beside the tenementes standing. In testemony of the truth of which particulers wee have hereunto sett our hands, this 18 day of July, 1656.

EDW. JERMAN.
JOHN TANNER.

Memorand. it is [def. in MS.] that who may take the ground to build after this manner, and soe acquitt the landlords from any charge therein, that the said landlords doe demise the said ground for the terme of forty or fifty yeers or more ; but for lesse tyme few will undertake the same: and it is further necessary that each builder bee tyed to a forme and scantling for such buildings.

EDW. JERMAN.
JOHN TANNER.

[Addressed]

For the Master or Warden
of Dullige, this.

FATE OF THE FORTUNE.

[The *Mercurius Politicus* for the week ending February 21, 1661, contains an advertisement for letting the ground, on which the Fortune stood, on a building lease, it being calculated (as appears by the preceding document, and as is stated in the advertisement) that twenty-three tenements might be constructed upon it. (See Hist. of Engl. Dram. Poetry and the Stage, iii. 311.) By what ensues we find that a builder had been found to undertake the work, who was to have a lease, with similar covenants to those contained in a lease granted to John Greenhill, who had taken some property then belonging to Dulwich College in Pye Alley, Bishopsgate Street, and which had been left to it by the Founder. These papers are quite new in the history of the Fortune, and clearly show what was its ultimate fate in less than forty years after it had been reconstructed by Alleyn.]

[Indorsed]

4º Mart. 61. Copy of the Order of Ct. of Assistants of the Fortune ground, &c. to Beaven.

At a Court of Assistants held at God's guift Colledge in Dulwich, the 4th day of March, 1661.

Whereas the Fortune playhouse, scituated betweene White-cross street and Goulding lane, in that part of the parish of St. Giles Creplegate which is in the County of Middx, hereto-

fore considerable part of the revenue of this Colledge, hath of divers yeares last past stood empty and bene utterly uselesse to the said Colledge, not yeilding any rent, but bene chargeable to it; by reason whereof the said playhouse was very ruinous, decayed and fallen downe, and is since totally demolished, noe man ever attempting to take the same to build on, although the members of the said Colledge have bene very industrious and carefull, and used their utmost endeavours by all lawfull wayes and meanes to promote the same. And whereas of late William Beaven, cit, and tiler and bricklayer of London, hath adventured on the designe, and hath at his owne proper costs and charges new built and erected on the ground whereon the said late playhouse stood, and on certaine other ground thereunto belonging, twenty messuages or tenementes with backsides, gardens, and other conveniences to them severally belonging: It is therefore ordered by this Court, in consideration of the great charge the said William Beaven hath laid out and expended in building of the said 20 messuages or tenementes, and of what further expences he shalbe hereafter at in erecting any other messuages or tenementes on the said ground, as also in pursuance of a decree in the high Court of Chancery, bearing date the 21st day of November now last past, that the said William Beaven shall have a lease in writing, under the Colledge seale, of all the said messuages or tenementes by him erected as aforesaid, with all lights, wayes, easementes, commodities, appurtenances whatsoever to them or any of them now belonging or appertaining, for the tearme of 21 yeares from Mids[r] last past, under the yearly rent of 34[li] 10[s] payable quarterly, or within 21 dayes next after every of the four usuall feast-dayes, by even portions; hee the said William Beaven, at his owne charge, defraying all taxes and impositions hereafter to be charged on the said premises: and hee to observe, performe, and keepe all such covenants, conditions, and agreements as are conteyned and expressed in one indenture of demise lately made from the said Colledge to John Greenhill of

certaine tenementes in Pye Alley, Bishopsgate streete: in which lease, to be made to the said William Beaven, the Colledge shall covenant for themselves and their successors to make and seale unto the said William Beaven, his exors, admors, or assignes, one other indenture of lease, in writing, under their common seale, of all the said premises for the tearme of 21 yeares more from the expiration of the first mentioned lease, at and under the said yearely rent of 34^{li} 10^s and covenantes in the said John Greenhill's lease comprised.

And at the end of the said second lease the Colledge, or their successors, shall make and seale unto the said William Beaven, his exors, admors, and assignes, one other lease, in writing, under their common seale, of the said premises, for the tearme of three yeares, to commence from the expiration of the said second lease, at and under the yearely rent of 34^{li} 10^s, and under the covenants in the said John Greenhill's lease specified; hee the said William Beaven, his exors, admors, and assignes, sealing, and in due form of law executing a counterparte of each lease or leases.

As to the exceptions and other covenants, not comprised in M. Greenhill's lease, I can say nothing.

INDEX.

	PAGE
Acrostic upon Philip Henslowe, by Richard Williams	38
Alleyn, Edward, his performance of Cutlack	vii
———, threat to	20
———, his property in Sussex	27
———, possible allusion to in "Ratsey's Ghost"	x
———, letter to, from Mrs. Anne Poyntz	31
———, new information regarding his property	xi
———, his Bill in Chancery against Sir Francis Calton	40
———, his money transactions with Sir Francis Calton	55, 56
———, his judgment in plays	60, 61
———, his property in the Blackfriars	83
———, address to from his Company	86
———, Lord of the Manor of Kennington	88
———, his marriage to Constance Donne	xx
———, his death	91
———, his last Will, copy of	xxi
Alleyn, John, (brother to Edward) Citizen and Innholder	2, 11
———, his dispute with Doctor Martin	4, 5, 7
———, letter from the Privy Council to the Lord Mayor, &c., in favour of	5
———, purchase by from Isaac Burgess	11
——— and Edward, their purchase of a cloak	12
———, release to	1, 2
——— and Edward, their debt to John Webster	14
———, his proposal of marriage	15
———, servant to Lord Sheffield and Lord C. Howard	1, 54
———, a witness for Henslowe in 1613	57

INDEX.

	PAGE
Alleyn, Mathias, E. Alleyn's kindness to	89
————, his letter to Edward Alleyn	ib.
————, Master of Dulwich College	95
Alleyn, Mrs. Edward, prayer and verses probably written by	88
————, her marriage to Harvey	xxi
Apparel, theatrical sale of	11, 12
Arraignment of London, a play	58, 64, 65
Articles of agreement between Actor and Manager, the earliest extant	75
———— of oppression against Philip Henslowe	80
Ashmore, Henry, his bear seized	34
Attwell, Hugh, the actor, a witness for Henslowe	57
————, fac-simile of his handwriting	87
Authors, dramatic, paid in part by the receipts at the doors	66
Bartholomew Fair by Ben Jonson, alluded to	67
Bear, belonging to Henry Ashmore, seized	34
Bear-garden, commission for	26
Beaven, William, his agreement for the ground on which the Fortune Theatre had stood	100
Bellingsley, Alderman of London	5
Bellman of London, a play	66
Ben Jonson, his "Richard the Third"	24
Birde, William, the actor, his letter to Alleyn respecting John Russell	32
————, his application to Henslowe for money	33
Bond given by Henslowe and Alleyn's deputy	81
Books, the foundations of plays, borrowed by dramatic poets	71, 73
Brewe, Patrick, his lease of the Fortune ground	17, 35
————, his letter to Alleyn on the ground-rent of the Fortune	34
————, his letter regarding the disputes of the Gills	36
Browne, Richard, inventory of his goods	3
————, Robert, his letter to Alleyn regarding an actor named Rose	51
Burbage, Richard, the actor of the principal characters in Shakespeare's plays	vi, xxx
Burgess, Isaac, his sale to John Alleyn	11
Burne, Mr., his daughter proposed for by John Alleyn	15
Calton, Sir Francis, Alleyn's Bill in Chancery against	40
————, his request of £5	55
————, money due to from E. Alleyn	ib.
Chettle, Hathway, and Smith, their play Too good to be True	25
Cloak and robe bought by John Alleyn	11

INDEX.

	PAGE
Clyffe, John, his sale of a cloak to J. and E. Alleyn	12
Composition, mode of with old dramatists	69
Conquest of Spain by John of Gaunt, a play	25
———— of the West Indies, a play	23
Corporation of Dulwich College, declaration by	95
———— of London, their dislike to plays, &c.	5
Cox, Robert, his release to John Alleyn	2
Crowe, Sir William, clerk	17
Croxted, E. Alleyn's projected purchases there	27
Cutlack, one of Edward Alleyn's characters	vii
Daborne, Robert and N. Field, their intended play	48
Daborne, R., his play of Machiavel and the Devil	56
————, his pecuniary claims upon Henslowe	57
————, his lawsuits	58
————, and Tourneur's Arraignment of London	ib.
————, his separation from his Wife	60
————, comparison of himself with Massinger	61
————, his daughter	62
————, his rapidity in composition	ib.
————, sale of his estate	63
————, his play, the Bellman of London	66
————, his threat to Henslowe	67
————, his preferment in the Church	68
————, his imprecations	71
————, his play of The Owl	72, 73, 74
————, his play called The She Saint	82
Dawes, Robert, a player, his theatrical "Articles"	75
Day, John, original lines by	24
————, plays by	23, 24, 25
Dekker, T., his share in Fair Constance of Rome	26
Deputy to Henslowe and Alleyn, bond given by	81
Dialogue, musical, in verse	29
————, theatrical, in verse	8
Donne, Constance, married to Edward Alleyn	xx
————, Dr. Edward, Alleyn's letter to	xxi
Dorset, Countess of	47
Doryngton, John, his Deputation to Alleyn and Henslowe	26
Drayton, Michael, his share in Fair Constance of Rome	ib.
Dulwich College, Introduction to the Statutes of	91

INDEX.

	PAGE
Dulwich College, petition of the Master and Warden of to Lord Keeper Littleton	96
———, purchase of by Alleyn from Sir F. Calton	40
Eastward Ho, a play acted by Henslowe's company	62
Egerton, Sir Thomas, Lord Keeper	20
Eglestone, an actor	78
English Players abroad	19
Fair Constance of Rome	26
Fawnte, William, his letter to Alleyn respecting Bulls for Paris Garden	31
Ferrex and Porrex, by T. Sackville and T. Norton	47
Field, Nathaniel, and R. Daborne's play	48
Field, Nathaniel, his letter to Henslowe	48
———, imprisonment of	65
———, an actor	79
Forkench, Richard, his letter to E. Alleyn	47
Furniture, inventory of	3
Fortune Theatre, and the ground on which it stood	17
———, the ground-rent of, letter respecting	34
———, non-payment of rent for	95
———, complaint against the tenants of	96
———, surveyor's report upon the state of in 1656	98
———, fate of the	100
Gatherers at Theatres	32
———, the wives of actors officiating as	51
Gill family and the Fortune Theatre	17, 34, 36
———, disputes between	36
Gosson, Stephen, his attacks upon players	ix
Gorboduc, a tragedy by T. Sackville and T. Norton	47
Greene, Robert, his play of Orlando Furioso	vi
Greenhill, John, his lease of property in Pye Alley	100
Griffin, Mr., mentioned by Daborne	63, 72
———, addressed by Daborne	72
Guilpin, Edward, his "Skialetheia," 1598	vii
Hallam, Henry, his "Introduction to the Literature of Europe"	47
Hamton, Robert, an actor, fac-simile of his handwriting	87
Harryes, John, draught of a bill in Chancery by	46

INDEX.

	PAGE
Harte, Lord Mayor of London	4, 5
Hathway, Day, and Haughton, their play of John of Gaunt	25
Hathway, and Day, their play of The Six Yeomen of the West	23
———, Day, and Smith's play, The Conquest of the West Indies	23, 24
Hebborne, John, his proposal to become Alleyn's tenant at Dulwich	48
Henslowe and Alleyn's rent to Doryngton	26
————, Philip, acrostic upon, by R. Williams	38
——————, his dispute with Wall about the Upper Pike Garden	49
——————, a broker between authors and actors	69
——————, his interest in some private theatre	72
——————, his dispute with his company	78
——————, Articles of Oppression against	80
Heywood, Thomas, his "Apology for Actors," 1612	19
Hired men among actors	80
Howard, Lord C., John Alleyn his servant	54
Jerman, Edward, and John Tanner's report on the state of the Fortune Theatre in 1656	98
John of Gaunt, a play	25
Johnson, Richard, his release to John Alleyn	1
Jones, Richard, his letter to Alleyn on going abroad with an English company of players	19
———, Robert, of the Blackfriars	83
Jonson, Ben, his intended play of Richard the Third	24
——————, his Bartholomew Fair alluded to	67
Kennington, E. Alleyn, Lord of the Manor of	88
King, the, his Players	67
Knave of Clubs, 1600, by S. Rowlands	vi, xxx
Langworth, Arthur	22
——————, John, Alleyn's advances to	ib.
Love-Verses, copy of	21
Luntley, John, landlord to Alleyn of property on the Bankside	90, 91
Machiavel and the Devil, a play, by R. Daborne	56
Malone and the MSS. at Dulwich	v
Marlowe Kit	8
Martin, Dr. Thomas, his dispute with John Alleyn	4, 5, 7

INDEX.

	PAGE
Massinger and Daborne	61
Mayor, Lord, of London, Letter of the Privy Council to, on behalf of John Alleyn	5
Meade, Jacob, Henslowe's partner	75
Mercurius Politicus, Advertisement in for letting the ground of the Fortune Theatre	100
Meridall, Richard, his gratitude to Mrs. Alleyn for education, &c. at Dulwich	83
Middleton, Henry, his letter to Alleyn	34
Minsheu, John, author of the Dictionary, a language-master	84
More, Thomas, a witness for P. Henslowe	59, 60
Musical Dialogue in verse	29
New Play, highest price of	64
Newton, John, fac-simile of his handwriting	87
Norris, William, Vicar-General of Man, his letter to Alleyn	34
————, Vicar-General of Man, death of his wife	37
Norton, Thomas, his share in Gorboduc	47
Nottingham, Lord, his letter in favour of John Alleyn	4
Orlando Furioso, a play, by Robert Greene	vi
Owl, the, a play, by R. Daborne	72, 73, 74
Page, Mr., of Croxted, Alleyn's tenant	27
————, his letter to Alleyn on his Sussex property	28
Pallant, Robert, the actor, a bad tenant	52
————, an actor	79, 82
————, his discontent	ib.
————, fac-simile of his handwriting	87
Paris Garden, letter regarding bulls for	31
————, supply of with dogs and bulls	50
Plays and Players, dislike of the Corporation of London to	5
Poor Northern Man, a play	25
Poyntz, Mrs. Anne, her letter to E. Alleyn	31
Radforde, Thomas, Deputy to Henslowe and Alleyn, his bond	81
Redmer, R., his letter to Alleyn	84, 85
————, his necessities	ib.
Release to John Alleyn	1, 2
Return from Parnassus, possible allusion to E. Alleyn in	viii
Richard the Third, an intended play, by Ben Jonson	24

INDEX.

	PAGE
Rivalry of Companies of Actors	67
Rose, an actor, and his wife	51
Rosseter, Philip	78
Rowlands, Samuel, his Knave of Clubs, 1600	vi, xxx
Rowley, Samuel, his letter respecting "The Conquest of the West Indies"	23
———, his letter respecting "The Six Yeomen of the West"	ib.
———, his letter regarding "John of Gaunt"	25
———, William, fac-simile of his handwriting	87
Russell, John, gatherer at the Fortune Theatre	32
Sackville, Thomas, Lord Buckhurst and Earl of Dorset, his share in Gorboduc	47
Shakespeare, William, the performance of the chief characters in his plays by Richard Burbage	vi, xxx
———, possible allusion to in "Ratsey's Ghost"	x
———, his property when he retired to Stratford-upon-Avon	xx
Shaw, Robert, the actor, his note to Henslowe	24
———, his letter to Henslowe regarding Fair Constance of Rome	26
Sheffield, Lord, John Alleyn theatrical servant to	1
She Saint, a play so called	82
Six Yeomen of the West, a play	23
Skialetheia, a collection of Epigrams and Satires, 1598, by Edward Guilpin	vii
———, reprint of, by Mr. E. V. Utterson	xxxi
Smyth, Anthony, the actor, fac-simile of his handwriting	87
Socklen, Elizabeth, a kinswoman to Alleyn, her letter	54
Tailors, defence of, in verse	13
Taming of a Shrew, the old, 1594	ix
Tarlton, Richard, the celebrated actor	13
Taylor, Joseph, not the first actor of Hamlet	86
———, fac-simile of his handwriting	87
Theatrical Dialogue in verse	8
Too Good to be True, a play, also called The King and the Poor Northern Man	25
Tourneur, Cyril, his aid to Daborne in The Arraignment of London	58, 64, 65
Townley, T., one of Alleyn's tenants, his letter	52

		PAGE
Tragedy, a new, by Daborne	. . . .	64
Traves, Edward, Alleyn's landlord of property in the Blackfriars	.	83
Tunstall, James, an actor	. . .	12, 13

Wall, Abraham, his dispute with Henslowe respecting the Upper Pike Garden 49
Webster, John, perhaps father to the dramatic poet . . 14
Wheeler, Lowe, and Handcock, their letter to Alleyn . . 20
White-lion prison in Southwark 90
Williams, Richard, his Acrostic upon P. Henslowe . . 38
Willoughby, Lord, his patronage of Daborne . . 68
Wilson, Munday, Hathway, Drayton, and Dekker, their play of Fair Constance of Rome 26

Upper Pike Garden, Henslowe's dispute with Abr. Wall regarding 49
Utterson, Mr. Edw. V., his reprint of Edw. Guilpin's Skialetheia, 1598 xxx

Verses, copy of love 21
——— by Richard Meridall, a poor scholar of Dulwich . 84

Yonge, Thomas, his letter respecting the supply of Paris Garden 50

THE END.

LONDON:
F. SHOBERL, JUN, 51, RUPERT STREET, HAYMARKET,
PRINTER TO H. R. H. PRINCE ALBERT.

www.bookjungle.com *email: sales@bookjungle.com fax: 630-214-0564 mail: Book Jungle PO Box 2226 Champaign, IL 61825*

The Codes Of Hammurabi And Moses
W. W. Davies

QTY

The discovery of the Hammurabi Code is one of the greatest achievements of archaeology, and is of paramount interest, not only to the student of the Bible, but also to all those interested in ancient history...

Religion **ISBN:** *1-59462-338-4* **Pages:** 132
MSRP $12.95

The Theory of Moral Sentiments
Adam Smith

QTY

This work from 1749. contains original theories of conscience amd moral judgment and it is the foundation for systemof morals.

Philosophy **ISBN:** *1-59462-777-0* **Pages:** 536
MSRP $19.95

Jessica's First Prayer
Hesba Stretton

QTY

In a screened and secluded corner of one of the many railway-bridges which span the streets of London there could be seen a few years ago, from five o'clock every morning until half past eight, a tidily set-out coffee-stall, consisting of a trestle and board, upon which stood two large tin cans, with a small fire of charcoal burning under each so as to keep the coffee boiling during the early hours of the morning when the work-people were thronging into the city on their way to their daily toil...

Childrens **ISBN:** *1-59462-373-2* **Pages:** 84
MSRP $9.95

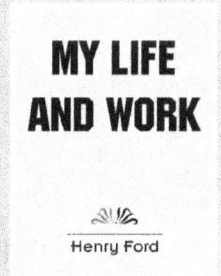

My Life and Work
Henry Ford

QTY

Henry Ford revolutionized the world with his implementation of mass production for the Model T automobile. Gain valuable business insight into his life and work with his own auto-biography... "We have only started on our development of our country we have not as yet, with all our talk of wonderful progress, done more than scratch the surface. The progress has been wonderful enough but..."

Biographies/ **ISBN:** *1-59462-198-5* **Pages:** 300
MSRP $21.95

www.bookjungle.com *email: sales@bookjungle.com fax: 630-214-0564 mail: Book Jungle PO Box 2226 Champaign, IL 61825*

The Art of Cross-Examination
Francis Wellman

I presume it is the experience of every author, after his first book is published upon an important subject, to be almost overwhelmed with a wealth of ideas and illustrations which could readily have been included in his book, and which to his own mind, at least, seem to make a second edition inevitable. Such certainly was the case with me; and when the first edition had reached its sixth impression in five months, I rejoiced to learn that it seemed to my publishers that the book had met with a sufficiently favorable reception to justify a second and considerably enlarged edition. ...

QTY

Reference   ISBN: *1-59462-647-2*   **Pages:412** *MSRP $19.95*

On the Duty of Civil Disobedience
Henry David Thoreau

Thoreau wrote his famous essay, On the Duty of Civil Disobedience, as a protest against an unjust but popular war and the immoral but popular institution of slave-owning. He did more than write—he declined to pay his taxes, and was hauled off to gaol in consequence. Who can say how much this refusal of his hastened the end of the war and of slavery ?

QTY

Law   ISBN: *1-59462-747-9*   **Pages:48** *MSRP $7.45*

Dream Psychology Psychoanalysis for Beginners
Sigmund Freud

Sigmund Freud, born Sigismund Schlomo Freud (May 6, 1856 - September 23, 1939), was a Jewish-Austrian neurologist and psychiatrist who co-founded the psychoanalytic school of psychology. Freud is best known for his theories of the unconscious mind, especially involving the mechanism of repression; his redefinition of sexual desire as mobile and directed towards a wide variety of objects; and his therapeutic techniques, especially his understanding of transference in the therapeutic relationship and the presumed value of dreams as sources of insight into unconscious desires.

QTY

Psychology   ISBN: *1-59462-905-6*   **Pages:196** *MSRP $15.45*

The Miracle of Right Thought
Orison Swett Marden

Believe with all of your heart that you will do what you were made to do. When the mind has once formed the habit of holding cheerful, happy, prosperous pictures, it will not be easy to form the opposite habit. It does not matter how improbable or how far away this realization may see, or how dark the prospects may be, if we visualize them as best we can, as vividly as possible, hold tenaciously to them and vigorously struggle to attain them, they will gradually become actualized, realized in the life. But a desire, a longing without endeavor, a yearning abandoned or held indifferently will vanish without realization.

QTY

Self Help   ISBN: *1-59462-644-8*   **Pages:360** *MSRP $25.45*

www.bookjungle.com email: sales@bookjungle.com fax: 630-214-0564 mail: Book Jungle PO Box 2226 Champaign, IL 61825

QTY

	Title	ISBN	Price
☐	**The Rosicrucian Cosmo-Conception Mystic Christianity** by *Max Heindel*	ISBN: 1-59462-188-8	$38.95
	The Rosicrucian Cosmo-conception is not dogmatic, neither does it appeal to any other authority than the reason of the student. It is: not controversial, but is: sent forth in the, hope that it may help to clear...		New Age/Religion Pages 646
☐	**Abandonment To Divine Providence** by *Jean-Pierre de Caussade*	ISBN: 1-59462-228-0	$25.95
	"The Rev. Jean Pierre de Caussade was one of the most remarkable spiritual writers of the Society of Jesus in France in the 18th Century. His death took place at Toulouse in 1751. His works have gone through many editions and have been republished...		Inspirational/Religion Pages 400
☐	**Mental Chemistry** by *Charles Haanel*	ISBN: 1-59462-192-6	$23.95
	Mental Chemistry allows the change of material conditions by combining and appropriately utilizing the power of the mind. Much like applied chemistry creates something new and unique out of careful combinations of chemicals the mastery of mental chemistry...		New Age Pages 354
☐	**The Letters of Robert Browning and Elizabeth Barret Barrett 1845-1846 vol II** by *Robert Browning* and *Elizabeth Barrett*	ISBN: 1-59462-193-4	$35.95
			Biographies Pages 596
☐	**Gleanings In Genesis (volume I)** by *Arthur W. Pink*	ISBN: 1-59462-130-6	$27.45
	Appropriately has Genesis been termed "the seed plot of the Bible" for in it we have, in germ form, almost all of the great doctrines which are afterwards fully developed in the books of Scripture which follow...		Religion/Inspirational Pages 420
☐	**The Master Key** by *L. W. de Laurence*	ISBN: 1-59462-001-6	$30.95
	In no branch of human knowledge has there been a more lively increase of the spirit of research during the past few years than in the study of Psychology, Concentration and Mental Discipline. The requests for authentic lessons in Thought Control, Mental Discipline and...		New Age/Business Pages 422
☐	**The Lesser Key Of Solomon Goetia** by *L. W. de Laurence*	ISBN: 1-59462-092-X	$9.95
	This translation of the first book of the "Lernegton" which is now for the first time made accessible to students of Talismanic Magic was done, after careful collation and edition, from numerous Ancient Manuscripts in Hebrew, Latin, and French...		New Age/Occult Pages 92
☐	**Rubaiyat Of Omar Khayyam** by *Edward Fitzgerald*	ISBN: 1-59462-332-5	$13.95
	Edward Fitzgerald, whom the world has already learned, in spite of his own efforts to remain within the shadow of anonymity, to look upon as one of the rarest poets of the century, was born at Bredfield, in Suffolk, on the 31st of March, 1809. He was the third son of John Purcell...		Music Pages 172
☐	**Ancient Law** by *Henry Maine*	ISBN: 1-59462-128-4	$29.95
	The chief object of the following pages is to indicate some of the earliest ideas of mankind, as they are reflected in Ancient Law, and to point out the relation of those ideas to modern thought.		Religion/History Pages 452
☐	**Far-Away Stories** by *William J. Locke*	ISBN: 1-59462-129-2	$19.45
	"Good wine needs no bush, but a collection of mixed vintages does. And this book is just such a collection. Some of the stories I do not want to remain buried for ever in the museum files of dead magazine-numbers an author's not unpardonable vanity..."		Fiction Pages 272
☐	**Life of David Crockett** by *David Crockett*	ISBN: 1-59462-250-7	$27.45
	"Colonel David Crockett was one of the most remarkable men of the times in which he lived. Born in humble life, but gifted with a strong will, an indomitable courage, and unremitting perseverance...		Biographies/New Age Pages 424
☐	**Lip-Reading** by *Edward Nitchie*	ISBN: 1-59462-206-X	$25.95
	Edward B. Nitchie, founder of the New York School for the Hard of Hearing, now the Nitchie School of Lip-Reading, Inc, wrote "LIP-READING Principles and Practice". The development and perfecting of this meritorious work on lip-reading was an undertaking...		How-to Pages 400
☐	**A Handbook of Suggestive Therapeutics, Applied Hypnotism, Psychic Science** by *Henry Munro*	ISBN: 1-59462-214-0	$24.95
			Health/New Age/Health/Self-help Pages 376
☐	**A Doll's House: and Two Other Plays** by *Henrik Ibsen*	ISBN: 1-59462-112-8	$19.95
	Henrik Ibsen created this classic when in revolutionary 1848 Rome. Introducing some striking concepts in playwriting for the realist genre, this play has been studied the world over.		Fiction/Classics/Plays 308
☐	**The Light of Asia** by *sir Edwin Arnold*	ISBN: 1-59462-204-3	$13.95
	In this poetic masterpiece, Edwin Arnold describes the life and teachings of Buddha. The man who was to become known as Buddha to the world was born as Prince Gautama of India but he rejected the worldly riches and abandoned the reigns of power when...		Religion/History/Biographies Pages 170
☐	**The Complete Works of Guy de Maupassant** by *Guy de Maupassant*	ISBN: 1-59462-157-8	$16.95
	"For days and days, nights and nights, I had dreamed of that first kiss which was to consecrate our engagement, and I knew not on what spot I should put my lips..."		Fiction/Classics Pages 240
☐	**The Art of Cross-Examination** by *Francis L. Wellman*	ISBN: 1-59462-309-0	$26.95
	Written by a renowned trial lawyer, Wellman imparts his experience and uses case studies to explain how to use psychology to extract desired information through questioning.		How-to/Science/Reference Pages 408
☐	**Answered or Unanswered?** by *Louisa Vaughan*	ISBN: 1-59462-248-5	$10.95
	Miracles of Faith in China		Religion Pages 112
☐	**The Edinburgh Lectures on Mental Science (1909)** by *Thomas*	ISBN: 1-59462-008-3	$11.95
	This book contains the substance of a course of lectures recently given by the writer in the Queen Street Hall, Edinburgh. Its purpose is to indicate the Natural Principles governing the relation between Mental Action and Material Conditions...		New Age/Psychology Pages 148
☐	**Ayesha** by *H. Rider Haggard*	ISBN: 1-59462-301-5	$24.95
	Verily and indeed it is the unexpected that happens! Probably if there was one person upon the earth from whom the Editor of this, and of a certain previous history, did not expect to hear again...		Classics Pages 380
☐	**Ayala's Angel** by *Anthony Trollope*	ISBN: 1-59462-352-X	$29.95
	The two girls were both pretty, but Lucy who was twenty-one who supposed to be simple and comparatively unattractive, whereas Ayala was credited, as her Bombwhat romantic name might show, with poetic charm and a taste for romance. Ayala when her father died was nineteen...		Fiction Pages 484
☐	**The American Commonwealth** by *James Bryce*	ISBN: 1-59462-286-8	$34.45
	An interpretation of American democratic political theory. It examines political mechanics and society from the perspective of Scotsman James Bryce		Politics Pages 572
☐	**Stories of the Pilgrims** by *Margaret P. Pumphrey*	ISBN: 1-59462-116-0	$17.95
	This book explores pilgrims religious oppression in England as well as their escape to Holland and eventual crossing to America on the Mayflower, and their early days in New England...		History Pages 268

www.bookjungle.com email: sales@bookjungle.com fax: 630-214-0564 mail: Book Jungle PO Box 2226 Champaign, IL 61825

QTY

The Fasting Cure by *Sinclair Upton* ISBN: *1-59462-222-1* **$13.95**
In the Cosmopolitan Magazine for May, 1910, and in the Contemporary Review (London) for April, 1910, I published an article dealing with my experiences in fasting. I have written a great many magazine articles, but never one which attracted so much attention... New Age/Self Help/Health Pages 164

Hebrew Astrology by *Sepharial* ISBN: *1-59462-308-2* **$13.45**
In these days of advanced thinking it is a matter of common observation that we have left many of the old landmarks behind and that we are now pressing forward to greater heights and to a wider horizon than that which represented the mind-content of our progenitors... Astrology Pages 144

Thought Vibration or The Law of Attraction in the Thought World ISBN: *1-59462-127-6* **$12.95**
by *William Walker Atkinson* Psychology/Religion Pages 144

Optimism by *Helen Keller* ISBN: *1-59462-108-X* **$15.95**
Helen Keller was blind, deaf, and mute since 19 months old, yet famously learned how to overcome these handicaps, communicate with the world, and spread her lectures promoting optimism. An inspiring read for everyone... Biographies/Inspirational Pages 84

Sara Crewe by *Frances Burnett* ISBN: *1-59462-360-0* **$9.45**
In the first place, Miss Minchin lived in London. Her home was a large, dull, tall one, in a large, dull square, where all the houses were alike, and all the sparrows were alike, and where all the door-knockers made the same heavy sound... Childrens/Classic Pages 88

The Autobiography of Benjamin Franklin by *Benjamin Franklin* ISBN: *1-59462-135-7* **$24.95**
The Autobiography of Benjamin Franklin has probably been more extensively read than any other American historical work, and no other book of its kind has had such ups and downs of fortune. Franklin lived for many years in England, where he was agent... Biographies/History Pages 332

Name	
Email	
Telephone	
Address	
City, State ZIP	

☐ Credit Card   ☐ Check / Money Order

Credit Card Number	
Expiration Date	
Signature	

Please Mail to: Book Jungle
PO Box 2226
Champaign, IL 61825
or Fax to: 630-214-0564

ORDERING INFORMATION

web: *www.bookjungle.com*
email: *sales@bookjungle.com*
fax: *630-214-0564*
mail: *Book Jungle PO Box 2226 Champaign, IL 61825*
or PayPal *to sales@bookjungle.com*

Please contact us for bulk discounts

DIRECT-ORDER TERMS

**20% Discount if You Order
Two or More Books**
Free Domestic Shipping!
Accepted: Master Card, Visa,
Discover, American Express

www.ingramcontent.com/pod-product-compliance
Lightning Source LLC
Chambersburg PA
CBHW080528170426
43195CB00016B/2506